Food Anxiety in Globalising Vietnam

Judith Ehlert • Nora Katharina Faltmann
Editors

Food Anxiety in Globalising Vietnam

palgrave
macmillan

Editors
Judith Ehlert
Department of Development Studies
University of Vienna
Vienna, Austria

Nora Katharina Faltmann
Department of Development Studies
University of Vienna
Vienna, Austria

ISBN 978-981-13-0742-3   ISBN 978-981-13-0743-0   (eBook)
https://doi.org/10.1007/978-981-13-0743-0

Library of Congress Control Number: 2018955436

Cover credit: Carina Maier

Published with the support of Austrian Science Fund (FWF): [PUB 506-Z29]

This Palgrave Macmillan imprint is published by the registered company Springer Nature Singapore Pte Ltd.
The registered company address is: 152 Beach Road, #21-01/04 Gateway East, Singapore 189721, Singapore

To Carina,
for her clarity, critical thinking and cheerfulness

Acknowledgements

This book would not have been possible without the generous support of the Austrian Science Fund (FWF). Its funding of our research project 'A Body-Political Approach to the Study of Food – Vietnam and the Global Transformations' (P 27438) marked the beginning of insightful research on Food Anxieties in Vietnam – a hot and yet underexplored social phenomenon – and inspired the idea for this edited volume. Thanks to the financial support of the FWF, we were able to bring together academics from various areas of scholarship united in their passion for food issues and empirical contexts. With first draft in hand, the contributors to this book met in person for a writer's workshop at the Department of Development Studies at the University of Vienna in March 2017. This intensive workshop was crucial in terms of co-reviewing the drafts, thereby refining the book's common thread of food anxiety and (hopefully) turning it into a coherent volume. Besides creating linkages between the individual chapters, the face-to-face discussions also established the necessary demarcation of thematically related chapters while creating inspiring dialogue about the particularities of the different disciplinary backgrounds of the authors. This workshop format offered an innovative space for in-depth scholarly debates and networking and – most of all – we definitely cherished the fun! As our get-together was hosted at the 'academic home' of the editors, we would like to thank our colleagues at the Department for Development Studies at the University of Vienna.

Thanks to Michaela Hochmuth for her crucial support in the early stages of the book idea through her thematic input, organisational help and overall contribution as a former research assistant on the project; Elke Christiansen for her great photographs of the workshop and Ines Höckner for the workshop documentation. We particularly want to thank head of department Petra Dannecker for her support throughout the book's genesis and her feedback on earlier drafts of the introduction (and especially for constantly pushing us to keep our own deadlines).

After the workshop, a couple of feedback loops on the drafts followed, before putting it all together in this edited volume. Thank you, Andrea Kremser, for the great work copy-editing the – at some point chaotic – script and for your flexibility, patience and attentive eye. Thanks to Joshua Pitt and Sophie Li at Palgrave/Springer Nature, who supported the process from proposal to reviews and final publication with reassuring ease. Also, we thank the anonymous reviewers for their encouraging and positively challenging comments at an early stage of the proposal, which undoubtedly helped to sharpen our concept ideas.

The biggest 'thank you' goes to Carina Maier. She has accompanied the whole process of the book from the workshop to manuscript submission as an undeniable organisational talent and reliable contact person for the book contributors and publishing house. Besides her resilience in putting up with all things bureaucratic, she has also provided the much appreciated analytical input and critical clarity at numerous stages of the book. We are also grateful for her photography skills, which produced the cover image of this book, the outcome of a joint motorbike trip through Ho Chi Minh City's back alleys. Carina always saw the bigger picture behind this project and cheerfully encouraged us in this endeavour of editorship.

Finally, the completion of this edited volume would also not have been possible without the great patience and support of our families and partners giving us the necessary grounding, rest and good food for bringing this project to an end.

Contents

Notes on Contributors

Nir Avieli holds a PhD in Cultural Anthropology and is working as a senior lecturer at the Department of Sociology and Anthropology at Ben-Gurion University, Israel. He is mainly interested in Vietnamese cuisine in its various guises, focusing on several relations of food and tourism, food and gender, and so on. He has been conducting anthropological fieldwork in the central Vietnamese town of Hoi An since 1998.

Nicolas Bricas holds a degree in socioeconomics and is working at CIRAD (Centre de Coopération Internationale en Recherche Agronomique pour le Développement) in Montpellier, France. His research focuses on food security, food safety and sustainable food systems. He is the director of the UNESCO World Food Systems Chair based in Montpellier.

Judith Ehlert is a sociologist and holds a PhD in Development Studies. She works as a post-doctoral researcher at the Department of Development Studies at the University of Vienna, Austria. She is the leader of the research project 'A Body-Political Approach to the Study of Food – Vietnam and the Global Transformations' funded by the Austrian Science Fund. Her main research interest lies in food sociology, body theories, knowledge and qualitative research methodologies.

Nora Katharina Faltmann is a PhD candidate in development studies at the University of Vienna and a member of the scientific staff of the research project 'A Body-Political Approach to the Study of Food – Vietnam and the Global

Transformations'. Her areas of research interest include food studies from production to consumption and food safety in connection to questions of social inequality.

Muriel Figuié holds a PhD in Sociology and is working at CIRAD in Montpellier, France. Her interests lie in food sociology and sociology of risk in relation to animals (meat consumption, zoonosis). She conducts research mainly in Southern countries (Asia, Southern Africa) focusing on health concerns, and trust-building in the context of globalisation.

Timothy Gorman is a PhD candidate in the Department of Development Sociology at Cornell University in Ithaca, New York, and conducts research on agrarian transformations, climate change and food security in Southeast Asia. His dissertation fieldwork in Vietnam was supported by the Social Science Research Council, the Rural Sociological Society, and USAID's Borlaug Global Food Security program. In the fall of 2018, he will be joining the faculty of Montclair State University, USA, as Assistant Professor of Sociology.

Sandra Kurfürst is Junior Professor of Cross-Cultural and Urban Communication at the Global South Studies Centre (GSSC), University of Cologne, Germany. Her research focuses on urbanism, development and media and communication in Southeast Asia, particularly Vietnam, and the Pearl River Delta.

Paule Moustier holds a PhD in Agricultural Economy and is working at CIRAD in Montpellier, France, where she is in charge of the MOISA (Markets, Organisations, Institutions and Stakeholders' Strategies) research unit. Her research focuses on the organisation and performance of food chains supplying African and Asian cities.

Nguyen Thi Tan Loc holds a PhD in Economics and is working at the Fruit and Vegetable Institute of Hanoi (Favri), member of Malica consortium. She has been working on the changes in food consumption and marketing in Hanoi for the last 15 years and is now in charge of the Economics and Marketing Department of Favri.

Erica J. Peters holds a PhD in History and is working as an independent food historian. She is Director of the Culinary Historians of Northern California. She received her graduate degree in history at the University of Chicago and is the author of *Appetites and Aspirations in Vietnam: Food and Drink in the Long Nineteenth Century* and *San Francisco: A Food Biography*. Her research interests are food history and French colonial history.

Jean-Pierre Poulain is a sociologist and anthropologist and holds the professorship of Food Studies: Food, Cultures and Health jointly set up by the University of Toulouse, France and Taylor's University in Kuala Lumpur, Malaysia. He conducts research on the links between food, cultures and health and is interested in food decisions and the transformation of food cultures and food habits.

Hongzhou Zhang is a research fellow with the China Programme at the S. Rajaratnam School of International Studies (RSIS), Nanyang Technological University, Singapore. His main research interests include China and regional resources security (food, water and energy), China's fishing policies and maritime security.

List of Figures

List of Tables

List of Boxes

1

Food Anxiety: Ambivalences Around Body and Identity, Food Safety, and Security

Judith Ehlert and Nora Katharina Faltmann

Imagine wandering around an open food market, tempted to satiate your appetite with something fresh and delicious. You come across a market vendor who displays a large pile of something on a silver tray. Given the view of a throng of curvy-shaped knotty things, you are puzzled to distinguish the actual boundaries between these nearly transparent objects. Only at second look, this bunch turns out to be a catch of dead shrimps with their visceral organs shining through, some with their heads torn off, some with intact bodies. Meanwhile a range of scents is in the air, some appetising, others perhaps more alien. Imagine being the viewer of this scene, what does it arouse in you? Depending on your perspective— eating habits and socio-cultural background, current sensation of hunger, perception of the quality, or knowledge of the surroundings—either delight or disgust.

This book is explicitly about such ambivalences of food ranging between delight and disgust. The described scenario could evoke anxiety in the viewer while others might be drawn to the food in question. At the

J. Ehlert (✉) • N. K. Faltmann
Department of Development Studies, University of Vienna, Vienna, Austria
e-mail: judith.ehlert@univie.ac.at; nora.faltmann@univie.ac.at

© The Author(s) 2019   **1**
J. Ehlert, N. K. Faltmann (eds.), *Food Anxiety in Globalising Vietnam*,
https://doi.org/10.1007/978-981-13-0743-0_1

same time, the scenario hints at the split seconds in which humans make something out as edible or not. According to the 'omnivore's paradox', human food consumption is navigated between the sheer abundance of things that could be eaten physiologically but are constrained by the social and cultural norms that define food and produce as edible or inedible, as symbolically enhanced or contaminated in the first place (Rozin 1976; Fischler 1988). Moreover, the categorisation of 'edible'/'inedible' is historically rooted in peoples' trial and error experiments with potentially harmful substances (Rozin 1976; Fischler 1988). Food can make you sick or keep you healthy, can leave you overindulged or hungry, can nurture social belonging but can also blatantly expose social exclusion. Historical and socio-cultural experiences, norms and discourses around material and symbolic quality can then mark food as pure or dangerous, and as friend or foe by the same token. This ambivalent nature of eating lies at the very heart of the human encounter with food as both matter and meaning and constitutes the lynchpin of this volume.

Whereas food is already amply discussed in terms of culinary 'delight' by putting at centre stage the role of food allocation in the creation and maintenance of social relationships, commensality, and cohesion,[1] this book rather engages with the conflictive externalities and local embeddedness of a globalised agri-food system, namely by bringing eating in Vietnam into perspective. The ambivalent and potentially disturbing nature that food can have is reflected in this volume's cover image[2]: photographed at an open market in Ho Chi Minh City (HCMC), with the depicted shrimps exemplifying the interconnectedness of global food systems and their embeddedness in Vietnam. With its cultivation at times competing with less lucrative rice growing, and subject to food safety concerns and as regimented item in global trade, shrimp commodity chains symbolise the complexity of global food trade.

Vietnam proves to be an excellent case to depict the diverse facets of food ambivalence given the country's historical context and compressed integration into global (food) markets. Its past—and in parts current—experience of food scarcity and hunger has created challenges of how to meaningfully manoeuvre in a context of emerging food abundance. Against this dynamic background in (urban) Vietnam, people's bodily integrity and identity, gendered and class-based consumption, and concerns of food safety and security all touch upon—in one way or another—the ambiguous nature of food itself, and also indicate discontinuities of broader social transformations.

Food anxiety is the book's common lens through which such ambiguities are considered. The very act of incorporating food constitutes the moment and the process in which materially and culturally transformed matter crosses the boundary of the body, thereby dissolving the dichotomy between 'inside' and 'outside', between the self and the world (Fischler 1988, 279). In this understanding, boundaries are crossed at various scales, connecting but also disconnecting the eating body with the multiple contexts it lives in. It is exactly the linking and disrupting quality of foodstuff—a food's transgressive capacity (Goodman and Sage 2014)—that accounts for its ambivalent nature and makes us speak of 'food anxiety'. Therein, we understand the lens of food anxiety as constitutive for unravelling social theoretical insights into the relationship between the individual and society.[3] What we observe in the vast field of food-related literature is that 'food anxiety' is more often than not used without further conceptual explanation or becomes boiled down to paramount incidences of food scandals.[4] We argue that 'food anxiety' has more to offer than being a descriptive term for the emotional and institutional management of food safety risks, as we will detail below. This volume brings together authors from various disciplines and while their contributions are united in that they all deal with dimensions of food anxiety in Vietnam, the authors follow their own distinct methodological and theoretical approaches to food. Likewise, this introductory chapter should be seen as *one*, namely the editors' interpretation of what follows in the outline of the book parts. By applying our lens of food anxiety, we will frame the three thematic dimensions along which the book is organised: 'Bodily Transgressions: Identity, Othering, and Self' (Part I), 'Food Safety: Trust, Responsibilisation, and Coping' (Part II), and 'The Politics of Food Security' (Part III).

When it came to naming this edited volume, food anxiety as the contributions' mutual lens quickly asserted itself into the title. Since all contributions focus on Vietnam, adding the country's name was also an easy decision. But then it took multiple attempts of testing the conceptual sound of 'Vietnam and beyond' and the like to finally come down with what is now the title of this book: *Food Anxiety in Globalising Vietnam*. In hindsight, the title seems almost inevitable as this book is not about a country *and beyond* but rather about the *(globalising) dynamics of beyond* in Vietnam. Bringing in our own perspective from the field of critical development studies, we find it important to stress the 'dynamics of beyond'. In the (food studies) literature we observe that the mentioned strong focus on the quality of food is very often connected with the Global North. It is, sometimes indirectly, sometimes more overtly assumed that 'the consumer' in the Global North is most concerned with quality and safety due to the food abundance provided by a modernised (agri-)food system. Thus, consumers in the Global North are presented as constantly calculating risks in their daily endeavour to eat clean and healthy food, whereas lack of food access—even though a social reality for many[5]—is much less discussed. By contrast, the Global South is generalised as struggling with not having enough to eat and set as an umbrella term essentialising deficiencies more generally. Yet, we find it more fruitful to contextualise such 'food struggles' along the lines of class, gender, and race and as symptoms of locally embedded capitalist structures bound up in the complex web of historical food trajectories. Besides the editors' innate interest in such dynamics around food availability and consumerism in Vietnam motivating the compilation of this edited volume, there was also a desire to contribute to literature given the relative paucity of existing research on this topic. Particularly from multidisciplinary angles, the area of food and anxiety in a wider sense has not yet received the academic attention that we believe it deserves in order to understand societal relations and transformations in Vietnam. Therefore, the twofold aim of this book is to contribute to research on the field of food in Vietnam as well as on phenomena of food anxiety more broadly.

Having made this point, it will become apparent throughout much of this book that many forms of food anxiety in current-day *globalising* Vietnam cannot be understood without the context of the country's rapid and recent economic integration into global agri-food systems and consumer markets. Therefore, we want to begin with examining the trajectories of the globalised agri-food system that Vietnam has grown to be increasingly intertwined with. We will then sharpen the lens of food anxiety conceptually. By portraying the book's contributions and the way they all speak—in yet different ways—to food anxiety, this will then lead us to discuss concrete examples of what it means to be anxious in terms of food consumption and production in Vietnam. The book ends with concluding remarks by Jean-Pierre Poulain in which he discusses the value of 'food anxiety' as a conceptual lens for understanding broader societal transformations. He argues that because food anxiety is able to capture contemporary crises ranging from food security and food fraud to social controversies, it offers the perspective for a more global analysis of the relation of humans to food.

Food in Globalising Vietnam

When speaking of an agri-food system of global dimensions, the question of what globalisation means in terms of food is inevitable. Depending on discipline and school of thought, the definitions of food globalisation and its beginnings vary widely. Referring to "food globalizations" (Inglis and Gimlin 2009, 4) in the plural mirrors the heterogeneous and at times contradicting dialectic relations of food matters with the social, economic, political, and cultural dimensions of globalisation (Inglis and Gimlin 2009, 9). While the travel of food has been a constant in human history and migration, it can be said that especially the nineteenth and twentieth centuries saw the spread of a mode of food production, distribution, and consumption that has become increasingly globe-spanning in nature (Inglis and Gimlin 2009, 13f.). The dissemination of industrial agriculture and factory farming, local integration into capitalist markets and trade liberalisation, food technology as much as global cargo transport were major factors in the spread of global agri-food systems (Beardsworth and Keil 1997).

These global dynamics also reflect—in locally unique manifestations—Vietnam's (agri-)food history which we will contextualise along with the global food regimes of political economists Friedmann and McMichael (Friedmann and McMichael 1989; McMichael 2009). Food regime theory problematises the capitalist evolution of globalised agriculture as the outcome of an unequal structural power play between different world regions. In general, the European ideology of racial superiority over 'backward' colonies in need of 'civilisation' marked the cornerstone of the development of a global yet highly unequal capitalist system of agricultural modernisation, industrialisation, and trade. During nineteenth-century colonialism, expanding projects of Western civilisation forced the world to participate in a market economy controlled by global colonial regimes, competing forcefully for the raw materials and markets in the colonised Global South. In Vietnam as elsewhere, colonial hegemonic power was ideologically based on constructed racial superiority, forcefully implemented on the bases of science, industrial might, and Christian norms (Jamieson 1995, 42). Industrialisation in Europe required the social reorganisation of labour from national agriculture into industrial factory work. In the 'colonial-diasporic regime'—as the first of three global food regimes—extensive land exploitation and mono-cropping in the colonies of the Global South literally fed the emerging national industries in Europe (Friedmann and McMichael 1989). In Vietnam, it was especially the rich resource base and the water-based transport potential of the Mekong Delta in the country's south that attracted the French colonial gaze.[6] Following the European 'masterplan' of capitalist growth, French colonial force was first imposed on the southern region of Vietnam in the 1860s before establishing rule in the central and northern regions later on.[7] Colonial domination triggered the First Indochina War (1946–1954), and finally culminated in the defeat of the French regime in 1954 and tore Vietnam in two, with the communist Democratic Republic of Vietnam in the north and the US-backed capitalist Republic of Vietnam in the south (Jamieson 1995, 232f.).

What then followed in terms of geopolitical struggles and agricultural developments in separated North and South Vietnam during the Second Indochina War (1955–1975)[8] could be subsumed under what Friedmann and McMichael coined the 'mercantile-industrial regime' ranging from the 1950s to the 1970s and founded in agro-industrialisation and state-protectionism (McMichael 2009, 143). During the second global food regime and the post-colonial independence in the Global South, the communist bloc and the 'free world' of the Cold War courted the newly independent nation-states to follow their respective models of agricultural modernisation. This included the transfer of Green Revolution technology, namely the introduction of large-scale monoculture and irrigation schemes, the reorganisation of agricultural land and labour as well as food aid from the communist bloc and the USA, respectively. During the decades of Vietnam's separation in which blatant food insecurity prevailed, both 'Vietnams' followed different agricultural strategies to feed the war-torn civilian populations as well as military personnel. While collectivisation of agriculture in the 1950s North Vietnam did lead to increased food security of the poorest rural populations, the anticipated increases in food production failed to materialise (Jamieson 1995, 367). The government of the North's Democratic Republic of Vietnam pursued a 'technical duality' which supported agricultural mechanisation while avoiding mechanical labour replacement (Fortier and Trang Thi Thu Trang 2013, 83). Meanwhile, agriculture in capitalist shaped South Vietnam was characterised by more intense mechanisation and commercial agriculture (Fortier and Trang Thi Thu Trang 2013, 83).

After the reunification of North and South Vietnam in 1976 when the Second Indochina War had been won by the communist North in the prior year, food scarcity remained a widespread threat in the face of the country's international isolation. Domestic food production met challenges in providing the Vietnamese people with sufficient food, with the country having relied on annual aid (e.g. in the form of fertilisers and food) primarily from other socialist countries ever since the 1960s (Dang Phong 2004, 21f). Moreover, the Communist Party's attempts to collectivise agriculture in southern Vietnam were met with resistance on the side of many farmers (Ngo Vinh Long 1993; Jamieson 1995, 367f.). With decreasing production and increasing food prices, the government feared unrest in urban areas; yet, governmental attempts to make farmers sell their rice yields at low prices resulted in hoarding and black market activities rather than the desired effect of low food prices (Jamieson 1995, 367f.). Eventually, it was the synergy of multiple factors that led the Vietnamese government to revisit its development strategies and policies more broadly:

> With agriculture stagnating, foreign exchange nearly exhausted, foreign aid low and shrinking, industrial capacity damaged by war, rebuilding stalled by a lack of capital, consumer goods in short supply, and per capita food consumption declining, the party began to sustain severe criticism and was forced to reverse its relentless pressure to transform Vietnam into its own vision of a utopian socialist paradise. (Jamieson 1995, 371)

Taking stock of the obstacles to the country's food security finally galvanised the Vietnamese Communist Party into reform. What followed were the economic reforms of *Đổi Mới* in 1986, marking a point of departure for the country's strong integration into global (food) markets (Beresford 2001; Beresford 2008). The *Đổi Mới* policy initiated the transition from a centrally planned economy, fixed prices, public ownership of the means of production, and state monopoly of foreign trade towards an open market economy with acceptance of private and foreign capitalist sectors (Dang Phong 2004, 21, 37). *Đổi Mới* mirrored a general gradual neoliberal trend in development politics of that time (McMichael 2012, 111ff.).

Sparked by the world financial crises of the 1970s and 1980s (McMichael 2009), international bodies like the World Bank and International Monetary Fund introduced further economic liberalisation and Structural Adjustment Programs (SAPs) to countries of the Global South as supposed remedies to the crisis. SAPs entailed the deregulation of the agricultural sector and cuts in governmental and donor expenditures, agricultural specialisation towards export crops plus the removal of agricultural tariffs (Mittal 2009). This gradually paved the way for corporate food power to emerge and to flourish. The third global food regime following the 1980s ('the corporate regime') constitutes the most recent one, providing the structural background against which most of the world's food production and consumption takes place today (McMichael 2009). The latest regime is driven by the monopolised corporate power of giant agribusinesses which dominate industrial-scale agriculture from the basis of agronomy research and agricultural patents over to mass-scale monocrop- and cash crop-production. The corporate landscape is complemented by large-scale industrial food producers and manufacturers monopolising the production and retail of packaged food and drinks on a worldwide scale. The popular term 'Big Food' is drawn on when referring to the power and control of such global agri-food giants sharply influencing what the world eats (Nestlé 2013; Clapp and Scrinis 2017).

Since Vietnam's gradual liberalisation in the mid-1980s and more recently with accession to the World Trade Organisation in 2007, emerging food markets in Vietnam are increasingly teeming with agri-food businesses trying to gain a foothold. The Green Revolution with its high inputs of pesticides, fertilisers, and growth hormones (Simmons and Scott 2007) is backed by global agribusinesses (see Zhang, this volume). While Vietnam boosted agricultural production in recent decades and switched from being a net importer of rice to one of the world's leading rice exporters (Tran Thi Thu Trang 2011), agriculture today faces other challenges. Agricultural land, especially in peri-urban areas, has seen land use conversions towards industrialisation and urbanisation, impacting farmers' livelihoods and—coupled with a growing population—creating pressure on agricultural productivity (Nguyen Van Suu 2009; Ehlert 2012). Moreover, the impacts of climate change are already palpable in agriculture, for example, in the shape of rising sea levels and salinity intrusion, effects that are predicted to worsen with climate change (Yu et al. 2010; Smajgl et al. 2015). Exposure to weather extremes and the importance of the agricultural sector makes Vietnam particularly vulnerable to these impacts which the government has so far mitigated through technological fixes such as dykes, irrigation systems, and resistant rice varieties in line with discourses of 'modernisation' (Ehlert 2012; Fortier and Trang Thi Thu Trang 2013).

With the vision of a 'modernised' food system also stretching into retail, the Vietnamese government strongly encourages foreign and domestic capital investments in the retail sector, opening the doors for corporate power to provide for domestic supermarket shelves (Hai Thi Hong Nguyen et al. 2013). Concomitantly, the food retail system was prominently altered by the emergence of supermarkets from the early 1990s which since have grown strongly in numbers in the country's major cities (Moustier et al. 2010, 72). Meanwhile, the prioritisation of formalised food outlets has implicated the marginalisation of informal street vendors and 'traditional' markets (Kurfürst 2012; Endres 2013).

Economic liberalisations in countries of the Global South produced a growing dependency of and vulnerability towards global markets and their prices (Mittal 2009). This became all the more apparent during the global food crisis in 2007/2008.[9] While not amongst the countries most affected and despite its recent food productivity gains, the impacts of the crisis did also resonate within Vietnam. The country's entanglements in a globalised food system in crisis showed in consumer anxieties over rising rice prices, in the re-evaluation of the country's food security strategy as well as in the risk of small-scale producers dropping out of the farming sector (Akram-Lodhi 2004, 2005; see Gorman, this volume).

From the Productivist Gaze to the 'Fruits' of Consumption

Against the background of the global corporate food regime, food distribution networks have become as globalised as they have become obscured, and a new quality of food safety concerns, health issues, and distrust towards food have emerged and certainly also constitute one of the most publicly denounced problems with food in contemporary Vietnam (see Part II, this volume). The global span of BSE (bovin spongiform encephalopathy) originating in Europe in the 1990s, large incidences of avian flu (Inglis and Gimlin 2009, 20), and the contamination of baby formula with melanin in China (Jackson 2015) are but a few of many contemporary food safety concerns. These are often seen as related to the globalised food system's structural characteristic of 'distanciation' between food production and consumption and between the realms of the rural and the urban (Bricas 1993; Wilk 2009; Figuié and Bricas 2010). In the same vein, Poulain (2017, 9) speaks of the characteristic of "[m]odern food" that "has been delocalized, in other words, disconnected from its geographical origins and the climatic constraints traditionally associated with them". In the face of growing complexity, it has then increasingly become the role of third parties to identify risks and guarantee product safety through a range of quality labels (Figuié and Bricas 2010). Despite regulatory bodies' function to provide highly controlled food production and trade, they may as well be contradictory or malfunctioning, resulting in mistrust (Inglis and Gimlin 2009, 19f). Also the role of science in food technology has become subject to growing scepticism as polarised public debates on genetically modified organisms (GMOs) exemplify (Wilk 2009; Poulain 2017, 68). On the international scene, such problems of industrial farming and manufacturing in the late 1970s became more and more apparent and were criticised, for example, by emerging environmental und feminist movements (Agarwal 1992; Moeckli and Braun 2001; McMichael 2012, 182ff.; Harcourt and Nelson 2015; Poulain

2017, 66). The demand for more transparency, the call on governmental and other regulatory mechanisms, and the enforcement of consumer citizenship rights (Brooks et al. 2013) started to address the perceived need to re-embed the externalities of living in a 'risk society' in which scientific progress and knowledge not only provided solutions and probabilities for rational management of food scares but also permanently unleashed new incalculable risks (Beck 1992). Meanwhile, neoliberal policy on a global scale led to the birth of 'the consumer'—understood as an individual supposedly acting in the commoditised system of food provision on the basis of individual choice, total information, and personal utility—and, by consequence, to the individualisation of healthy and safe food choice (Parsons 2015).

In Vietnam, concerns over the safety of food have mounted with people being anxious about the effects of feeding their bodies with harmful food. Thus, while economic growth and gains in food productivity have meant a reduction in the prevalence of undernourishment in the country (Marzin and Michaud 2016), one now increasingly finds widespread concerns over food safety related to the harmful effects of the overuse of agricultural inputs as well as regarding the insufficient traceability of food. Correspondingly, consumers at times assess that while the variety of meals has improved, the quality of food products has diminished as has the trust in food regulation bodies to detect substandard produce (see Figuié et al., this volume). Faced with an emerging commoditised food system, the 'invention' of the consumer in Vietnam in recent decades coincided with described neoliberal economic paradigms on the international scene, standing in stark contrast to the prior governmental food rationing system and general discouragement of conspicuous consumption of foreign goods (Vann 2005, 468).

With the general surplus that emanated from industrial production in many world regions and "the majority of the populace hav[ing] access to the ever-growing consumerist fruits of the productivist tree" (Corrigan 2011, 1), food consumption gradually became key for social differentiation as well as for food scholars engaging with food-related identities symbolically as well as in terms of its material conditions (e.g. Goody 1982; Klein 2014). 'Consumer culture', 'consumer society', and 'lifestyle' became common conceptual foci through which scholars aimed to describe central organising principles of social reality and identity. This focus breaks with class and occupation as the paramount lens to understand social inequality and change (Warde 1997, 7ff). Whereas some attest that the major goal of consumption lies in the expression of self-identity (e.g. Bauman 1988), others understand lifestyles as part of a social class' habitus (e.g. Bourdieu 1984). Again others see lifestyle not as a coherent function of identity but rather in terms of fluid and conflictive plural lifestyles in post-modernist consumer culture (e.g. Featherstone 1990).[10] Global agri-food industries and leisure economies in manifold shapes provide services, products, and imaginaries through which to express social belonging and demarcation. In this regard, the role of transnational companies inspired controversial studies on food globalisation conceptualised in terms of processes leading either to culinary and cultural homogenisation (e.g. Ritzer 1993) or to the localisation of global food consumerism creating culinary heterogeneities (e.g. Watson 1997).[11] Often seen as symbols of US-American cultural imperialism and a threat to cultural peculiarities, such transnational brands are at times met with protest and hostility (Wilk 2009).

When following the workings of 'Big Food' monopolising complete global food chains, as discussed earlier, it does not come with surprise that respective food businesses eventually moved on from saturated markets in the Global North to emerging market-terrain such as Vietnam and other Southeast Asian countries. Western-style formats of fast food restaurants and coffee houses tend to appeal, for example, to Asian middle classes and become locally adapted as spaces for leisure and recreation, as family events or as spaces for business opportunities (Higgins 2008; King et al. 2008; Yan 2008; Earl 2014; Ehlert 2016).

Whereas for decades Vietnam was driven by the concern of providing adequate amounts of food, the symbolic meaning of food has come more and more into focus. This transformation in society's relation with food from scarcity to the increasing relevance of consumerism is also expressed in the Vietnamese proverb 'cơm no, áo ấm; cơm ngon, áo đẹp'—"enough food and warm clothing; delicious food and beautiful clothing" (Ehlert 2016, 71). Questions of access to the material and symbolic quality of foodstuff options turns food into an ever-growing marker for social differentiation, inclusion, and exclusion in the context of rising standards of living, newly emerging middle classes, and related growth of socio-economic disparities (Taylor 2004, xi; Van Nguyen-Marshall et al. 2012; Earl 2014). Growing prosperity also stands in relation to the country's nutrition transition which is characterised by a general increased calorie intake and growing shares of animal products, sugar, and processed foods in people's diets (Baker and Friel 2014). In contrast to the earlier times of shortages, Vietnam nowadays suffers from the so-called double burden of malnutrition (Walls et al. 2009; Vietnam Ministry of Health 2012; see also Sobal 1999, 178): cases of underweight prevail (Nguyen Cong Khan and Ha Huy Khoi 2008), while at the same time diet-related diseases of affluence such as obesity and heart-related diseases are on the rise (Avieli 2014). In this regard a strong divide between rural and urban areas can be observed with aspirational food-related lifestyles as well as overweight predominantly being phenomena of the cities (TQ Cuong et al. 2007) and child malnutrition often being a rural phenomenon (Nguyen Cong Khan and Ha Huy Khoi 2008). What Featherstone (1991), for example, accredits to a sheer overwhelming range of dietary, slimming, and other 'body-work' products on the shelves of supermarkets in the Global North, proliferated through advertisements, the popular press, and motion pictures can, without doubt, also be found in (urban) Vietnam. Drummond (2004) for instance describes the social construction of the Vietnamese woman in popular women's magazines. Miss Coca-Cola beauty contests in Hanoi and HCMC start to put female body work on public display (Drummond and Rydstrøm 2004, 12) and with the emergence of the urban fitness sector in the late 1990s, exercising has become a symbolic and physical expression of a modern lifestyle for (women of) the urban middle classes (Leshkowich 2012). What can be observed in urban Vietnam is the growing significance of the body being discursively turned into a gendered consumer object and that proliferates as prime 'locus' of self-discipline (see Ehlert, this volume).

As one can see, there is a lively debate going on in terms of bringing together consumption with different forms of identity construction that ranges from the extremes of the liberal idea of the freedom of choice to being an irreversible corollary of the socio-political context and the material conditions one lives in. The growing divide between insufficient access to (quality) food for some and oversupply of food for others makes

Vietnam particularly vital for the study of food anxieties since people more and more have to manoeuvre between certain paradoxes: in the midst of growing food abundance, they, by eating, manoeuvre between health and illness, pleasure and displeasure (Beardsworth and Keil 1997), and social belonging and exclusion (Bourdieu 1984). In the Vietnamese context of neoliberal market transformation and rampant consumerism (Schwenkel and Leshkowich 2012), fast developing urbanisation, the modernisation of the agricultural and food industries as well as the emergence of certain health, beauty, and lifestyle trends, consumers are thus increasingly confronted with the insecurity of what they symbolically and physiologically ingest via their food options and deprivations. In contrast to the dominant definition of 'the consumer' described as driven by preferences, freedom of choice, and free information in neoclassical economics, the following book contributions all work on contextualisation (Kjærnes et al. 2007), namely on the socio-cultural processes and the structural power that the consumption and production of food and related social anxieties in urban Vietnam is embedded in.

The Transgressive Nature of Food: Conceptualising Food Anxiety

What is on one's plate (or not) is by many means complex given the transgressive nature of food. Goodman and Sage establish that for the human body "there are few things more essentially transgressive and boundary-crossing than food" (2014, 1). In the widest sense of the term, 'transgression'—being an established concept in social theory—refers to the delineation, crossing, and exceeding of spatial, discursive, behavioural, and material boundaries (Jenks 2003). We understand such boundaries as fluid 'areas' marked by relational interaction between blurred rather than supposedly clear-cut categories (Lamont and Molnár 2002).

The complexity of food then lies in its characteristic of bounding diverse scales in one's own mouth. Through the lens of food one can connect the past with the present, the individual with society and the domestic household with the world economy (Belasco 2007, 5). Yet, the complexity of food does not end on the plate. It is rather nurtured again by the very act of incorporation of food *into* the body (e.g. Fischler 1988, 279; Probyn 2000; Carolan 2011; Abbots and Lavis 2013; Lavin 2013; Abbots 2017). Eating thus constitutes the intersection of the body and the 'Self' (see Lupton 1996) or the 'objectified' and the 'lived' body (Gugutzer 2012). Correspondingly, the body is more than an object regulated by social norms and structural relations but constitutes the immediate site of the visceral and sensory experience of 'being-in-the-world' (Csordas 1990).

We, the editors, conceptualise food anxiety as evolving from transgressing diverse scales that lace the visceral being of the self with societal norms, political dynamics, and economic structures. The constant negotiation of such boundaries provokes essential questions, even poses threats, to relational integrity at different levels (Lavin 2013, xii). These internalised or unconscious as well as conscious negotiation processes are also captured through the concept of food neophilia and neophobia—the openness/affection towards respectively the distrust/fear of new food (Rozin 1976; Fischler 1988; Wilk 2009). Related to the 'omnivore's paradox', humankind's relationship to food is inherently contradictory, alternating between the search for diversification and mistrust of potential danger (Fischler 1988). In contrast to the terms 'uncertainty' or 'fear', which are rather confined to risks regarding food quantity, quality, and palatability, 'anxiety' captures more fundamental struggles over identity, difference, and power (Hayes-Conroy and Hayes-Conroy 2008). 'Anxiety' reflects not only on questions of integrity in terms of material 'realities' but also regarding the transgression of discursive structures. What one consumes and produces, can access or is excluded from tells something about one's class-based, gendered, racialised, and historical embeddedness in global capitalist systems of food production, distribution, and consumption. Furthermore, what one eats or refrains from needs to be seen in the context of diverse local social norms and taboos of food provisioning and responsibility (DeVault 1994) as well as understood as embedded in codes of body conduct, attractiveness (Lupton 1996; Probyn 2000; Cairns and Johnston 2015), and productivity (e.g. Foucault 1977, 1978; Featherstone 1991). Historical trajectories of food scarcity, emotions, and memories of food desire as well as imaginaries of abundance are imparted over generations (Sutton 2001). As such, food demarcates as well as crosses physical, symbolic, and imagined boundaries, and as the process of incorporation is so closely linked with subjectivity, it constitutes a great source of anxiety and risk in general (Lupton 1996, 16). Food anxiety in its symbolic and material dimensions, then, emerges as an effect of fundamental social processes and structures bound in relationality and the essential process of boundaries constantly being made and unmade (Lamont and Molnár 2002; Jenks 2003).

In the following presentation of the book structure, the reader will be introduced to the various dimensions of food anxiety as resonating at different intersections at stake. The editors' lens of food anxiety on the case studies will reflect on how and which boundaries are transgressed, negotiated, kept elastic, or reinforced. The book is organised in three parts, reflecting on different boundary crossings and respective food anxiety facets. Part I focuses on bodily transgressions and questions of (colonial) identity, gender, and power. Part II puts centre stage the boundaries between the supposed fixed triangle of state, market, and society by discussing questions of trust, responsibilisation, and coping regarding food safety. The final Part III turns to the politics of food security by elaborating on transgressions of territorial agricultural boundaries and volatile global food markets.

Part I—Bodily Transgressions: Identity, Othering, and Self

Part I of this book makes central the interface of the eating body, the subjective self and broader society. It discusses identity construction as a process strongly mediated through food consumption, deprivation, and body work. Eating offers insights into the ways in which identity, difference, and power are inscribed upon the body be it as formulated, for example, in Bourdieu's concept of the class-based habitus (1984) or by Foucault's techniques of self-discipline and optimisation (1988; Parsons 2015), as socialised into gendered bodies (Butler 1993; Lupton 1996) or as racialised 'Others' (Hall 1997; Slocum and Saldanha 2013). Furthermore, the focus on eating throws light on agency and the "micropractices of contestation and acceptance" (Abbots 2017, 14) towards the structural, discursive, and material forces working on the body. Embodiment—as the sensory, visceral, and emotional dimensions of bodies as 'being-in-the-world' (Csordas 1990)—draws attention to the very sensual experiences of being regulated in terms of gender, class, and race but also to embodiment as a potential site of resistance (Abbots 2017, 20f.).

Eating as a project of negotiating identity is fundamental. The positioning vis-à-vis 'foreign' food either through hostility or openness can be an expression of a perceived threat towards an imagined culinary origin as much as the demonstrated consumption of the unfamiliar can be an expression of distinction or sophistication (Wilk 2009; see Peters, this volume). As we will see with the first contribution by Erica J. Peters, this colonial power play very subtly materialised in people's everyday foodways. Peters's chapter 'Power Struggles and Social Positioning: Culinary Appropriation and Anxiety in Colonial Vietnam' opens this section by providing an in-depth historical portray of food-related anxieties as rooted in different power constellations. By focusing on Vietnam's precolonial and colonial culinary history, Peters lays the groundwork for the subsequent book chapters which concentrate primarily on food anxieties in contemporary Vietnam. The choice to integrate a historical perspective in this volume was made in order to avoid assumptions about the historical singularity of phenomena (Inglis and Gimlin 2009, 11). Peters's historical account elaborates on the central point of food becoming a powerful vehicle to rise in and to demarcate one's social status as well as to exclude others from social mobility. The chapter deals with anxiety on the part of the colonial power(s) in Vietnam. Anxiety here is triggered by colonised bodies incorporating French foods. French colonisers perceived the Vietnamese elite and general population eating French food according to French etiquette as acts of bodily and symbolic transgressions by the 'uncivilised'. To the contrary, the Vietnamese colonial elite actually played with such dichotomies of the 'civilised' and the 'backwards' by displaying the sophistication of their own food etiquette and gustatory traditions. Through demonstrations of the French's inability to handle, for example, chopsticks, the Vietnamese relativised narratives of 'civilisation' and, therewith, turned the embodiment of Vietnamese food into a potential site of resistance towards the colonial regime. Besides examining food anxieties during the French colonisation of Indochina both on the side of the colonisers and on the colonised society, Peters also takes a look at intra-societal conflicts and anxieties along the lines of class, location, and political views. She uses food as a lens to show how the complex social boundaries, for example, between the rural 'backwards' and the local (urban) elite, were constantly transgressed, reinforced, reproduced, and challenged along matrixes of constructed 'superiority' and 'inferiority'. Peters's contribution shows the intimate relationship between food and claims of social and political authority as a means to assure oneself and one's own identity against the respective Other. She closes with the argument that anxiety evolves on the part of the colonisers because their power feels illegitimate and vulnerable more generally. This would make the constructed demarcation line between the refined 'culinarily civilised' and the 'rawness' of the colonised bodies becoming more and more porous.

Whereas anxiety in Peters's chapter is triggered by supposedly clear-cut identities of the powerful and the subordinate becoming transgressed through food practices, the subsequent chapter by Nir Avieli relates to anxiety as a matter of transgressing food taboos and social norms of food restrictions. In his chapter 'Forbidden from the Heart: Flexible Food Taboos, Ambiguous Culinary Transgressions, and Cultural Intimacy in Hoi An, Vietnam' Avieli brings the reader's attention to contemporary Vietnam and presents an ethnographic study conducted in the central Vietnamese town of Hoi An. Avieli's ethnography zooms into the catering and consumption of he-goat meat and 'jungle' meat, both subject to certain food taboos. He describes the food venues where these 'forbidden' meats are served as strongly marked by the symbolic display of extreme masculinity, characterised by both vague and blatant associations with sexual services and female suppression as well as the abuse of political and social power. In the two case studies and along the cultural symbolism of meat, the essence of the patriarchal system of dominance and power as in men over women and men over animals and nature unfolds through the incorporation of the female sexualised Other and of 'forbidden' meats (Twigg 1983; Adams 2000; see also Probyn 2000). Another momentum of masculine 'might' shows in the abuse of the law through the incorporation of the 'wild' flesh of legally protected forest animals. The dense atmospheric description of respective food venues imparts to the reader the strong ambivalence that accompanies the consumption of such symbolically contaminated meats (Rozin 1976). Avieli tickles out the conflictive affair of eating between lust and disgust. Being aware that their culinary practice is ambivalent as it transgresses social and moral imperatives, the eaters of tabooed meat escape to what he describes with Herzfeld as 'cultural intimacy' (Herzfeld 2005). This notion constitutes that the act of transgression itself creates new boundaries of social bonding in these arbitrary culinary places. There, cultural intimacy becomes based on essentialised maleness through the subordination and symbolic consumption of the female and the wild. The transgression of such food taboos loaded with gendered notions of masculinity and femininity becomes even reinforced by social condemnation. Thus, the chapter illustrates the relationality of boundaries at play with the discussed meats being subject to taboos and anxiety in some and desirable and identity-instilling in other contexts.

Part I closes with a chapter by Judith Ehlert titled 'Obesity, Biopower, and Embodiment of Caring: Foodwork and Maternal Ambivalences in Ho Chi Minh City'. According to the World Health Organisation, obesity constitutes one of the major food anxieties as the threat it poses is global in scale. It is supposed to put public health systems as well as the productive labour force of whole economies under pressure (WHO 2000). In this vein, fatness is considered a moral transgression and obese people conceived as supposedly unable to restrain themselves for the public good and in the name of idealised personal responsibility (LeBesco 2011; Lupton 2013; Cairns and Johnston 2015, 89ff.). For the first time in recent history following the opening-up of the economy, obesity and being overweight have also entered the public health discourse in Vietnam relating it to general dietary changes towards the increasing consumption of processed, convenience, and high-calorie foods (Vietnam Ministry of Health 2012). The government addresses the global 'obesity epidemic'[12] through national programmes on nutrition and health education and public awareness campaigns. The obesity discourse and the media's and the food industry's diverging appeals of 'consume and abstain' serve the author as a scaffold for her empirical study on how mothers experience the conflicting social norms and practices of feeding children amidst the prescription of certain body and beauty ideals for children. She elaborates how food femininities are constructed through discourses and practices of mothering and rooted in the embodiment of caring for oneself and one's children. Ehlert argues that food anxiety on the side of mothers and mothers-to-be arises from the conflicting demands being placed on them. First, a whole food industry co-opts the practice of feeding and caring as it promotes their products tainted with paramount symbols of love and care for profit-making purposes. Second, and simultaneously, public health campaigns urge mothers to regulate their children's unhealthy appetites, coupled with social media fora and lifestyle blogs pandering to 'modern' and responsible mothering. Third, intergenerational conflicts regarding the regulation of children's nutrition add to the complex demands that frame the 'correct' feeding of children as a mother's obligation and as essential to her 'moral personhood'. These conflicts materialise in certain ways to discipline the child's body and leads to mothers exerting self-discipline on their own bodies. The chapter shows that the correspondence with social norms addressing femininity and the child's body as object in terms of its shape and physical constitution are inevitably internalised as well as embodied in the phenomenological sense (Crossley 2012). The conflicting demands of caring become embodied and arouse sensual ambivalences wielding socially structured food anxiety.

Part II—Food Safety: Trust, Responsibilisation, and Coping

By addressing food safety, the contributions in the second section touch upon an aspect of food anxiety of high societal relevance and one of the most prevailing contemporary food concerns in Vietnam. The empirical basis of this section counters the academic bias that discusses concerns for food quality and safety predominantly as phenomena of the Global North. Against the structural framework of the capitalist system of food production and provision, Part II deals with subjective feelings and discourses on food anxiety that actors experience in the face of decreasing transparency in global food chains that reaches down to local urban markets. Moreover, this section centres on the relational power between society, state, and the market in terms of food safety as it articulates questions of how people negotiate the described intransparency and lack of accountability when eating food that is perceived as hazardous. Related to the previously mentioned sweeping changes in food provisioning are transformations in qualification processes of food. Whereas in wet markets quality is observed directly and sensorily on the basis of embodied food knowledge, in supermarkets third-party labels on often pre-packaged foods are supposed to be quality guarantors (Figuié and Bricas 2010, 187). Concomitantly, trust is negotiated very differently in the face of third-party institutions. At the same time the relation between state and society has seen a change in character: while under central planning consumerism was officially frowned upon and possible mostly on an illicit black market, post Đổi Mới citizens are expected to embody their roles as consumers (Vann 2005). And while structurally the government continues to exercise power over the conditions of the food system, its role is now more indirect in terms of decision-making. Rather, policy interventions and market paradigms position the individual as responsible for behavioural change regarding (food) shopping based on the execution of choice (Wertheim-Heck 2015). As stated, it is particularly anxieties that touch on the safety of food that are examined under Part II. Besides issues of food hygiene, it is especially the question of chemical contamination that concerns people regarding their health and bodily integrity. Through mismanagement of (at times illegal) agricultural inputs, preservatives in food processing and chemicals used in food scams, unclear amounts and types of substances make their way into food and eventually into people's bodies. To a certain degree, people are 'blindfolded' when eating as they cannot retrace the origin and the quality of the food they ingest on a daily basis, stirring people's insecurity in terms of harming one's health and bodies.[13]

This second part begins with the chapter 'Trust and Food Modernity in Vietnam' by Muriel Figuié, Paule Moustier, Nicolas Bricas, and Nguyen Thi Tan Loc, and provides an overview of the food safety concerns that exist in current-day Vietnam. This contribution presents empirical research into Vietnam's transforming food system and the anxieties associated with this. By specifically drawing on the notion of trust in consumers' search for quality food, this chapter examines people's strategies of coping with a food system in transition. It builds on the idea that there exist three types of food systems—traditional food systems, modern food systems, and late modernity systems—with very different risks as well as qualification processes of food. Due to the speed of changes in terms of industrialisation, urbanisation, and economic liberalisation in recent decades, the authors hypothesise that the food system in Vietnam shows characteristics of all three types of food systems as it has been transformed by a 'compressed modernity'. Traditional food systems are characterised by small-scale farming as well as small local markets where food quality is assessed directly through the senses and based on trust in familiar sellers. In the face of industrialised food production and lengthened food chains in modern food systems, then, the gap between a highly specialised food sector and the population not involved in food production is bridged by institutions who guarantee the quality of food through formalised labels. As such a liberalised food system produces sustainability and safety issues that cannot be assessed by consumers directly and thus are less acceptable to them, the authors then speak of food systems of late modernity in which the negative consequences behind the achievements of modernisation such as productivity increases become visible. It is under these intransparent and complex circumstances that food safety becomes a major concern of consumers since neither direct qualification nor governmental controls seem to be able to offer sufficient trust in food. Consequently, consumers diversify their ways of building trust in food sources and navigate between them depending on the context. Figuié et al. describe how the boundaries between the different and coexisting systems are at times fluid and how they are negotiated by consumers while posing a source of anxiety at the same time. The exceptionally rich empirical basis for this chapter composes data from 12 years of research in Vietnam. By conceptually marrying questions of trust with modernisation processes of the food system, the chapter offers insights into the sources of and dealings with current-day food anxieties in Vietnam.

The following chapter 'Between Food Safety Concerns and Responsibilisation: Organic Food Consumption in Ho Chi Minh City' by Nora Katharina Faltmann focuses on one specific response to food anxieties in the form of eating organically produced food. This chapter examines emerging organic food consumption in urban Vietnam and contextualises it within the country's current food safety situation. Faltmann's empirical research on Ho Chi Minh City indicates that while environmental concerns do not play a role in organic consumption, personal health concerns and food anxieties in light of the prevailing food safety issues do all the more so. With this, consumers' individual motivations for buying organic products in urban Vietnam differ widely from the emergence of organic food consumption as part of wider environmental movements in the Global North that still often informs Western-centric understandings of organic consumption. The chapter points out that whereas organic sectors in Global North contexts have seen strong corporatisation and conventionalisation tendencies in past decades, environmental protection continues to serve as the official rationale behind many foreign-financed organic initiatives in Vietnam. Yet in the context of the country's food safety issues, Vietnamese consumers rather seek organic food as an individual response to food safety concerns, particularly in terms of chemical contamination. With the clientele of Ho Chi Minh City's high-priced organic niche market most prominently being highly educated, well-earning, and female in familial care positions, organic food consumption is moreover structured along the lines of class and gender. Opting for organic food, thus, poses an individual strategy to achieve safe food provisioning for oneself or one's family within the realms of market logic. Similarly, the chapter identifies the recent growing interest of the Vietnamese state in the development of the organic sector as clearly corporate-driven whereas the governmental emphasis on productivity-oriented agriculture and overall food security persists. The at times contradicting influences of neoliberal consumer discourse, the socialist state as well as contemporary food safety issues simultaneously structure the organic sector and produce food anxieties that Faltmann illustrates based on the narratives of organic food consumers. It is in this vein that the author embeds her findings on organic consumption within changing societal discourses that mark a shift in the relations between the government, the market, and the individual.

Notions of what constitutes safe food and ways to acquire such are also an element of the next chapter, this time with a focus on (informal) practices of urban gardening in Hanoi. In this chapter, Sandra Kurfürst links her own empirical research on urban gardening practices and rural-urban food supply in Vietnam's capital with conceptions of the rural and the urban. 'Urban Gardening and Rural-Urban Supply Chains: Reassessing Images of the Urban and the Rural in Northern Vietnam' argues that while binary categories of the rural and the urban in Vietnam persist in imaginaries, the boundaries between them are oftentimes transgressed in practices of everyday life. The author recalls the symbolic meanings of the urban as a hub of modernity, political power yet also as polluted and disorderly in contrast to the countryside which is regarded as a socially intact place of tradition, in touch with nature and source of safe and fresh food, yet also designated as potentially backward. These binary categories are continuously reproduced in social interaction while at the same time being resolved in everyday practices (in the city). These practices are then worked out by Kurfürst in relation to prevailing food anxieties and urbanites' quest for safe and fresh food. Through, for example, growing food in urban space on sacred pagoda land, in private spaces prior dedicated to ornamental rather than edible plants or in public spaces, ideas of what constitutes inherently urban or rural practices and spaces are negotiated. In the case of gardening on public land in Hanoi that the government increasingly transforms from agricultural to construction land, citizens—so the author argues—make (subversive) usage of space purposed for economic activities, hence actively shaping their urban environment. With such interim usage often being tolerated by local authorities, 'mediation spaces' occur in which the boundaries between public and private, economic and agrarian, are re-negotiated and fluid while on a national level, policies for the re-zoning of agricultural land into investment land for development projects (see Gorman, this volume) intend more clear-cut determinations of the functions and value of land through concomitant classifications. Another realm that expresses fluidity between rural and urban conceptions in Vietnam's urbanising society lies in relations urbanites maintain with kin in their rural place of origin. The source of knowledge for cultivating food in the city often lies in the rural biographies of urban gardeners. Moreover, such rural-urban ties also function as provision systems for urban residents with food from the countryside. Other than food from the in-between spaces of vast peri-urban areas providing Hanoi with food, products directly from the countryside are trusted as safe and fresh. This applies all the more so if this food is acquired through direct personal relations even though the end consumers might know little about the conditions of production or origin. Thus, the chapter shows that on the one hand the rural/urban binary continues to inform the way people imagine space as well as safe food, while on the other hand their practices often prove the fluidity and ambivalence of such imagined boundaries.

Part III—The Politics of Food Security

Part III touches on the most basic anxiety around food: food security—namely the adequate availability and accessibility of food not only to meaningfully fuel one's body but to avoid malnutrition and chronic hunger. At the 1996 World Food Summit in Rome, food security was defined as "exist[ing] when all people, at all times, have physical and economic access to sufficient, safe and nutritious food that meets their dietary needs and food preferences for an active and healthy life" (FAO 1996). Critical debates on food security often take a swipe at the concept's apolitical core and its technocratic understanding of 'feeding the world' from the top-down (Holt Giménez and Shattuck 2011). The genuine political nature of food safety, however, comes into light when relating it more closely to the path-dependency of colonial exploitation, the unequal conditions of global trade, and mass production and mass consumerism bearing most severely on marginalised groups to cater for their food needs. The political dimension of food security also plays in as much as food provision and accessibility are crucial in terms of national sovereignty and political authority, providing the essential backbone for a regime's legitimacy (Bohstedt 2016).

Part III of this book centres on such political dimensions of food security when it discusses questions of national sovereignty and the limits of protecting domestic production markets amidst global food provisioning systems. The chapters in this book part portray how, despite the general abundance of food on a global scale and increase in consumer affluence, structural deficiencies of the agri-food system continue to work to the detriment of marginalised groups. Food security as a basic need seemed almost forgotten in Vietnam, tranquilised as it was by the heydays of economic growth and agricultural boom. On the basis of its agricultural output records in recent decades, Vietnam not only provides for the domestic market but contributes significantly to the global food provisioning system through its agricultural export orientation. However, the global food crisis that reached fever pitch in 2007/2008 exposed Vietnam's shaky interconnectedness with volatile agricultural commodity markets. Although much less than elsewhere, when the food crisis hit Vietnam it sharply called the assumed steadfastness of food security into question. As will be shown, China plays a dominant role for the development and future of the Vietnamese agricultural sector. Besides the relationality of the food security strategies of both countries, they are strongly connected in terms of food safety issues. What will become most apparent in the two chapters in Part III is the class-based dimension of having enough (safe) food to eat—no matter on which side of the national borders one is. The permeability of both national agricultural sectors towards global agri-food trends is highlighted by the following chapters whereas food anxiety will show in reinforcing class-based boundaries. This is what will be focussed as the politics of food security in this book part.

In his chapter 'From Food Crisis to Agrarian Crisis? Food Security Strategy and Rural Livelihoods in Vietnam', Timothy Gorman begins with a scene of food panic that economic analysts would not have dared to suspect; as the food price crisis of 2007/2008 swept Vietnam, anxious consumers queued up to buy food and hoarded supplies of rice. As one economist exclaimed in disbelief: "In Ho Chi Minh City, for heaven's sake, the centre of the second-largest rice exporting surplus in the world, supermarkets and rice markets got cleaned out in two days" (Timmer in Charles 2011). Gorman takes this alarming outcry as basis for his meticulous inspection of the post-crisis national food security strategy as defined in Resolution 63. His discourse analysis brings to light the specific cultural, political, and historical pathway that the document was formulated on and the government's priority to shield the Vietnamese population from falling back into historical times of rice insecurity. Whereas panic buying of urban consumers in 2007 constitutes the starting point for Gorman to illustrate the reactions to the global food crisis in Vietnam, in his chapter, he reconstructs the rationale of why the government responded in the way it did. According to him, the legacy of food shortages in Vietnam translates into the historical promotion of production- and supply-oriented rice agriculture as a means to prevent political unrest throughout the different times and regimes (see also Peters, this volume). In connection with this, the chapter discusses Confucianist norms of sovereignty, based on the teleological power of the sovereign to provide for its people, the deeply entrenched symbolism of rice for the Vietnamese diet and identity as well as rice constituting the major foodstuff for the rural poor and urban working classes as crucial drivers of the post-crisis rice policy. The chapter then brings together the implementation measures of Resolution 63 with a broader agrarian crisis. In his case study, the author discusses how the resolution has affected the social conditions and peasants' class struggles more broadly in the rice-growing areas in the Mekong Delta. Gorman summarises the externalities of the modernised and production-oriented rice and food policy by describing a 'general air of agrarian crisis in the countryside'. This 'general air' on the part of small-scale peasants speaks of their anxiety regarding the insecure and blurry options they have when dropping out from the agricultural sector with not too many options for being meaningfully absorbed by other economic sectors. With his chapter and from the standpoint of critical agrarian studies, Gorman retraces food-relationality between various scales—from the volatile bubble of global trade markets to the territorially bounded nation-state aiming to provide food security down to the risky livelihoods of small-scale farmers in the Mekong Delta. This implies food, in this case rice, to travel between the boundaries of highly abstract food markets, over fairly concrete physical and territorial boundaries to the embodied boundaries of food producers and consumers alike. Furthermore, this chapter covers the historical interconnectedness of time-related boundaries when it brings together the collective memory of food scarcity of the past that carries on as an imperative for the party's resolution to provide food in a self-sufficient and production-oriented manner within own territorial boundaries.

In his chapter 'When Food Crosses Borders: Paradigm Shifts in China's Food Sectors and Implications for Vietnam', Hongzhou Zhang assumes that it would be politically, diplomatically, and practically challenging for

Vietnam to repeat the ban of rice exports, as was done in 2007/2008, in the case of another crisis. With China being the biggest rice consumer in the world and Vietnam supplying an enormous share, Zhang analyses the implications of China's overall food security strategy and changing consumer food preferences for the Vietnamese agri-food market and for global agricultural developments more broadly. Due to its growing production gap China turns to alternative measures to assure growing domestic demand and national food security in staples. As in Vietnam's agricultural policy (see Gorman, this volume), China also prioritises farmland concentration to the dead end of small-scale agriculturalists. Besides further exploitation of the aquatic and marine resources which has recently triggered a lot of geopolitical conflict between Vietnam and China, China heavily invests in agricultural technology developments in the form of GMOs. This is backed by China's economically powerful merger and acquisitions of business giants in the agri- and pharmaceutical sectors which are likely to shape the GMO agenda for the global agri-food industry as a whole (Zhang 2016). In the same vein, China's agriculture going global relies on land-based investments outside of its national territory—a strategy often criticised as neocolonial land grabbing (Hofman and Ho 2012). Zhang then zooms in on domestic food consumption leading the focus to food safety issues in China as well as beyond its borders in Vietnam. Part II of this book on food safety portrays Vietnamese consumers being suspicious towards the consumption of Chinese food produce. Given Vietnam's suspicion towards the 'Big Brother China', the ambivalences arising in Vietnam are twofold: on the one hand, the Vietnamese discourse condemns Chinese food[14] as it is perceived harmful for a person's health as well as for national integrity more generally; on the other hand though, the relative affordability of Chinese imported produce caters to a substantial demand for cheap food of the working class and destitute groups in urban and rural society in Vietnam. Zhang's data shows that counterfeit and substandard food products legally and illegally entered the Vietnamese consumer market. Furthermore, China's increasingly harsher environmental policies drive Chinese low-end food manufacturing, fertiliser, and pesticide sectors out of the domestic market, which resettle in emerging markets like Vietnam. Just like for the Vietnamese case, broader changes in dietary patterns in

China expose strong class-based differences and rural-urban divides. Whereas high- and middle-income consumers turn to (partly organic) imports from neighbouring Southeast Asian countries which are perceived as safer, consumers who cannot afford to go the safe way suffer from sharply rising domestic retail prices and substandard food supply to the detriment of their health. Evidently, food anxiety for price-sensitive consumers on both sides of the border in China and Vietnam relate to food security as well as food safety concerns. The food legally and illegally traded in both directions of the national borders show how food risk is passed on domestically and across the land borders to poorer groups who structurally make up the major 'recipients' of such food risks endemic to the domestic as well as global food systems.

Notes

1. For an overview, see Mintz and Du Bois 2002; on Vietnam, see Avieli 2012.
2. We thank Carina Maier for providing us with this photo as it captures the essence of this book so well.
3. By approaching food as a paramount physical and social requirement of human existence, it was anthropological and sociological scholars in particular who lifted food out of its perceived irrelevance for scientific discovery (e.g. Lévy-Strauss 1997; Mintz 1985; Mintz and Du Bois 2002; Murcott 1983; Mennell et al. 1992; Counihan and Kaplan 1998; Poulain 2017).
4. For detailed works engaging with food anxiety theoretically and empirically see, for example, Abbots 2017; Jackson 2015; Lavin 2013.
5. For an example on an intersectional approach to issues of food access in the USA, see Alkon and Agyeman 2011.
6. Of course, Vietnam's colonial history pre-dates the arrival of the French colonial regime as much as the formation of the nation-state itself involved the forced subordination of diverse ethnic groups by the ethnic Vietnamese (*Kinh*) majority in the pursuit of arable land to fight hunger in scarcity-prone areas (see Peters, this volume). Since ethnic Vietnamese (*Kinh*) gained rule over Chinese power in 939 AD and claimed rule in the Red River Delta in the North (*Bắc Bộ*), the Vietnamese "slowly inched their way through the centre (*Trung Bộ*) into the South (*Nam*

Bộ), opening new land to colonisation and encouraging migration from older areas" (Popkin 1979, 84). During the great "advance to the south" (*Nam tiến*) (Hickey 1967, 2) first Vietnamese and Chinese settlers reached the Mekong Delta in the 1600s (see Peters, this volume; Biggs 2004, 79; Brocheux 1995, 10ff.). This claim of new frontier land involved the forced colonisation of diverse ethnic populations in the areas defeated by the ethnic Vietnamese (Taylor 2007; Scott 2009) and marked the beginning of a decades-long internal food transfer from the southern delta for fighting hunger in the scarcity-prone regions (Biggs 2004; Brocheux 1995).

7. The French colonial terms for these regions were *Cochinchina* for the southern, *Annam* for the central, and *Tonkin* for the northern region.

8. Also known in the USA as the 'Vietnam War'.

9. At the peak of the crisis skyrocketing prices for staple food resulted in menacing levels of food insecurity and malnutrition and sparked protests and food riots in a number of countries in the Global South. Revealing the instability of the global food system through the volatility of world market prices, the crisis was caused by the interplay of a variety of short-term factors including financial speculation in agricultural commodity markets, export restrictions, decreasing global grain stocks, and bad harvests. These were coupled with long-term shifts including land competition between crops for food and crops for livestock feed and so-called biofuels and rising fuel prices in fossil fuel dependent agrarian systems (Mittal 2009; Weis 2013).

10. For a summary of the debate, see Warde 1997.

11. Ritzer's work on the McDonaldisation of Society (1993) discusses rationalisation as a principal structural driving force of modernisation in general and in the field of food consumerism specifically, predicting a certain trend of culinary homogenisation. Watson (1997) confronted Ritzer's rather pessimistic outlook regarding the loss of culinary diversity. Along with empirical case studies on the localisation of fast food markets, Watson highlights that the structural expansion of McDonaldisation does not inevitably lead to cultural homogenisation but rather to the localization of this structural imperative—fostering global culinary heterogeneity.

12. For a critical perspective of the social construction of the 'obesity epidemic' in China, see Greenhalgh 2016; for a critical account of the 'obesity epidemic' and neoliberalism, see, for example, Guthman 2009 and Metzl and Kirkland 2010.

13. The chapters in this section have set their primary focus on perceptions and practices of urban consumers, while food safety of course also relates to the realms of the rural. While (harmful) agricultural practices are part of the general food safety debate and academic focus, farmers' perspectives are often given less room despite their central role in and direct contact with food production. Whereas Part III of this volume zooms in on the major changes in domestic agriculture in the course of agricultural restructuring policies of the government, rural perspectives on issues of food safety are not part of this volume, posing one of its limitations. We certainly would have liked to integrate such work and are convinced that perspectives *of* rather than *on* those growing the food would deepen insights into the country's food safety debate and require further academic attention.

14. Suspicion towards the safety of Chinese food imports is not confined to Vietnam (for Japan, see Walravens 2013).

References

Abbots, E.-J., 2017. The Agency of Eating: Mediation, Food and the Body. Contemporary Food Studies: Economy, Culture and Politics. London; New York: Bloomsbury Academic.

Abbots, E.-J., Lavis, A. (eds.), 2013. Why We Eat, How We Eat: Contemporary Encounters between Foods and Bodies. Farnham; Burlington: Ashgate (Critical Food Studies).

Adams, C. J., 2000. The Sexual Politics of Meat: A Feminist-Vegetarian Critical Theory. 10th anniversary ed. New York: Continuum.

Agarwal, B., 1992. The Gender and Environment Debate: Lessons from India. *Feminist Studies* 18(1), 119–158.

Akram-Lodhi, H. A. 2004. Are 'Landlords Taking back the Land'? An Essay on the Agrarian Transition in Vietnam. *European Journal of Development Research* 16(4), 757–789.

Akram-Lodhi, H. A. 2005. Land Markets and Rural Livelihoods in Vietnam. ISS/UNDP Land, Poverty and Public Action Policy Paper No. 4. The Hague: Institute of Social Sciences (ISS).

Alkon, A.H., Agyeman, J. (eds.), 2011. Cultivating food justice: race, class, and sustainability, Food, health, and the environment. Cambridge: MIT Press.

Avieli, N., 2012. Rice talks: food and community in a Vietnamese town. Indiana University Press, Bloomington.

Avieli, N., 2014. Vegetarian Ethics and Politics in Late-Socialist Vietnam. In: Jung, Y. (ed.). Ethical eating in the postsocialist and socialist world. Berkeley: University of California Press, 144–166.

Baker, P., Friel, S., 2014. Processed foods and the nutrition transition: evidence from Asia: Processed foods and nutrition transition in Asia. *Obesity Reviews* 15(7), 564–577.

Bauman, Z., 1988. Freedom. Concepts in Social Sciences Series. California: University of Minnesota Press.

Beardsworth, A., Keil, T., 1997. Sociology on the menu: an invitation to the study of food and society. London; New York: Routledge.

Beck, U., 1992. From Industrial Society to the Risk Society: Questions of Survival, Social Structure and Ecological Enlightenment. *Theory, Culture & Society* 9(1), 97–123.

Belasco, W. J., 2007. Appetite for change. How the counterculture took on the food industry. Ithaca: Cornell University Press.

Beresford, M., 2001. Vietnam: The transition from central planning. In: Rodan, G., Hewison, K. and Robison, R. (eds.). The political economy of Southeast Asia: conflict, crises and change. Melbourne: Oxford University Press, 206–233.

Beresford, M., 2008. *Doi Moi* in review: The challenges of building market socialism in Vietnam. *Journal of Contemporary Asia* 38(2), 221–243.

Biggs, D. A., 2004. Between the Rivers and Tides: A Hydraulic History of the Mekong Delta, 1820–1975. Ph.D.-Thesis, University of Washington.

Bohstedt, J., 2016. Food riots and the politics of provisions from early modern Europe and China to the food crisis of 2008. *The Journal of Peasant Studies* 43(5), 1035–1067.

Bourdieu, P., 1984. Distinction. A Social Critique of the Judgement of Taste. London: Routledge and Kegan Paul.

Bricas, N., 1993. Les caractéristiques et l'évolution de la consummation alimentaire dans les villes africaines. In: Muchnik, J. (ed.). Alimentation techniques et innovations dans les régions tropicales. Paris: L'Harmattan, 127–160.

Brocheux, P., 1995. The Mekong Delta: Ecology, Economy, and Revolution, 1860–1960. Madison: University of Wisconsin (Madison Monograph No. 12).

Brooks, S., Watson, D. B., Draper, A., Goodman, M., Kvalvaag H., Wills W., 2013. Chewing on Choice. In: Abbots E.-J., Lavis, A. (eds.), 2013. Why We Eat, How We Eat: Contemporary Encounters between Foods and Bodies. Farnham; Burlington: Ashgate, 149–168 (Critical Food Studies).

Butler, J., 1993. Bodies That Matter: On the Discursive Limits of 'Sex'. New York: Routledge.

Cairns, K., Johnston J., 2015. Food and Femininity. London; New York: Bloomsbury Publishing (Contemporary Food Studies: Economy, Culture and Politics).

Carolan, M. S. 2011. Embodied Food Politics. Farnham; Burlington: Ashgate (Critical Food Studies).

Charles, D., 2011. How Fear Drove World Rice Markets Insane. In: All Things Considered, National Public Radio.

Clapp J., Scrinis G., 2017. Big Food, Nutritionism, and Corporate Power. *Globalizations* 14(4), 578–595.

Corrigan, 2011. The Sociology of Consumption: An Introduction. London; Thousand Oaks: Sage Publications.

Counihan, C., Kaplan, S. L. (eds.), 1998. Food and Gender: Identity and Power. Food in history and culture. London: Routledge.

Crossley, N., 2012. Phenomenology and the Body. In: Turner, B.S. (ed.). Routledge Handbook of Body Studies. New York: Routledge, 130–143.

Csordas, T., 1990. Embodiment as a Paradigm in Anthropology. *Ethos* 18(1), 5–47.

Dang Phong, 2004. Stages on the Road to Renovation of the Vietnamese Economy: A Historical Perspective. In: Beresford, M., Angie Ngoc Tran (eds.). Reaching for the Dream: Challenges of Sustainable Development in Vietnam. Copenhagen: NIAS Press (NIAS Studies in Asian Topics 33), 19–50.

DeVault, M. L. 1994. Feeding the Family: The Social Organization of Caring as Gendered Work. Chicago: University of Chicago Press (Women in Culture and Society).

Drummond, L. 2004. The Modern "Vietnamese Women": Socialization and Women's Magazines. In: Drummond, L., Rydstrøm, H. (eds.). Gender Practices in Contemporary Vietnam. Singapore: Singapore University Press, 158–178.

Drummond, L., Rydstrøm, H. (eds.), 2004. Gender Practices in Contemporary Vietnam. Singapore: Singapore University Press.

Earl, C., 2014. Vietnam's New Middle Classes: Gender, Career, City. Copenhagen: NIAS Press (Gendering Asia 9).

Ehlert, J., 2012. Beautiful Floods. Environmental Knowledge and Agrarian Change in the Mekong Delta, Vietnam. Berlin: Lit.

Ehlert, J., 2016. Emerging consumerism and eating out in Ho Chi Minh City, Vietnam. The social embeddedness of food sharing. In: Sahakian, M., Saloma, C.A., Erkman, S. (eds.). Food Consumption in the City: Practices and patterns in urban Asia and the Pacific, Routledge studies in food, society and the environment. London; New York: Routledge, 71–89.

Endres, K.W., 2013. Traders, markets, and the state in Vietnam: Anthropological perspectives. *ASEAS – Austrian Journal of South-East Asian Studies* 6(2), 356–365.

FAO – Food and Agriculture Organization of the United Nations, 1996. Rome Declaration on World Food Security. Document adopted at the 1996 World Food Summit, http://www.fao.org/docrep/003/w3613e/w3613e00.htm, last accessed on 03.03.2018.

Featherstone, M., 1990. Perspectives on Consumer Culture. *Sociology* 24(1), 5–22.

Featherstone, M., 1991. Consumer Culture and Postmodernism. London: Sage.

Figuié, M., Bricas, N., 2010. Purchasing Food in modern Vietnam: When supermarkets affect the senses. In: Kalekin-Fishman, D., Low, K.E.Y. (eds.). Asian Experiences in Every Day Life: Social Perspectives on the Senses. Burlington: Ashgate, 177–194.

Fischler, C., 1988. Food, self and identity. *Social Science Information* 27, 275–292.

Fortier, F., Tran Thi Thu Trang, 2013. Agricultural Modernization and Climate Change in Vietnam's Post-Socialist Transition. *Development and Change* 44(1), 81–99.

Foucault, M., 1977. Discipline and Punish: The Birth of the Prison. New York: Vintage Books.

Foucault, M., 1978. The History of Sexuality. New York: Vintage Books.

Foucault, M., 1988. Technologies of the Self. In: Martin, L. H., Gutman, H., and Hutton, P. H. (eds.). Technologies of the Self: A Seminar with Michel Foucault. London: Tavistock, 16–49.

Friedmann H., McMichael, P., 1989. Agriculture and the State System: The Rise and Decline of National Agricultures, 1870 to the present. *Sociologia Ruralis* 29(2), 93–117.

Goodman, M. K., Sage, C., 2014. Food Transgressions: Making Sense of Contemporary Food Politics. London; New York: Routledge (Critical Food Studies).

Goody, 1982. Cooking, Cuisine and Class: A Study in Comparative Sociology Cambridge: Cambridge University Press.

Greenhalgh, S., 2016. Neoliberal science, Chinese style: Making and managing the 'obesity epidemic'. *Social Studies of Science* 46(4), 485–510.

Gugutzer, R., 2012. Verkörperung des Sozialen. Neophänomenologische Grundlagen und soziologische Analysen. Bielefeld: Transcript.

Guthman, J., 2009. Teaching the Politics of Obesity: Insights into Neoliberal Embodiment and Contemporary Biopolitics. *Antipode* 41(5), 1110–1133.

Hai Thi Hong Nguyen, Wood, S., Wrigley, N. 2013. The emerging food retail structure of Vietnam. Phases of expansion in a post-socialist environment. *International Journal of Retail & Distribution Management* 41(8), 596–626.

Hall, S., 1997. The Spectacle of the 'Other'. In: Hall, S. (ed.). Representation: Cultural Representations and Signifying Practices. London; Thousand Oaks; New Delhi: Sage, 223–279.

Harcourt W., Nelson I. L., 2015. Practising Feminist Political Ecologies: Moving Beyond the 'Green Economy'. Chicago: University of Chicago Press.

Hayes-Conroy A., Hayes-Conroy J., 2008. Taking Back Taste: Feminism, Food and Visceral Politics. *Gender, Place & Culture* 15(5), 461–73.

Herzfeld, M., 2005. Cultural intimacy: Social poetics in the nation-state. New York: Routledge.

Hickey, G. C., 1967. Accommodation in South Vietnam: The key to Sociopolitical Solidarity. Santa Monica: The RAND Corporation.

Higgins, R. 2008. Negotiating the Middle: Interactions of Class, Gender and Consumerism among the Middle Class in Ho Chi Minh City, Viet Nam. Doctoral dissertation submitted to the Department of Anthropology, University of Arizona.

Hofman, I., Ho, P., 2012. China's 'Developmental Outsourcing': A critical examination of Chinese global 'land grabs' discourse. *The Journal of Peasant Studies* 39(1), 1–48.

Holt Giménez, E., Shattuck, A., 2011. Food crisis, food regimes and food movements: rumbling of reform tides of transformation? *The Journal of Peasant Studies* 38(1), 109–144.

Inglis, D., Gimlin, D. L., 2009. Food Globalizations: Ironies and Ambivalences of Food, Cuisine and Globality. In: Inglis, D., Gimlin, D.L. (eds.). The Globalization of Food. Oxford; New York: Berg, 3–44.

Jackson, P., 2015. Anxious Appetites: Food and Consumer Culture. London; New York: Bloomsbury.

Jamieson, N. J., 1995. Understanding Vietnam. Berkeley: University of California Press.

Jenks, C., 2003. Transgression. Key Ideas. London: Routledge.

King, V., Phuong An Nguyen, Nguyen Huu Minh, 2008. Professional middle class youth in postreform Vietnam: Identity, continuity and change. *Modern Asian Studies* 42(4), 783–813.

Kjærnes, U., Harvey, M., Warde, A., 2007. Trust in food: a comparative and institutional analysis. Basingstoke; New York: Palgrave Macmillan.

Klein, J.A., 2014. Introduction: Cooking, Cuisine and Class and the Anthropology of Food. In: Klein, J., Murcott, A., Goody, J. (eds.). Food consumption in global perspective: essays in the anthropology of food in honour of Jack Goody. Consumption and public life. Basingstoke; New York: Palgrave Macmillan, 1–24.

Kurfürst, S., 2012. Informality as a strategy: Street traders facing constant insecurity. In: McFarlane C., Waibel M. (eds.). Urban Informalities: Reflections on the Formal and Informal. Farnham: Ashgate, 89–111.

Lamont, M., Molnár V., 2002. The Study of Boundaries in Social Sciences. *Annual Review of Sociology* 28, 167–195.

Lavin, C., 2013. Eating Anxiety: The Perils of Food Politics. Minneapolis: University of Minnesota Press.

LeBesco, K., 2011. Neoliberalism, Public Health, and the Moral Perils of Fatness. *Critical Public Health* 21(2), 153–164.

Leshkowich, A., 2012. Women, Buddhist, entrepreneur: Gender, moral, values, and class anxiety in late socialist Vietnam. *Journal of Vietnamese Studies* 1(1–2), 277–313.

Lévy-Strauss, C., 1997. The Culinary Triangle. In: Counihan, C., Van Esterik, P. (eds.). Food and Culture. A Reader. London; New York: Routledge, 28–35.

Lupton, D., 1996. Food, the Body, and the Self. London; Thousand Oaks: Sage Publications.

Lupton, D., 2013. Fat. Abingdon; New York: Routledge.

Marzin, J., Michaud, A., 2016. Evolution of Rural Development Strategies and Policies. Lessons from Vietnam. Document de travail ART-Dev 2016-5, http://agritrop.cirad.fr/582603/1/Marzin%20Michaud%202016%20Rural%20development%20strategies%20Vietnam%20def.pdf (accessed 27.02.2018).

McMichael, P., 2009. A food regime genealogy. *The Journal of Peasant Studies* 36(1), 139–169.

McMichael, P., 2012. Development and Social Change. A global perspective. 5th ed. London: Sage.

Mennell, S., Murcott, A., Otterloo, A.H. van, 1992. The sociology of food: eating, diet, and culture. London; Newbury Park: Sage.

Metzl, J., Kirkland R. A. (eds.), 2010. Against Health: How Health Became the New Morality. Biopolitics, Medicine, Technoscience, and Health in the 21st Century. New York: New York University Press.

Mintz, S. W. 1985. Sweetness and Power: The Place of Sugar in Modern History. New York: Viking Penguin.

Mintz, S. W., Du Bois, C. M., 2002. The Anthropology of Food and Eating. *Annual Review of Anthropology* 31, 99–119.

Mittal, A., 2009. The Blame Game: Understanding Structural Causes of the Food Crisis. In: Clapp, J. and Cohen, M. J. (eds.). The Global Food Crisis: Governance Challenges and Opportunities. Waterloo: Wilfrid Laurier University Press, 13–28.

Moeckli, J., Braun, B., 2001. Gendered natures: feminism, politics and social natures. In: Castree, N., Braun, B. (eds.). Social Nature: theory, practice and politics. Malden: Blackwell. 112–132.

Moustier, P., Phan Thi Giac Tam, Dao The Anh, Vu Trong Binh, Nguyen Thi Tan Loc, 2010. The role of farmer organizations in supplying supermarkets with quality food in Vietnam. *Food Policy* 35(1), 69–78.

Murcott, A. (ed.), 1983. The Sociology of food and eating: essays on the sociological significance of food. Aldershot: Gower.

Nestlé, M. 2013. Food politics. How the Food Industry Influences Nutrition and Health, Revised and Expanded Tenth Anniversary Edition. Berkeley; London: University of California Press.

Ngo Vinh Long, 1993. Reform and Rural Development: Impact on Class, Sectoral, and Regional Inequalities. In: Turley, W.S., Selden, M. (eds.). Reinventing Vietnamese socialism: doi moi in comparative perspective. Boulder: Westview Press, 165–207.

Nguyen Cong Khan, Ha Huy Khoi, 2008. Double burden of malnutrition: the Vietnamese perspective. *Asia Pacific Journal of Clinical Nutrition* 17(S1), 116–118.

Nguyen Van Suu, 2009. Industrialization and Urbanization in Vietnam: How Appropriation of Agricultural Land Use Rights Transformed Farmers' Livelihoods in a Peri-Urban Hanoi Village? Final Report of an EADN Individual Research Grant Project, EADN Working Paper 38.

Parsons, J. M., 2015. Gender, class and food: families, bodies and health. London; New York: Palgrave Macmillan (Palgrave Macmillan Studies in Family and Intimate Life).

Popkin, S. L., 1979. The Rational Peasant. The Political Economy of Rural Society in Vietnam. Berkeley; London: University of California Press.

Poulain, J.-P., 2017. The Sociology of Food: Eating and the Place of Food in Society. London; New York: Bloomsbury Academic.

Probyn, E., 2000. Carnal Appetites: Food sex identities. London; New York: Routledge.

Ritzer, G., 1993. The McDonaldization of Society. Newbury Park: Pine Forge Press.

Rozin, P. 1976. The Selection of Foods by Rats, Humans, and Other Animals. In: Rosenblatt, J. S., Hinde, R. A., Shaw, E. and Beer, C. (eds): Advances in Study of Behaviour, Volume 6. New York, San Francisco, London: Academic Press, 21–76.

Schwenkel, C., Leshkowich, A.M., 2012. Guest Editors' Introduction: How Is Neoliberalism Good to Think Vietnam? How Is Vietnam Good to Think Neoliberalism? *positions* 20(2), 379–401.

Scott, J. C., 2009. The Art of Not Being Governed: An Anarchist History of Upland Southeast Asia. New Haven: Yale University Press (Yale Agrarian Studies Series).

Simmons, L., Scott, S., 2007. Health concerns drive safe vegetable production in Vietnam. *Leisa Magazine* 23(3), 22–23.

Slocum, R., Saldanha A. (eds.), 2013. Geographies of Race and Food: Fields, Bodies, Markets. Farnham; Burlington: Ashgate (Critical Food Studies).

Smajgl, A., To Quan Toan, Dang Kieu Nhan, Ward, J., Nguyen Hieu Trung, Le Quang Tri, Van Pham Dang Tri, Pham Thanh Vu, 2015. Responding to rising sea levels in the Mekong Delta. *Nature Climate Change* 5, 167–174.

Sobal, J., 1999. Food System Globalization, Eating Transformations, and Nutrition Transition. In: Grew, R. (ed.). Food in Global History. Boulder: Westview Press, 171–193.

Sutton, D. E., 2001. Remembrance of Repasts. An Anthropology of Food and Memory. Oxford: Berg.

Taylor, P., 2004. Preface. In: Taylor, P. (ed.). Social inequality in Vietnam and the challenges to reform. Singapore: Institute of Southeast Asian Studies, xi–xii.

Taylor, P., 2007. Cham Muslims of the Mekong Delta: Place and Mobility in the Cosmopolitan Periphery. Honolulu: University of Hawaii Press (ASAA Southeast Asia Publications Series).

TQ Cuong, Dibley, M.J., Bowe, S., Tran TM Hanh, TT Loan, 2007. Obesity in adults: an emerging problem in urban areas of Ho Chi Minh City, Vietnam. *European Journal of Clinical Nutrition* 61(5), 673–681.

Tran Thi Thu Trang, 2011. Food Security versus Food Sovereignty: Choice of Concept, Policies, and Classes in Vietnam's Post-Reform Economy. *Kasarinlan – Philippine Journal of Third World Studies* 26(1–2), 68–88.

Twigg, J., 1983. Vegetarianism and the meanings in meat. In: Murcott, A. (ed.). The sociology of food and eating: essays on the sociological significance of food. Aldershot: Gower, 18–30.

Van Nguyen-Marshall, Drummond, L. B. W., Bélanger, D. (eds.), 2012. The Reinvention of distinction: modernity and the middle class in urban Vietnam. Dordrecht: Springer (ARI –Springer Asia Series).

Vann, E. F., 2005. Domesticating consumer goods in the global economy: Examples from Vietnam and Russia. *Ethnos* 70(4), 465–488.

Vietnam Ministry of Health. 2012. General Nutrition Survey 2009–2010. Hanoi: Medical Publishing House.

Walls, H. P., Peeters, A., Pham Thai Son, Ngoc Quang Nguyen, Nguyen Thi Thu Hoai, Do Doan Loi, Nguyen Lan Viet, Pham Gia Khai, Reid, C. M., 2009. Prevalence of underweight, overweight and obesity in urban Hanoi, Vietnam, *Asia Pacific Journal of Clinical Nutrition* 18(2): 234–239.

Walravens, T., 2013. Japan facing a rising China: food safety as a framework for Japanese identity formation. *Acta Asiatica Varsoviensia* 26, 115–135.

Warde, A., 1997. Consumption, Food and Taste. Manchester: Sage Publications.

Watson, J. L., 1997. Golden Arches East: McDonald's in East Asia. Stanford: Stanford University Press.

Weis, T., 2013. The Meat of the Global Food Crisis. *Journal of Peasant Studies* 40(1), 65–85.

Wertheim-Heck, S. C. O., 2015. We have to eat, right? Food safety concerns and shopping for daily vegetables in modernizing Vietnam. Ph.D.-Thesis, Wageningen University.

WHO – World Health Organization, 2000. Obesity: Preventing and Managing the Global Epidemic. Report of a WHO Consultation. Geneva: World Health Organization.

Wilk, R., 2009. Difference on the Menu: Neophilia, Neophobia and Globalization. In: Inglis, D., Gimlin, D.L. (eds.). The Globalization of Food. Oxford; New York: Berg, 185–196.

Yan, Y. 2008. Of Hamburger and social space: Consuming McDonald's in Beijing. In: Counihan, C., Esterik, P. van (eds.). Food and Culture: A Reader. New York: Routledge, 500–522.

Yu, B., Zhu, T., Breisinger, C., Nguyen Manh Hai, 2010. Impacts of climate change on agriculture and policy options for adaptation. IFPRI (International Food Policy Research Institute) Discussion Paper 01015.

Zhang, H., 2016. The GMO Controversy in China: More than Food Security. In: IPP Review, 15.03.2016, http://ippreview.com/index.php/Home/Blog/single/id/70.html (accessed 11.05.17).

Part I

Bodily Transgressions: Identity, Othering, and Self

2

Power Struggles and Social Positioning: Culinary Appropriation and Anxiety in Colonial Vietnam

Erica J. Peters

Introduction

Jean Anthelme Brillat-Savarin wrote in 1825 "Tell me what you eat, and I will tell you what you are." Those first two words, "tell me," are key: what we say about what we eat reveals so much about how we see ourselves and others (Ferguson 2004, 31–33). Since food is a relatively affordable part of everyone's daily life, food choices signify more than just economic decisions. People send many signals when they talk about what they eat and what they refuse to eat. People also reference food when signaling what they think of others. In Vietnam during the French colonial period, language about food uncovered people's anxieties about the changing social hierarchy.

People saw themselves as having more options than their grandparents, and their choices spoke about their aspirations and anxieties for where they and their children would end up in the colonial order. That is not to say that Vietnamese people ate French food to assimilate into French

E. J. Peters (✉)
Independent Food Historian, Culinary Historians of Northern California, Mountain View, CA, USA
e-mail: ejpeters@chonc.com

© The Author(s) 2019
J. Ehlert, N. K. Faltmann (eds.), *Food Anxiety in Globalising Vietnam*,
https://doi.org/10.1007/978-981-13-0743-0_2

society, that a Chinese husband ate his Vietnamese wife's local dishes to feel Vietnamese, or that French people at a Vietnamese banquet were trying to "go native." Eating unfamiliar food does not lead to assimilation; more often people try new dishes or ingredients out of necessity, curiosity, or in an effort to rise in social status.

The French incorporated Vietnam into the larger Southeast Asian colony of French Indochina, along with Cambodia and Laos. Cities flourished in the new colony and people of very different backgrounds jostled each other in the streets every day. Everyone in this colonial world—whether Vietnamese, French, Chinese, Indian, Cambodian, Hmong, Malay, Cham, or a mix of ethnicities and cultural experiences—saw other people eating different foods with different table manners. They recognized that they could borrow from each other's cuisines, whether with careful preparation and significant expense or else spontaneously, in the street, away from one's home village and the judgment of one's extended family. One was only limited by the prices charged in stores and restaurants in relation to one's purse, by anxiety over others' views, and by one's willingness to try the unfamiliar.

Textual evidence suggests French people bore the most anxiety in the colonial environment, as seen in the cultural norm they established against eating local dishes. After losing to the Prussians in 1870, French national pride tumbled. As they tried to rebuild, French nationalists relied on touchstones such as the international reputation of grand French cuisine (Ferguson 2004, 124; Laudan 2013, 280–290).

In colonial Indochina, French people wrote about their French dining practices as if they had accurately recreated familiar dishes in the colony, eliding the many culinary compromises they had to make due to the distance from France. French hotels in the colony, for instance, avoided any trace of Asian cuisine on their menus. In 1894 one French publisher stressed to readers back in France that white people in the colony only ate proper French food: "we do not live on rice, fish and bananas" (*Le Mékong*: April 2, 1894, 2).[1] As late as 1927, a young French soldier refused to try a bowl of *phở*, writing to a friend that although the soup looked appetizing, "I wouldn't taste it 'for an empire'" (Tardieu and Heurgon 2004, 76). The jocular idiom he chose has a bitter aftertaste, since he had come to Hanoi as an active agent of French imperial power.

Cultural theorists such as Stuart Hall, Michel Foucault, and Gayatri Chakravorty Spivak have analyzed how power is never univocal, never only exerted by the rulers upon the ruled. Resistance and power are two faces of the same phenomenon, as social actors struggle over control, collusion, and consent (Hall 1997, 50–51; Spivak 1981, 158–171). The overt exercise of power—in the form of tax collectors, policemen, or a French woman running a household of Asian servants—has a systemic effect on ordinary people who encounter that power and respond to it, which in turn means that everyday decisions to avoid or engage, to complain or challenge, to taste new dishes or refuse them have real consequences on social structures. French imperialism developed its harshest aspects out of anxiety over colonial populations who undermined the hierarchical division between colonizer and colonized, casting the French as illegitimate foreign usurpers rather than a powerful master race on a civilizing mission. The same "mission civilisatrice" which justified French colonialism also provided grounds for criticizing the French regime when it did not deliver on its promise to protect the local people from hardship (Conklin 1997, 145).

As a historian, I use contemporary advertisements, travel narratives, administrative reports, ethnographies, folktales, missionary correspondence, and newspaper editorials as the source material to investigate how new food practices disrupted rigid social hierarchies, whether those hierarchies had long been in place or emerged during the colonial era. This chapter does not claim that French colonial cuisine reflected a uniquely French kind of anxiety. The point is rather that people in positions of power and command are especially prone to anxiety around their food practices at those moments when their hold on power feels illegitimate and vulnerable. Food represents what we are willing to incorporate into our bodies, and those aspiring to rise in society expressed more openness toward trying new ingredients and new dishes than those fearful of losing their social position.

Culinary Accommodations Before the French Conquest

In the region we now call Vietnam, colonial forms of dominance started long before the French military arrived in the nineteenth century. The Việt people originally inhabited the Red River Delta and faced sporadic imperial incursions from China even after formal Chinese rule in the region ended in the early tenth century. The Chinese brought a culture of wet-rice agriculture and chopsticks to a region where people had eaten sticky rice wrapped in fragrant leaves, along with molluscs, root vegetables, fruits, and meat from hunting (Lien 2016, 35). The Việt people then carried the wet rice and chopsticks culture further south as they themselves colonized regions which had been Cham, Malay, Khmer, or controlled by uplanders, part of ongoing shifts in local control in mainland Southeast Asia (Tana 1998, 145).

As we will see below, the French would later seize control, taking the southern region (then called Cochinchina) in the 1860s and 20 years later the central and northern regions (Annam and Tonkin). By the turn of the twentieth century, the unified colony of French Indochina, comprising what we now consider Vietnam along with Cambodia and Laos, would be overseen by a French administration in Hanoi (Goscha 2016, 87). In the days of French colonialism, however, local memories of long vanished invaders would serve to undermine French claims to be building something permanent. Food sometimes played a key role in these narratives (Fig. 2.1).

In a folktale supposedly dating back to the period when the Bạc Liêu/Sóc Trăng region of the Mekong Delta was under Khmer (Cambodian) control, for instance, the storytellers represented food practices as anxiety-producing even for the powerful. When the Siamese military invaded Angkor in the fifteenth century, the Khmer king fled further south to the Mekong Delta. He took as a wife a very talented cook, named Căn. Her background was probably Khmer Krom, a people who lived in maritime villages along the southern coast. Their villages had long served as outposts for the otherwise land-locked Khmer empire in far-off Angkor.

As the king's consort, Căn used her long nails to measure out seasonings, preparing all her dishes precisely to his taste. The king found her food amazing and sent spies to watch her in the kitchen. Horrified by her methods, he condemned her to death. In turn Căn cursed any king who came to the region, then or in the future. In memory of her fiery nature and her populist curse, the people in that region supposedly gave her name to a kind of shellfish shaped like a fingernail (Son-Diệp 1903, 80–81). The local memory of resistance against external control endured

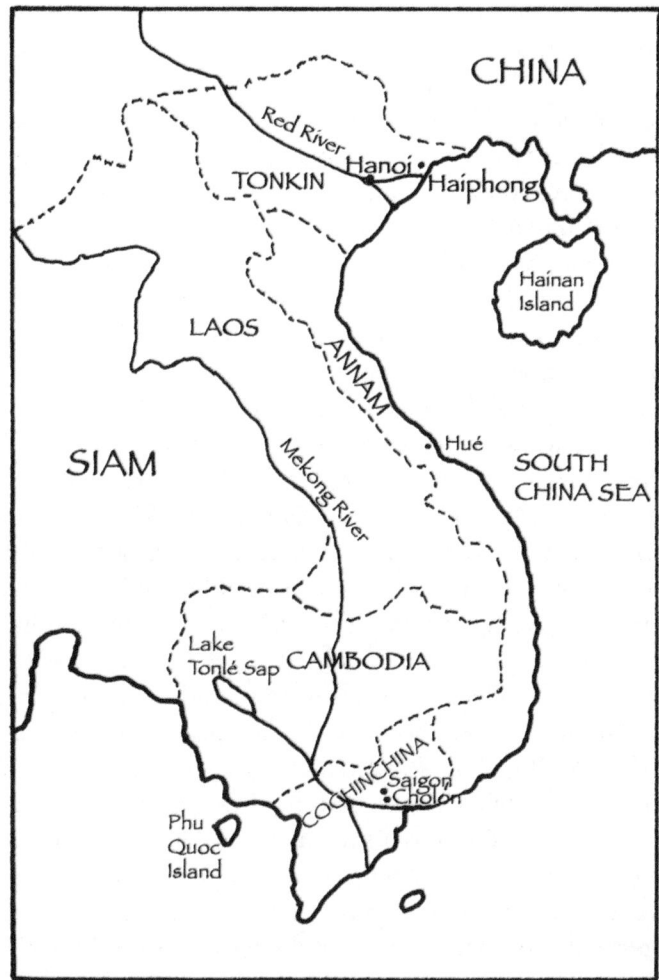

Fig. 2.1 Map of French Indochina. (Source: Peters (2012, 24). Reprinted by permission of AltaMira Press)

for centuries, as this folktale was eventually collected by a colonial administrator of Khmer Krom ethnicity in the early twentieth century. People in the region seem to have noticed parallels between French rejection of indigenous foodways and the retelling of a folktale about an occupying oppressor who reacted violently to an unfamiliar aspect of local food expertise.

In the early nineteenth century, a strong Vietnamese state established direct rule over most of the regions which now make up the country Vietnam. One ambitious ruler, Minh Mạng, held power from 1820 to 1841 and worked to unify the nation culturally. He issued decrees forcing people in his realm to adopt Vietnamese culture, and in particular, Vietnamese food and agriculture. The emperor established firm expectations around culinary customs, based on the premise that white non-sticky rice should be at the heart of all meals. That premise relied on the wet-rice method of rice cultivation and also on a particular way of eating: a tray of shared food, with an individual bowl for each diner, full of the kind of rice one enjoys with chopsticks.

To Minh Mạng, conflicting customs revealed the "barbarian habits" of minorities within his new empire. No longer satisfied with indirect rule, Minh Mạng planned to change people's daily life: "[Khmer] people have no knowledge of agriculture," he announced in 1834. "Teach them to grow more rice, teach them to raise mulberry trees, pigs and ducks … [Vietnamese] table manners must also be followed" (Chandler 2009, 152–153). Minh Mạng authorized a wholesale transformation of other ethnicities' ways of eating—particularly targeting using one's fingers to consume sticky rice. Vietnamese officials also told Cham people to ignore their Hindu values and eat beef and buffalo meat; Muslims were told to eat pork (Wook 2003, 50–55).[2] Even though Minh Mạng hoped to consolidate power through a shared culture, these impositions also seem to have galvanized opposition to his regime (Goscha 2016, 57).

In the official narrative, only the non-Việt people in the south should have needed coaching in Vietnamese culinary customs. But ethnically Việt people in the south themselves hardly acted like northern Vietnamese after decades of acclimation to a new environment. They had learned from their neighbors to enjoy new dishes and try new ingredients in familiar dishes (Wook 2004, 139). Sometimes they ate with their fingers, enjoying fruit, rice cakes, and skewered meat (Brown 1861, 252). Imperial Vietnamese sources anxiously avoided that uncomfortable topic, as chopsticks had come to symbolize civilization in their realm (Phan Thuận An 1991, 39–41). Vietnamese people eating without chopsticks disrupted the narrative: they were supposed to act civilized.

Similarly, administrators from northern or central Vietnam were surprised to find that their distinguished counterparts from other apparently civilized cultures did not know how to use chopsticks (Tana 1998, 65; Anonymous 2007, 151; Wook 2004, 145). In the late eighteenth century the governor in Huế, Phạm Ngô Cầu, gave a grand dinner to mark the occasion of a British trade mission. Servers brought out many bowls containing assorted vegetables, fish, pieces of meat (chopped pork and slices of water buffalo meat), different kinds of rice, and various sauces. The hosts watched for a long moment and commented with amusement as the British trade envoys fumbled awkwardly with the ivory chopsticks at their places. The governor then called for porcelain spoons and little bamboo sticks, split at one end, to help the envoys enjoy the meal. Governor Cầu could have instructed the servers to set out all possible implements at the same time they brought out the food. He seems, however, to have wanted to put the Europeans in the situation of having to make do with chopsticks, to test whether it was really true that they did not know how to use them. In the British report, the envoys noted their own clumsiness during the banquet (Chapman 1817, 121).

An even more discomfiting topic for Vietnamese administrators was the recurring inadequacy of the rice harvest. One reason Minh Mạng wanted to transform the foodways of the south was to increase that region's rice production by expanding southern rice fields significantly and thus provide greater food security for the whole realm. He criticized southerners (of any ethnicity) for "despising the value of rice" in comparison with northern Vietnamese (Wook 2004, 69–73, 102–103). Severe food shortages were still common in early nineteenth-century Vietnam. Terrible famines hit north-central Vietnam in 1823–1824, the Red River Delta in 1827, central Vietnam in 1835, northern Vietnam in 1840, and central Vietnam in 1841. Food scarcity exacerbated cholera epidemics in 1806, in the 1820s, and the 1840s, as well as after Minh Mạng's reign in the 1860s and 1870s (Nguyễn Thế Anh 1967, 13–14; Nguyễn Thế Anh 1992, 19–21). Vietnamese officials tried to find structural solutions. Minh Mạng's minister for land development, Nguyễn Công Trứ, organized the large-scale recuperation of flood plains through dikes and drainage, adding hundreds of square kilometers to Vietnam's agricultural resources in the north (Lê Thành Khôi 1955, 358–365). A few decades later, the Catholic Nguyễn Trường Tộ returned from travels to Hong Kong, Canton, Italy, and France full of ideas to improve agriculture and protect the population from famine. Trứ and Tộ both spoke out against corruption that sometimes illicitly diverted state aid from those who were hungry (Peters 2016, 65). Tộ also proposed teaching hygiene and nutrition as well as shifting rice from alcohol production to food needs during hard times as "one cannot sate one's hunger by drinking" (Chương Thâu 1993, 485). Administrators worked to address these terrible periods of famine for humanitarian reasons as well as to reduce the chance of rebellions (Goscha 2016, 61).

Vietnamese rulers collected taxes in kind and stored the collected rice in granaries for ordinary state needs as well as for bad harvests. Aware of the political dangers of running out of food, Minh Mạng and the other nineteenth-century Nguyễn emperors improved the sturdiness of their granaries (see Gorman, this volume). A brick-walled granary might be 1500 meters square and 25 meters high. Their roofs were no longer thatched as they had been in the eighteenth century. Now they were tiled to protect against fire. Not only did granaries keep the rice safe from fire and bandits, but administrators could also store troops and arms in the granaries when necessary (Aurillac 1870, 22–23; Brown 1861, 206–207, 267).[3]

Nguyễn officials faced difficult choices about how to use their stores of rice. Their first choice when the harvest failed was to reduce the taxes people owed in that region. That left more rice in the village to feed locals, without offering handouts which might attract people from a neighboring region. Hunger alone usually did not convince officials to give out food, unless it was accompanied by the possibility of rebellion. Threatening rebellion was, however, a dangerous tactic for a region. In one incident, the Nguyễn army destroyed crops in order to starve rebels in the south after Minh Mạng's death (Nguyễn Thế Anh 1967, 11, 17, 20–22).[4] Control of the harvest was key to state power. But local rebellions created administrative anxiety about whether the state could control the harvest. Poor harvests provided opportunities for the government to demonstrate its effectiveness in responding to crises; the Vietnamese government established its legitimacy along these lines more than the French colonial government ever would. The French should have been more concerned about stories ordinary people told each other about government overreach, incompetence, and illegitimacy, as in the Khmer Krom folktale of a king who killed a woman for cooking too well.

The French Conquest and Chopstick Challenges

By the early 1860s, the French gained military control of the southern part of the Vietnamese realm, the Mekong Delta and the greater Saigon region. By the 1880s, they had extended their control through the Red River Delta in the north as well. French anxiety about their own legitimacy permeated the colonial period, and how French people wrote about colonial dining practices revealed these concerns. As mentioned, before the French conquest, Vietnamese officials like Huế governor Phạm Ngô Cầu were intrigued to learn that Europeans did not know how to use chopsticks. After defeat at French hands, one might think Vietnamese people would be circumspect in pointing out French ineptitude. Yet Vietnamese elites who were scorned by many of their countrymen for eating and working with the French occupiers still hosted events where they pushed chopsticks on their French guests. This gesture may have acted to challenge the French claim to a civilizing mission by reminding those present—and those who heard about it later—that civilization was a relative term: these French military victors did not even know how to use chopsticks.

In 1888 when the Vietnamese governor of the northern city of Nam Định gave an official luncheon, the mixed crowd of French and Vietnamese elites faced a meal served "half French-style and half Vietnamese-style" (*L'Avenir du Tonkin*, Sept. 15, 1888, 4).[5] The host mixed elements from each culture's formal banqueting style, cleverly relying on the premise that the meal was early in the day and thus could bend the formal rules. A French reporter who wrote up the event noted his compatriots "struggling" to eat the Vietnamese dishes with chopsticks, caught off-guard and embarrassed by the Vietnamese governor (*L'Avenir du Tonkin*, Sept. 15, 1888, 4).

In the 1890s, the well-traveled southern administrator Đỗ Hữu Phương gained a reputation for inviting influential French officials and businessmen to lavish banquets at his home. When the guests arrived, the very Western-style table was set "Vietnamese-style," at least to French eyes, with "an infinity of little bowls" containing different delicacies. Each setting featured a small plate, a bowl of rice, a porcelain spoon, and chopsticks.

One guest, the French administrator Pierre Nicolas, was so dismayed by the chopsticks that the utensils began to overwhelm his narrative of the occasion, recurring in his description again and again: "armed with two ivory sticks," he wrote, the French guests tried to dip into the bowls with their "little sticks," to pull out at random "a bit of still-born pig" or "palm-tree worms, grilled to perfection" (Barrelon 1893, 244). Then, "still using the chopsticks, you put the morsel on your rice, and with the little spoon, you add some *nước mắm* [Vietnamese fish sauce]." Then picking up the rice bowl, "you use the two sticks to place the tidbit in your mouth, then shovel the rice in with the help of your ivory chopsticks." He admitted they were let off easy in the end, fed European food to make sure no one went home hungry:

> After everyone has struggled their best [literally: *escrimé* ("fenced")] with these little sticks, less dangerous than our fork and our knife, but also less convenient … the table is reset in European style, and servers bring out huge steaks for those not satisfied with the previous offerings. (Barrelon 1893, 244–246)[6]

The martial imagery Nicolas used, describing the guests as "armed," and "fencing" with their chopsticks, led to his comparison that at least chopsticks were "less dangerous than our fork and our knife." He left the impression that the French might turn to force—even in the middle of a dinner party—to resolve internal anxiety about their role in the colony. The overall defensiveness of the story suggests French people worried that they looked foolish muddling through awkwardly with chopsticks and that they feared their Vietnamese hosts enjoyed watching the French display their incompetence. Đỗ Hữu Phương clearly owned forks, after all, and could have placed them on the table from the start, rather than just bringing them out with the steaks toward the end of the meal. Like Governor Cầu a century earlier or the governor of Nam Định in 1888, maybe the Vietnamese administrator simply wanted to see how these Europeans would handle the uncomfortable situation. Food may seem apolitical and innocent, but negative stories about someone's food choices or cutlery skills can affect a person's public image. The French may have found it hard to challenge these micro humiliations without looking petty.

French Resistance to Cross-Cultural Cuisine

Unlike these powerful Vietnamese, ordinary villagers were less prone to challenging a French guest's skill with chopsticks. A French text from 1862 notes that women in the southern region prepared food for village banquets: "all the talented old women, whatever their rank or wealth, would set to the task" (Cortambert and de Rosny 1862, 61). They boiled pork, chicken, and geese with a few vegetables and they mixed cane sugar with eggs, rice flour, or corn to make treats for the whole village. The women put bowls of this food out on trays five or six hours before the feast; they do not seem to have eaten with the men. In front of each guest sat a bowl of boiled rice, two chopsticks, and a little cup for rice liquor— except that visiting Frenchmen received a spoon alongside the chopsticks, without having to ask for it or wait at all.

Within rural villages, these public banquets held a great deal of weight socially and were fraught with anxiety for those who hosted the feasts as well as for Frenchmen who sometimes attended. In 1861 the colonial administrator Lucien de Grammont attended a feast in the market town of Thủ Dầu Một, in Cochinchina (southern Vietnam). He praised the mayor's wife, who had organized the feast, saying "she had undertaken the task with understanding and perfect taste" (Grammont 1863, 246). Trays were spread out along the porch of the communal hall; each tray held a substantial dish, accompanied by an array of sauces of different colors and tastes. The dishes included:

Roasted peacocks, displayed in their feathers, flattened ducks, deboned chickens, minced pork, minced buffalo, bits of meat boiled with vegetables or cooked in gelatinous fat; fish stews, eggs streaked with fat or beaten with sugar; aromatic green herbs; pale noodles, some firm, some quivering; potatoes coated with corn flour; yams roasted in their skins; dried mushrooms; acacia pods cooked with tomatoes; beans from My-tho; rice cakes of many colors and textures; grilled pistachios, green bananas, slices of papaya and star fruit, purple mangosteens, yellow mangos, coconut creams, boiling hot tea, scented rice alcohol, and immense bouquets of pineapples. (Grammont 1863, 247)

Grammont's praise might lead one to think that he ate and enjoyed the meal. In fact, he and the few other French guests did not touch the food: "We tried to put a good face on it, by sipping our tea from time to time. As dubious and intense smells began drifting up to us, we began to find the atmosphere a bit oppressive" (Grammont 1863, 248). By refusing to join in the feasting, Grammont knew he was offending his hosts; their displeasure probably added to his sense that the festive mood was clouding over.

French missionaries had long noted that eating village food was one of the best ways to build relationships with the Vietnamese community. "These nice people are so happy when we eat the food they have brought," noted one missionary. "I hear them repeating to each other: 'The Father tasted everything'" (Monteuuis 1894, 264).[7] Grammont probably worried more that the other Frenchmen might view him as soft toward the natives if he admitted to eating any of the food there. As we will see, that would be a reasonable concern for someone in his situation, since French people in the colony tried hard to avoid eating like the local population and wrote about their efforts.

French texts reverberate with refusals to eat rice, or try the fish sauce, *nước mắm*, or try any kind of street food. In practice, colonials could not get the same fresh ingredients they had in France, so they made do with canned and preserved imports. The French colonial diet was a shaky simulacrum of French cuisine, rather than an accurate reproduction. As argued elsewhere, as a small minority dominating this foreign space and uncertain how long the status quo would last, the French let fear and anxiety drive their determination to "eat French," rather than being motivated by pride, taste, or health concerns (D'Enjoy 1897, 145; Peters 2012, 150).

One might think French people worried about getting sick from local food. Colonial newspapers were full of advertisements for medical treatments and nostrums—but so were newspapers back in France (Stewart 2001, 60). In the colonies, French people ignored contemporary Western nutritional recommendations to avoid alcohol, canned goods, and meat consumption in the tropics (Neill 2009, 9–11). When the French turned to canned asparagus over local vegetables, ate expensive steaks regularly, and drank to excess—it was not for health reasons. It was to represent themselves as fundamentally different from those they had colonized.

For similar reasons, French texts repeatedly returned to the fear that Vietnamese people might eat French food—particularly household servants: "They claim in a whine to 'eat only rice,' but treat themselves to the scraps from our tables, when they do not filch the best bits beforehand" (*La France d'Asie*, Nov. 7, 1901, 2.) A prominent French newspaper in Hanoi asserted that Asian cooks routinely prepared too much food for their French employers in order to have leftovers to bring home to their own families (*L'Avenir du Tonkin*, Aug. 15, 1900, 1). The impressive feat of putting many different dishes on the table every night was reconceptualized in that story as theft. The next day, the same newspaper issued another iteration of this imagery: "If you go on a trip [...] and then return without warning, you will find your servants, their families and their friends [...] as drunk as Poles." And if you confronted them, they would blatantly lie about drinking their employer's liquor: "Us no can drink same thing French; no eat same thing" (*L'Avenir du Tonkin*, Aug. 16, 1900, 1). This deception, attributed to an imagined Vietnamese servant, reveals some of the anxiety of the French at the idea of Vietnamese people consuming the same food and drink as the French. Many French colonizers wanted to feel they were completely different from (and superior to) the people whose country the French seized by force.

Culinary Tensions in the Colonial Countryside

Anxieties about food also emerged among the colonial Vietnamese population, but the root causes were different. People worried about getting enough to eat or strategized how to build social networks with food.

Journalist and social critic Phan Kế Bính reported on village feasts in the early twentieth century, noting that all men hosted in turn, unless they were destitute (Peters 2016, 67–68). Sometimes the expectation was that the host paid the banquet costs out of savings; other villages lent the money up front and then the host reimbursed the costs over time; another possibility was for village men to make regular payments into a fund covering the expense of the animal sacrifice, the pigs, chicken, or buffalo slaughtered in honor of local spirits. In those cases, the particular host would pay for vegetables, rice, and firewood (Phan Kế Bính 1975, 146–148).[8]

At the feast, one's seat was assigned based on one's rank in the village. The food was portioned out onto many different trays. There were trays for those who officiated at the ceremony, trays for elders, trays for village notables. If one belonged to more than one category, one might be entitled to three or four shares. Some received so much that they could not eat it all at once, and brought home meat and cakes. Others received only a small portion and the honor of joining in the village feast: "a bite sitting on a mat in the middle of the village is worth a meal in one's own kitchen" (Phan Kế Bính 1975, 148). As Phan Kế Bính interpreted that saying, villagers appreciated the opportunity to display their portion of rice and meat in public. Even the lowest-ranked feaster could hold up his head before village boys not yet old enough for a seat at the banquet, not to mention the girls and women who generally were not invited to the formal feasts. Yet the visibility of everyone's rank at the feast probably also increased anxiety about one's position and prospects.

There were other opportunities for villagers to share food besides the formal village-wide feasts and those excluded from the latter found other ways to get noticed. Village women prepared regular offerings of rice cakes, bananas, betel nuts, and rice liquor for village spirits. In the rainy season, a Buddhist monk might lead a more elaborate ceremony offering food to local spirits in exchange for their help with the weather (Phan Kế Bính 1975, 85). Villagers anxious about the contrasting dangers of floods or drought would pile offerings on an altar: rice in many shapes and consistencies, prepared in many ways, as well as fruit, sweet potatoes, and assorted candies. After the ceremony, the poor came and made off with the food, a custom known as "cướp cháo thí," which literally meant "looting the charity porridge" (Phan Kế Bính 1975, 118).

The food from some ceremonies was divided according to established village hierarchies; other ceremonies led to more anarchic distributions. Ethnographer Lê Văn Phát described villages in the south holding banquets for "cô hồn" (wandering souls). These unsettled spirits would be invited to a grandiose spread, with butchered whole pigs or huge hunks of roasted meat lying next to enormous cones made of rice cakes in many colors, with baskets of other foods nearby. Each basket had an elegant scroll indicating the name of its donor. Village authorities then turned a blind eye while the baskets and food offerings were systematically pillaged by hungry younger villagers, who were called the "cô hồn sống" (the living wandering souls):

> Crowds of them fight each other for the food, and serious accidents sometimes arise from these fights. The next day, a smaller feast is offered up ... This one was reserved for those who were late the day before, or who had been too weak to take part in the first meal. (Lê Văn Phát 1907, 43–45)

The first day's festivities were apparently a free-for-all among the boys of the village, those who were not old enough to sit at the formal banquets. The following day, the boys shoved aside at the first feast were invited back to gather up the scraps for themselves.

A precolonial tradition had involved gangs of young men maintaining village norms by confiscating the livestock of those accused of theft, assault, or seduction: "They bring the animals to the communal hall [đình], where there are always knives ready for the slaughter" (La Bissachère 1920, 145). The meat was then divided among villagers according to rank. Other times the young bands avoided that hierarchical division by not returning to the communal hall. Instead, they tied up the alleged wrongdoer, beat him with sticks, and roasted his pig with his own fuel, in his own courtyard, and enjoyed a feast right there. A spontaneous feast like that carried a distinct claim about power in the village (La Bissachère 1920, 139–145, 158–161; Peters 2016, 67). By the colonial period, village offenders were more likely to face monetary fines than to lose their pigs in the dark of night. Village elites presumably forbade informal pig confiscations at least in part in order to limit the power of village youth, who were no longer able to reintegrate a wrongdoer into the community by seizing and eating his pig (Papin 1997, 15, 19).[9] Instead village boys fought among themselves to get the food that was set out for "wandering souls." Lê Văn Phát's colonial-era text made intergenerational conflict in the village sound neatly contained by such ceremonial food distribution.

Food could also be a proxy for other kinds of disputes, some of which had histories stretching back to the earlier moment of Vietnamese colonialism in the south. Ethnographer Lê Văn Phát also described stories of feasts in the rural countryside with anxious overtones about dispossession and defiance. Vietnamese settlers with Vietnamese military support had taken southern lands from Cham and Khmer residents, often turning the former landowners into farmhands or sharecroppers. Local resentment ran high, and certain feasts seem to have been designed to soothe hard feelings.

A large part of Annam and Lower-Cochinchina [central and southern Vietnam] used to belong to aborigines: the Cham and Khmers whom we pushed into the bush and whose land we took. But the dead are still here. The vanquished use their last resources to reclaim their property ... and to avenge their brutally dominated brothers. They engage in a guerrilla war without truce or respite, and create all sorts of hardships and troubles. When members of a [Vietnamese] family fall victim to wasting illnesses, or when the livestock die in large numbers, one does not hesitate to attribute these misfortunes to the vengeance of the "chúa-ngu ma-nương" [Cham spirits], the name given to the original owners of the land [now deceased]....

To appease the expropriated spirits, one serves them a feast, prepared to their taste, with large fish skewered from mouth to tail with a bamboo stick and roasted over a high flame. During the meal, with gentle, reasonable words, one tries to calm the spirits' anger and ask them to renounce their claims....

If all that does not work ... then one turns to magicians or sorcerers. In all legal matters, the law requires both parties to be present.... Two people who are unknown to the sorcerers (so they cannot collude with each other) represent the husband and wife, the former owners of the land in dispute.... The sorcerers use incantations, gestures, and cabalistic phrases to enchant [the stand-ins] ... [until] they are completely brutish, dishevelled, in rags, with dirt smeared all over their bodies and faces.... Then one gives them baskets, utensils and wooden bowls such as the aborigines used. They receive them with signs of satisfaction....

Then the sorcerers pressure the *chúa-ngu ma-nương* [Cham spirits] to sell the disputed land for some money and livestock. The savages try to refuse, with many tears. But in the end, they usually accept.... [The buyers] give them food, and pay them in paper-money and pictures of animals which are then burnt.... When the spirits do refuse, a long-term lease is signed instead.

In our time, sales and leases of this kind are rare. Most of the lands were acquired by more or less arbitrary and underhanded methods ... One still sees these ceremonies sometimes in the remote countryside, either when a well-off property owner wants to protect his farmers and animals, or when someone has been clearing new crop land, gets a fever from the virgin soil, and thinks that demons have attacked him. (Lê Văn Phát 1907, 32–36)[10]

Superficially, the ethnographer acted as if these spirits were real, engaging in "guerrilla war" and expressing their dissatisfaction with what they were offered. He explicitly wrote that these feasts and ceremonies happened in the "remote countryside," revealing his discomfort with the practice of eating with so-called ghosts. His rhetoric asserts that people living in towns or cities would not participate in these customs or feel a need to appease the expropriated spirits.

Lê Văn Phát's story provides a perspective on culinary practices in a disputed territory. Some of the farmers mentioned in the last section of the quote may have been grandchildren or other descendants of the original inhabitants of the land (Baurac 1899, 246; Hardy 2009, 118–119; Wheeler 2006, 186–187). In that case, providing the symbolic feast would have allowed the rich Vietnamese property owner to cater to his fieldhands' culinary heritage and pride by hosting a somewhat appropriate feast.[11] It also reveals the upper-class ethnographer's anxiety at the idea that his rural compatriots did talk about sitting down to eat with ghosts.

Chinese Compradores Coping in a Vietnamese Setting

As discussed below, the same Vietnamese ethnographer also addressed a local legend which related to marriages between male Chinese immigrants (or their male children) and Vietnamese women. These relationships could look like a business relationship, but they could also be more intimate. Cultural differences might strain these marriages, but one can also see traces of significant cultural accommodations—particularly in family meals.

The regions south of Huế had a significant Chinese community since at least the seventeenth century, when many Chinese men fled Guangdong and Fujian after the fall of the Ming dynasty. They brought tea, cloth, farming implements, and porcelain from China and exported pepper, ginger, cardamom, cinnamon, sugar, sugar-candy, dried shrimp, and a great deal of rice to China, Singapore, and Bangkok. By the early nineteenth century, more than 30,000 Chinese lived in the southern regions of Vietnam, and there were well over a 100,000 by the early twentieth century, not counting untold populations of mixed Sino-Vietnamese ethnicity (Tana 2004, 3–9).

For the most part, Chinese immigrants married local women, and relied heavily on their wives' networks, language skills, and business acumen in establishing and running their commercial ventures. A Chinese trader might set up a different wife in different trading posts, seeking each one's help in dealing with her local community and trusting her with his accounts (Hocquard 1999, 71, 340). He might also have a legal wife back in China, with whom he intended to retire in old age (Ha 2009, 199). The sights, sounds, and smells of Chinese cuisine proliferated in and around Vietnam's port cities. Vendors from different regions in China spoke in different dialects—Cantonese, Hainanese, Teochiu, Hakka, and Hokkien—but the majority of the Chinese restaurateurs and soup vendors were Cantonese (Garros 1905, 290; Nguyễn Tùng and Krowolski 1997, 168).

Meanwhile, Hokkien-speaking traders were most likely to marry Vietnamese women in the countryside and engage directly with the farmers bringing in the rice harvest (Tsai Maw Kuey 1968, 87–104). They established warehouses and small shops along Vietnam's rivers and coasts, selling goods such as pans, cutlery, and farm tools, alongside seed for farmers, ordinary needs such as *nước mắm*, salt, sugar, rice wine, and new treats such as durians, mangosteens, pineapples, and Siamese bananas (Tana 2004, 9; Barton 1977, 72–74).

In describing the Vietnamese culinary preparation of crocodile meat—"we make it a treat with spicy sauces" (Lê Văn Phát 1908, 13)—ethnographer Lê Văn Phát described a local legend saying that the Chinese had driven all crocodiles out of China to prevent them from eating Chinese people. The legend insisted that Chinese people living in southern Vietnam (Cochinchina) were culturally forbidden from eating crocodile meat, lest the reptile return to China and start eating Chinese people again:

> Some of [the Chinese] are completely assimilated to the locals from their long stay in Cochinchina, where they have married Annamese women, and they eat everything – except crocodile meat. They even manage to accustom their wives to regard this meat with disgust. (Lê Văn Phát 1908, 14–15)[12]

Between the fantastical lines of this story about different cultural views on eating crocodiles, Lê Văn Phát provides a rare glimpse of men whom he identified as ethnically Chinese, who apparently ate Vietnamese meals at home. At the same time, he pointed out that their wives also compromised in some ways, adapting to their Chinese husband's anxiety about eating crocodile meat. A Vietnamese wife would also sometimes hire a Chinese chef to cook an important meal for her husband's Chinese business associates (Lefèvre 1989, 170). Sino-Vietnamese families perceived a broad range of food options, and husbands and wives were capable of negotiating family meals keeping in mind each person's social relations, memories, cultural anxieties, and taste.

Despite these internal negotiations, Chinese who lived with or married Vietnamese women raised anxiety in outside observers. Writers portrayed Chinese compradores cohabitating with multiple Vietnamese women while in the colony, then abandoning them and returning to their original wives and children in China with a sizable fortune (Bineteau 1864, 58; Bouinais and Paulus 1885b, 508; Chivas-Baron 1927, 54). In 1898, a Vietnamese bureaucrat told the following story of an apparently happy Sino-Vietnamese arrangement:

> In Hải Dương province, a poor widow sold her daughter – a ravishing creature, thirteen or fourteen years old – to a rich Chinese merchant. The

child was dressed and adorned with uncommon luxury, and her new master treated her with great solicitude and a surprising degree of respect, for a Celestial.

A Vietnamese student suspected that the Chinese man wanted to transform the young virgin into a guardian spirit to watch over his wealth. Acting on his advice, the widow secretly told her daughter to leave a trail of rice behind if her master escorted her out of the house. One morning … the widow learned that her daughter had been gone for quite some time.

Frightened, she told the student, who summoned the police; they found the trail of rice the girl had thrown behind her, and followed it to an isolated mountainside with freshly turned dirt. Digging, they found her still alive, walled up with her master's treasure. The Chinese man was sentenced to death, while his victim was awarded his property; naturally, she married the Vietnamese student. (Basset 1898, 214–215)

The folktale revealed a tension in Vietnamese villages, torn between the pragmatic benefits of a match with a successful Chinese entrepreneur and the competing fear of losing their daughters and future grandchildren to a foreign culture. Vietnamese mothers might feel a sense of foreboding even though a daughter seemed to be well fed and treated with respect by her Chinese husband, as in the beginning of the story. Rice serves as the link, connecting the daughter back to her family of origin.

The mother secretly told her daughter to leave a trail of rice for the mother to follow, creating a bond between mother and daughter through food. The instruction also acknowledged, however, that the younger married woman now had the resources to throw rice on the ground, to use rice for communication, rather than just for food. Many Vietnamese mothers had to endure years of quiet submission to their own Vietnamese mother-in-law before gaining more control of the household. The story expressed their anxiety about their daughters in these different marriages, free of abusive mothers-in-law, but also lacking maternal guidance. Their daughters might never be able to stand up to their Chinese husbands and gain some control over family resources, since they were metaphorically "walled up"—shut away from their Vietnamese families and culture.

Anxiety about Chinese economic power also led to rhetoric describing Chinese men getting fat off the backs of the poor Vietnamese. French authors sometimes took the stereotype seriously, as when a well-considered text explained to Parisian readers that the Vietnamese were "generally less obese than the Chinese" (Bouinais and Paulus 1885a, 228). The French colonial administrator Pierre Nicolas noted a folktale about a stout Chinese man who turned into a round teapot from overindulging in that hot beverage (Nicolas 1900, 144).[13] The implications were that the Chinese were gluttonous and that they were overindulging while the local population went hungry. Contemporary rhetoric portrayed Chinese as obese parasites, feeding directly on the region's resources. One French editorial complained in 1910 that the Chinese were "a parasitical organism, established between us and the Annamese" (*L'Avenir du Tonkin*, Feb. 5, 1910, 5). In 1907, the anticolonial activist Phan Bội Châu had made a similar analogy, but lumping in the French as well:

> We are so stupid to spend all our money on these foreign imports. We feed to the foreigners the resources Heaven and Earth have given us. Today we buy French merchandise; tomorrow we purchase Chinese goods. (Phan Bội Châu 2000, 116)

That parallel raised problems. The French were anxiously aware that many of the Vietnamese viewed French colonial interests much the same as the Chinese, two different kinds of parasites feeding off Vietnam's human and material resources. French colonizers did not like that comparison, especially since the Chinese often seemed to be more successful at exploiting the Vietnamese economically (Lanessan 1889, 455).

Ambition and Anxiety About New Urban Foods

Despite exhortations such as the ones by Phan Bội Châu, many Vietnamese were eager to explore new culinary opportunities, especially in the growing colonial cities. The French colonial government neither mandated nor banned the use of European products, so even the lower classes could try new tastes, eating bread instead of soup or *xôi* [cooked sticky rice] in the morning, or an occasional beer, lemonade, or banana-flavored drink

(*L'Opinion*, May 26, 1908, 3). Arriving in Saigon in 1909, a French travel writer noticed "natives in every street taking for breakfast half a roll [petit pain] with black coffee or café au lait" (Jafe 1910, 21). By the 1910s, French writers reported widespread Vietnamese appreciation for French bread, butter, and Gruyère cheese, in addition to Western drinks from milk to coffee to beer, wine, and champagne (Brébion 1913, 295).

Middle- and upper-class Vietnamese parents introduced their children to dairy products in particular, which had not been part of the local cuisine. This was part of a larger project to support their children learning culinary practices that might help them advance in the colonial administration, from using a knife and fork to chewing silently (Peters 2012, 196–197). At first fresh milk was sold door to door in wealthy neighborhoods by Tamil milkmen, but by 1914 advertisements in the Vietnamese-language newspaper *Lục Tỉnh Tân Văn* (News of the Six Provinces) promoted imported *La Petite Fermière* brand milk in place of fresh milk. One rendition of the ad had a Vietnamese servant standing at the gate of a grand house, scolding a dark-skinned person holding milk in glass bottles: "Go away! Your milk smells like hairy goat, and this house drinks only *La Petite Fermière* milk." The ad glossed over the employers' ethnicity; the point of the ad was the Vietnamese servant's scorn for the Tamil milkman and his milk (*Lục Tỉnh Tân Văn*, Jan. 7, 1915, 8).[14] Another version showed two Vietnamese women on the street: one has baskets and a bamboo pole, while the other has a chubby child. The first praises the baby's weight, and the other replies that she only gives him *La Petite Fermière* milk. The ad promises that drinking this particular condensed milk will promote the child's health and good fortune (*Lục Tỉnh Tân Văn*, Feb. 25, 1915, 3). Even without knowing sales numbers, the text and imagery of this widely read advertising campaign illustrates Vietnamese anxiety about how to get one's children established in colonial society.

On the one hand, cost prevented most working-class Vietnamese from giving their children imported milk or eating imported foods very often. Food took up three-quarters of the average unskilled laborer's income in the 1920s (Leurence 1924, 1, 5). On the other hand, workers and even villagers did get occasional urban treats. They came to the cities to sell in the market or for temporary work and city residents made regular trips back to their original village for celebrations, bringing gifts of food. In

January 1895, a French observer in Cholon, the Chinese business district near Saigon, commented on the "interminable lines of villagers, coming to make their purchases for Tết," the lunar new year (Monnier 1899, 36). In the north, the journey from Haiphong to Hanoi became a quick day-trip once the railroad line was finished for the 1902 Hanoi Exposition. Many classes of travelers used the colonial train service. The train was "a wandering market on wheels, full of rice, millet, vegetables, fruit, fish, and all kinds of other merchandise … [J]ust as in one of the market halls of the Tonkin towns, … people are bargaining, selling and buying" (Baelz 1902, 11–12). Whether the trip to the city was for commerce or employment, the Vietnamese appreciated the new sights, sounds, and tastes.

Not all new urban tastes were imported from outside Vietnam. There were many new drinks available in the city: nước hột é (cold water with sugar and basil seeds, which swelled up like tapioca pearls), herbal teas, or drinks made from oleaginous plants in many colors, red, yellow, green, or purple (Brébion 1913, 297; D'Enjoy 1897, 142). Each village probably had its own local herbal tea, but only in the cities could people taste so many different beverages. Vietnamese workers may not have been able to afford French cafés or Chinese restaurants, but they could enjoy a wider variety of foods than they were used to in the countryside: fresh and dried seafood; new fruits and vegetables; sweet and savory bean jellies; and a diversity of sticky rice cakes, from smooth rectangles of sweetened rice flour (*bánh khảo*), to firm round silver-dollar-sized cakes (perhaps like bánh bèo, but with a jujube filling), to marzipan-like cakes colored pink, blue, yellow, or green, to breast-shaped soft rice dumplings (bánh vú), to many more. There were numerous candies as well, white and yellow rock candies, candied fruit, peanut nougat, sugared water lily seeds, caramel taffy, and more (Hocquard 1999, 93; Bourde 1885, 250).

In 1909, a French newspaper reported workers panicking when two northern Vietnamese died after eating pineapple; one of them collapsing after having only two little pieces of the fruit: "We are now hearing Vietnamese and Chinese insisting French authorities ban the sale of pineapples in the city's markets … [The locals] deem pineapple a dangerous fruit, containing a powerful poison" (*L'Independance Tonkinoise*, July 22, 1909, 2). The French journalist mocked their anxiety, but the anecdote reveals how new pineapple was to northern Vietnam. People feared the fruit, when perhaps the tragedy came from eating an unripe pineapple or contaminated piece of fruit, or from an undiagnosed allergy. Parisians had enjoyed pineapple since the middle of the nineteenth century, whether imported fresh from Brazil and Havana; canned from Martinique; or grown in greenhouses in Parisian suburbs like Versailles and Meudon (Husson 1856, 364–377). For the Vietnamese and Chinese living in northern Vietnam, however, this fruit was exotic and disconcerting. They asked in vain for the colonial government to respond to their concerns. More Vietnamese fell ill after eating pineapple, experiencing itching, acid reflux, stomach pains, sometimes followed by sweating, sensory problems, and finally coma (Mouzels 1912, 618–619). It is not clear if this rash of medical issues was due to allergies to the pineapple itself or to reactions to some kind of fungus on the pineapples, as French administrators did not explore how to address the problem. To this day the Vietnamese are especially particular about peeling their pineapples, carefully removing all the skin and the eyes before eating the flesh (Avieli 2012, 50).

While pineapple moved from south to north, *phở*, the aromatic beef-based noodle soup, moved in the opposite direction. It originated in the north at the beginning of the twentieth century and only gradually made its way south to Huế and Saigon (Greeley 2002, 80). *Phở* was marked as a particularly Vietnamese dish from very early on. By 1919, Jean Marquet reported hearing "Yoc Pheu!" called out on the streets of Hanoi by Vietnamese selling beef soup with flat rice noodles, competing with Chinese vendors of chicken soup or duck soup with wheat noodles. This may be the earliest representation in print of *phở* as an essentially Vietnamese dish (Marquet 1922, 76).[15] For decades, *phở* was a northern dish. By 1950, however, *phở* was also available in Saigon (Arnold 1950, 10). Then the 1954 Geneva Accords brought a flood of northern refugees to southern Vietnam, and with them a sharp increase in *phở* consumption (Peters 2010, 161).[16]

Wartime Anxieties About Food and Power

Phở became a complicated symbol of the then-divided nation. In 1957 a prominent northern Vietnamese essayist named Nguyễn Tuân wrote a notorious essay on *phở* (Nguyễn Tuân 2000 [1957]). Communist Party officials had just admitted some serious missteps regarding the controversial land reform program, and they looked vulnerable (Goscha 2016, 292–296).[17] The very first issue of the northern literary journal *Văn*, on May 10, 1957, included the first part of Nguyễn Tuân's playful but provocative essay, which went much further in poking the Communist Party than one might expect from a piece on *phở*.

He spent much of the piece praising the soup in all its many delightful variations, but the essayist went on to mention that some people could not afford meat in their *phở*. The criticism was not subtle, as Nguyễn Tuân portrayed the government of North Vietnam failing to care for the population. In a similar vein, he wondered what *phở* would be like, if people had to start making it with a broth made from rat meat. He then bitterly brought up the innovative ways that rich people—even under Communism—were enjoying *phở*, made with duck, with pork, with five spice or sesame seeds. Nguyễn Tuân even affected to worry that the country was relying so heavily on industrial foods imported from the Soviet Union (mostly potato flour and wheat flour) that soon people might find themselves eating canned *phở*. Soon after the Party shut down the journal and made Nguyễn Tuân apologize for his supposedly "frivolous" essay. Yet the political thrust of the essay became even clearer over time, as *phở* lost its flavor under continued Communist rule.

The frame of Nguyễn Tuân's essay was the author reminiscing about *phở* while he was overseas and missing his country. So Nguyễn Tuân used *phở* as a symbol of Vietnam as a whole, but without homogenizing it or pretending there was one authentic, timeless *phở*. He mentioned a variety of different ways to prepare *phở*, including how it was still evolving on the streets of Saigon. He also stated how he himself preferred the soup. In the process he highlighted the idea that getting into arguments over the best kind of *phở* was part of what made *phở* so Vietnamese.

Vũ Bằng was another northern writer who avoided the mode of timeless nostalgia about *phở*, even as he, like Nguyễn Tuân, reminisced about the dish at a distance. In the late 1950s he was living in Saigon, spying for the north, and writing an essay remembering Hanoi's *phở*. He said:

> To some people, *phở* is no longer just a dish – they are addicted to it, the way others are addicted to tobacco … These fans do not easily step into any *phở* shop on their path. To them, enjoying *phở* is a process of inquiry and experiments … They each have a favorite *phở* shop. (Vũ Bằng 1990, 19)

The rhetoric of addiction offered a way of talking about the craving for *phở* without being sentimental.

There was very little to be sentimental about during the American war. After 1964 people in the north used the phrase *"phở không có người lái,"* joking about having to eat *phở* "without a pilot" (i.e., without the meat), as they mocked the official version of *phở*. The phrase riffed on current events—at the time the United States was using unmanned planes, flying at very low altitudes, to take photos of North Vietnam for intelligence purposes (Vietnam Studies Group online listserv, February 2000). People in North Vietnam may not have enjoyed their cheap *phở* very much in those days, but they connected it with the modern world around them. *Phở* was not an age-old, traditional dish, but a creation of living Vietnamese, making something delicious from a new source of scraps. It was invented to be cheap, nourishing street food, but now the government had taken even that away. People resented having to pay a high price on the black market if they hoped to find a rich, tasty *phở* (Xuan Phuong and Mazingarbe 2004, 170).

Conclusion

Over centuries, Vietnamese taste preferences evolved as new ingredients and new dishes became available. People in power made evolving claims about what foods Vietnamese people ought to eat, or ought to avoid. The disjunction between what a person ate (or wanted to eat) and what society said they should eat—based on their class, gender, or ethnicity—was definitely a source of anxiety. Had a youth outgrown the right to pillage the "wandering souls" offerings? Was it nurturing for a wife to adjust meals to her Chinese husband's tastes or a sign she was losing her culinary culture? Was feeding milk to one's children just maternal love, or a sign of collaboration with the French? Despite such concerns, for many Vietnamese in the nineteenth and twentieth centuries the larger problem was simply getting enough food to eat.

When the French controlled the region, individual French people felt little concern about where their next meal was coming from. Instead, the blatant illegitimacy of their rule led to protracted anxiety about losing control and being forced to leave. Erecting a rhetorical bright line between the foods of the colonizer and those of the various local colonized people made the French feel different from (and superior to) those they ruled. The frequency of stories about the wrong people eating French food reveals how much anxiety went into pretending that bright line was real—until the line was gone, and with it the colonial moment.

Notes

1. For hotel menus, see advertisements in, for instance, *Petites Affiches Saigonnaises*: 4 Oct. 1888, 2; *La France d'Asie*: 3 Jan. 1905, 3; *L'Opinion* (Saigon): 3 Jan. 1911, 3.
2. For more discussion of the foodways of non-Việt ethnicities living under Minh Mạng, see Alexander Woodside (1971, 96, 134, 254–255); Po Dharma (1987, 121–130); Jean Moura (1883, 383); Trịnh Hoài Đức (1863, 129); Charles Wheeler (2006, 163–193, 184–186).
3. On poor quality eighteenth-century granaries, see Lê Quý Đôn (1977 [1776], 239); on granaries in the nineteenth century, see also Van Nguyen-Marshall (2008, 23–26).
4. On problems of famine migration, see David Arnold (2008, 117–139, 125).
5. Another banquet with mixed French and Vietnamese food and diners is described in Charles Édouard Hocquard (1999 [1892], 300–2).
6. The author did not include diacritical marks on the word *nuớc mắm*. On the engagement party of Đỗ Hữu Phương's daughter, catered by the French *Hôtel de l'Univers* with a largely European guest list, see *La Semaine Coloniale* (Saigon), 19 September 1896, 2.
7. For the experiences of other missionaries, see Jean-Charles Cornay (1989 [1809–1837], 143) and a letter from Mgr. Retord published in *Annales de la propagation de la foi* (1847, 325).
8. On current public feasts and animal sacrifices in Vietnam, see Nir Avieli (2012, Chap. 6).
9. This shift also emphasized that the offender had not nourished the village in the same way that an ambitious villager might ceremonially feed everyone at a feast. This transition happened much later in some villages than in others.
10. On spirits and materiality in Vietnam, see Léopold Cadière (1944, 17–19); Heonik Kwon (2008, 104–107); Nir Avieli (2008, 129–130).

11. See discussion of transferring oxen, buffalo, and pigs to settle disputes with *chúa-ngu ma-nương* spirits in Philip Taylor (2016, 354–355).

12. The term "Annamese" referred to the local Vietnamese women. Vietnamese people did eat crocodile meat when they could get it. See, for instance, Albert Bouinais and A. Paulus (1885a, 239) and Gaston Darboux et al. (1906, 296).

13. See also the image of fat Chinese men in Saigon, in Aloïs d'Huncks (1908, 522). Throughout Southeast Asia the Chinese were described in similar terms.

14. Immigrants from French commercial cities in India such as Pondicherry ran most of the dairies in Cochinchina; see Natasha Pairaudeau (2016, 215).

15. Jean Marquet's novel, *Du village à la cité: moeurs annamites*, was serialized in *La Revue indochinoise* in 1919 before being published in Paris in 1922.

16. In 1954, representatives of Cambodia, China, France, Laos, the United Kingdom, the United States, the Soviet Union, the Communist Vietnamese government and the rival anti-Communist Vietnamese government all met in Geneva, Switzerland, to settle the crisis in Vietnam. They divided the country temporarily at the 17th parallel until a projected election and reunification in 1956. During the cease-fire of 1954–1955, about 800,000 people moved south to escape Communist rule, and about 120,000 people moved north. The country was not in fact reunified until the US withdrawal in 1975 (Goscha 2016, 267–270, 280).

17. Starting in 1953 the Communist-run Democratic Republic of Vietnam initiated a land reform campaign in the zones it controlled, with the goal of redistributing land from the rich to the poor. Ad hoc courts encouraged villagers to denounce their neighbors, which led to violent attacks based more on intravillage rivalries than strict measures of wealth. By 1957, the atrocities were public knowledge and embarrassing to the Communist regime.

References

Anonymous (2007) [1838] "The Customs of Cambodia" in N. Cooke and L. Tana (eds.) *Chinese Southern Diaspora Studies* 1, 148–157.

Arnold, D. (2008) "Vagrant India: Famine, Poverty, and Welfare under Colonial Rule" in A.L. Beier and P. Ocobock (eds.) *Cast Out: Vagrancy and Homelessness in Global and Historical Perspective* (Athens: Ohio Univ. Press).

Arnold, H. (1950) "Gastronomie viêtnamienne", *Sud-Est asiatique* 16, p. 10–12.

Aurillac, H. (1870) *Annamites. Moïs. Cambodgiens* (Paris, Challamel, 1870).

Avieli, N. (2008) "Feasting with the Living and the Dead: Food and Eating in Ancestor Worship Rituals in Hội An" in P. Taylor (ed.) *Modernity and Re-Enchantment: Religion in Post-Revolutionary Vietnam* (Lexington Books).

Avieli, N. (2012) *Rice Talks: Food and Community in a Vietnamese Town* (Bloomington, IN: Indiana Univ. Press).

Baelz, Dr. E. (1902) "A Report on a Visit to Tonkin", *Transactions of the Asiatic Society of Japan* Vol. XXX, 11–12.

Barrelon P. [pseudonym of P. Nicolas] (1893) "Saigon", *Tour du monde*, vol. 34, no. 2, 225–256.

Barton, C. G. (1977) "Credit and Commercial Control: Strategies and Methods of Chinese Businessmen in South Vietnam" (Cornell University: Ph.D. dissertation in anthropology).

Basset, A. (1898) "Notes sur quelques traditions et superstitions annamites", *Bulletin de la Société dauphinoise d'ethnologie et d'anthropologie* Vol 5, no. 3&4: 214–15.

Baurac, J. C. (1899) *La Cochinchine et ses habitants* (Saigon).

Bineteau, H. (1864) "Cochinchine Française", *Bulletin de la Société de géographie*, Ser. 5, Vol. 7 (Paris): 55–71.

Bouinais A. & A. Paulus (1885a) *L'Indochine française contemporaine Vol. 1: Cochinchine, Cambodge* (Paris).

Bouinais A. & A. Paulus (1885b) *L'Indochine française contemporaine Vol. 2: Tonkin, Annam* (Paris).

Bourde, P. (1885) *De Paris à Tonkin* (Paris: Calmann Lévy).

Brébion, A. (1913) "Boissons et mets indochinois", *Revue Indochinoise* XVI:3, 286–298.

Brown, E. (1861) *Cochin-China, and My Experience of it: A Seaman's Narrative of his Adventures and Sufferings during a Captivity among Chinese Pirates* (London: Charles Westerton).

Cadière, L. (1944) *Croyances et pratiques religieuses des Annamites* (Hanoi: Impr. d'Extrême-Orient).

Chandler, D. P. (2009) *A History of Cambodia*, 4th edn (Boulder, CO: Westview Press).

Chapman, C. "A Voyage to Cochin China in 1778" (Part 6), *The Asiatic Journal and Monthly Register for British India and Its Dependencies* Vol. 4 (August, 1817), pp. 121–126.

Chivas-Baron, C. (1927) *Confidences de métisse* (Paris).

Chương Thâu (1993) "Réformes Agricoles et Rurales Préconisées par Nguyễn Trường Tộ", in Phan Huy Lê, et al. (eds.) *Le Village Traditionnel au Vietnam* (Hanoi: Thế Giới), 477–485.

Conklin, A. (1997) *A Mission to Civilize: the Republican Idea of Empire in France and West Africa, 1895–1930* (Stanford: Stanford University Press).

Cornay, J.-C. (1989) *Le premier martyr français du Tonkin: Saint Jean-Charles Cornay (1809–1837)* (ed.) G. Jubert (Paris: TEQUI).

Cortambert E. and L. de Rosny (1862) *Tableau de la Cochinchine* (Paris: Le Chevalier).

D'Enjoy, P. (1897) *Tap-Truyen: récits à la bouche* (Paris: C. Mendel).

D'Huncks, A. (1908) "Visages de pierres", *Grande Revue* 51 (10 oct. 1908), 522.

Darboux G. et al. (1906) *L'Industrie des pêches aux colonies* (Marseille: Barlatier).

Dharma, P. (1987) *Le Panduranga (Campa) 1802–1835; Ses Rapports avec le Vietnam*, vol. 1 (Paris: Ecole Française d'Extrême-Orient, 1987).

Ferguson, P. P. (2004) *Accounting for Taste: The Triumph of French Cuisine* (Chicago: University of Chicago Press).

Garros, G. (1905) *Les Usages de Cochinchine* (Saigon: Coudurier & Montégout).

Goscha, C. (2016) *Vietnam: A New History* (New York: Basic Books).

Grammont, L. de (1863) *Onze mois de sous-préfecture en Basse-Cochinchine* (Paris, Challemel Ainé).

Greeley, A. (2002) "Pho: The Vietnamese Addiction", *Gastronomica* Vol. 2, No. 1, 80.

Ha, M.-P. (2009) "The Chinese and the White Man's Burden in Indochina" in E. Yee Lin Ho and J. Kuehn (eds.) *China Abroad: Travels, Subjects, Spaces* (Hong Kong: Hong Kong UP).

Hall, S. (1997) "The Work of Representation", in Hall (ed.), *Representation: Cultural Representations and Signifying Practices* (London: Sage).

Hardy, A. (2009) "Eaglewood and the Economic History of Champa and Central Vietnam" in Hardy, A. et al. (eds.) *Champa and the Archaeology of Mỹ Sơn (Vietnam)* (Singapore: NUS Press).

Hocquard, Dr. C.-E. (1999) [1892] *Une campagne au Tonkin* (ed.) P. Papin (Paris: Arléa).

Husson, J. C. A. (1856) *Les consommations de Paris* (Hachette).

Jafe [pseudonym for A. Jourdain] (1910) *Impressions d'Indochine* (Paris: V. Polgar).

Kwon, H. (2008) *Ghosts of War in Vietnam* (Cambridge: Cambridge University Press).

La Bissachère (1920) [1807] *Relation sur le Tonkin et la Cochinchine* (Paris: Eduoard Champion).

Lanessan, J.-L de (1889) *L'Indo-Chine française: étude politique, économique et administrative sur la Cochinchine, le Cambodge, l'Annam et le Tonkin* (Paris: F. Alcan).

Laudan, R. (2013) *Cuisine and Empire: Cooking in World History* (Berkeley: University of California Press).

Lê Quý Đôn (1977) [1776], *Toàn Tập: Tập I: Phủ biên tạp lục* (Complete works, Vol. 1: Miscellaneous chronicles of the pacified frontier), transl. from Chinese characters into quốc ngữ by Đào Duy Anh (Hanoi: NXB Khoa Học Xã Hội).

Lê Thành Khôi (1955) *Le Viêt-nam: Histoire et civilisation* (Paris: Les Editions de Minuit).

Lê Văn Phát (1907) "La vie intime d'un Annamite de Cochinchine et ses croyances vulgaires", *Bulletin de la Société des Etudes Indo-Chinoises de Saigon*, Vol. 52, 3–142.

Lê Văn Phát (1908) "Croyances Diverses", *Bulletin de la Société des Etudes Indo-Chinoises de Saigon*, Vol. 54, 5–52.

Lefèvre, K. (1989) *Métisse Blanche* (Paris: Barrault).

Leurence, F. (1924) *Note sur deux indices du coût de la vie pour les indigènes à Hanoi* (Hanoi: Imprimerie d'Extrême-Orient).

Lien, V. H. (2016) *Rice and Baguette: A History of Food in Vietnam* (London: Reaktion).

Marquet, J. (1922) [1919] *Du village à la cité: moeurs annamites* (Paris: Delalain).

Monnier, M. (1899) *Le Tour d'Asie* (Paris: Librarie Plon).

Monteuuis, L'abbé G. (1894) *L'âme d'un missionnaire: Vie du Père Nempon* (Paris: Retaux et Fils).

Moura, J. (1883) *Le royaume du Cambodge* (Paris: E. Leroux).

Mouzels, Dr. (1912) "Sur trois cas d'intoxication par le fruit de l'ananas", *Annales d'hygiène et de médecine coloniales* no. 15, 618–619.

Neill, D. (2009) "Finding the 'Ideal Diet': Nutrition, Culture, and Dietary Practices in France and French Equatorial Africa, c. 1890s to 1920s", *Food and Foodways* 17:1, 1–28.

Nguyễn Thế Anh (1967) "Quelques aspects économiques et sociaux du problème du riz au Vietnam dans la première moitié du XIXe siècle," *Bulletin de la Société des Etudes Indo-Chinoises de Saigon*, N.S. 42, 5–22.

Nguyễn Thế Anh (1992), *Monarchie et fait colonial au Viêt-Nam (1875–1925)* (Paris: Harmattan).

Nguyễn Tuân (2000) [1957] "Phở" in Nguyễn Đăng Mạnh (ed.) *Tuyển Tập I* (Hanoi: Nhà Xuất Bản Văn Học).

Nguyễn Tùng and N. Krowolski (1997) "Some notes on Vietnamese alimentary practices and foreign influences", *Vietnamese Studies* (special issue on Gastronomic heritage of Vietnam) 55:3, 151–90.

Nguyen-Marshall, Van (2008) *In Search of Moral Authority: The Discourse on Poverty, Poor Relief, and Charity in French Colonial Vietnam* (New York: Peter Lang Publishing).

Nicolas, P. (1900) *Notes sur la vie française en Cochinchine* (Paris: Flammarion).

Pairaudeau, N. (2016) *Mobile Citizens: French Indians in Indochina, 1858–1954* (Copenhagen: NIAS Press).

Papin, P. (1997) "Food references and monetary equivalents in ancient village conventions (hương uóc)", *Vietnamese Studies* (special issue on Gastronomic heritage of Vietnam) 55:3, 5–24.

Peters, E. J. (2010) "Defusing Phở: Soup Stories and Ethnic Erasures, 1919-2009", *Contemporary French and Francophone Studies* 14:1, 159–167.

Peters, E. J. (2012) *Appetites and Aspirations in Vietnam: Food and Drink in the Long Nineteenth Century* (Lanham, MD: Alta Mira Press).

Peters, E. J. (2016) "Rice, Pork and Power in the Vietnamese Village, 1774-1883" in I. Banerjee-Dube (ed.) *Cooking Cultures: Convergent Histories of Food and Feeling* (Delhi, India: Cambridge University Press).

Phan Bội Châu (2000), "'The New Vietnam' (1907)" in Truong Buu Lam (ed.) *Colonialism Experienced* (Ann Arbor: University of Michigan Press).

Phan Kế Bính (1975) [1915] *Việt-Nam Phong-Tục* (Vietnam's Social Life and Customs) vol. I (transl. and ed.) N. Louis-Hénard (Paris: Ecole Français d'Extrême-Orient).

Phan Thuận An et al. (1991) *Có gì lạ trong cung Nguyễn?* (Anything Novel in the Royal Palace of the Nguyen Dynasty?) (Hue: Thuan Hoa Publishing House).

Retord, Mgr. (1847) "Letter to M. Laurens, curé de la paroisse de Salles près Lyon", *Annales de la propagation de la foi* Vol. 19 (Lyon), 325.

Son-Diêp (1903) "Légendes du pays de Bassac (Cochinchine)", *Premier Congrès International des Etudes d'Extrême-Orient: Compte rendu analytique des séances* (Hanoi), 80–81.

Spivak, G. C. (1981) "French Feminism in an International Frame", *Yale French Studies*, No. 62, pp. 154–184.

Stewart, M. L. (2001) *For Health and Beauty: Physical Culture for Frenchwomen, 1880s–1930s* (Baltimore, MD: JHU Press).

Tana, L. (1998) *Nguyễn Cochinchina* (Ithaca: Cornell Univ. Press).

Tana, L. (2004) "The Water Frontier: An Introduction" in N. Cooke and L. Tana (eds.) *Water Frontier: Commerce and the Chinese in the Lower Mekong Region, 1750–1880* (Singapore: Rowman & Littlefield Publishers).

Tardieu, J. and Heurgon J. (2004) "Correspondance 1922–1944" in D. Hautois (ed.) *Le ciel a eu le temps de changer* (Paris: Institut mémoire de l'édition contemporaine).

Taylor, P. (2016) *Connected and Disconnected in Viet Nam: Remaking Social Relations in a Post-socialist Nation* (Acton, Australia: ANU Press).

Trịnh Hoài Đức (1863) *Histoire et description de la basse Cochinchine* (transl.) G. Aubaret (Paris: Impr. Impériale) [orig. written in Chinese in 1820].

Tsai Maw Kuey (1968) *Les chinois au Sud-Vietnam* (Paris: Mémoires de la section de géographie).

Vietnam Studies Group online listserv (2000) "Soup Without the Pilot" thread accessed at https://sites.google.com/a/uw.edu/vietnamstudiesgroup/discussion-networking/vsg-discussion-list-archives/vsg-discussion-2000/soup-without-the-pilot on July 30, 2017.

Vũ Bằng (1990) *Miếng Ngon Hà Nội* (Hà Nội: NXB Văn học) [orig. published in Saigon in the late 1950s].

Wheeler, C. (2006) "One Region, Two Histories: Cham Precedents in the History of the Hội An Region", in N. T. Tran and A. Reid, eds. *Việt Nam: Borderless Histories* (Madison: University of Wisconsin Press).

Woodside, A. (1971) *Vietnam and the Chinese Model: A Comparative Study of Nguyen and Ch'ing Civil Government in the First Half of the Nineteenth Century* (Cambridge: Harvard University Press).

Wook, C. B. (2003) "Vietnamisation of Southern Vietnam during the First Half of the Nineteenth Century", *Asian Ethnicity* 4:1, 47–65.

Wook, C. B. (2004) *Southern Vietnam under the Reign of Minh Mạng (1820–1841)* (Cornell: SEAP).

Xuan Phuong and D. Mazingarbe (2004) *Ao Dai: My War, My Country, My Vietnam* (transl.) Lynn M. Bensimon (Great Neck, New York: EMQUAD International).

3

Forbidden from the Heart: Flexible Food Taboos, Ambiguous Culinary Transgressions, and Cultural Intimacy in Hoi An, Vietnam

Nir Avieli

Non-Asian tourists visiting the lively market of Hoi An, a town in central Vietnam where I have been conducting ethnographic research since 1998, are often surprised by the huge array of aquatic and amphibian creatures of shapes and sizes they have never seen before, often sold live, skinned and gutted on the spot. They stare in horror at the slaughtering of chicken and ducks, and the handling of fresh non-refrigerated flesh. They are visibly disgusted by the sale of internal organs such as hearts, lungs, kidneys, guts, claws, hooves, or ears, which are rarely consumed in their countries of origin. A recurrent topic on any market visit is dog meat (which is not sold in Hoi An's markets, and see Avieli 2012a). Visitors seem to be most eager to find what they consider tabooed flesh (such as that of reptiles, amphibians, or dogs), and when they do, they take a picture, stare for a while, and leave disgusted. One comment I have heard repeatedly in such circumstances was that "they eat everything".

N. Avieli (✉)
Department of Sociology and Anthropology, Ben-Gurion University,
Beersheba, Israel
e-mail: avieli@bgu.ac.il

© The Author(s) 2019
J. Ehlert, N. K. Faltmann (eds.), *Food Anxiety in Globalising Vietnam*,
https://doi.org/10.1007/978-981-13-0743-0_3

Such comments are hardly trivial. While Mary Douglas (1975) argued that food taboos are important components of any categorization system, Marvin Harris (1987) suggested that they are the rational outcome of material considerations (see also Meyer-Rochow 2009 for a comparative functional approach). Interpretative anthropologists stressed the symbolic meanings of food taboos and their role in reinforcing and/or undermining power relations (Mintz and Du Bois 2002). A social group accused of having no food taboos is actually suspect of complete lack of categorization processes, rational decision-making, social boundaries, and/or moral framework. If "they eat everything", "they" must be uncivilized, savage, and, in fact, cultureless.

Food taboos are usually understood as rules that should never be lapsed (Lien 2004; Meyer-Rochow 2009), and when transgressed, cause inevitable pollution and call for retribution and ritual purification (Douglas 2003 [1966]). Many years of studying foodways and food taboos in different cultures lead me to the understanding that such notions of taboo as a total prohibition are not universal but, rather, culture specific. In fact, the idea that specific foods, or as is most often the case—the flesh of specific animals, is completely forbidden and should be avoided under any circumstances, is found mostly in cultures where monotheism prevails.[1]

Indeed, the term *taboo*, originally *tapu* in Tongan language, introduced into English by James Cook in the late eighteenth century, "has been the source of much scholarly analysis ever since, but the logic behind a word that can be applied to many disparate and apparently contradictory things continues to puzzle the scholars" (Shirres 1982: 29). Shirres points out that *tapu* "can be applied equally to high descent, ritual and sacred lore, and to death, darkness menstrual blood and filth", associations which make sense for the Maoris, but "has eluded scholarly [Western] analysis" (Shirres 1982: 29). Gilmore et al. (2013: 332) point out that "taboo commonly [in English] refers to things which are culturally proscribed for symbolic rather than pragmatic reasons … *Tapu*, however, is a much more complex concept which, in Polynesia, is intrinsic to a cultural worldview which places people, objects, places and activities under the protection of the *atua* [gods, spirits] and, therefore, as sacred, or apart from the ordinary". So, when the term "taboo" was adopted into common usage in the English vocabulary and as an important anthropological term, it was preloaded with misunderstandings regarding its meaning and cultural function: rather than "total prohibition", its original denotation had to do with sacredness and uniqueness (Gilmore et al. 2013: 336; Calder 1999; Sachdev 1989).

In Vietnam, where âm dương (Chinese Yin-Yang), completing-oppositions that maintain a dynamic balance, govern the cosmos and everything within it (Jamieson 1995; Avieli 2012b), and where the unity and oneness of God are hardly the rule, food regulation and temporary restrictions are common (Manderson and Mathews 1981; Mathews and Manderson 1981), but total food prohibitions rarely exist. Indeed, though Manderson and Mathews (1981) use the term "food taboos" in the introductory parts of their articles, when it comes to the culinary practices themselves, they describe temporary prohibitions and restrictions during pregnancy and post-labor. Thus, their findings too suggest that in Vietnam, food restrictions are context dependent and temporary, in line with the Polynesian idea of *tapu* rather than the total prohibition implied by the Western notion of taboo.

Buddhism does call for total avoidance of animal products due to the compassion that must be cultivated toward all living beings, yet only a few Hoianese (and for that matter, relatively few Buddhists elsewhere) practice complete veganism. What is very common in Hoi An is part-time veganism: "full moon" and "black moon" (*ngày rằm* and *mùng một*) veganism or other temporal patterns of animal-flesh avoidance. Elsewhere (Avieli 2014) I elaborate how such patterns of temporal veganism are adopted by increasing numbers of Hoianese as a consequence of—and an antidote to—modernity. The important point, however, is that meat avoidance is considered by most Buddhists as a temporal restriction rather than complete and total prohibition. Here again, *tapu* rather than *taboo* is the organizing principle.

Buddhism further advocates abstinence from "ten forbidden meats": human, elephant, horse, dog, snake, lion, tiger, leopard, bear, and hyena (Tambiah 1969). Yifa (2002: 56) mentions "dragon" too—an idea to which I return shortly. Thus, despite the call for complete veganism, Buddhism actually acknowledges the fact that many adherents do eat the flesh of living creatures, and sets further prohibitions regarding the flesh of the specific animals mentioned above. In this sense, Buddhist meat prohibitions are relative and fluid. Here again, my Hoianese interlocutors adhere to these prohibitions only to a certain extent and would be willing and even eager to gorge over most of these meats during certain times and in specific contexts, and abstain in others.

"We do have one total food taboo", pointed out one of my most knowledgeable friends, "dragon meat is taboo!". When I asked her to elaborate, she explained: "dragons have alligator-heads, snake bodies, fish scales and parts of many other animals. We can eat alligators, snakes and fish, but not dragons." This remark is the exception that makes the rule: Vietnamese do follow a total food taboo, but only when it comes to the flesh of an animal that does not exist (or, perhaps, whose flesh is unavailable). This remark is extremely important as it exposes the ambiguous approach to total food prohibitions in Vietnam: the principle is acknowledged, but the actual culinary practices are flexible.

In this chapter I discuss culinary establishments that specialize in the flesh of animals that should be avoided in Hoi An, at least in principle: he-goat meat (*thịt dê*) and jungle meat (*thịt rừng*), and their complex relations with the taboo on "eating human flesh" (*ăn thịt người*). Some Hoianese, mainly male members of the emerging middle class, may gorge on jungle meat and he-goat meat in specific circumstances in the context of increasing affluence, modern consumerism, and class distinction. Eating these meats expresses wealth and sophistication. Food venues that serve these meats mainly attract groups of men, some in the company of their female mistresses or lovers, but not their spouses and children. These venues also offer hostess services, which may include paid sex. These culinary spaces are therefore arenas for the performance of hyper-masculinity, associated with excessive drinking, smoking, potency, and illicit sexuality.

Many of my Hoianese friends, women and men, were critical of these food venues and the culinary transgressions they entail when discussing them in public. However, male and some female interlocutors who admitted in private to frequenting such restaurants were clearly ambivalent. They were excited yet ashamed at partaking in what they themselves described as repulsive, illegal, and, perhaps, immoral culinary practices that expressed gluttony, greed, violence, lust, and unfaithfulness. Desire and fear were often mentioned concomitantly when discussing these preferences and when dining at these restaurants. Along the chapter, I point to the social components that underlie this ambivalence.

In order to make sense of these Hoianese flexible food taboos, I conclude by drawing on Michael Herzfeld's concept of "cultural intimacy". Cultural intimacy is "the recognition of those aspects of a cultural identity that are considered a source of external embarrassment but that nevertheless provide insiders with their assurance of common sociality ... This can take the form of ostentatious displays of those alleged national traits ... that offer citizens a sense of defiant pride in the face of a more formal or official morality and, sometimes, of official disapproval as well" (Herzfeld 2005: 3).

While Herzfeld emphasizes relations with the state and its officials, I show how cultural intimacy may also be experienced among members of specific social echelons in their relations with members of other social groups. In this sense, flexible food taboos and ambiguous culinary transgressions, despite their explicit negative image, are perceived positively by the practitioners, at least to a certain extent. However, such transgressions and the ambivalence they entail involve a measure of anxiety that seems to spice up the food and make it uniquely palatable.

Quán Nhậu (Rice Liquor Shops): Sites of Transgression

Places that serve he-goat meat and jungle meat in Hoi An belong to the culinary category of *quán nhậu* (liquor shops): drinking establishments where men consume alcohol and *dương* (yang) charged dishes, made with ingredients and spices that are considered warming (*nong*) and libido enhancing (basically animal flesh seasoned with ginger, garlic, and chili, fried and/or rich dishes). In the late 1990s, there were only a few *quán nhậu* in Hoi An. The most common places where men would drink alcohol were dingy makeshift sheds set in back alleys serving cheap rice alcohol (*rượu gạo*) or beer and chicken or duck rice gruel (*cháo gà* and *cháo vịt*), mainly to blue-collar men. Most of my Hoianese friends, members of the tourism-related nascent middle class, avoided these venues, and the common explanation had to do with the drunkenness of the patrons as well as the coarseness of the food and setting. Male drunkenness was presented as violent and dangerous, especially for women. These culinary establishments were avoided also by those who could afford more refined dining options and locations.

These venues, just like the more elaborate restaurants with which I deal in this chapter, were operated by women. I ate at some of them and observed what I later realized were the general patters of men-to-men and men-to-women interactions in culinary establishments that involved libido and masculinity enhancing foods, excessive consumption of alcohol, and a measure of social competition. Drinking entailed increasing (or escalating) tensions: competition and challenge among men, which led at times to actual violence; and sexual tension and desire harbored by the men toward the women who operated the stalls. These women were clearly very experienced in handling their clients, making sure that the men paid for their food and drink while keeping them at bay; at the same time—some measure of feminine interest and attraction, or at least, some exchange of sexually charged semi-joking comments were part of the service. As far as I could tell, these were essentially professional maneuvers by the female owners intended at attracting and maintaining male clientele.

While drunkenness was criticized by almost every Hoianese with whom I discussed this issue, male binge drinking (easily discerned in the flushed faces of the drunk men) was the rule in all major social/ritual gatherings, ancestor worship events, and weddings, and was clearly tolerated by all those present. As tables in such events were gender segregated, most of the drunk interaction was among men, who turned increasingly competitive and abusive the more they drunk. Nasty comments were sometimes exchanged, and wild bursts of laughter became at times angry and abusive. In some cases, drunk men would become violent, but since they were so drunk, this never resulted in more than attempted punches and perhaps a turned-over table. These drunk men were easily overcome by somewhat less drunk companions, who would drag them away.

As public violence was so rare in Hoi An, I was surprised and intrigued when I witnessed such incidents early in my fieldwork. I was surprised by the violence and intrigued by the setting: though overt violence was very rare in daily public interactions and spheres, it was almost expected in important social rituals, which seemed to me completely inappropriate spaces for such transgression. When I inquired about this public display of what I felt was total breach of proper social conduct, these public acts were dismissed as unimportant. I was told that these men were drunk, which made their lack of control negligible and tolerable. I gradually realized that the expression and containment of drunkenness and violence in public events was an elaborate mechanism that allowed the articulation of negative sentiments in public, specifically among relatives and friends, while defining them as petty and insignificant.

Rising incomes set the ground for the proliferation and popularity of ever more sophisticated *quán nhậu* that offered beer and even imported (or at least bootlegged) alcohol and increasingly more elaborate and exotic dishes. Many of these new places specialized in fish and seafood, while others served the expensive animal flesh attributed with virility, strength, and sexual potency, such as he-goat or that of wild animals. The virility and potency embedded in the flesh of these animals was further exacerbated by the *nóng* (hot/piquant), libido-enhancing spices such as chili, lemongrass, ginger, and *rau răm* (Vietnamese coriander).

McNally (2003), Nguyen-vo (2008), and Horton and Rydstrom (2011) address similar establishments, termed *karaoke ôm* ("hugging karaoke"), where "girls serve food and drinks to customers, select the songs that they wish to sing, and allow the men to touch, hug, and kiss them" (Horton and Rydstrom 2011: 552), suggesting that these venues were practically brothels. While *karaoke ôm* are extremely common in Vietnam, the local authorities in Hoi An have been very effective in curbing them. *Quán nhậu* differ from *karaoke ôm* in their emphasis on food and drink rather than karaoke, and in the sexual tone, which is less pronounced.

One of the outcomes of the increasing affluence in Vietnam, and of the booming tourism industry in Hoi An during the last two decades is the emergence of a new socioeconomic elite, composed mostly of successful business people, as well as high ranking government employees and officials who manage to get a piece of the economic cake, legally and illegally. Many of the members of this new local elite are deeply involved in conspicuous consumption and use their newly acquired means so as to celebrate and enhance their status. The more affluent purchase cars (rather than the ubiquitous motorbikes), travel to ever more remote and expensive destinations abroad, build large mansions and villas with luxurious gardens and pools, and send their children to overseas schools and universities. Bearing in mind that cars, villas, overseas schooling, and expensive trips abroad remain too expensive for most members of the Hoianese expanding middle class, they tend to invest their newly acquired capital in branded motorbikes, large houses, trips to Southeast Asian countries and universities for their children in Hanoi and Saigon and, perhaps, Singapore.

They are also eager to try new and exotic food in ever more refined settings, hence the flourishing and upgrading of *quán nhậu*. One version is that of restaurants that are set in simple, even coarse setting, but serve high-quality food cooked to order, along with beer and other alcoholic drinks, inclusive of *rượu gạo*. A more upscale version is that of open-air garden (*vườn*) restaurants, located at the margins of town, overlooking countryside, river or beach scapes, serving expensive, rare, power, libido and status-enhancing dishes accompanied by local and imported alcoholic drinks. While the cheaper *quán nhậu* were, and still are, a male-only affair, these new culinary establishments attract couples and even whole families, who uneasily share the culinary space with a majority of male-only groups, often drunk, loud, aggressive, and rude. These establishments, like their less sophisticated predecessors in the late 1990s, are mostly owned and managed by women, and employ female waitresses. The new garden restaurants are also mostly female-run, though many are family businesses, with male family members involved in the operation.

One prominent aspect of contemporary *quán nhậu* is the employment of *gái bia* (beer-girls). These women are employed by the beer companies and not by the restaurants, and are paid commission for the beer they sell. They are provided by the beer companies to the restaurants for free. However, as the beer-girls' income depends on the amount of beer consumed rather than the food eaten, they "push" beer rather than food, hence the structural tension between the restaurant owners, who are eager to use free manpower but boast and profit from the food they cook (Avieli 2012a). The beer-girls usually dress in very daring and sexy outfits, at least by Hoianese standards, wear heavy makeup and offer a variety of services to their male costumers beyond the actual serving of food and drinks: they pour the drinks, light cigarettes, wipe the customers' faces with cold towels, feed them, and even sit on their laps. They often drink and smoke with the clients, flirt with them, and allow different measures of physical contact. At least some of them engage in paid sex, while others double as kept mistresses. *Gái bia* are considered in Hoi An a notch above *gái ôm* ("hugging girls" or sex workers). Arguing that someone is a *gái bia* is a serious insult and admitting that one's relative is one is very embarrassing.

Women, be it beer-girls waitresses or lovers, have a pivotal role in the process of masculinity enhancement that takes place in *quán nhậu*: they encourage the consumption of *dương* (yang), *nóng* (warming) dishes, and alcohol and excite their clients with a combination of feminine submission (lighting cigarettes, wiping sweat, using respectful female grammar, and childlike, high-pitched tone) and assertive sexuality (dressing daringly, drinking, smoking, and flirting). These women are also the target of the resulting excessive masculinity: they allow their clients different measure of physical contact and, ultimately, if having sex with them, literally incorporate the excessive *dương* (male energy), serving as receptive utensils into which this excess is ejaculated.

Meat, Spiciness, and Masculinity

While all *quán nhậu* are spaces where men drink, consume *dương* foods, and engage in sexually charged extramarital relations, all of which are *social* transgressions, they do not necessarily entail *culinary* transgression. The flesh of fish, seafood, chicken, pork, and at times beef, served in these restaurants is not forbidden or otherwise frowned upon. In fact, these are the kinds of flesh commonly eaten at home, in public, and ritual meals. What makes the food served in such establishments different and masculine (besides the excessive consumption of alcohol) is the relatively large amounts of animal flesh (when compared to home eaten meals), and the *nóng* (hot/piquant) seasoning, which differs from the balanced, delicate seasoning common in Hoianese home cooking.

Scholars researching the interface of food and culture have long emphasized the strong links between meat, physical power, social dominance, and masculinity. Nick Fiddes (2004: 65) argues that eating meat is, above all, symbolic: "Killing, cooking and eating other animals' flesh is the ultimate authentication of human superiority over the rest of nature", while Carol Adams (2015) reminds us that the British Royal Guards are called "Beefeaters" because of their food of choice, designated to ensure their physical strength as members of a crack unit (that should be "as strong as oxen"), as well rewarding them with high status food, otherwise reserved to the upper classes.

Meat eating also represents socioeconomic and political power. In his classic article on "political types in Melanesia and Polynesia", Sahlins (1963) argues that pork sharing in public feasts constitutes a key physical and symbolic resource in the political game. Far from being exclusively an act of generosity and cooperation, he shows that meat is also a token in the social competition over status and prestige. Twigg (1983: 21) suggests that "meat is the most highly prized and culturally significant of foods", while Elias (1978) shows how in Medieval Europe members of the higher classes ate prodigious amounts of meat, while peasants ate very little of it, if at all. Bourdieu (1984) too argues that meat is indicative of economic wealth and high social status, and that eating certain kinds of meat is a symbolic action that expresses economic, cultural, and symbolic capital.

Eating meat is clearly a gendered practice. Michael Herzfeld (1985) describes how meat is central to the meal of every Cretan who considers himself a man, while Twigg (1983) suggests that the blood that gives red meat its color is expressive of power, aggression, passion, and sexuality—attributes that are desirable for men but considered offensive when it comes to women. Willard (2002: 112–113) thus concludes: "Because physical power is historically associated with masculinity and virility … meat has been perceived as a masculine subject."

Feminist critiques such as Twigg (1983) and Adams (2015) suggest that specific symbols related to meat are situated in a concentric hierarchy: culture above nature, humans above animals, and men above women. While Twigg (1983) suggests that the association of vegetarian and dairy foods with femininity indicates weakness and passiveness (as in the use of the term "vegetable" so as to describe a comatose person), Fiddes (2004: 210) argues that "meat exemplifies, more than anything, an attitude: the masculine worldview that ubiquitously perceives, values and legitimates hierarchical domination of nature, of women and of other men". Collectively, these scholars point out that there is no biological or nutritional connection between meat and masculinity. Rather, it is the violent act of asserting one's power and privilege by the killing of another creature and consuming its flesh that makes meat so appealing to men, not the actual building of a strong and muscular body.

When it comes to spiciness, its association with masculinity is not as clear. Herzfeld (2009: 191), in a text that celebrates culinary ambiguity, notes: "it is always tempting to associate high spice with an ideology of masculine pride ... [Indeed] the appearance of an intense spice quickly develops into a test of masculinity, while women claim to be horrified by the very idea of eating anything so spicy. But there is no necessary biological connection between spiciness and masculinity and it is not clear that such connections are found in all human societies." Herzfeld's ambiguous text therefore suggests that spiciness is associated, at least in Thailand, with working-class masculinity. Spiciness, like meat, have very little to do with the biological aspects of masculinity. Clearly, it is all about competition and the demonstration of bodily control that make spicy food masculine, at least in Thailand.

In Hoianese homes, food is rarely spicy, though diners may add (or bite into) hot chili. Spicy food as such is usually served only in *quán nhậu*, which up until recently served only working-class men. Thus, just like in Thailand, spicy food was associated with working-class masculinity. It should be noted, however, that most members of the Hoianese elite and middle class grew up in working-class families and their taste and habitus are those of the working class, despite their recent affluence.

While spicy food and large amounts of meat are considered masculine in Hoi An, it is the establishment, *quán nhậu*, along with the social relations it entails, that induces a sense of transgression. Let us now turn to the flesh of specific animals considered forbidden, or at least, inappropriate: he-goat and jungle meat.

He-Goat Meat

A group of Hoianese friends with whom I used to have lunch every now and again often played a food/word game that, at first, I couldn't figure out. One of the diners would pick up a morsel of food, say a piece of *rau muống* (water morning-glory), and ask: "*ăn rau bổ gì?*" ("[when] eating greens/vegetables, what gets nourished?"). After a short reflection, one of the co-diners would reply: "*ăn rau bổ râu!*" ("[when] eating vegetable, [the] beard [is] nourished!"), and everyone would burst in loud laughter. After a while, another diner would pick up a different food item, say a shrimp, and ask: "when eating shrimp, what gets nourished?" The answer would be: "when eating shrimp, the shrimp is nourished" ("*ăn tôm bổ tôm!*"), stirring yet another burst of laughter. Things could get even more incomprehensible, as when someone would ask: "when eating shrimp, what gets nourished?", to which the answer would be: "when eating shrimp, the banana is nourished!" ("*ăn tôm bổ chuối!*").

As my language skills improved, I realized that this confusing food/word game was actually very sophisticated and had an erotic/sexist undertone, which was well known to the participants and the reason for their laughter: each bite of food insinuated a sex-related body organ. The word *rau*, which means "vegetable", was replaced by *râu*, which means "beard" but is also used for body hair and for pubic hair. The meaning of the sentence was: when eating greens, the pubic hair is nourished. *Tôm* (shrimp), my friends explained, represented the vagina due to its curvilinear shape. However, when eaten by men, it nourishes their "banana" or penis. I also learned that when *sữa chim* or "bird's milk" was offered, usually by one of the men to either of the women, he was actually referring to semen and was thus suggesting oral sex, as *chim*, or "bird", is commonly used for the penis. Another double-edged invitation would be to eat "clams" (*nghêu*), which stand for the vulva.

Thus, while having lunch, these friends were conducting an anatomically detailed conversation about sex, using only food terms, demonstrating the Vietnamese ability to maintain virtuous and chaste façade despite the great interest in, and practical engagement with sex—both within and beyond marriage. This was summarized by a female friend, merely 18 at the time, who realizing my surprise at the juicy piece of gossip she shared with me about a mutual friend who was apparently having a very sexually active affair with a married partner, commented: "Nir, we have everything in Hoi An, but quietly".

But this tendency to maintain sexual discourse quiet or camouflaged had one salient exception: goat meat restaurants. When it came to these food venues, things were much more explicit and direct—*thịt dê* (goat meat) was an aphrodisiac and men would dine in places that specialized in this kind of meat as a way of enhancing their sexual potency.

Coming from the Middle East, where goat meat is quite common but hardly an aphrodisiac, I was intrigued by the idea that the meat of this specific animal was attributed with so much libido. Indeed, the word *dê* or "goat" is routinely used in Hoi An for "horny" (and note the connotation to the he-goat horns in English too[2]), and one's 35th birthday (which I celebrated in town) is termed *ba lăm dê* (35 [years old] goat—in reference to the Vietnamese zodiac) is the source of endless jokes about one's state of sexual arousal. When I wondered why goat meat was considered such a powerful aphrodisiac, a friend explained: "have you ever seen goats in the mountains: there are some forty or fifty female goats and a single he-goat. This male goat may mount any of the females any time, and can actually do it." The he-goat condition was therefore described as ideal from the male perspective: a very large number of available, submissive (and perhaps interested) females; no competition with other males; and no less important: potency to engage in unlimited number of sexual intercourses. This perception depicts the he-goat as the essence of masculinity.

Hoianese Goat meat restaurants, like all *quán nhậu*, were essentially drinking places. However, they were attributed with specific kind of aura and/or sleazy character: men who frequent these venues were explicitly seeking sexual potency. I asked several friends, men and women, to eat in one of these places but my invitations were all declined with a surprised frown. Eventually, an Australian female tour guide who spent months in town told me that she was craving for mutton and we went for goat meat instead. We came quite late for dinner, and there was only a single man eating alone by one of the tables. This in itself was quite unusual, as in a small town such as Hoi An, meals are very rarely eaten alone, even when one goes alone to the restaurant: there are always people around with who to share the table.

We ordered roast goat meat by the weight, and spent the evening chewing the tough stringy meat. We were surprised to find out that despite the universal refusal of our friends to frequent this place the actual practices were so innocent (at least during that evening).

A few months later, a friend who was an alcoholic and used any excuse to drink, overheard my questions about goat meat and suggested that my wife and I join him and his spouse for a meal at a goat meat place he knew on the way to Da Nang. His wife was first angry and reluctant, arguing that he was just using a pretext as an excuse to drink, but he used a combination of smiles, soothing voice, and seduction—arguing that this was a rare chance to try goat meat, and that the place he knows serves very tasty dishes, and eventually she half-heartedly agreed.

A few days later we drove to the restaurant. We arrived by late afternoon, just in time for early dinner. The restaurant was a small place of some four tables in the first floor of a family house. A skinny goat was tied by the door on the pavement, serving as a commercial and a proof of authenticity and freshness. We ordered *lẩu dê* (goat hotpot) and the proprietor asked whether we wanted red or white wine. This was an unusual offer in the early 2000s, when wines were rare and expensive, and hardly a routine component of a meal at a restaurant that catered to low-income clients. My friend explained that "red" was rice liquor mixed with fresh goat blood, while "white" was the same liquor in which the goat testicles were soaked. He ordered glasses of "white" for both of us, but not for the women, and when I declined—drunk mine as well.

We cooked the thinly sliced goat meat in goat-bones broth served in a hotpot, with our friend consuming several beer bottles. His wife was exceedingly distressed and upset, both because of his drinking and because the group of men that occupied another table made offensive comments about her and about my wife. The scene became increasingly uncomfortable and we were relieved to leave. We never experienced this kind of abusive attitude in a restaurant previously, and though such behavior may be tolerated when it comes to drunk men, this was probably one of the most aggressive reactions toward women I have experienced in Vietnam. It was clear to us that the setting—that is, a goat meat restaurant, was a place where such behavior may occur, as it never happens elsewhere.

I partook in goat meat meals in two other instances that further complicated the sense of transgression and ambiguity surrounding this meat. Not very long after the meal in Da Nang I traveled to visit a friend in Hanoi. I asked my host and her brother to go for goat meat. They took me to a very large and busy restaurant where multi-generational families and large groups of men and women were roasting goat meat over charcoal grill built into the table. When I commented that in Hoi An goat meat is a male-affair, my hosts were surprised. They said that in Hanoi goat meat is considered a specialty and served in specific restaurants, but is not considered masculine or an aphrodisiac. Moreover, though drinking in Hanoian goat meat restaurants was common, these venues were not associated with illicit or paid sex. In fact, my hosts pointed out, one delicacy served in Hanoian goat meat restaurants was goat udders. Along the meal, I realized that the udders were, once more, a subject of double speak and laughter, but this was clearly focused on the notion of udders as a form of female breats (*vụ*). In Hanoi, I realized, goat meat was a special food, but was not associated with explicit masculinity and sexuality but, rather, with femininity and the consumption of the human female body. The transgression here had a somewhat different meaning, but was associated with power relations and sexuality, though the composition of diners (women, children, families) implies more implicit eroticism of the meal.

The forth goat meat meal took place under very different circumstances. An Indian restaurant was set up in Hoi An, and we invited our Vietnamese teacher along with three of her colleagues, two female teachers and a male teacher, to try this new place and experience the new food. Wrongly assuming that our guests were unfamiliar with Indian food, I suggested that I would explain the menu and order the food. I picked some starters and bread, and suggested several vegetarian dishes as main courses, but the male teacher asked if we could have *cà ri dê* (goat curry). I was surprised by his request, as I never had goat curry in India or in Indian restaurants elsewhere (though I did eat mutton curry). I responded that I didn't think the restaurant served *cà ri dê*, but the male teacher insisted it did—and was right. We ordered the goat curry and though our guests were quite cautious and ambivalent before and after tasting the goat curry, this dish was clearly the one all our guests, male and female, were interested in.

Here I should add that the male teacher was a notorious womanizer. Whenever I met him in public, those present at the meeting would tell me later about his intimate relationships with his (high school) students. They were very critical of him not only because of the students but also because they felt angry and ashamed by the way he treated his wife, who was well aware of her husband's exploits, and was hurt and upset. I was told several times that he was *dê* (goat, i.e., horny), and between me and my teacher, we nicknamed him "Mr. dê". Oddly enough "Mr. dê" insisted that we ordered *cà ri dê*. It was also odd, however, that the female teachers, his spouse included, were all eager to try the dish. My understanding was that this was a chance to try this kind of meat in a setting that was socially acceptable or, at least, not male and sex oriented, but rather a place that offered exotic and odd food, where everyone could pretend that no transgression was going on. The event, however, became tense once we ordered the goat curry, with our guests becoming quiet, carefully biting into the goat meat and looking at each other with what seemed to me a combination of fear and embarrassment. The tension eased only once the main course were cleared and we turned to order desserts.

My experience with goat meat in these different settings suggested that this was one salient example of ambiguous culinary transgression. In Hoi An, goat meat was attributed with male potency. It was served in specializing restaurants that catered to men. The meat was either roasted, condensing and augmenting the potency it embodied, or cooked in a broth that ensured that every bit of it was consumed to the fullest. Goat blood and testicles, the essence of its masculinity, were consumed in rice liquor, further increasing the potential masculinity consumed by the diners. Restaurants that served goat meat catered only to men and any woman present was perceived as a legitimate target for sexual approach, exploitation, and abuse, as we realized when such comments were made at our female companions.

Goat meat was perceived by my Hoianese friends as tempting yet problematic. Men were eager to consume it so as to enhance their masculinity. Yet both women and men agreed that this was not the fare appropriate for normative people under normal circumstances. Women were especially critical and deterred from goat meat and the places that served it, but they too were willing (perhaps eager) to try it in circumstances that somehow removed the meal from the realm of blunt male potency and sexuality, such as the Indian restaurant.

In Hanoi, goat meat was considered a specialty, but not a blunt vessel of masculine sexuality. In fact, female-goat udders were highlighted, while the testicle-liquor was not offered. The udders were related to female sexuality, but the mixed clientele and multi-generational families suggested that these were respectable (or at least acceptable) dining venues.

Ambiguity was most clearly observable in the Indian restaurant. This place catered mainly to foreign tourists, and was not marked as masculine and/or inappropriate for women. Thus, I could invite four teachers from the town's only high school, all of them well known in town, to have a meal at this food venue. But precisely because this was a tourist-oriented establishment and was not considered locally as a goat meat venue, with all the negative implications such definition entails, the male teacher could ask for goat meat in the presence of his female colleagues inclusive of his wife, while the female teachers, who would otherwise refuse to dine in a goat meat restaurant, were quite enthusiastic to try it. Goat meat in Hoi An was both repulsive and appealing, shunned in public, but thought after by men, and in some contexts, by women. Eating goat meat was a transgression, but one which many Hoianese wanted to experience.

Jungle Meat

Jungle meat (*thịt rừng*), the flesh of animals hunted in the forest and the wild (or whatever is left of it in Vietnam), is also served in *quán nhậu* style establishments and is associated with masculinity and male competitiveness, alcohol, beer-girls, and sex. But while goat meat is consumed because of the he-goats' alleged potency, jungle meat is associated with sexuality somewhat less directly. Forest animals are thought-after because their flesh is imbued with the power of the wild. I was told that snakes and other reptiles such as large lizards (*con kỳ đà*) may enlarge penis size and strengthen erection because of their shape. Deer is associated with erection because of its long straight horns. Other forest animals, such as the tiger, are consumed because, just like the he-goat, they demonstrate outstanding sexual abilities. But generally speaking, wild animals are strong and wild and consuming their flesh would make the eater stronger and wilder. Eating the flesh of such wild animals also expresses the subjugation of nature. Jungle meat is therefore associated with wilderness and untamed power, *and* with the taming of this power.

Another important feature of jungle meat has to do with the fact that most of it is hunted and traded illegally. Men who eat jungle meat defy both nature and culture: they overcome the wild animals and consume their power, while ignoring the law and the social order. It is hard to think of a blunter statement of masculine confidence and power.

One important aspect of jungle meat restaurants is that the killing should be done on spot and in full view of the clients. The violent ritual of public killing, which often involves draining the blood (and at times the gall) into rice alcohol for immediate consumption, further enhances the sense of power and taming of the wild associated with jungle meat meals. Hoianese jungle meat restaurants therefore display some of the animals whose flesh they offer in cages, and the customers witness the slaughtering.

Killing the animal on the spot also allows clients to observe that the promised meat is not only fresh but also what they paid for. Jungle meat is rare, expensive, and illegal, and I was often told how these restaurants substitute the meat of wild animals with that of domestic ones, which is abundant, cheaper, and legal. Some substitutes are symbolic and even acceptable and declared, for example, serving cat meat instead of tiger (at times under the nickname of "little tigers"[3] or *hổ con*). In other instances, domestic pork is served instead of boar. But at times, any cheap and available meat would substitute any promised jungle meat. Killing and cooking the animal in front of the costumers reduces, at least to a certain extent, the potential for cheating.

At the same time, taking part in an illegal activity, even if only by ordering the meat and watching the killing, exacerbates the defiance of the law and thus spices up and invigorates the transgression and the power it entails: *here I stand in front of everyone and in broad day light—break the law; I am scared of no one.*

I found this public defiance of the law especially intriguing because whenever I attended a jungle meat restaurant in Hoi An, some of the clients were public officials, along with their friends, colleagues, and business partners (the latter actually paying for the meal, drinks, and hostess services). The jungle meat meals I observed were therefore events in which law makers (politicians) and law officers (policemen) ritually and publically broke the law they were charged with upholding and enforcing.

Since in many cases those paying for the meal were potential partners for illicit or corrupt deals, my understanding is that the meal, alcohol, and sex paid by the hosts were not only a direct form of bribe but also a conduit to future relations: the co-diners were breaking a relatively unimportant law together, creating bonding, trust, and mutual dependency that would stabilize ongoing cooperation.

While I never shared a meal with corrupt officials, my interlocutors described these culinary events several times, shifting from condemning attitude toward the official corruption, to the description of their own pleasure during these meals and accompanying activities. They made it clear that they felt blackmailed by the officials, who made them pay for the expensive food and services in return for things such as licenses and permits, which they were entitled too in any case, or for things that were clearly illegal, such as the postponing of military draft. In most cases I was told that they did not like the company of the officials themselves who were greedy and took advantage of their position. But when I asked about the food, they often commented that it was very delicious. In some cases, they also mentioned that the food had an impact on their libido and their sexual relations with the beer-girls. The comments about the good food and sexual relations were often followed by inviting me to join such a meal. I was first confused by this shift: how was it possible that they felt blackmailed and yet enjoyed the food, drink, and sexual services so much? And why would they want to repeat this experience with me? I gradually realized however, that this combination of shame, guilt, and pleasure was very attractive, and that one way of dealing with the negative aspects of shame and guilt was by arguing that everyone (i.e., all men) take part in such practices. I was invited to join in to not only share the pleasure with me but also the shame and guilt—share the burden as it were and relieve my friends of some of it.

An invitation to dine at a jungle meat restaurant (and to a lesser extent—at a goat meat restaurant) is therefore an invitation for male bonding reinforced by partaking in activities that are both illegal (hunting wildlife is banned) and morally problematic (overindulgence, drunkenness, and extramarital paid sex).

Following my working rule of "accepting every invitation" (Avieli 2012b), I never refused an invitation to join in a jungle meat restaurant or jungle meat meal cooked at home, though I generally prefer to stay away from illegal activities, and despite my objection to wild life hunting. I also found it very hard to eat the flesh of animals whose death I witnessed.

This turned out to be awkward: joining the table but avoiding the meat was not merely a refusal to "break bread", but also abuse of the trust bestowed upon me by my hosts. They allowed me to observe them breaking the law and transgress moral standards, but my refusal to eat the food and embody the transgression, as it were, meant that now I had potentially implicating information about my hosts, but since I did not partake in the actual eating, they did not have the same kind of implicating information about me. My hosts were therefore adamant that I eat or, at least, try the meat, and were visibly upset when I refused.

This dynamic was also common in cases were hostesses and potential paid sex were involved. Engaging in paid sex is perhaps the least kept secret of Hoianese men. The subject would come up in many male-only conversations and meetings, usually as a joke or a comment. But if I wouldn't protest or otherwise signal reservation, the conversation would very quickly turn into straightforward discussion of the potential of the waitress or some other women as a sex partner. This would often develop into an ambiguous invitation to pursue sex. I was interested in the subject and the discourse surrounding it, so I usually "passed" the first stage, with jokes turning into serious conversations regarding sexual practices, qualities, choices, availability, and price. However, the fact that I took notes and my eventual refusal to engage in paid sex were often met with dismay and discomfort. If I would have avoided the subject or presented a critical/moralistic position to begin with, it would probably be ok. But engaging in a conversation and asking for details that only practitioners would know, and later refuse to take part in the activity itself, was not only surprising but also perceived negatively by people who did not know me well.

Several taboos were breached when eating jungle meat in Hoi An: the Buddhist prohibition to consume the flesh of wild animals, which may turn the eater into a wild beast; the public act of killing, which is a violent expression of power; and the public defiance of the law. The context of corruption and abuse of power exacerbated the transgression, while excessive drinking, extramarital erotic relations, and paid sex further removed the event from the realm of the normative into that of the extraordinary and forbidden.

At this point, I would like to address another important food taboo that was transgressed in these meals: the taboo on human flesh. As pointed out earlier, human flesh is one of the ten forbidden meats in Buddhism. It is also a universal taboo. The ethnographic data on cannibalism is very problematic and mostly unreliable but the few authoritative sources distinguish between endo and exo cannibalism, suggesting that much of it is ritual and internal—when some flesh of a deceased ancestor is consumed by relatives to ensure continuity. Ethnographic descriptions of such events detail the great difficulty and distress suffered by the participants, who often collapse vomiting by the end of the ritual.

In Hoi An, however, quite a few men with whom I discussed their food preferences responded to my question about their favorite meats by pointing out that they liked human flesh (*thích thịt người*). This remark was yet another word game where food and sex were interchanged: "I like human flesh" meant "I like sex", and the fact that human flesh is forbidden insinuated for the kind of sex these men were talking about: the forbidden kind of sex—with lovers, mistresses, and sex workers. In goat and jungle meat restaurants, forbidden meat and forbidden sex were reflections of each other, and both were practiced even though it was clear to all those involved that these were social and moral transgressions.

The point, of course, is that such transgressions were context dependent, relative, and flexible. People may argue that one should not eat jungle food, avoid cruelty toward animals, should not pay for the meals of corrupt officials to gain actual or potential benefits, be faithful to their spouses, and avoid paid sex. Yet the very same people, in specific circumstances and company, may be sympathetic and even enthusiastic about these practices.

Culinary Ambivalence and Cultural Intimacy

Eating goat meat and jungle meat in Hoi An are ambiguous culinary practices. The men who partake in such meals are well aware that they are socially and morally problematic and may be illegal. At the same time, they find them very appealing. This ambivalence is the source of the unease and anxiety that were always felt when discussing these culinary practices and when partaking in them. The ad hoc solution for this anxiety may be found in the sense of cultural intimacy that prevails among the diners in these meals.

Cultural intimacy is "the recognition of those aspects of a cultural identity that are considered a source of external embarrassment but that nevertheless provide insiders with their assurance of common sociality" (Herzfeld 2005: 3). In other words, cultural intimacy prevails among members of a specific culture who partake and indulge in specific cultural activities, which they perceive as their own, but at the same time find them embarrassing and therefore actively hide them from outsiders.

The prime example Herzfeld uses is the Greek government's attempt to ban plate-breaking in restaurants that attract both locals and tourists: "not only is the practice 'not Greek' despite all the evidence to the contrary, but it is humiliating for some Greeks to realize that tourists – Northern Europeans especially – see this custom as quintessentially Greek. Plate smashing becomes a site of 'cultural intimacy' for Greeks in relation to German observers … Whether Germans really do look down on Greeks for smashing plates does not matter; the intimacy that emerges in this context of self-recognition is decidedly Greek" (Shryock 2004: 10).

Another example Herzfeld uses is Cretan sheep theft. According to Herzfeld, sheep stealing, as well as many other illegal activities such as tax evasion, are vehemently denied in public contexts and during official interaction with state representatives, but are celebrated privately as representations of cultural traits that signal out Greek or Cretan (or a specific village) distinctiveness. In one instance, Herzfeld describes how the Cretan shepherds he was studying invited a police team investigating sheep theft to a lavish feast. Meal over, the shepherds informed the police officers that they have just eaten the evidence (i.e., the stolen sheep).

Somewhat different from plate smashing, the Cretan state representatives took part in the cultural intimacy of the revelation, even though they were the target of the scam. The police officers were fooled into accomplishment, but in this apparently negative status, were accepted as peers with whom cultural intimacy may be shared.

Herzfeld discusses cultural intimacy and its manifestations on the national level (as in "Greeks" vs. "Germans"), or as a relationship between citizens and the state (as with the sheep thieves and police officers). My data suggests for further realms where cultural intimacy defines relations and shapes their content.

The first realm is that of gender. Dishes made of he-goat and jungle meat were "men only" affairs. Men consumed them in the company of other men in an explicit attempt to enhance their sexual prowess. The women who shared the space and, at times, the food were either mistresses, beer-girls, or sex workers. Wives and girlfriends were excluded from this space of cultural intimacy. In fact, in the presence of wives, female friends and female relatives, or in mixed-gender company, men would frown upon these meats and food venues or dismiss the food.

But the very same men would be much more enthusiastic in the company of other men or in a quite corner, away from women. The smile that often accompanied the discussion of he-goat meat and jungle meat among men was similar to the smile that accompanied conversations about extramarital affairs or paid sex, as well as discussions of illegal transactions of money in the form of bribe. Such smiles seemed to express a strong sense of ambivalence: *I know it's wrong—but I love it; are you in it with me?*

The second realm of cultural intimacy may be set between state officials and other men. Yet while Herzfeld depicts a scene where local farmers fooled the police officers into cultural intimacy, Hoianese officials established social bonds with other men in the setting of these culinary establishments, where partaking in dodgy activities (enhanced sexuality, extramarital relations), which were at times illegal (prostitution, forbidden kinds of meat, corruption, and bribe), set the ground for cultural intimacy among the co-diners. In these meals, cultural intimacy was the outcome of a shared sense of transgression: *we are all naughty boys; we now know each other's secrets; we are all in it together.*

Cultural intimacy is therefore the remedy for the anxiety involved in the context of such socioculinary transgressions. This remedy, however, is context dependent and bound in space and time: it allows those men sharing cultural intimacy to temporarily inhibit their reservations, partake in the transgression, and indulge in it. However, in the presence of those with whom such sense of cultural intimacy is not possible (spouses or "official" girlfriends, mixed-gender groups, elders, and other people who may be critical of such transgressions), frequenting he-goat and jungle meat restaurants would be criticized, denied, or dismissed.

Finally, a word is due about the essence of food anxieties (see Ehlert and Faltmann, this volume). Usually, the material and practical dimensions of food anxieties are those highlighted in the public discourse and the academic research; the most immediate and common are unhygienic foods or those polluted by poisons that may affect the eaters' short- and long-term well-being. In this chapter I argue that food anxieties are always contextualized in social and cultural circumstances and that at times, perhaps often, have very little to do with material considerations or with the physical effect on the diners' bodies. Rather, food anxieties may emerge in situations where social norms are transgressed and where symbolic interpretations define the meanings of specific situations and interactions. They are, indeed, forbidden from the heart.

Notes

1. This tendency may be the outcome of the assumption that there is only one true god and that all other gods are false. This binary of "true" versus "false" evolves into an ever-expanding set of moral binaries: right and wrong, holy and profane, allowed and forbidden, and so on. In the culinary sphere, it is extended into the binaries of clean and polluted, or edible and taboo. These culinary binaries are central to monotheistic thought and practice no less than the binaries of life and death, men and women, good and evil, or nature and culture highlighted by Lévi-Strauss (1963, 1966). In non-monotheistic cultures such as Vietnam, these dichotomies are less clear-cut, and a more flexible and relativistic attitude prevails when it comes to the perception of death, gender, moral

standards, and the place of humans in the cosmological order. This flexibility is also the rule in the culinary sphere. Perhaps, as my colleague Uri Shwed suggested, it is the other way round: a cultural tendency for binaries leads to monotheism *and* to total food prohibitions, while more flexible and relativistic cultures are susceptive to the multiplicity of gods and to laxer food regimes.

2. The term "old goat" in English and Hebrew stands for someone who is lecherous. It implies though that there are also "young goats", that is, acceptably libidinous young people. In any case, he-goat is associated with sexual desire in other cultures too.

3. http://www.inquisitr.com/1379070/little-tiger-vietnams-taste-for-cat-meat/, sampled 13.12.16.

References

Adams, C.J., 2015. *The sexual politics of meat: A feminist-vegetarian critical theory*. London: Bloomsbury.

Avieli, N., 2012a. Dog meat politics in a Vietnamese town. *Ethnology*, 50, 1: 59–78.

Avieli, N. 2012b. Rice Talks: Food and Community in a Vietnamese Town. Bloomington: Indiana University Press.

Avieli N., 2014. Vegetarian Ethics and Politics in Postsocialist Vietnam. In Yuson Jung, Jakob Klein, and Melissa Caldwell (eds.) *Ethical Eating in the Postsocialist and Socialist World*. Berkeley: University of California Press. Pp. 144–166.

Bourdieu, P., 1984. *Distinction: A social critique of the judgement of taste*. Cambridge: Harvard University Press.

Calder, A. 1999. The Thrice Mysterious Taboo: Melville's Typee and the perception of culture. *Representations* 67: 27–43.

Mary, D. (1975). *Implicit Meanings: essays in anthropology*. London: Routledge and Kegan Paul.

Douglas, M. 2003 [1966]. *Purity and danger: An analysis of concepts of pollution and taboo*. London: Routledge.

Elias, N., 1978. *The civilizing process. Vol. 1: The history of manners*. New York: Pantheon.

Fiddes, N., 2004. *Meat: A natural symbol*. New York: Routledge.

Gilmore, H., Schafer, C. and Halcrow, S., 2013. Tapu and the invention of the "death taboo": An analysis of the transformation of a Polynesian cultural concept. *Journal of Social Archaeology*, 13, 3: 331–349.

Harris, M., 1987. *The Sacred Cow and the Abominable Pig: riddles of food and culture*. Simon and Schuster.

Herzfeld, M., 1985. *The Poetics of Manhood*. Princeton: Princeton University Press.

Herzfeld, M., 2005. *Cultural intimacy: Social poetics in the nation-state*. New York: Routledge.

Herzfeld, M., 2009. Serving Ambiguity: Class and Classification in Thai Food at Home and Abroad. In Kim, K.O. ed., 2015. *Re-orienting Cuisine: East Asian Foodways in the Twenty-first Century*. New York and Oxford: Berghahn Books, 186–201.

Horton, P. and Rydstrom, H., 2011. Heterosexual masculinity in contemporary Vietnam: Privileges, pleasures, and protests. *Men and Masculinities*, *14*(5), 542–564.

Jamieson, N.L., 1995. *Understanding Vietnam*. Berkeley: Univ of California Press.

Lévi-Strauss, C. 1963. *Structural Anthropology*. London: Basic Books.

Lévi-Strauss, C. 1966. The Culinary triangle. *New Society*, 8, 221: 937–940.

Lien, M. 2004. Dogs, Whales and Kangaroos: Transnational activism and food taboos. In Lien, M. and Nerlich, B. (eds.). *The Politics of Food*. London: Berg Publishers, pp. 179–199.

McNaIIy, S., 2003. Bia om and karaoke: HIV and everyday life in urban Vietnam. In Drummond, L.B.W. and Thomas, M. (eds.), 2003. *Consuming Urban Culture in Contemporary Vietnam*. London: Routledge Curzon.

Nguyen-vo, Thu-huong, 2008. *The Ironies of Freedom: Sex, Culture, and Neoliberal Governance in Vietnam*. Seattle: University of Washington Press.

Manderson, L., & Mathews, M. 1981. Vietnamese behavioral and dietary precautions during pregnancy. *Ecology of Food and Nutrition*, *11*(1), 1–8.

Mathews, M., & Manderson, L., 1981. Vietnamese behavioral and dietary precautions during confinement. *Ecology of Food and Nutrition*, *11*(1), 9–16.

Meyer-Rochow, V. B. (2009). Food taboos: their origins and purposes. *Journal of Ethnobiology and Ethnomedicine*, *5*(1), 1.

Mintz, S.W. and Du Bois, C.M., 2002. The anthropology of food and eating. *Annual review of anthropology*, *31*(1), 99–119.

Sachdev, P. S. 1989. Mana, Tapu, Noa: Maori cultural constructs with medical and psychosocial relevance. *Psychological Medicine* 19: 959–969.

Sahlins, M.D., 1963. Poor man, rich man, big-man, chief: political types in Melanesia and Polynesia. *Comparative studies in society and history*, 5(3), 285–303.

Shirres, M.P. 1982. Tapu. *The Journal of the Polynesian Society*, 91, 1: 29–51.

Shryock, A., 2004. *Off stage/on display: intimacy and ethnography in the age of public culture*. Stanford: Stanford University Press.

Tambiah, S.J., 1969. Animals are good to think and good to prohibit. *Ethnology*, 8(4), 423–459.

Twigg, J. (1983). Vegetarianism and the meanings in meat. In Murcott, A., 1983. The sociology of food and eating: essays on the sociological significance of food. Aldershot: Gower, 18–30.

Willard, B.E., 2002. The American story of meat: Discursive influences on cultural eating practice. *The Journal of Popular Culture*, 36(1), 105–118.

Yifa. (2002). *The origins of Buddhist monastic codes in China: an annotated translation and study of the Chanyuan qinggui*. University of Hawaii Press.

4

Obesity, Biopower, and Embodiment of Caring: Foodwork and Maternal Ambivalences in Ho Chi Minh City

Judith Ehlert

Introduction

An article titled "Alert: children with fat bellies" in a local newspaper[1] published in 2015 drew public attention to the growing phenomenon of obesity in children in Ho Chi Minh City (HCMC). Besides the lack of physical activity, the article points to the increase of high-calorific food consumption as one reason for this development. The economic reforms of *Đổi Mới* in 1986 went hand in hand with the modernisation of the food system, with dietary patterns gradually changing towards the consumption of more processed, convenience, and high-calorie foods (see Ehlert and Faltmann, this volume). With growing economic affluence and dietary patterns changing, Vietnam is said to be undergoing a phase of nutrition transition. For the first time in the country's history being overweight and obesity especially in children proliferate as public health concerns and make the Vietnamese government respond by a comprehensive mission for their eradication by 2030. Health and nutrition

J. Ehlert (✉)
Department of Development Studies, University of Vienna, Vienna, Austria
e-mail: judith.ehlert@univie.ac.at

© The Author(s) 2019
J. Ehlert, N. K. Faltmann (eds.), *Food Anxiety in Globalising Vietnam*,
https://doi.org/10.1007/978-981-13-0743-0_4

education programmes first and foremost target parents of children under the age of five years and the children themselves living in urban areas—a cohort that was found most at risk (Vietnam Ministry of Health 2012).

The World Health Organization (WHO) defines obesity as "abnormal or excessive fat accumulation that may impair health" (WHO 2018). While it used to be considered a problem of the Global North, obesity is perceived as the nearest future concern of low- and middle-income countries, with Asia already being highly affected (WHO 2018). Scholars from the broad field of critical health, obesity, and fat studies criticise the medicalised discourse of 'obesity' on the basis of it constructing fatness as a unidirectional health problem. This critical scholarship argues that the dominant discourse constructs obesity as one of the major food anxieties of our time that supposedly puts public health systems as well as the productive labour force of whole economies under pressure (WHO 2000; Guthmann 2009; Metzl and Kirkland 2010; LeBesco 2011; Lupton 2013). For the context of China, critical voices on obesity argue that the 'obesity epidemic' deemed culturally favoured body fatness in children pathological (Greenhalgh 2016).[2] Similarly in Vietnam, the chubby shape of a child's body becomes vested with conflicting meanings, ranging from the beauty of chubby children to "children with fat bellies" perceived as "alarming", as exemplified in the headline of the local newspaper above. Whereas the medical and nutrition sciences dominate research on child obesity in Vietnam, a critical social science perspective on the topic hardly exists.

Therefore, the emerging obesity discourse in Vietnam constitutes the scaffold for the following empirical study. Coming from the background of sociology and critical development studies, the author's interest lies in deconstructing the discourse by engaging with the everyday routines, social relations, and practices of mothers' foodwork[3] in urban Vietnam. The chapter develops the argument that food anxiety derives from the ambivalences that women experience in their daily practices as 'caring' mothers. Socio-cultural norms articulated in public health discourses, taken up by the food industry, discussed in social media platforms, as well as emphasised by family, friends, and neighbours all address very different expectations regarding a child's body shape and health status. These conflicting discourses are not only inscribed on the child's body but work on and in the mother's body as well.

This chapter is in keeping with Cairns and Johnston (2015, 25) in their sociological approach to food femininities, which establishes the link between individual food and body performances at interpersonal and emotional levels and the social structures and institutions these are embedded in. In general, the regulation of food, food-related entitlements, and responsibilities are structured along gendered lines, strongly associating foodwork with feminine identity (Charles and Kerr 1988; DeVault 1991; Counihan 1999). To this end, however, it is by no means to say here that women[4] are considered as 'naturally' caring, nor that something like a general motherhood experience exists. By contrast, the chapter aims to better contextualise how women in HCMC manoeuvre dominant socio-cultural discourses that essentialise maternal love by connecting it with food and body work (Collins 1994). The following study thus brings in the perspectives of married women in their 20s to 40s, all holding a university degree, working in full-time employment, and having one to three children. Given their social 'middle-class'[5] position, they command the (economic) means to participate in the emerging lifestyle, food, and body industries in the city. The concise focus of the study implies its very limitation at the same time, namely the exclusion of perspectives of women who are structurally deprived of access to certain spaces of urban consumption.

This chapter draws on data from different periods of field research in HCMC between 2014 and 2017. The main data for this study was gathered in the summer months of 2015. Back then, the author was pregnant herself—a circumstance that surely helped open up access to other women and ample opportunities for informal discussions on the research topic. Through the regular attendance in a prenatal class the author met women sharing ideas of what they considered good for their (unborn) babies and on how they regulated their food consumption during pregnancy. The contact to this prenatal class in the hospital was provided by Loan,[6] the owner of a women's spa in HCMC specialising in services for mothers and mothers-to-be. Furthermore, interviews[7] were conducted with Ly, a female editor of a popular women's and family lifestyle magazine to get a first-hand idea on 'modern' mothering and feeding trends. Thi, interviewed in her capacity as staff of a local market research institute, shared insights not only into urban consumption trends but also on her personal experience of mothering. This chapter also refers to the narratives of Veronique—a French woman with two kids and married to a Vietnamese—a representative of a supermarket chain. Back then, she had just had her first baby and the discussion naturally diverted to her personal observations of women 'stuffing' their children. This was the first time that the topic of child 'obesity' and the ideal of plump body figures in children popped up as a dimension of this research. An interview with a representative of the Nutrition Centre in Hanoi,[8] with a medical doctor as well as a personal fitness coach complements the subjective experiences of the mothers interviewed by bringing in perspectives of the public health sector and fitness industry. Participant observation in condominium blocks, restaurants, shopping malls, and supermarkets enriched the data collected. Moreover, this chapter builds on internet research that explored the role of social media platforms and online forums on child nutrition. Local online newspapers were scanned by search engine tools to investigate the use of terms like 'feeding practices' (*cách thức cho trẻ/bé ăn*) and 'a good mother' (*một người mẹ tốt*) in media discussions.

Biopower, Obesity, and Maternal Caring

This section briefly introduces the background of nutrition transition and related weight gain of children in urban Vietnam. Its main goal is to provide a conceptual framing for the understanding of the local phenomenon of obesity—as discourse. The public health sector and the role of the food industry are addressed in terms of their biopower over children's health. Furthermore, the public debate on childhood obesity is put in perspective through pinpointing the dominant narrative of 'proper mothering' assigning women with a 'natural' responsibility for feeding their children in contemporary Vietnam.

Biopower Over Eating Bodies

Biopower in the Foucauldian sense refers to the regulation of bodies through appeals to life, risk, and responsibility (Monaghan et al. 2010).

Whereas historically this power was executed by the sovereign invested with the right to decide over death and life of his subjects, biopower turns into a more abstract mechanism to rationally organise and control the vital character of contemporary societies (Foucault 1977). No longer is power understood as the asset of a sovereign entity but as relationally bound in and oscillating between different bio-authorities. Their authority is embedded in (several) truth discourses towards human existence and in their acknowledged capacity of problematising and strategising rational interventions in the collective body of the population in the name of controlling and fostering its life and health (Rabinow and Rose 2006). Moreover, modes of subjectification are central elements of bio-power "through which individuals are brought to work on themselves, under certain forms of authority, in relation to truth discourses, by means of practices of the self, in the name of their own life or health, that of their family or some other collectivity, or indeed in the name of the life or health of the population as a whole" (Rabinow and Rose 2006, 197).

In Foucauldian-coined governmentality studies, biopower is oftentimes drawn on to explain the effect of neoliberal political-economic contexts (Harvey 2005) on self-governing subjects in relation to food. In a self-disciplining mode, individuals unconsciously embody discourses stressing consumer choice and individual responsibility for well-being, health, and happiness when engaging with the food system as 'free consumer subjects' (Parsons 2015, 7; Cairns and Johnston 2015, 33). This theoretical lens is prominently drawn on by scholars to understand, for example, organic food consumers pursuing safe and healthy food options as a way to navigate food system risks (Cairns et al. 2013; see Faltmann, this volume) and in their creation of healthy bodies through self-care regimes and health optimisation (Lupton 1997; Shilling 2002). Besides, critical obesity studies are strongly framed within the same parlance of neoliberal governmentality. In Foucauldian critique, scholars, for example, focus on the social (de)construction of the self-indulging body as abject and morally transgressive—the incapacity of a person's self-discipline, the lack of individual responsibility towards his or herself and society as a whole reflected in the fat body (e.g. Wright and Harwood 2009; Metzl and Kirkland 2010; LeBesco 2011; Abbots 2017, 139). Critical obesity scholars focus on the categorisation of pathologic bodies and 'normal' bodies along the truth regimes provided for by, for example, the medical and nutrition sciences and their matrixes, statistics, and indices such as the Body Mass Index (BMI) (Monaghan et al. 2010, 47ff.).

Given the way obesity is critically addressed in studies—mainly pertaining to contexts in the Global North—this chapter provides in the following for the contextualisation of such an approach in the Global South. It does so by stressing the complexity, ambiguities, and differing rationales of bio-authorities which work on the child's body in Vietnam. There, the discursive construction of normal and abject children's bodies is way less clear-cut than the dichotomy of the fat/'abject' body and the healthy/'normal' body for neoliberal contexts would commonly suggest. In a first step, however, the context of the study needs to be established by outlining the obesity discourse and its prominent authorities of truth in Vietnam.

Obesity, Public Health, and the Economy of Caring in Vietnam

After decades of food insecurity affected by the country's war-torn history, Vietnam's economic upswing came along rapid processes of industrialisation and urbanisation that also provided for a restructuring of the food sector as a whole (see Ehlert and Faltmann, this volume; see Figuié et al., this volume). The food distribution and retail sector today constitutes one of the hottest markets attracting domestic and foreign direct investments (Mergenthaler 2008, 6f.; Hai Thi Hong Nguyen et al. 2013). Supermarkets in major cities such as HCMC offer convenience and globally branded products (Cadhilon et al. 2006). They are usually integrated with huge shopping malls and, especially at nights and weekends, frequented for leisure and recreational purposes (Ehlert 2016). Next to the retail sector, the gastronomic sector constitutes a vibrant and expanding market, with Western-style fast food especially constantly gaining in popularity (Q & Me Vietnam Market Research 2016). In summary, 'Big Food'—a popular term subsuming the corporate power of global food companies dominating food chains from production to retail on a worldwide scale (Nestlé 2013; Clapp and Scrinis 2017)—has long seized the economic potential of the Vietnamese market (see Ehlert and Faltmann, this volume).

Đổi Mới's 'open door' policies of the mid-1980s (Beresford 2001, 2008) have stimulated the development of new food consumption patterns, most strikingly in urban areas. Vietnam is said to have entered a phase of "nutrition transition" (Sobal 1999, 178) as a consequence of the changing local food and nutrition system (Nguyen Cong Khan and Ha Huy Khoi 2008; Walls et al. 2009). Dietary patterns are changing due to increased consumption of processed and convenience foods, meat, as well as of high-calorie foods (Vietnam Ministry of Health 2012).

Unknown before 1995, overweight and obesity have turned into major public health issues in Vietnam recently. According to findings of the nutrition sciences, overweight and obesity is growing rapidly among children under the age of five living in urban centres (Vietnam Ministry of Health 2012). In response to such emerging food-related health concerns, the government launched a National Nutrition Strategy for 2011–2020, including a vision for its eradication by 2030 (Socialist Republic of Vietnam 2012). Through nutrition and health education and public awareness campaigns, the government aims to correct such pitfalls of rapid market integration. Organisations such as Vietnam's Nutrition Association (VNA) or the National Institute of Nutrition (NIN) periodically survey the food-related health problems of the population. The medical system is vested with the authority to confront the country's nutrition transition problems. Regular health, weight, and BMI statistics professionalise the obesity discourse (Vietnam Ministry of Health 2016), which is widely taken up by local press. However, as we will see, this medical discourse of an alarming rise in child obesity is not fully embedded in the everyday realities of feeding children, but rather is just one of the competing truth discourses on the body ideal for children.

In this context of emerging consumerism, food advertisements are omnipresent in providing lifestyle imaginaries of 'free' consumer choice in HCMC (see Ehlert and Faltmann, this volume). Advertisements framing the city roads, TV ads, and popular magazines, the food and lifestyle industries constantly call for the consumption of convenient foods, fast food, and dairy products, enjoying beverages and confectionary (on China, see Jing 2000) (Fieldnotes, 09/2014). On fast food consumption, Thi explained:

So because we have money and then we just want to make our baby, our kid happy. And then, you know it is also a good place for a family catch up, for a family hang out. So I can go there with my friend's family. So kids can play together and everyone is happy. So that is why we still go there. Even when we know it is not good. And then you know [in Vietnam], we have more money so we can afford more things to the kid and just want to make the kid happy. (Interview, 09/2015)

The quote by Thi points to the conflict that resonates in the felt need to make "the kids happy" and, at the same time, being aware that the food offered in respective places "is not good". In her critical approach to the 'obesity epidemic' in China, Greenhalgh (2016, 487) takes up this ambivalence tainted with conflictive emotions as being a structural characteristic of 'Big Food', 'Big Soda', and 'Big Pharma'. According to her, huge profits in newly emerging lifestyle industries—ranging from the food and beverage industries over the gastronomic sector to diet and fitness markets—back up the 'obesity epidemic'. The same globally operating economic system that calls for relentless consumption offers the products to fight the externalities that it creates in the first place. The food and diet industries, that structurally condition and boost each other, co-opt emotions when working with 'maternal affection' and 'love' to symbolically enrich the products they sale. This can be referred to as the 'economy of caring'. The industrialised, large-scale conventional food system subjects eating bodies by craving them into certain food tastes and emotions (Carolan 2011). 'Big Food' symbolically sells the truth of happiness and well-being. For consumers, who failed in their "agency" to choose "wisely" (Parsons 2015, 7), 'Big Food' puts them back on the 'right', self-responsible track. Depending on the specific beauty and body ideals in a given local market, 'Big Food' is able to provide tailor-made products producing certain kinds of bodies—for example, dieting products to lose weight or high-calorie food to explicitly gain weight.

The Dominant Mothering Discourse

With children overeating supposedly turning into a public health problem, the government calls on the family's responsibility to educate and socialise children in a way that aligns with the ideal of a healthy and harmonious Vietnamese society. State equality discourses following *Đổi Mới* picked up the family as "a bulwark against the disintegrative effects of market change" and shifted attention of gender equality in terms of social equity to gender relations within the family (Werner 2009, 75). Families were promoted as anchors for managing the post-*Đổi Mới* vagaries of social disintegration. Women were acknowledged as "most efficient link in family culture: they are the soul of the family and the warm sentimental fire of the family"—herewith addressing women's responsibility for childcare and caring for the elderly (Werner 2009, 75, referring to Resolution 42. 04/TW of the Communist Party of Vietnam).

In a survey conducted by the VNA in 2013 on feeding children, generally 'the parents' were addressed in their role of food socialisation. The interview with the Secretary General of the VNA presenting the survey, however, shows the continuance of discursively domesticising women and foodwork, the latter perceived as a symbol for the affection between mother and child:

> Nowadays, many mothers are only present at the family's dinner. This has led to difficulties in the children's eating. Children want to eat the food cooked/prepared by their mothers, because no one else can understand them as well/ be as close to them as their mothers. (Tuổi Trẻ Online 2013)[9]

The quote by the nutritionist represents the approach of the public health sector prioritising family meals as important factor for properly socialising children into food experiences. This perspective holds that children desire to have their mothers involved in their food encounters at home. Being present at and preparing for family meals becomes set as a bar of 'good motherhood'. A woman's foodwork thus persists being considered one of the paramount performances of her femininity.

Contemporary discourses on femininity in Vietnam are rooted in Confucianist norms[10] of the woman of virtue[11] (Ngo Thi Ngan Binh 2004) intertwined with socialist ideals of gender equality (Rydstrøm 2011). Both engrain the female and the male body in the cosmological and social order. The relativist system of Yin and Yang in Confucianism draws on female and male bodily dispositions and forces through which the 'natural' characters of women and men can be inferred. Similarly, state-driven gender discourses channelled through the state-organised Women's Union (Waibel and Glück 2013) deduce female traits, capabilities, and social functions strongly from women's biological sex and physiological disposition. The reproductive function of the female body in terms of, for example, her childbearing and breastfeeding capacity assigns the woman with a "natural vocation" (*thiên chức*) (Rydstrøm 2004, 2011, 174f.). From the basis of her corporality she is expected to develop into a woman of virtue as would show in herself-controlled and self-sacrificing responsibility for the nurturing of the family (Ngo Thi Ngan Binh 2004). Bélanger (2004), in her study on childless and single women in Vietnam, brings to the fore the social construction of motherhood and caring conceived of as *the* intrinsic parts of a woman's identity in patrilineal context extending beyond the family. Moreover, women's reproductive and caring roles are emphasised as crucial for the reconstitution and revitalisation of the nation (Drummond and Rydstrøm 2004, 3). The subjectification of the dominant motherhood discourse makes women work on themselves in the name of their children and that of the Vietnamese nation (Drummond and Rydstrøm 2004, 3; Rabinow and Rose 2006, 197).

This section provided an overview against which the further narratives of the female interviewees should be read. It has been shown that the 'problem' of obesity strongly aligns with a dominant mothering discourse, which first and foremost holds women responsible for socialising their children into healthy eaters. At the same time, the bio-authority of the economy of caring—stylised here as 'Big Food'—co-opts both the discourses on obesity and proper motherhood, as we will see in the following.

Biopower and the Embodiment of Caring

As suggested by Shilling (2012, 44), "[t]he spotlight shines on certain aspects of the body leaving others obscured". He refers to a division between those scholars who focus on the body as object that is rendered passive from without by changing regulating authorities and modes of biopower in the Foucauldian sense, and on the other side those engaging with the body as a 'lived' space of subjective, sensual experiences of "being-in-the-world" as conceptualised in the phenomenology of the body (Csordas 1994, 10). In reference to food consumption, the latter means that "eating [and being fed] is an experience through which people materially and viscerally taste, smell, feel and sense food" (Abbots 2017, 19f.).

Thus far, obesity has been introduced as a discourse, marking the 'obese' against the 'normal' body and the respective role assigned to women in producing such kinds of children's bodies. The following will integrate these notions of the 'outer' and the 'inner' body—or 'body as object' and the 'lived body'[12]—by discussing how subjective embodied experience and socio-cultural frames are entangled in the mundane practice of eating and feeding others.

This section highlights both the child's and the mother's bodies as objects addressed by different bio-authorities; and approaches the lived experiences of these bodies. In keeping with Abbots (2017, 142) what is perceived as normal/abnormal children's bodies and what as 'good mothering' is more than just a social construction but always and deeply related to the materiality of bodies and the way one feels from within. The latter will be discussed in terms of emotions such as failure and shame of not having reached the mothering ideal, shyness because of one's own body, as well as along bodily sensations such as taste, satiety, and hunger (Crossley 2012, 139f.). It will be argued that a more contextualised understanding of socially structured food anxieties in contemporary urban Vietnam is only possible through reference to both biopower and the embodiment of caring.

Embodiment of Motherhood (Discourses): The Milk of Love

As will be shown in the following ideals of motherhood, public health recommendations and 'Big Food's' economy of caring already intimately work on the pregnant body of mothers-to-be, who start regulating their own bodies and appetites when carrying their unborn children.

In a social media forum,[13] a young mother gave vent to her discomfort about the way society and the food industry in Vietnam intrude on mothers by instructing them on how to bring up their children in ways to make them gain weight fast. Being overconcerned with baby's weight gain (see detailed below), mothers-to-be already start to compare their foetuses' weights in ultrasound scans. Since a woman's capacity to breast-feed her newborn properly is rendered an essential feature of her femininity (see above), women easily "get scolded" for having breastmilk that is too "weak and fluid" after birth. As consequence of the mother's bodily incapacity, the baby would fail to accumulate fat. In sympathetic response to this social media user's thread, many other young women recalled similar intimidating experiences of being blamed and feeling ashamed for having 'weak' breastmilk and thus being considered unable to properly nurture their newborns. Young mothers would be accused of "not having eaten well enough" or of having "been too lazy to eat properly" during pregnancy—hence the failure of the baby to put on fat. This is why women, already during pregnancy, would try hard to ensure that "all nutrition will be absorbed by the foetus and not by the mother's body". The social media user criticised food companies for co-opting the social pressure faced by young mothers and for turning their distress into profit by "launch[ing] various types of pregnancy milk and vitamins … in order to facilitate 'fat children and beautiful mothers' or 'smart children and slim mothers'" (Vietnam's Nutrition Association 2017a[14]).

Similar to the huge variety of infant formula, supermarkets promote a nearly unmanageable range of liquid milk products—from foreign imports to domestic brands, over flavoured snack-like drinks to ultra-heat treated and sugar-added fresh milk. What is interesting is the availability of diverse brands and prices of pregnancy formula (Fieldnotes, 08/2015). Besides this, the dairy industry finds its way into the public health system via product placements. Very often commercial pregnancy formula and breastmilk substitutes are marketed in promotion areas near hospitals where women used to come for regular pregnancy check-ups (Interview, editor, 09/2015; Fieldnotes prenatal class, 10/2015).

The consumption of dairy in Vietnam in general has a long history in regards with social status aspiration. Milk was unavailable and foreign to local diets before French colonisation. In the late nineteenth century, cows bred for providing milk were for the first time imported from southern India when Tamil-owned dairies opened in Saigon. Back then, the

French as well as the colonial Vietnamese middle-class preferred pasteurised, condensed, and fresh milk imports from France to the natural fresh milk available locally. Concerns for hygiene but especially claims of racial and social superiority led Vietnamese consumers to buy imported milk (Peters 2012a, 190–197). Under French colonialism, advertisements for a French brand of condensed milk promised the plump child's future fortune and the parents' urban sophistication. The advertisement clearly pronounces strong class differences as written upon the portrayed child's body: in times scourged by the hardship of food scarcity for 'ordinary' people, the plump child symbolised the distinct power of an urban bureaucratic elite setting itself apart from 'backward' agrarian life and labour (Peters 2012b, 46ff.). Social status and economic means determined access to food and showed in well-fed bodies as compared to poverty and social marginalisation inscribed on meagre bodies. Seen in historical perspective, since its emergence in colonial urban Vietnam, milk used to symbolise upward mobility, the ability to personal advancement, and the connection with European etiquette.

Respective manufacturers seize on this strong historical association of milk consumption and social status aspiration as a crucial element in their marketing strategies. Whereas nearly every household uses baby formula, pregnancy milk formula is consumed by about 60%–70% of all households in the panel study for HCMC conducted by the local market research institute (Interview, representative research market institute, 09/2015).

Coming to the narratives of the informants of the research for this chapter, the owner of the spa explained that her customers "believe that if they drink the special milk for mamas, their baby will become more intelligent, and healthier" (Interview, 08/2015). Similarly, Veronique tells about her pregnant colleagues' practice of drinking milk. The women "really believe this is a kind of a rule – that a women needs to drink milk [no matter in what form] everyday" to aid the development of the unborn child (Interview, 08/2015). My, who worked in a hotel restaurant and was five months pregnant at the time of the research, had flavoured pregnant formula in the mornings and a glass of fresh milk in the evenings. Although she did not like the taste of the formula at all, she drank it regularly following the recommendations of her doctor and husband (Interview, 09/2015).

The body ideal for pregnant women exhibits certain discrepancies. It is not uncommon that women gain between 20 and 25 kilogrammes during pregnancy (Fieldnotes, 09/2015). A woman the author met during pregnancy class, working in the TV business, had put on respective weight. She had to stop working in front of the camera early during her pregnancy, as her body was perceived as too big to be presented publicly. However, she followed her mother's and mother-in-law's advice to gain weight as this was supposed to be transferred to the developing foetus and ensure that she would have enough and solid breastmilk after delivery. Given that female adult bodies are socially valued for their slenderness (Leshkowich 2012), other women rejected pregnancy formula precisely because of its high calories and turned towards fresh milk instead (Fieldnotes, 09/2015). During pregnancy, on the one hand, the female body is pressured into weight gain by mothers and mothers-in-law. On the other hand, pregnant women try to comply with the slim female body ideal as well as with public health recommendations on reasonable weight gain (Mecuti n.d.). They aim for 'fat children and beautiful selves', for which the food and diet industry have 'tailor made' solutions, as was criticised by the social media user above.

In a context in which having children is deeply associated with being a 'proper' woman (Bélanger 2004), pregnancy constitutes a pivotal moment that make women work hard on their bodies for the sake of their unborn babies. The consumption of (flavoured) milk formula or liquid dairy products is regarded essential for the bodily connection between the pregnant woman and the unborn baby. The consumption of milk exhibits a strong dogmatic practice exemplifying technologies of the Self (Foucault 1988). Hence, its consumption even arouses negative visceral sensation and bodily indisposition within, some dislike the taste, and, yet, they self-discipline themselves to have it (Abbots 2017, 142). Through the example of milk in its various forms, it becomes visible how the family of the pregnant woman, the food industry, and the public health system all spotlight the pregnant body. For the mother-to-be, her own body turns into a contested space of social discourses and also becomes an object to herself that she regulates and moulds according to conflictive expectations. And these social expectations and pressures mothers-to-be sensually experience inside their bodies. When the breastmilk of the mother is disqualified for not being nurturing enough, feelings like shame and distress make themselves felt inside her body (Crossley 2012, 140). Embodying such discrepancies, women ingest the social expectations being placed on them as 'natural' caregivers. They are not only responsible for regulating the child's food—to which this chapter will turn to next—but also their own diets, appetites, and bodies.

Body Ideals in Children: 'When the Dog Is Too Skinny, the Owner Should Feel Ashamed'

"When the dog is too skinny …"[15]—this Vietnamese saying was used by the social media user introduced above. It summarises the rationale behind the feeding of babies and young children in contemporary urban Vietnam (Vietnam's Nutrition Association 2017a). As will be shown, it captures an essential female concern: a child's skinny body physically exposes the maternal incapacity of caring for the ones most dependent.

Against the background of the country's war-torn past and the experience of famine and food scarcity deeply engraved into collective memory, the 'skinny dog' might also stand for former times dominated by a general lack of means for appropriate foodwork. Whereas the chubby child depicted in colonial advertisements (see above) aimed to impart the idea of colonial and urban exceptionalism (Peters 2012b, 46ff.), the increasing weight ratio of children today represents the general economic betterment and a more decent and luxurious urban life.

Loan explains that "[a] mother in HCMC likes her children fat" (Interview, 08/2015). Ly elaborates further on the association between body weight and health of the child:

> The standard of a healthy child in our country is that of the fat child. When two mothers come together, they just care about how many kgs the child has. They don't care whether they [the children] are healthy or sick. Just how much food [the child eats] or how tall it is. (Interview, editor, 09/2015)

The societal importance assigned to well-nurtured children becomes apparent in this common greeting ritual. In many discussions with mothers and pregnant women it was repeated that when two mothers meet with their kids the first question is "how many kgs [kilogrammes does your child weigh]?" (Interview, representative research market institute, 09/2015; Fieldnotes, 08/2014).

As mentioned in an interview with Thi, herself a mother of a two-year-old daughter, she explained that when a child or baby is perceived as "underweight, people like your neighbours or your parents in law think that you are not a good mum" (Interview, 09/2015). She stresses that what falls into the 'normal' body range according to global biomedical body indices, qualifies as 'underweight' by the perception of her neighbours and in-laws. She articulates the pressure faced by mothers to regulate their children's bodies in ways to live up to the local norms of social status, health, and bodily beauty, which certainly do not coincide with the image of a 'skinny dog'.

Beauty in children becomes particularly manifest in bigger body sizes symbolising physical attractiveness, health, and socio-economic status—the bigger, the higher the social prestige, and the 'skinnier'—as in the metaphor of the dog—the more to be looked down at the supposed lack of a mother's accountability towards her loved ones. In this process of social normalisation of the child's body, weight gain and the accumulation of fat become the top criteria not only for numerically measuring the development of the child but also for measuring the mother's quality of foodwork. The notion of 'a good mum' (*một người mẹ tốt*) constitutes a paramount marker inscribed onto the child's body. This is the way maternal care and affection supposedly materialise physically, as will the failure of maternal foodwork show in 'skinny dogs'. Being in sharp contrast to the official public obesity discourse fostering the healthy child, the presented weight-gain discourse normalises the child's chubby body shape—but into the opposite direction. It constitutes a competitive powerful discourse of truth carried on by family, in-laws, friends, and neighbours as bio-authorities.

Feeding Practices: Between 'Raising Pigs' and Self-Determined Eating Subjects

To achieve this body ideal in children requires certain ways of feeding the babies and toddlers. This obviously relates to the kind of food as well as to the quantities and the ways of being fed. A survey of 3000 parents[16] in urban areas conducted by the VNA in 2013 suggested that "65% of parents did not feed their children properly" (Tuổi Trẻ Online 2013). Main reasons found were parents having too little time and grandparents taking on the role of caregiver, and the use of force and diversion when feeding children. In her outcry "[d]on't apply the mentality of raising … pigs when raising your children"[17] the social media user set off an avalanche of online forum discussions about the proper way and common practices of feeding children in urban Vietnam. Her comparison deploys the analogy of raising children with industrially fattening pigs. The social media user recalls a typical morning at a food vendor shop when grandmothers, babysitters, and mothers come to have breakfast with their kids:

> you will notice that someone will be bawling at, then soothing a crying baby and stuffing, forcing him/her to eat at all costs. The mothers would argue that 'if we leave it [eating] up to them, they will not at all be hungry all day long'. There are babies who are forced to eat on a daily basis five main and supplementary meals, then an extra six to seven times [feeding on] milk, to gain weight well and fast. (Vietnam's Nutrition Association 2017a)

She stresses the quantities eaten as well as the use of force applied to make the child eat. A common way of feeding children, substantiated in the data, can be called 'mobile feeding'. In many discussions women reported that grandmothers or babysitters would run with the spoon after the kids (Fieldnotes, 09/2014). Personal observations around the condominium bloc during the research stay matched such accounts of mobile feeding (Fieldnotes, 08/2015). By running after the kids with a bowl of congee and spoon, food is constantly being made available in order to guarantee the ingestion of 'enough' food. The use of TV and toys are other common means to distract the child's attention away from being stuffed while turning eating into a minor matter (Tuổi Trẻ Online 2013). On the issue of force, Thi explains further:

> You can easily observe how mums feed their baby in Vietnam. Sometimes they force the babies to eat. So it is very different from other countries, especially in Europe. Because I heard lately, [there] they just feed the babies

what they need. And just give them the food they can eat or they can say 'no'. But here we force them to eat … and the kid or baby will be punished if they don't eat. (Interview, 09/2015)

The social media user shares her observation of mothers giving pills and medicines to their children to increase their appetites (Vietnam's Nutrition Association 2017a). Children vomiting because of overfeeding is nothing uncommon (Interview, Veronique, 08/2015). At the same time it is suggested to mothers that they discipline their child's eating behaviour by conditioning them to be hungry at certain times (Tuổi Trẻ Online 2014). Through the regulation of overindulgence, and vomiting as a consequence of being stuffed, the embodied feeling of satiety inside the body is naturally levelled out. The child's body as object is conditioned to eat and the subjective bodily and sensual experiences of taste and appetite externally retained while felt within.

The approach of feeding children 'properly' holds a strong generational dimension. While parents update with the modern parenting knowledge and practices, grandparents depend on their experiences to raise children (Tuổi Trẻ Online 2013), thus oftentimes causing conflicts of the clashing ideas of how to feed and what the child actually needs. As elaborated earlier on, for the older generation which grew up in food-insecure times, the paramount expression of a female's ability to care for her child is the constant provision of food to nurture the child's body well and therewith to project the child's successful future (Peters 2012b, 48). According to Loan, mothers would feel overwhelmed by the sheer mass of information to which they have access nowadays. Information on feeding practices and food socialisation styles provided on the internet and social media becomes overwhelmingly abundant and calls the feeding practices of the older generation into question:

It is the old thinking when the child is fat, it is healthy. Now they change it, it changes. More people now they change thinking. For example, they share about the Japanese way to take care of the baby. Now we have a lot of information, from the internet. How to take care of your baby for health reasons, not fat. So now, for the modern mother it is difficult. More difficult to take care, because there are a lot of [conflictive] information. (Interview, 08/2015)

Online research conducted for this study backs Loan's perspective on women struggling with overwhelming loads of diverse and oftentimes conflicting information as channels of food and nutrition knowledge have generally multiplied, as obviously have the recommendations for children's dieting methods. New truth discourses regarding the feeding of children proliferate and contradict the dominant weight-gain discourse. The desk study for this chapter revealed that nutrition counselling seems to be a professional and lay sector on the upswing. Medical intuitions such as hospitals and institutions under the Ministry of Health still dominate the scene (Interview, medical nutrition doctor, HCMC, 08/2017). However, online press and popular periodicals featuring food and nutrition columns have led to an explosive increase in the amount of accessible information. Blogs run by amateurs, such as 'experienced' mothers and so-called lifestyle influencers, social media forums, home-made online tutorials, and 'expert corners' on the websites of food companies make up the widening landscape of nutrition counselling which women, like Loan, consume for advice. The online research brought to light new trends of feeding babies and toddlers that divert from the 'mobile feeding' of blended congee as was described earlier on. Although the latter is still very popular, the so-called Japanese-style and the baby-led weaning methods are strongly gaining in popularity (Vietnam's Nutrition Association 2017b). Following the Japanese style (*phương pháp ăn dặm kiểu nhật*), food is cooked and offered in its solid form when the child is three to five months old and breastfed in parallel.[18] The method of baby-led weaning (*phương pháp ăn dặm bé chỉ huy*) offers solid food and puts the baby or toddler in charge of choosing what to eat from the plate and how to eat it—supposed to stress the discovery of the meal according to the child's own demand.[19] According to the newspaper Tuổi Trẻ, children nutrition training programmes had started to include this method due to the high rates of 'anorexic' (*biếng ăn*) and picky eaters (*kén ăn*) in children from six months to five years old (Tuổi Trẻ Online 2017).

The internet is full of debates introducing, promoting, and condemning such emerging trends. The use of force when feeding babies and toddlers is increasingly called into question (Tuổi Trẻ Online 2013; VietNamNet 2015) as a way of passively 'stuffing' children. In the debate, 'choice' comes in assigning to the child the ability to choose 'naturally' what feels best for it. The study of the Vietnam Nutrition Association argued that it would be common for parents to keep on feeding their children when they are over two years old and that this method would inevitably lead to a lack of independence in children and a feeling of being forced to eat at others' will (Tuổi Trẻ Online 2013).

In sum, on the one hand, women are captives of the two metaphors comparing children with 'skinny dogs' and 'fattening pigs' strongly guiding maternal foodwork. On the other hand, mothers are confronted with clashing feeding models given the diffusion of new 'options' via the internet. Besides the mothers' 'duty' to stuff their children they are increasingly called on to socialise their children into making self-informed food choices. This latter feeding model of the child as eating subject focuses the child's attention towards its subjective embodied feelings of appetite and hunger and the bodily experience of taste. The different approaches locate women's foodwork between the extremes of forcing objects to eat and to let subjects chose. The latter resembles what is discussed as the quality of being a good mother in neoliberal parlance in the Global North, namely, in which mothers are held responsible for turning their children into self-experiencing subjects prepared for neoliberal ideals of choice and individual responsibility (Cairns et al. 2013). In this ambivalent context, mothers' biopower which resonates from nurturing their children becomes more complex and conflictive as does the fear of failure being regarded a 'good mother'. What is more, the qualities that make up a 'good mother' in the first place are negotiated and challenged through emerging competitive feeding practices.

Normalisation of Bodies Growing(-up)

> Looking at a fat adult [in Vietnam], people will often criticise that the person is lazy, slow and doesn't exercise, or that he/she eats a lot or judge them in a more comforting way such as 'kind-hearted, gentle looking'. On the contrary, children are increasingly stuffed to be fat or even overweight. (Vietnam's Nutrition Association 2017a).

In her quote, the same social media user relates to the social construction of what counts as normal and abject bodies being different for children and for (female) adults. The dominant weight-discourse materialising in chubby children's bodies invites the question of when the cuteness of growing bodies reaches a threshold that turns the chubby body into an abject fat teenaged or adult body. The process of normalisation of bodies as mentioned here refers to the categorisation of what is perceived as beautiful in body shapes, backed up by truth discourses that apply differently to a body's lifespan from childhood to adulthood.

In this regard, Loan considers the upbringing of her two daughters who are now teenagers. When they were children, they were taken care of by her mother-in-law while Loan was working. Because she was the first baby in the family, other people and her mother-in-law cared a lot about her oldest daughter by feeding her "a lot of everything, a lot of sweet and a lot of delicious foods". Nowadays, the first daughter has, according to Loan, to fight being overweight. Loan designed a workout programme for her to lose weight but she senses that her daughter "is not happy [at all], [as] she feels taught and controlled [by the workout programme]". But since they talked about the need to lose weight, her daughter would accept it. One of the arguments for losing weight mentioned by Loan to her daughter was that her daughter would feel "shy" about her body when having a first boyfriend. A similar reference to the overweight female body regarding amiableness, love, and potential for sexual relationships was brought up in an online video produced by a local TV production company, which focuses on urban lifestyle issues. Teenagers were interviewed on the topic of overweight. In small question and answer statements they shared perspectives and personal experiences with being addressed as 'overweight' in society. When asked whether her family would complain about her weight, one of the female interviewees shared with the audience: "my mom said no one would ever marry me, cause he wouldn't possibly be able to afford enough food for me" (*Vì Sao Mập?* [Why are you fat?] 2017). Loan describes her second daughter as an absolute contrast. Put under the same feeding regime of the older generation, she nowadays "hates food. Hates [!]. This is the reason she now is very thin" (Interview, 08/2015).

On the one hand, mothers are supposed to feed their kids and let go control of foodwork when giving the children to the grandmother to pursue wage labour. Concurrently, later on they are responsible for curbing the 'unhealthy appetites' of their adolescent children. As indicated in the opening quote by the social media user, the slim body ideal expects body control and containment from women (Ngo Thi Ngan Binh 2004) which is dissonant with the ideal of overweight children symbolising cuteness. Growing children partly reject the feeding regime applied on them as is seen, for example, in teenagers starting to hate or refuse food. Others go on diets and work out as they start feeling shy about their bodies, which seem no longer to correspond to the beauty ideal of slimness of their age. In a way, they become bio-authorities over their own bodies—but remain framed by conflicting socio-cultural images of ideal bodies. At the same time, mothers like Loan feel responsible for working on their child's body, for example, through preparing workout programmes for them. They direct their bio-authority over their children in the perceived need to prepare them for the next stage of adolescent body norms. An interview with a personal fitness coach depicted the growing demand of mothers registering their teenaged kids for rigorous body workout programmes with the main goal to slim them down (Interview, fitness coach, HCMC, 08/2017). In an interview with the Nutrition Centre in Hanoi it was indicated that anorexia nervosa is developing into an issue amongst teenagers feeling overweight and trying to avoid eating "to be in a good shape" (Interview, 09/2016). Oftentimes and beyond Vietnam, female teenagers find themselves struggling with the passage from childhood to adolescence, a struggle of the Self, in which the body becomes a central reference point (Bordo 1993). The rapid development from food scarcity to food abundance in the country poses intriguing questions regarding the connections between food consumption and body regulation, eating disorders, and body alienation. Whereas eating disorders such as anorexia nervosa are not covered by the truth discourse of the medical sciences or taken up by popular media in Vietnam yet,[20] this does not say much about the social realities and experiences of lived bodies and their pursuit of embodying and rejecting discursive 'normalisation'. How this is elaborated in urban Vietnam constitutes an issue for further research.

Conclusion: Ambivalent Maternal Foodwork

What runs like a thread through the narratives of the interviewees is the generational conflict between the mother and her own mother or mother-in-law. Under the auspices of the older female generation in the household they feel urged to 'feed up' their infants as a "mum in Vietnam is influenced quite strongly by family, and from parents" (Interview, Thi, 09/2015). Ly describes doing things differently in terms of children's nutrition as an ambiguous endeavour. In the end, because of their insecurities, women would oftentimes comply with the common standards of feeding, because: "when I tried to do something different, I just felt like me against the world" (Interview, 09/2015).

Besides complying with the expectation to fatten up their children, they are confronted with contrary discourses that shift the eating child from the position of the passive body to an eating subject with intrinsic preferences and the freedom to choose. What is more, mothers increasingly do not only need to provide 'enough' and in a proper way for their children, but food should also qualify as safe since the navigation of food safety risks increasingly plays a role in responsible 'mothering' (see Faltmann, this volume; see Kurfürst, this volume).

The interview narratives showed the mundane ways that individuals used to govern themselves in everyday practices of eating and feeding (Foucault 1994). A tendency of technologies of responsibilisation crystallised, but not only in the sense of neoliberal governance and in its pursuit of health and well-being (Cairns and Johnston 2015, 33) but, contradictorily, for fatness and weight gain at the same time. It is in this context of conflicting and dynamic truth discourses regarding ideal body standards, norms of health, and feeding that mothers and mothers-to-be manoeuvre in. The child's body constitutes a contemporary contested object over which norms of health and beauty, food regulation, and responsibility are fought. Aligned with this dynamic is the negotiation of socio-cultural discourses on what constitutes 'a good mother'. Thus, both, the mother and the child embody these ambivalences and ambiguities through their lived experiences. The embeddedness of routinised and reflective female feeding practices at different scales revealed biopower as oscillating between different authorities and truth regimes. These are malleable and contested and in this way create a diffuse sense of anxiety on the side of mothers regarding their responsibility of feeding their children. Through daily foodwork routines and the approach of food femininities, this chapter uncovered links between individual food and body performances at interpersonal and emotional levels and showed its embeddedness in wider social structures. Food as material matter crossed the bodily boundaries of the mother and the child. Feeding practices spoke to the "symbolic boundary of what it means to be seen as a 'good mother'" as well (Cairns and Johnston 2015, 70). As was seen, the constant comparison with other mothers aimed for inclusion and exclusion in the boundary of 'good mother'. At the same time, the sympathy of many mothers expressed towards the social media user's critique of the diverse forms of pressure faced by women, adumbrates the alternative views on food femininities and the spaces for resistance against dominant truth discourses.

Overall it became clear that obesity is more than just a management problem to be tackled by a global set of intervention measures. This chapter aimed to uncover the local social complexities, interests, and conflicts beyond the medical categorisation of 'abject' and 'normal' bodies.

Acknowledgements This research was made possible through the generous support of the research project 'A body-political Approach to the Study of Food – Vietnam and the Global Transformations' (P 27438) by the Austrian Science Fund (FWF). I deeply thank my colleagues in the project, Nora Katharina Faltmann and Carina Maier, for the engaged and inspiring feedback loops on various chapter drafts. Also thanks to Nir Avieli for his valuable input to this work. Furthermore, I want to express my gratitude to Thi Linh Hoang, who so reliably supported the online desk study for this chapter and for being an important gate-keeper to the field.

Notes

1. Vietnamese title '*Báo động trẻ béo bụng*', Tuổi Trẻ Online 2015.
2. For in-depth discussions on body discourses and practices in Asia, see Zheng and Turner 2009.
3. This chapter focuses on feeding as one aspect of foodwork, entailing cooking, shopping, planning for mealtimes, and so on, and understands it as labour and emotional and mental engagement (DeVault 1991).

4. When using the term 'woman' in the following, it is used as understood by the dominant local discourse on femininity drawing strongly on biological dispositions. This is not necessarily the author's own understanding but drawn on to make sense of the local context rather than reflecting on the author's personal view.

5. For an in-depth discussion of middle classes in Vietnam, see Van Nguyen-Marshall et al. (2012); Welch Drummond (2012); Earl (2014); Ehlert (2016).

6. All following names are changed for reasons of anonymisation.

7. Most interviews were conducted in English. If otherwise, a Vietnamese interpreter supported the interview.

8. Thanks to Nora Katharina Faltmann, who conducted the interview as team member of the same research project 'A Body-Political Approach to the Study of Food – Vietnam and the Global Transformations'.

9. Quotes from newspaper paper articles and online documents in Vietnamese were translated into English.

10. In general, in Confucianist thinking society is glued together through moral obligations of control and deference between the ruler and the subjects, between parents and children, between husband and wife (Drummond and Rydstrøm 2004, 6ff.).

11. The Confucian concept of the four virtues (*tứ đức*) defines the moral obligations for women to correctly behave bodily and verbally towards men and the elderly in society. The first virtue (*công*) refers to her domestic skills, the industriousness, and the selflessness of the woman. The second virtue (*dung*) defines the proper, modest outward appearance for woman. The third virtue (*ngôn*) demands female self-control in speech and emotions. Finally, the fourth virtue (*hạnh*) constitutes the ultimate outcome of a long process of self-control, self-sacrifice, and self-cultivation of a 'virtuous' woman (Ngo Thi Ngan Binh 2004).

12. See, for example, Crossley (2004) on why the common distinction in social theory of the body between the 'inscribed' (e.g. Foucault 1977) and the 'lived' body (e.g. Merleau-Ponty 1962) cannot be maintained.

13. The social media user posted her discussion in Vietnamese, which was translated into English (see also next endnote).

14. Her blogpost was word by word reprinted with her permission on the website of the Vietnam's Nutrition Association. Many other social media users, also young mothers, have reposted her social media thread supporting her critical views on mothers being scolded by society for their feeding practices (e.g. of having too fluid mother's milk or babies which are not considered chubby enough).

15. The English translation from Vietnamese of "*Chó gầy hổ mặt người nuôi*".
16. By focusing on parents and the household level, gendered food allocation and responsibilities and gender inequalities within the household do not seem to have been appropriately considered in the large-scale survey (Charles and Kerr 1988; DeVault 1991).
17. The English translation from Vietnamese of "*Nuôi con, đừng up dụng tư duy nuôi … lợn*".
18. The quantitative content analysis with an online search engine noted first entries on this feeding method in Vietnam in 2012, and ever since it is widely discussed online in terms of its pros and cons (e.g. Marry Baby 2017).
19. The term baby-led weaning started to appear online in Vietnam in 2015.
20. The online research using keywords like 'anorexia' (*biếng ăn*) did not yield significant matches. The author is aware that such a quantified approach can only be a first and very superficial step calling for the development of a qualitative research design to approach this sensitive topic in future research.

References

Abbots, E.-J., 2017. The Agency of Eating: Mediation, Food and the Body. Contemporary Food Studies: Economy, Culture and Politics. London; New York: Bloomsbury Academic.

Bélanger, D., 2004. Single and Childless Women of Vietnam: Contesting and Negotiating. Female Identity? In: Drummond, L., Rydstrøm, H. (eds). Gender in Contemporary Vietnam. Singapore: Singapore University Press, 96–116.

Beresford, M., 2001. Vietnam: The transition from central planning. In: Rodan, G., Hewison, K. and Robison, R. (eds.). The political economy of Southeast Asia: conflict, crises and change. Melbourne: Oxford University Press, 206–233.

Beresford, M., 2008. *Doi Moi* in review: The challenges of building market socialism in Vietnam. *Journal of Contemporary Asia* 38(2), 221–243.

Bordo, S. 1993. Unbearable Weight: Feminism, Western Culture, and the Body. Berkeley: University of California Press.

Cadilhon, J.-J., Moustier, P., Poole, N. D., Phan Thi Giac Tam, Fearne, A. P., 2006. Traditional vs Modern Food Systems? Insights from Vegetable Supply Chains to Ho Chi Minh City (Vietnam). *Development Policy Review*, 24(1), 31–49.

Cairns, K., Johnston, J., MacKendrick, N., 2013. Feeding the 'organic child': Mothering through ethical consumption. Journal of Consumer Culture 13, 97–118.

Cairns, K., Johnston J., 2015. Food and Femininity. London; New York: Bloomsbury Publishing (Contemporary Food Studies: Economy, Culture and Politics).

Carolan, M. S. 2011. Embodied Food Politics. Farnham; Burlington: Ashgate (Critical Food Studies).

Charles, N., Kerr, M., 1988. Women, Food and Families. Manchester and New York: Manchester University Press.

Clapp, J., Scrinis, G., 2017. Big Food, Nutritionism, and Corporate Power, Globalizations, 14:4, 578–595.

Collins, P.H., 1994. Shifting the Center: Race, Class and Feminist Theorizing about Motherhood. In: Bassin, D., Honey, M., Kaplan, M. (eds.). Representations of Motherhood. New Haven, CT: Yale University Press, 56–74.

Counihan, C., 1999. The Anthropology of Food and Body. London: Routledge.

Crossley, N. 2004. Body-subject/body-power: agency, inspiration and control in Foucault and Merleau-Ponty. In: The Aberdeen Body Group (ed.). The Body. Critical Concepts in Sociology, 219–235.

Crossley, N., 2012. Phenomenology and the Body. In: Turner, B.S. (ed.). Routledge Handbook of Body Studies. New York: Routledge, 130–143.

Csordas, T.J., 1994. Introduction: The body as representation and being in the world. In: Csordas, T.J. (ed.). Embodiment and Experience: The Existential Ground of Culture and Self. Cambridge: Cambridge University Press, 1–26.

DeVault, M. L. 1991. Feeding the Family: The Social Organization of Caring as Gendered Work. Chicago: University of Chicago Press (Women in Culture and Society).

Drummond, L., Rydstrøm, H. (eds.), 2004. Gender Practices in Contemporary Vietnam. Singapore: Singapore University Press.

Earl, C. 2014. *Vietnam's New Middle Classes: Gender, Career, City, Gendering Asia*. Copenhagen: NIAS.

Ehlert, J., 2016. Emerging consumerism and eating out in Ho Chi Minh City, Vietnam. The social embeddedness of food sharing. In: Sahakian, M., Saloma, C.A., Erkman, S. (eds.). Food Consumption in the City: Practices and patterns in urban Asia and the Pacific, Routledge studies in food, society and the environment. London; New York: Routledge, 71–89.

Foucault, M., 1977. Discipline and Punish: The birth of the prison. New York: Random House.

Foucault, M., 1988. Technologies of the Self. In: Martin, L. H., Gutman, H., and Hutton, P. H. (eds.). Technologies of the Self: A Seminar with Michel Foucault. London: Tavistock, 16–49.

Foucault, M., 1994. The Political Technology of Individuals. In: Faubion, J. (ed.). Michel Foucault: Power. New York: The New Press.

Greenhalgh, S., 2016. Neoliberal science, Chinese style: Making and managing the 'obesity epidemic'. *Social Studies of Science* 46(4), 485–510.

Guthman, J., 2009. Teaching the Politics of Obesity: Insights into Neoliberal Embodiment and Contemporary Biopolitics. *Antipode* 41(5), 1110–1133.

Hai Thi Hong Nguyen, Wood, S., Wrigley, N. 2013. The emerging food retail structure of Vietnam. Phases of expansion in a post-socialist environment. *International Journal of Retail & Distribution Management* 41(8), 596–626.

Harvey, D., 2005. A Brief History of Neoliberalism. New York: Oxford University Press.

Jing, J., (ed.), 2000. Feeding China's Little Emperors. Stanford: Stanford University Press.

LeBesco, K., 2011. Neoliberalism, Public Health and the Regulated Body. London: Sage.

Leshkowich, A.M., 2012. Finances, Family, Fashion, Fitness, and … Freedom? The Changing Lives of Urban Middle-Class Vietnamese Women. In: Van Nguyen-Marshall, Drummond, L. B. W., Bélanger, D. (eds.), 2012. The Reinvention of distinction: modernity and the middle class in urban Vietnam. Dordrecht: Springer (ARI –Springer Asia Series), 95–114.

Lupton, D., 1997. The Imperative of Health and the Regulated Body. London: Sage.

Lupton, D., 2013. Fat. Abingdon; New York: Routledge.

Marry Baby. 2017. *Tập cho bé ăn dặm kiểu Nhật như thế nào? (How to train your baby to eat solid food using the Japanese method?).* [online] Available at: http://www.marrybaby.vn/nuoi-day-con/an-dam-kieu-nhat-thuc-don-va-phuong-phap-an-dam [Accessed 30 March, 2018].

Mecuti: Kiến thức nuôi con – làm đẹp cho phụ nữ Việt. (n.d.). *Mẹ bầu tăng bao nhiêu cân là chuẩn - Mức tăng cân trong thời kỳ mang thai các mẹ bầu nên biết (How much weight should a pregnant woman gain? Recommended weight gains during different stages of pregnancy which mother-to-be's should know).* [online] Available at: https://mecuti.vn/me-bau-tang-bao-nhieu-can-la-chuan-muc-tang-can-trong-thoi-ky-mang-thai-cac-me-bau-nen-biet.html [Accessed 3 Apr. 2018].

Mergenthaler, M., 2008. The Food System Transformation in Vietnam: Challenges for the Horticultural Sector Posed by Exports and By Changing Consumer Preferences. Dissertation, Universität Hohenheim.

Merleau-Ponty, M., 1962. The Phenomenology of Perception. London: Routledge.

Metzl, J.M., Kirkland A. (eds.), 2010. Against Health: How Health Became the New Morality. New York: New York University Press.

Monaghan, L.F., Hollands, R., Pritchard, G., 2010. Obesity Epidemic Entrepreneurs: Types. Practices and Interests. *Body and Society*, 16(2), 37–71.

Nestlé, M., 2013. Food politics. How the Food Industry Influences Nutrition and Health, Revised and Expanded Tenth Anniversary Edition. University of California Press.

Ngo Thi Ngan Binh, 2004. The Confucian Four Feminine Virtues (tu duc): The Old Versus the New – Ke thua Versus Phat huy. In: Drummond, L., Rydstrøm, H. (eds.). Gender Practices in Contemporary Vietnam. Singapore: Singapore University Press, 47–73.

Nguyen Cong Khan, Ha Huy Khoi, 2008. Double burden of malnutrition: the Vietnamese perspective. *Asia Pacific Journal of Clinical Nutrition* 17(S1), 116–118.

Parsons, J. M., 2015. Gender, class and food: families, bodies and health. London; New York: Palgrave Macmillan (Palgrave Macmillan Studies in Family and Intimate Life).

Peters, E.J., 2012a. Appetites and Aspiration in Vietnam: Food and Drink in the Long Nineteenth Century. Plymouth: AltaMira Press.

Peters, E.J., 2012b. Cuisine and Social Status Among Urban Vietnamese, 188–1926. In: Van Nguyen-Marshall, Drummond, L. B. W., Bélanger, D. (eds.), 2012. The Reinvention of distinction: modernity and the middle class in urban Vietnam. Dordrecht: Springer (ARI –Springer Asia Series), 43–58.

Q & Me Vietnam Market Research, (2016). Asia Plus Inc. [online] Available at: https://qandme.net/en/report/Fast-food-eating-behavior-and-popular-chains.html [Accessed 03 April, 2018].

Rabinow, P., Rose, N., 2006. Biopower today. *BioSocieties*, 1, 195–217.

Rydstrøm, H., 2004. Female and Male "Characters": Images of Identification and Self Identification for Rural Vietnamese Children and Adolescents. In: Drummond, L., Rydstrøm, H. (eds). Gender in Contemporary Vietnam. Singapore: Singapore University Press, 74–95.

Rydstrøm, H., 2011. Comprised Ideals: Family Life and the Recognition of Women in Vietnam. In: Rydstrøm, H. 2011: Gendered Inequalities in Asia. Configuring, Contesting and Recognizing Women and Men. Copenhagen: NIAS Press.

Shilling, C., 2002. Culture, the "sick role" and the consumption of health. *British Journal of Sociology*, 53(4), 621–638.

Shilling, C., 2012. The Body & Social Theory. 3rd ed. London: Sage.

Sobal, J., 1999. Food System Globalization, Eating Transformations, and Nutrition Transition. In: Grew, R. (ed.). Food in Global History. Boulder: Westview Press, 171–193.

Socialist Republic of Vietnam, 2012. National Nutrition Strategy for 2011–2020, with a Vision toward 2030. Hanoi: Medical Publishing House.

Tuổi Trẻ Online. (2013). 65% cha mẹ cho con ăn không đúng cách, vì sao? (65% of parents did not feed their children properly, why?). [online] Available at: https://tuoitre.vn/65-cha-me-cho-con-an-khong-dung-cach-vi-sao-544280.htm [Accessed 30 Mar. 2018].

Tuổi Trẻ Online. 2014. Con ăn giặm, mẹ chớ vội (Mums should not hurry while feeding babies solid food). [online] Available at: https://tuoitre.vn/%E2%80%8Bcon-an-giam-me-cho-voi-640483.htm [Accessed 30 Mar. 2018].

Tuổi Trẻ Online. 2015. Báo động trẻ béo bụng (Alert: children with fat bellies). [online] Available at: https://thethao.tuoitre.vn/tin/comment/964332.html [Accessed 30 March, 2018].

Tuổi Trẻ Online. 2017. Cho trẻ ăn dặm Theo phương pháp bé chỉ huy (Applying the baby-led weaning method to feeding babies sold food). [online] Available at: https://tuoitre.vn/cho-tre-an-dam-theo-phuong-phap-be-chi-huy-1309392.htm [Accessed 30 Mar. 2018].

Van Nguyen-Marshall, Drummond, L. B. W., Bélanger, D. (eds.), 2012. The Reinvention of distinction: modernity and the middle class in urban Vietnam. Dordrecht: Springer (ARI –Springer Asia Series).

Vietnam Ministry of Health. 2012. General Nutrition Survey 2009–2010. Hanoi: Medical Publishing House.

Vietnam, Ministry of Health. 2016. National Survey on the Risk Factors of Non-Communicable Diseases (STEPS) Vietnam 2015. Hanoi: General Department of Preventive Medicine.

VietNamNet. 2015. 10 lời khuyên dinh dưỡng mọi bà mẹ cần biết (10 pieces of advice on nutrition and feeding practices which mums should know). [online] Available at: http://vietnamnet.vn/vn/doi-song/10-loi-khuyen-dinh-duong-moi-ba-me-can-biet-273023.html [Accessed 30 Mar. 2018].

Vietnam's Nutrition Association (Hội Dinh Dưỡng Việt Nam). (2017a). Nuôi con, đừng áp dụng tư duy nuôi lợn (Don't apply the mentality of raising pigs when raising your children). [online] Available at: http://hoidinhduong.vn/be-yeu/nuoi-con-dung-ap-dung-tu-duy-nuoi-lon-905.html [Accessed 30 Mar. 2018].

Vietnam's Nutrition Association (Hội Dinh Dưỡng Việt Nam). 2017b. Phương pháp ăn dặm khoa học (The scientific method of feeding). [online] Available at: http://hoidinhduong.vn/be-yeu/phuong-phap-an-dam-khoa-hoc-862. html [Accessed 03 April, 2018].

Waibel, G., Glück, S., 2013. More than 13 million: mass mobilisation and gender politics in the Vietnam Women's Union. *Gender & Development* 21(2), 343–361.

Walls, H. P., Peeters, A., Pham, Thai Son, Nguyen, Ngoc Quang, Nguyen, Thi Thu Hoai, Do, Dan Loi, Nguyen, Lan Viet, Pham, Gia Khai, Reid, C. M., 2009. Prevalence of underweight, overweight and obesity in urban Hanoi, Vietnam, *Asia Pacific Journal of Clinical Nutrition*, 18(2), 234–239.

Welch Drummond, L. B., 2012. Middle Class Landscapes in a Transforming City: Hanoi in the 21st Century. In: Van Nguyen-Marshall, Drummond, L. B. W., Bélanger, D. (eds.), 2012. The Reinvention of distinction: modernity and the middle class in urban Vietnam. Dordrecht: Springer (ARI – Springer Asia Series), 79–94.

Werner, Jayne, 2009. Gender, Household and State in Post-Revolutionary Vietnam. Oxon, New York: Routledge.

WHO – World Health Organization, 2000. Obesity: Preventing and Managing the Global Epidemic. Report of a WHO Consultation. Geneva: WHO.

WHO – World Health Organization, 2018. Obesity and overweight. Fact sheet. [online] Available at: http://www.who.int/mediacentre/factsheets/fs311/en/ [Accessed 03 January, 2018].

Wright, J., Harwood, V. (eds.), 2009. Biopolitics and the 'Obesity Epidemic': Governing Bodies. New York: Routledge.

Zheng, Y., Turner, B.S., 2009. The Body in Asia. New York: Berghahn Books.

Video

Vì Sao Mập? [Why are you fat?]. (2017). [video] Directed by BomTV. Vietnam: BomTV. Available at: https://www.youtube.com/watch?v=ofvVarfHNJw [Accessed 30 Mar. 2018].

Part II

Food Safety: Trust, Responsibilisation, and Coping

5

Trust and Food Modernity in Vietnam

Muriel Figuié, Paule Moustier, Nicolas Bricas,
and Nguyen Thi Tan Loc

Introduction

Studies conducted in European countries (Eurobarometer 2006) have shown a growing anxiety generated by food among consumers. Sociologists, as mentioned later, have analysed the reasons for this trend. One set of reasons is related to the changing nature of risks making these risks less acceptable for eaters: risks are noncontrollable, new, unknown, controversial, with few benefits for eaters (Slovic 1987). Another set is related to the industrialization and globalization of food systems and, as a consequence, the growing physical and cognitive distance between eaters and food (Bricas 1993). Other reasons are related to changing and oftentimes nontransparent relations between the stakeholders of the food

M. Figuié (✉) • P. Moustier • N. Bricas
CIRAD, UMR MOISA, Montpellier, France
Université Montpellier, Montpellier, France
e-mail: muriel.figuie@cirad.fr; paule.moustier@cirad.fr; bricas@cirad.fr

Nguyen Thi Tan Loc
Fruit and Vegetable Research Institute (FAVRI), Hanoi, Vietnam

© The Author(s) 2019
J. Ehlert, N. K. Faltmann (eds.), *Food Anxiety in Globalising Vietnam*,
https://doi.org/10.1007/978-981-13-0743-0_5

139

systems (producers, food industries, traders, consumers, state agencies, experts, all suspected to privilege their own interests over food quality) and their impacts on the process of trust building between consumers and their food, in particular in relation with safety issues (Poulain 2012; Fischler 1990). These changes, characteristic for the food sector, have been called alternately second modernity, late modernity (Fonte 2002), or hypermodernity (Ascher 2005).

In a context of emerging economies like those found in Asia, the rapidity of processes such as industrialization, urbanization, and economic liberalization causes the development of first modernity and the transition to a second one to be almost simultaneous, resulting in a "compressed modernity" (Beck and Grande 2010; Kyung-Sup 2010). Even if we consider that there is not a linear transition from first to second modernity (Beck and Lau 2005), we can admit an overlap of both modernities where individuals navigate from one world of meanings to another, or combine and mix eclectic features from both worlds. What then is the impact on food anxiety?

We propose in this chapter to describe these developments in the context of Vietnam. The food sector in Vietnam is undergoing sweeping changes: end of shortages, development of an agri-food sector, and supermarket distribution. These changes come about through the impact of the combined forces of rapid economic liberalization, urbanization, improved living standard of the people, and the transformation of social and cultural norms. Households are seeing a diversification of the products consumed and changes in consumption practices: their own production of food decreases both in urban and rural contexts. (The self-consumption decreases with the urbanization process and the specialization of farms (Moustier et al. 2003)) as well as the preparation with the increasing consumption of processed food and the development of out-of-home consumption (Ehlert 2016). We hypothesize that these changes are not just a shift imposed by globalization, from traditional to modern, or from local to global food systems, but that they are also driven by the stakeholders of the food systems who mix elements from the traditional food system (see below) as well as from different stages of modernity; these changes can be analysed through the evolution of consumers' concerns towards their food.

Our purpose in this chapter is to analyse the modernization of the Vietnamese urban food system, its impact on food anxiety and on the way for consumers to build trust in their food, and to recognize it as edible. This analysis relies on data originating from different studies (see Table 5.1)[1] conducted over nearly 15 years through the framework of MALICA,[2] a France-Vietnam research consortium (French Agricultural Research Centre for International Development (CIRAD), Vietnam Academy of Agricultural Sciences (VAAS), Institute of Policy and Strategy for Agriculture and Rural Development (IPSARD)). Given the many facets of the food issues tackled in those studies, many different methods have been required to collect data (person-to-person questionnaires, qualitative and quantitative surveys, focus group discussions, and free

Table 5.1 List of the consumers' surveys conducted by the MALICA consortium and quoted in this chapter

Surveys/Projects	Date	Main topic	Sampling	Methodology
S1. CIRAD/IOS (Figuié et al. 2004)	2002	Relation between food/health	200 households in Hà Nội 40 households in Mông Phu	Semi-structured questionnaires
S2. Susper (Figuié 2007)	2003	Trust in vegetables' quality and labelling	55 consumers and 4 focus groups of 10 consumers	Free listing and focus group discussion
S3. Markets4poor (Moustier et al. 2006; Figuié and Moustier 2009)	2005	Food purchasing practices	100 low-income households in Quỳnh Mai area, Hà Nội	One week monitoring
S4. ACI project (Figuié and Mayer 2010)	2006	Trust in food labelling and retailing points	537 households in Hà Nội	30 in-depth interviews 507 structured interviews
S5. ANR SustainApple (Nguyen Thi Tan Loc et al. 2016; Moustier et al. 2014)	2014	Perception of apple quality in relation with their origin Apple market chain	54 consumers in in Hà Nội and 49 in Hải Dương, on 6 focus groups 25 retailers and 34 wholesalers of apple in Hà Nội and Hải Dương	Focus group discussions Interviews (39) and in-depth interviews (20)

Source: Authors' own

listing) and to sample surveyed persons (urban and rural households (survey 1 in Hà Nội and Mông Phu), income levels (survey 2 in focus groups), focusing on poor households and their foodscape (survey 3 in Quỳnh Mai district, in Hà Nội), customers from different retailing points (survey 4 looking at street markets, official open markets, shops, supermarkets), or stakeholders along the market chain (survey 5 on the apple market chain)).

Men were underrepresented in our surveys: most of these surveys focused on food purchasing and food preparation practices (rather than food consumption), and men in Vietnam are not much involved in these tasks (as food customers or traders). We did not conduct any survey aiming at comparing age groups. Yet we guess from what we collected indirectly that this could have been valuable. We believe that this diversity of surveys, by their objectives, methods, sampling strategies, does not weaken our demonstration but on the contrary provides a comprehensive overview of the changes affecting the Vietnamese food system, from different points of view on its social spaces.

In the first section, the main concepts used for this analysis are exposed: food system, distanciation distanciation and conventions of quality. In the second one, we describe the accelerated modernization of the Vietnamese food system in the last 30 years. In the third, we analyse the impact of this modernization on the strategies of Vietnamese urban consumers to build trust in their food, in particular in relation with food safety issues.

Food Systems, Distanciation, and Quality in the Light of Modernity

Food Systems and Food Modernity

A food system can be defined as "the series of technological and social structures which, from the field to the kitchen, via the various stages of production and processing, enable the food to reach the consumer and to be recognised as edible" (Poulain 2017, 206). A food system is a useful concept to analyse at each stage (including purchasing, cooking, and eating stages) how stakeholders mobilize knowledge, representations, and social interactions to recognize the quality of their food. It provides a framework to analyse how the eaters at the end of this chain decide to trust their food or not, the technologies embedded in it, the stakeholders involved in its delivery, and how people finally consume it or not. This process may vary according to the different food systems and their respective local embeddedness.

Three different food systems have been identified, in relation with the modernization process (Fonte 2002; Malassis and Padilla 1986): the traditional, the modern, and the late modernity food systems.

In the *traditional food system,* food production relies on numerous and small-scale farming units, involving a high proportion of the population. Production units are also consumption units since self-consumption dominates. The market is limited to local trade of rough products and the proximity between producer and consumer constitutes the basis of trust (Fonte 2002). The system is characterized by its simplicity and frugality. *The modern food system* developed in Western countries through the agricultural industrialization experienced during the twentieth century. In its most advanced phase, it is characterized by a highly specialized, industrial production sector involving a small part of the population. This system enables important growth of production and reduction of food shortages. Self-consumption is low, mass consumption prevailed based on standardized products, a so-called Fordist diet (Friedmann and McMichael 1989). Processed food is provided via the market over long distances and via a large number of specialized actors (Fonte 2002). In addition to these two models (traditional and modern), Fonte (2002) identifies a third model, referred to as the *late modernity system,* which has been emerging since the 1970s. It is a consequence of the crisis of the previous ones in relation with raising issues of sustainability and safety (e.g. the "mad cow" crisis linked to the emergence of a new zoonotic disease, Bovine spongiform encephalopathy—BSE—in the 1980s) and in a context of reflexive modernization that means "the possibility of a creative (self-)destruction for an entire epoch: that of industrial society" (Beck 1994, 2). It is characterized by satiety, compared to the shortages of the traditional model, and growth (in food intake and in food market) of the modern one. Satiety is characterized by a saturation of energy intake (with an increasing burden of diseases related to obesity, diabetes, hypertension, etc.) and the stabilization of food expenditure over total household expenditure. The industrialization of the food chain is more generalized and includes a preparation stage (households buy processed food). Consumption patterns are more individualized, with consumption outside the home playing an important role. At the same time, traditional techniques are re-evaluated and niche markets develop for fair-trade, organic, local products and the like in order to respond to growing consumer concerns (see Faltmann, this volume).

As Fonte mentioned, the shift from one system to the other does not imply the complete disappearance of the preceding one; different models may co-exist. This "overlap" may be important in countries where the process of modernization is rapid, such as is the case in "compressed modernity" (Kyung-Sup 2010). Each food system is characterized by a dominant consumption model, involving the various stages of purchasing, transporting, storing, cooking, sharing, eating, and managing wastes. Knowledge, representations, and the social interactions that consumers mobilize at each of these stages to recognize food as safe and edible are impacted by the process of modernization. The concept of "distanciation" is useful to understand this impact.

"Distanciation", a Challenge for the Modern Eater

Urbanization and industrialization contribute to increase the distance between production and consumption, between products and consumers. This process can be summed up by the concept of "distanciation" (Bricas 1993). This "distanciation" process results from the following trends:

1) With the development of a food industry, consumers have to be able to distinguish food products within an increasingly diverse choice. At the same time, however, consumers lose knowledge of processes of food production and transformation, which have become complex. It is no longer possible to identify food with a particular place or actor (family, neighbours or known sellers). Food becomes "delocalised" and

loses its identity. Consumers are faced with what Fischler (1990) refers to as an "unidentified edible object" (OCNI—French acronym).

2) Although, during modernity, science has proved itself capable of overcoming shortages, in late modernity, science is no longer seen by consumers as a source of progress but as a source of new risks (Beck 1994). These new risks are related to the industrialization of production and transformation processes, for example, pesticide residues, mad cow disease. That means in the words of Giddens (1991) that they are manufactured risks, implying culpability and responsibility rather than random events. Moreover, late modern risks are complex, with time-lag effects, and are referred to as being "invisible", or out of reach of the senses of the layperson. The consumer can only rely on third parties who act as intermediaries between the consumer and the product and who can guarantee the safety of the product.

3) The modernization of the food system is accompanied by a generalization of pre-packed food. Buyers no longer choose among foodstuffs but among packages (Cochoy 2002). Pre-packed food satisfies the needs of transportation, hygiene, self-service, and product identification. Packaging carries new kinds of information: brand, label, information on origin, and so on. However, while pre-packed food can provide buyers with a great deal of information, it also hides certain factors: by preventing direct contact with the foodstuffs, it contributes to depriving the consumers of their capacities for assessing the foodstuffs using their senses (Figuié and Bricas 2010).

In this modernization and distanciation process there is a shift of consumers' expertise: it moves away from the knowledge of a product's intrinsic characteristics towards the analysis of information relating to its brand, label, and point of sale as well as the reliability of this information and those providing it. The qualification process of food is transformed. In the traditional food system qualification relies on direct procedures; these procedures stimulate the sensory capacities of the subject to evaluate the physical characteristics of the product (Bricas 1993).[3] With the modernization process of the food system, consumers have to deal with more indirect qualification procedures: trust in food relies increasingly on trust in the numerous stakeholders involved in the food system such as in science, the food industry, and supermarkets. In the late modernity system, consumers' trust in food cannot longer be taken for granted (de Krom 2010; Kjaernes et al. 2007).

Assessing the Safety of Food: A Matter of Convention

Food safety becomes a major concern for the consumer in a late modern food system. At the same time, the process of food qualification by consumers is transformed. It becomes more indirect. This is even more pronounced in the case of sanitary quality. In late modernity, food risks refer to the presence of pesticide or antibiotic residues, bird flu, and so on. These characteristics cannot be assessed by the consumers themselves (or only in the very long term). They are related to what has been named "credence attributes" (Darby and Karni 1973),[4] that is, signs that are not connected to the products themselves, but which are more indirect such as a veterinary stamp, a label, or a brand. That raises questions of trust in a third party capable of giving credibility to these signs.

To identify the different ways to build trust in food quality, we can use the grid proposed by Sylvander (1995). It is based on the typology of conventions defined by Boltanski and Thevenot (1991). Sylvander identifies "quality conventions", that is, a set of common beliefs between the purchaser and the seller, making it possible to come to an agreement on the quality of the products and therefore conclude the transaction. He proposes four quality conventions: the market convention where price is a means of indicating quality; the industrial convention in which compliance with a set of specifications built on scientific knowledge, formalized by a label, is the basis for trust in the quality; the domestic convention or interpersonal convention where the consumer's trust is based on a personal relationship with the supplier; and the civic convention where the commitment of an institution guaranteeing the public good, such as the government, also formalized by a label, reduces consumer uncertainty (Sylvander 1995).

In this chapter we analyse the Vietnamese food system and we focus on the purchasing stage. We analyse how Vietnamese urban consumers build trust in purchased food. We propose that the Vietnamese food system is transformed by a "compressed modernity". This transformation increases the distance between the food and the consumers. This distance imposes consumers redefining their way to build trust in food, in order to face their growing anxiety towards food safety.

Evolution of the Food System in the Vietnamese Context

The food sector in Vietnam is undergoing sweeping changes under the impact of the combined factors of economic liberalization, urbanization, and the improved living standard of the people. These changes (see Box 5.1) have been initiated with the adoption of *Đổi Mới* policy in 1986 characterized by an economic and political opening. As a consequence, Vietnam's GDP increased substantially during the past 30 years, from USD 14.1 billion in 1985 to USD 193.6 billion in 2015.[5] Per capita GDP doubled in seven years to USD 1560 in 2012 (ranked 155th globally). Vietnamese urban middle and upper classes re-emerged, driving consumerism as the number of middle class households has nearly doubled over the past decade from 1.2 million in 2003 to 2.3 million in 2012 (USDA 2008). These changes are coming with important transformations of Vietnam's food system affecting food markets and food safety (see Ehlert and Faltmann, this volume).

Box 5.1 Prominent Trends That Will Shape the Growth of Vietnam's Modern Retail Sector over the Next Few Years, According to US Department of Agriculture (USDA 2013)

- A growing number of Western-minded consumers, especially large numbers of young consumers in urban areas.
- A growing middle class, where both parents are working and less time is available for food shopping.
- A high number of women in the workforce, with increased disposable incomes to purchase higher-value food products for their children and families.
- A wide range of products offered by large supermarkets, attracting even lower-income consumers.

- Increasing consumer acceptance of processed and packaged products. Many products traditionally sold in bulk are now readily available pre-packaged.
- More concern about and willingness to pay for nutrition, quality, hygiene, and food safety.
- Brand loyalty, but still receptive to new products.
- Weekly shopping at modern retailers versus daily shopping at traditional markets.

USDA Foreign Agricultural Service, 2013. Vietnam retail foods; Sector report 2013. Gain Report VM 3062. Hanoi, USDA.

A Food System Under Modernization

Until the *Đổi Mới* policy began bearing fruit, food distribution of staples produced locally or sourced from Soviet food, aid was taken care of through a system of ration vouchers, and also through the black market. Since then, the food market in Vietnam experienced sharp growth. In 1992–1993, it accounted for USD 3.4 billion or VND 51,500 billion; excluding the value of out-of-home consumption, not available for that "period".[6] Ten years later, that market had almost doubled, accounting for over USD 7.2 billion (VND 91,000 billion, and nearly VND 110,000 billion including out-of-home consumption) (Moustier et al. 2003). A prospective study estimated the Vietnam food and beverage market at USD 66 billion in 2017 (USDA 2008).

This trend reflects a growth in the quantities of food consumed at the individual level, along with a decreasing rate of undernutrition (Tuyen Le Danh et al. 2004) and at national level, both in rural and urban population. It also reflects a decrease in households' self-consumption, in relation to a growing share of urban population (it grew from 14.5 per cent in 1985 to 30.8 per cent in 2015)[7] and rural households increasingly depending on markets for their supply (in food and agricultural inputs) and for commercializing their production. This growing food market is mainly to the advantage of local producers despite the rapid increase in imports. In 2001, imports represented only about 6 per cent of the food market in Vietnam compared with 19 per cent in 2006

(USD 0.44 billion and USD 2 billion respectively for the value of imports, according to FAOstat) (Vorley et al. 2015). Food imports mainly originate from China, Australia, and other ASEAN countries (USDA 2008). In Hà Nội metropole, the peri-urban agricultural production meets an important part of the needs of the population with 69 per cent of meat, 32 per cent of fish, 38 per cent of rice, 60 per cent of vegetables, and 18 per cent of fruits produced in this area, according to an official of Hà Nội City department of agriculture (quoted in Vorley et al. 2015).

The growth of agricultural production observed in Vietnam over the past 20 years relies on an intensification of agricultural production, in particular through an increasing use of chemical inputs (fertilizer, pesticides, preservatives, etc.). For example, the use of pesticides has sharply increased in Vietnam during the last years. The volume of imports has increased five times from 1990 to 2007, mainly coming from China, partly relying on a black market where vendors illegally import proscribed pesticides (Pham Van Hoi et al. 2013). Food processing has also been industrialized, as has the retail sector through supermarket development. The modern retail sector accounts for a small share of the distribution system but that sector is growing rapidly: it accounts for 14 per cent of food market share in 2008 (USDA 2008) compared with 5 per cent in 2002 (Figuié and Moustier 2009). From zero modern grocery outlets in 1990, by 2012 Vietnam had 421 supermarkets, 23 hypermarkets, and 362 convenient stores (USDA 2013).[8]

With this increasing dependence on the market for food supply, the lengthening and industrialization of food chains, and the increasing use of pesticides all contribute to rising food safety issues. Food crisis and food scandals multiply. They can be interpreted as signs of late modernity in the food system.

Food Scandals and Crises As Signs of Late Modernity

The modernization process of the Vietnamese food system operates in a context of a lack of control capacity from authorities. Controls are scarce, and when they exist have a low level of trust given the frequency of misleading information (Ginhoux 2001). With this lack of official control and information, media are the main source of information for consumers. Most of these media are controlled by the state, and behave as the voice of the leading Communist Party (Kerkvliet 2001). On several occasions, they have revealed and exposed criticisms towards the practices of stakeholders of the food system, like street vendors, or local authorities, for example, regarding the local implementation of state regulation, in the case of avian flu crisis (Tuong Vu 2010; Guénel and Klingberg 2010). Moreover, social media and the internet may facilitate whistle blowers as they did during the measles crisis in 2014,[9] or function as a "social amplifier of crisis".

The *phở* crisis is a good example of that situation. *Phở* is a culinary specialty of Hà Nội; consumed at any time of the day (see Peters, this volume). This is a beef broth poured over strips of beef and rice noodles, fragrant star anise, and ginger. In 1999, controls made in various street restaurants revealed the presence of formaldehyde in seven samples out of ten. Formaldehyde is toxic to humans. It is used to preserve noodles and keep them soft.

These revelation by the press (*Nhân Dân*, 6 Jan. 2000) caused what has been called "*phở* crisis". In the days that followed, *phở* consumption fell by up to 80 per cent. After this, consumers progressively resumed their consumption habits.

The use of formaldehyde is probably not new. What is new is the role of the press in the uncovering the massive scale of formaldehyde contamination, and the way to interpret it. Using formaldehyde was characterized as a serious crime against the national gastronomic culture, a crime motivated by the pursuit of profit by a few individuals at the expense of the general interest. Indirectly, the criticisms point out that economic liberalization adopted in 1986 has allowed private entrepreneurship and capitalist values to develop. A similar interpretation can be applied to the revelation by the press of mass food poisoning affecting workers employed by foreign companies in Vietnam as a consequence of these reforms.

The *phở* crisis may be the first food scandal of the second modernity: a scandal largely mediatized, affecting consumers' behaviours massively, but with no (registered) victims. It illustrates a crisis in trust between consumers and the other stakeholders of the food system (sellers, authorities, etc.). The press also regularly reports cases of mass poisoning. For example, during the first four months of 2007, the journal *Thanh Niên News* reported a case of 1000 workers suffering food poisoning after eating at their company canteen, 250 workers the following month, and then 172 school children affected in April at their school cafeteria. They have played up the results of alarming analyses, such as in June 2006, when it was revealed that 30 per cent of pork meat sold contained clenbuterol, a prohibited antibiotic. In 2007, in Ho Chi Minh City, one quarter of the rice noodles sampled was said to contain borax or formaldehyde (like during the *phở* crisis). That same year, the press (*Nhân Dân*, March 2007) alerted consumers regarding problems with water morning glory—the most widely consumed vegetable in Vietnam—produced in Hà Nội's Thanh Tri district. It was found to have heavy metal contamination, causing a severe drop in its consumption. Examples of fraud and counterfeit products are numerous. For example, reconstituted powdered milk was sold as fresh milk (Vietnamnet 2014), or imported milk from China which was adulterated with melamine in 2008. The press also contributes to report certain stories that are more a matter of rumour: hormones in meat reportedly leading to homosexual behaviour or artificial eggs (again, from China) sold in the markets.

Apple safety is one of the recent subjects for Vietnamese consumer concerns (Nguyen Thi Tan Loc et al. 2016). It also illustrates the characteristics of a food scandal of the second modernity. In 2012, media reported that Chinese farmers from Yantai prefecture used prohibited toxic pesticides (Tuzet, Asomate) and arsenical fungicide to coat bags for apples (see Box 5.2). China is the main country of imports of apples in Vietnam and Vietnamese consumption of Chinese apples has been deeply affected by this revelation. Media headlined the issue of "toxic apples",[10] "toxic Chinese fruits",[11] and "Chinese low quality and toxic products".[12] Despite the problem being localized to one Chinese prefecture, it affected the trust in all apples, all fruits, and then all products imported from China in a context of a general mistrust in food coming from this country (see Box 5.2). It remained even after the announcement that the company which disseminated the toxic bags was sanctioned. As a consequence, imports of Chinese apples to Vietnam decreased strongly from 162,848 tons in 2009 to 83,623 tons in 2011 and 81,556 tons in 2013 (to the benefit of imports from USA and New Zealand) (Nguyen Thi Tan Loc et al. 2016).

These food scandals at times come along with massive environmental pollutions provoked by industries, such as the pollution provoked in 2016 by a Taiwanese company, Formosa, set up in Vietnam, at the origin of a massive sea pollution, leading to high fish mortality and protest marches in Hà Nội (Mullman 2016).

No sooner than the Vietnamese modern agro-industrial sector emerges, than it already shows characteristics of late modernity such as large-scale food scandals associated with new technologies (hormones, pesticides, etc.) or the influential role of media in the food system. What are the reactions and the practices of Vietnamese consumers facing these scandals and uncertainties?

Box 5.2 "Toxic Chinese Apple", the Socio-cultural Dimension of Food Anxiety

Fruits are largely consumed in Vietnam (citrus, banana, apples, litchi, watermelon, guava) (Figuié 2004). They are not only food, they also have symbolic functions, being used as presents for ancestor worship (the 1st and 15th days of the lunar month) or for festive meals (weddings, mournings, festivals, etc.). Fuji apples originating from China, are traditionally popular in Vietnam (Nguyen Thi Tan Loc et al. 2016). They have beautiful brightness, a glossy shell, a crunchy flavour, and they are cheap.

Nevertheless, there is a growing concern about the use of chemicals for fruit production and conservation (S5, S6). This concern was expressed by half of the people surveyed in Hà Nội in 2004 (S1). Following the Chinese apple scandal in 2012, 100 per cent of people surveyed in Hà Nội expressed their concern about chemical residue in Chinese apples (and 67 per cent of consumers in Hai Duong), (S5). This concern is fed by media reports but also originates from a direct experience: many consumers report experiences of conserving apples at home for weeks or even months as a proof of the massive use of chemical conservatives.

The head of the Hà Nội Plant Protection Department announced recently (2016)[13] that local authorities strictly control the majority of Chinese fruits imported to Vietnam, including control of pesticide residues and preservatives. He mentioned recent samplings of Chinese apples, with 30 per cent of samples containing pesticide residues, but under the allowable level.

Nevertheless, consumers remain anxious and many of them declared that they avoid buying apples from China (which is confirmed by the drop in

Chinese imports of apple): "We do not believe in the quality of (Chinese) apples, so that we do not buy them. Although they are stickered by stamps and labels of exporters, we think that they use more preservatives or these stamps and labels are fake" (focus group in 2014). Sixty-five per cent (S5) declare that they would not buy organic Chinese apples if made available, for lack of trust.

Some consumers report that they prefer buying apples with a sticker indicating a US or New Zealand origin (indeed fruit imports from the USA and New Zealand have increased in recent years). That said, avoiding Chinese apple is not easy since consumers lack reliable information on the origin of the products they buy: "When purchasing imported apples, we do not care about stamps and labels stuck on these products ... because we do not trust them. We only trust sellers because they are familiar and they would not lie with us" (S5).

Distrust in Chinese apples is embedded in a complex relationship between China and Vietnam. It is reported that China supplies the Vietnamese market with all of the low-quality goods that it cannot dispose of on its own market, despite it being considered quite lax in terms of health regulations (see Zhang, this volume). It is noteworthy that the same distrust is expressed by Cambodian consumers with regard to products from Vietnam (Sipana and Moustier 2004). Chinese products are associated with many evils (low quality, counterfeit, poisoned food, etc.) probably echoing thousands of years of rivalry between the two countries. And this instance of distrust may be interpreted as the desire to emphasize one's identity, as "you are what you eat" as would have said Brillat-Savarin.[14]

Trust in Food in Vietnam

Food Anxiety Among Consumers

Changes in the Vietnamese food system have affected the representation of food, in particular in relation with health.

Traditionally in Asia (Blanchon 1995; Simoons 1991), eating is perceived as a way to prevent or cure certain diseases. Foods are seen to fit into three categories—cold, hot, or neutral. The individual must consume the proper combination of each of type to ensure the right balance of the two vital body strengths—yin and yang. Such a classification is not specific to Asia although it exists only residually and latently in Western societies in the form of dishes such as the pairing of cantaloupe and Port wine (Flandrin 1992). In Vietnam, among the elderly, it is still the basic rule in deciding what food combination to choose. Younger people, although knowing the principle, rarely know how to put foods into those categories (Lepiller 2005). Regardless, a survey conducted in Hà Nội (S1, Table 5.1) shows that for a very great majority (86 per cent), diet is vital for health. While Asian tradition holds that diet is indeed considered as a way of maintaining good health, or even as therapeutic, what seems new is the perception of the dark side of the diet/health relationship: food can also make one sick. Consumers in Hà Nội (93 per cent of them) (S4) feel that the quality of their meals has improved over the last ten years (food is considered to be more abundant and more varied). But over half of the persons surveyed felt that food product quality had regressed. So much so that 65 per cent of them claim that food products today are unsafe for the health.

Consumer concerns involve the nutritional quality of the food. Some foods have recently acquired a sharply negative nutritional image with urban consumers (S1): sugar is associated with being overweight and diabetes. Yet, just a few years ago, there was a striking image of it as a fortifier, with many street venders selling it in front of hospitals to families who had come to visit sick relatives. The same is true with animal fats and, to a lesser extent, meat, the consumption of which is associated with the emergence of being overweight, obesity, unhealthy cholesterol levels, and high blood pressure (S1).

The main concern, however, relates to the use of artificial chemicals and their residues present in vegetables, fruit, meats, and fish, a concern confirmed by many different surveys (S1–S6). It indicates a pronounced "chemophobia"[15] among consumers. Regarding meat, the main concern involves the use of *lợn tăng trọng* or stimulants (a rather vague term used by consumers, seemingly to refer to antibiotics, hormones, and other growth-promoting agents used in pork feeds). Fish and other aquatic products (shrimp, crab) are also seen as potentially unsafe products because of the use of preservatives (urea, formaldehyde, borax). For fruit and vegetables, the probable presence of pesticide residues is highlighted. Regarding fruit (mainly for those from China), the use of preservatives adds to this problem as mentioned above. Data measuring presence of chemical residues in foodstuffs are scarce (see section "see above") but indicate that chemophobia is not baseless. Nevertheless, consumers of course keep on purchasing, cooking, eating, and sharing food. What knowledge, representations, and social interactions do they mobilize to recognize food as being edible in such a context? As shown below, consumers have numerous ways to build trust in food; these ways change with the modernization of the food system.

Building Trust in the Vietnamese Food System

In spite of the dangers associated with the main foodstuffs, consumers are not concerned when they eat at home (S1). Most of them think that the meals they prepare themselves present little or no danger. The home is considered a safe place[16] (see Kurfürst, this volume). To justify their answers (low risk of getting sick when eating at home despite numerous dangers associated to foodstuffs), consumers evoke their knowhow (S1, S2). This knowledge deals with their method of preparing food at home. This presupposes ways of making foodstuffs safe to eat by soaking, washing, peeling vegetables, and prolonged cooking of meat. These practices aim at eliminating impurity, including chemical residues, and to reduce the food related risks at short term (such as food intoxications) and at long term (such as cancer). It deals also and overall with their way of selecting foods at retailing places. This selection relies on direct qualification procedures but also on diverse conventions of quality.

Food Selection in Traditional Markets

The "traditional" sector very much predominates in fresh food distribution. According to Wertheim-Heck et al. (2014), supermarkets in Hà Nội account for less than 2 per cent of the vegetable market. People in charge of purchasing food for households (mainly women), of all social backgrounds, purchase their food daily at open-air markets in order to be sure of the freshness of the produce (S2, S3, S4). The freshness of products is by far the first guarantee of safety. It is also associated with the sensory quality of food such as its taste and firmness.

Buyers purchase food preferably early in the morning (from 6 a.m.) in order to find the freshest products (Figuié et al. 2004). Selecting food may involve a whole set of tests that engage the senses. Consumers in a hurry, sometimes without even getting off their motorbike (the most widespread urban form of transport), head straight for their usual vendor with whom they exchange only a few words. Others go from stall to stall, compare products, touch them, smell them, or even taste them.

Traditional open-air markets offer a wide range of small animals, fish, poultry, rabbits, frogs, that consumers can buy alive; and the word (*sống*) can serve to express that a "food" is raw or that it is living (e.g. alive fish). Larger animals, such as pigs (pork meat is the most consumed meat in Vietnam) are slaughtered in the night in slaughterhouses located in the city (but that the authorities are increasingly trying to move to the outskirts) and are offered for sale on market stalls in the following hours. To assess the freshness of pork meat, buyers smell the meat or touch it to check if it doesn't stick to your finger (Figuié et al. 2004). It should not be cold which would mean that it has been stored cool so that the animal would not come directly from the slaughtering house. So whereas in French the word "fresh" means both "newly produced, yet unaltered" and "slightly cold", the Vietnamese language distinguishes these two feels (*tươi* meaning newly produced and *mát* meaning slightly cold).

Besides freshness, buying at the usual retailers is also a way to guarantee the quality of a food purchase. "I trust the quality of the vegetables I buy because my seller is a member of the Party", one elderly lady declared (S2). But for the most part, domestic convention has the upper hand through reference to the "woman I usually buy from". Faithfulness to the purchaser is the counterpart of the seller's honesty.

Changes in the food market have limited the possibility of direct qualification of the product using the senses because of pre-packaging and the complexity of modern food attributes. Consumers must use indirect qualification where different conventions can be used. At the same time liberalization of the market has eroded the civic convention as the basis of trust. Supply practices are changing, and other ways of building trust are now developing, with the emergence of supermarkets.

Of course, the idea is not for consumers to idealize the quality and in particular the safety of foods previously available in the market. Older people relate, for instance, that in times of shortage (occurring up into the 1980s), wheat (shipped in from the USSR) and rice had a high proportion of weevils, stones, and other impurities (S1). Although there was probably a risk also present, it was somehow more "acceptable". Firstly because of the context, namely war and shortages. Moreover, the respondents felt that today's problems are completely different in nature, linked to the fraudulent practices of economic actors selfishly out for personal gain to the detriment of the common interest.

Anxiety may also be related to increasing offers of products that were still unknown to Vietnamese consumers only ten years ago (sweet products, oil, etc.), pre-packed (conserves, frozen food, etc.) and originating in distant countries (e.g. French products in Cora supermarkets). Although legislation requires that essential information indicated on packaging such as the list of ingredients, expiry date, and so on, be translated, many products continue to break this rule.

Supermarket Development, a New Qualification Process

With the development of a modern retail sector, and in particular the development of supermarkets, the qualification process is changing rapidly. The supermarket is a sanitized, cold, and impersonal place. Freshness does not mean that the product was recently harvested but that it is stored in a cold chain with an "expiration date". Most of the products are sold pre-packaged or served by gloved employees. The direct contact with the products is broken. The staff of vendors there is often renewed, preventing the creation of relations of familiarity. The buyer needs to redefine how to check quality and to delegate the assessment of food quality to a trusted third party.

Nevertheless, supermarkets are viewed favourably by consumers who trust the quality of the products sold in them, particularly their health quality. Recent crises, such as the avian flu crisis and the influx of buyers to the supermarkets during this crisis (Figuié and Fournier 2008), showed that supermarkets were able to give trust to consumers. That trust is associated with the high prices charged in supermarkets: "In supermarkets, products cost more. So we trust them more" (S3), referring to a market convention. That is also the industrial convention applied to brand name or reputable products: "Supermarket products are more reliable because maintaining prestige is an issue" (S3).

This analysis shows the diversity and the evolution of trust strategies mobilized by Vietnamese urban consumers when purchasing food.

Despite mistrust in the food system's industrialization process, linked to a growing chemophobia, trust in supermarkets is high (Figuié and Mayer 2010). It refers to both an industrial convention (trust in brand) and a market convention (trust in the high prices at the supermarkets). It is likely however that an excessive trust is granted to supermarket quality, even if food safety is not objectively always better than in wet markets,[17] and even by those who cannot afford to purchase food there, and then have no experience of it (Figuié and Mayer 2010). Vietnamese policy makers rely on supermarket development to improve food safety and deliver food safety guarantees (Wertheim-Heck et al. 2015). Incidents like the bird flu outbreak in 2005 caused consumer chicken and egg purchases to increase in supermarkets due to Ministry of Health statements recommending that purchases be made at supermarkets where poultry products were considered safe (Figuié and Fournier 2008). This delegation by a Communist government of the protection of its citizens to capitalist companies[18] may be surprising. Delegating management of a health risk to the supermarket distribution sector in that way illustrates the challenges inherent in setting up a public control system, based on civic convention, when facing an accelerated modernization of the food system. While some consumers' reactions in Western countries are seen as a rejection of the modern industrialized food sector (Setbon et al. 2005), reactions in Vietnam reveal that sanitary crises can, on the contrary, generate major opportunities for the development of an industrialized food sector. That illustrates the role of food safety as a "Trojan horse" for supermarkets breaking into the food markets in developing countries.

The larger portion of urban consumers cannot afford to purchase food in supermarkets, but this segment is decreasing with economic growth and the development of a middle class. They develop numerous practices at home to improve the safety of the products they buy (washing, soaking, etc.). When they purchase food, domestic convention, as typical of a traditional food system and based on face-to-face relationships, still prevails.

Conclusion

In Western societies, food systems have evolved from the traditional to the modern, and then to late modern systems. Late modern systems are characterized by consumers' distrust in food linked to a distanciation process (cognitive and physically) and a distrust in industrialized techniques. In late modernity, features of the traditional systems are revalorized (e.g. farmers markets) and reintroduced in the food systems, in order to reconstruct consumers' trust in food.

The rapid evolution of the Vietnamese food system has gone hand in hand with the emergence of a consumer with both the characteristics of the traditional system (cooking practices to improve food safety, importance of domestic convention), the modern one (attraction for the abundance of standardized goods offered by supermarkets) and the late modern one (low acceptability of "industrial" risks). Vietnamese consumers have some of the features of the "hypermodern eater" described by Ascher (2005). This means that the consumer has the capacity to shift from one world to another, from one kind of convention to another, illustrating the compressed modernity facing the country.

Notes

1. It is partially based on Figuié et al. (2014) which has been updated with some recent research.
2. http://www.malica-asia.com
3. Direct qualification refers to "body cues". The indirect qualification procedures can be defined as being those processes which link the subject and the object through the intermediary of a third party enabling the quality of the product to be evaluated. It can also refer to the atmosphere of the place of sale, as perceived by the senses (music, smell, light), namely "situational cues". The modernization process requires shoppers to deal with more indirect qualification procedures, with an increasing number of situational cues and a decreasing number of direct body cues.
4. Along with credence attributes, Darby and Karni (1973) identify two others types of attributes (the attributes refer to the properties or characteristics of a product) enabling consumers to rate the products: attributes

of research or knowledge, and attributes of experience. The research or knowledge attributes can be assessed directly by the consumer at the time of purchase. Experience attributes can be assessed only at the time the products are prepared or consumed.

5. http://data.worldbank.org/country/vietnam
6. These figures reflect the value of the currency in 1998. "Food market" means all purchases (food items, beverages) made by households to feed themselves. It therefore does not include the value of what the households produce for their own consumption that is self-consumption (Moustier et al. 2003).
7. http://www.indexmundi.com/facts/vietnam/urban-population—based on national statistics and World Bank population estimates.
8. In the Vietnamese supermarket business, it is estimated that approximately 55 per cent of total supermarket sales are food, of which imported food accounts for a small percentage ranging from 5 per cent to 15 per cent of total food sales.
9. In 2014, the revelation by social media (Facebook, blogs) of a massive rise in the number of Measles cases in Vietnam forced the Ministry of Health to be more transparent.
10. Beijing news, 12 June 2012, http://www.bbc.com/news/world-asia-china-18406012
11. Thanh Niên News, May 2014 http://www.thanhniennews.com/society/vietnam-turns-away-500-tons-of-toxic-chinese-fruit-26701.html
12. VietNamNet Bridge, May 2013, http://english.vietnamnet.vn/fms/business/74358/vietnam-turning-chinese-refuse-tip-.html
13. http://www.tinmoi.vn/tao-fuji-trung-quoc-boc-tui-doc-ban-tran-lan-01934589.html
14. Brillat-Savarin (1755–1826) is a well-known French gastronome and author of many gastronomic essays.
15. The word "chemophobia" appeared at the end of the 1970s in the community of chemists (see abstracts of the meeting of the American Chemical Society in the 1970s and 1980s). It refers to the supposed exaggerated and irrational fear of chemicals by the public. Chemophobia is associated with the rise of the environmental movement in the USA and the publication of Rachel Carson's *Silent Spring* in 1962, which is accused of "demonizing" chemicals. We use it here in a neutral sense without judging if this fear is exaggerated or not.
16. It is interesting to compare the perception of the home as a safe place with the data provided by the Vietnamese Ministry of Health at the same

period: 60 per cent of food-borne outbreaks occurred following family meals, 6 per cent in canteens, 21.5 per cent at parties, 9.5 per cent in street restaurants, and 3 per cent in school canteens. This comparison may lead, through a psychological approach of risk, to the identification of a layperson's optimism bias, and of a lower acceptability of suffered risks (i.e. suffered by the restaurant customers) compared to self-imposed risks (Slovic 1987). But data from the Ministry of Health only take into account food poisoning, while surveyed consumers take into account all kind of risks. Moreover, it may also be explained by the fact that, when quoting dangerous places for eating, people refer to a probability of being sick based on their own experience (and so, they take into consideration the ratio number of "bad" meals to number of meals taken at this place, while the Ministry of Health refers to the ratio number of bad meals at this place to the total number of bad meals).

17. A study conducted by ILRI, the International Livestock Research Institute, and quoted by Vorley et al. (2015) proceeds to a comparative analysis of pork sold in supermarkets and wet markets in Hà Nội. It shows that while most pork sold did not meet safety standards in both retailing places, meat was found to be highly contaminated more frequently in supermarkets, probably due to the fact that meats tend to sit longer on supermarket shelves for sale, allowing bacteria to multiply.

18. There are state-owned supermarkets in Vietnam but during the peak of the avian flu outbreak, only the supermarket Metro was allowed to sell chicken in Hanoi.

References

Ascher, François. 2005. Le mangeur hypermoderne. Paris: Odile Jacob.

Beck, Ulrich. 1994. "The reinvention of politics: Towards a theory of reflexive modernization." In *Reflexive modernization: Politics, tradition and aesthetics in the modern social order* edited by Ulrich Beck, Anthony Giddens and Scott Lash, Stanford, California: Stanford University Press. pp. 1–55.

Beck, Ulrich, and Edgar Grande. 2010. Varieties of second modernity: The cosmopolitan turn in social and political theory and research. *British Journal of Sociology*, 61 (3): 409–443.

Beck, Ulrich, and Christoph Lau. 2005. Second modernity as a research agenda: theoretical and empirical explorations in the 'meta-change' of modern society. *British Journal of Sociology*, 56 (4); 525–557.

Blanchon, Flora. 1995. *Asie. Savourer, Gouter*. Edited by CREOPS. Paris: Presse universitaire de Paris Sorbonne.

Boltanski, Luc, and Laurent Thevenot. 1991. *De la justification. Les économies de la grandeur*. Paris: Gallimard.

Bricas, Nicolas. 1993. "Les caractéristiques et l'évolution de la consommation alimentaire dans les villes africaines." In *Alimentation, techniques et innovations dans les régions tropicales.*, edited by J. Muchnik, 127–160. Paris: L'Harmattan.

Cochoy, Franck. 2002. Une sociologie du packaging ou l'âne de Buridan face au marché. Paris: PUF.

Darby, Michael R., and Edi Karni. 1973. "Free Competition and the Optimal Amount of Frau." *Journal of Law and Economics* 16:67–88.

de Krom, Michiel. 2010. "Food risk and consumer trust. European governance of avian influenza." PhD, School of Social Sciences, Wageningen: Wageningen University.

Ehlert, Judith. 2016. "Emerging Consumerism and Eating Out In Ho Chi Minh City, Vietnam: The Social Embeddedness of Food Sharing." In *Food Consumption in the City. Practices and patterns in urban Asia and the Pacific*, edited by Marlyne Shakian, Czarina Saloma and Suren Erkman, 71–89. London: Routledge.

Eurobarometer. 2006. Risk Issues. European Commission.

Figuié, Muriel. 2004. La consommation de fruits au Vietnam. Tieu dung qua tai Viêt Nam. Hanoi: Malica (CIRAD/IOS/RIFAV/VASI).

Figuié, Muriel. 2007. "Vegetable consumption behaviour in Vietnam." In *Final summary report of SUSPER (Sustainable development of peri-urban agriculture in South-East Asia)*, edited by Paule Moustier, 100–102. Hanoi: Thê Gioi publishers.

Figuié, Muriel, Nicolas Bricas, and Paule Moustier. 2014. "Nouvelles pratiques de consommation alimentaire, perceptions des risques et de la qualité des aliments par les consommateurs urbains vietnamiens." In *Viêt-Nam en transition*, edited by G. de Terssac, An Quoc Truong and M. Catlla, 123–140. Lyon: ENS Editions.

Figuié, Muriel, Nicolas Bricas, Vu Pham Nguyen Thanh, and Nguyen Duc Truyen. 2004. "Hanoi consumers' point of view regarding food safety risks: An approach in terms of social representation." *Vietnam Social Sciences* 3:63–72.

Figuié, Muriel, and Tristan Fournier. 2008. "Avian influenza in Vietnam: chicken-hearted consumers?" *Risk Analysis* 28 (2):441–541. doi: https://doi.org/10.1111/j.1539-6924.2008.01039.x.

Figuié, Muriel, and Julie Mayer. 2010. "A qui se fier quand les aliments font peur? Labels, points de vente et décontamination symbolique au Vietnam." *Working Paper Moisa* 211004.

Figuié, Muriel, and Paule Moustier. 2009. "Market appeal in an emerging economy: supermarkets and poor consumers in Vietnam." Review of diffusion sans restriction. *Food Policy* 34:210–217. doi: https://doi.org/10.1016/j.foodpol.2008.10.012.

Figuié, Muriel, and Bricas Nicolas. 2010. "Purchasing food in modern Vietnam: when supermarkets affect the senses." In: Kalekin-Fishman, D., and Low, K. E. Y. (eds.). Everyday Life in Asia: Social Perspectives on the Senses, 177–194. Aldershot, Hants: Ashgate.

Fischler, Claude. 1990. *L'homnivore*. 2001 ed. Paris: 0. Jacob.

Flandrin, Jean-Louis. 1992. *Les chroniques de platine*. Paris: Odile Jacob.

Fonte, Maria. 2002. "Food systems, consumption models and risk perception in late modernity." *International Journal of Sociology of Agriculture and Food* 10 (1):13–21.

Friedmann, Harriet, and Philip McMichael. 1989. "Agriculture and the state system: the rise and fall of national agricultures, 1870 to the present." *Sociologia Ruralis* 29 (2):93–117.

Giddens, Anthony. 1991. *The Consequences of Modernity*. Stanford, California: Stanford University Press.

Ginhoux, Valérie. 2001. Etude de la sensibilité des consommateurs urbains de viande porcine (Ha Noi et Hai Phong, Vietnam). GRET, VASI, VSF, CIRAD, Programme Fleuve Rouge.

Guénel, Anne, and Sylvie Klingberg. 2010. "Press Coverage of Bird Flu Epidemic in Vietnam." In *Liberalizing, Feminizing and Popularizing Health Communications in Asia*, edited by Liew Kai Khiun. Farnham: Ashgate.

Kerkvliet, Benedict J. Tria. 2001. An Approach for Analysing State-Society Relations in Vietnam. *Journal of Social Issues in Southeast Asia* 16 (2): 238–278.

Kjaernes, Unni, Mark Harvey, and Alan Warde. 2007. *Trust in Food. A Comparative and Institutional Analysis*. Hampshire: Palgrave Macmillan.

Kyung-Sup, Chang. 2010. The second modern condition? Compressed modernity as internalized reflexive cosmopolitization. *British Journal of Sociology*, 61 (3): 446–464.

Lepiller, Olivier. 2005. "Les mutations de wla société urbaine de Hanoi (Viêt Nam) – Illustration par des portraits de mangeurs." Mémoire DESS "Sciences Sociales Appliquées à l'Alimentation" (mémoire encadré par Poulain J.-P., Figuié M). Université Toulouse de Mirail, Toulouse.

Malassis, Louis, and Martine Padilla. 1986. *Economie Agro-Alimentaire*. Vol. III: L'Economie mondiale. Paris: Cujas.

Moustier, Paule, Dao The Anh, and Muriel Figuié eds. 2003. *Food markets and agricultural development in Vietnam*. Hanoi: The Gioi.

Moustier, Paule, Jia, Xiangping, Nguyen Thi Tan Loc, Marie-Vivien Delphine. 2014. Exploratory results on food safety management in Chinese apple chains. Montpellier, Cirad report. https://agritrop.cirad.fr/583383/

Mullman, Steve. 2016. "A Taiwanese Steel Plant Caused Vietnam's Mass Fish Deaths the Government Says." Quartz. 30 June 2016, retrieved 8 July 2016. https://qz.com/718576/a-taiwanese-steel-plant-caused-vietnams-mass-fish-deaths-the-government-says/

Nguyen Thi Tan Loc, Sau Nguyen Thi, Hang Ngo Thu, Thinh Le Nhu, and Anh Hoang Viet. 2016. Situation of the apple market and consumption in Vietnam. Hanoi: Sustainapple project, FAVRI, CIRAD, MALICA.

Pham Van Hoi, Arthur Mol, and Peter Oosterveer. 2013. "State governance of pesticide use and trade in Vietnam." *NJAS – Wageningen Journal of Life Sciences* 67:19–26.

Poulain, Jean-Pierre. 2012. "Risques et crises alimentaires." In *Dictionnaire des cultures alimentaires*, edited by J.-P. Poulain, 1168–1185. Paris: PUF.

Poulain, Jean-Pierre. 2017. *The Sociology of Food. Eating and the Place of Food in Society*. Translated by Augusta Dörr. London: Bloomsbury Publishing.

Setbon, Michel, Jocelyn Raude, Claude Fischler, and Antoine Flahault. 2005. "Risk perception of the 'mad cow disease' in France; determinants and consequences." *Risk Analysis* 25 (4):813–826.

Simoons, Frederick J. 1991. *Food in China. A cultural and historical inquiry*. Boston: C.R.C Press.

Sipana, Chan, and Paule Moustier. 2004. Socio-economic strategies and results of vegetable traders in Phnom Penh (Cambodia). Montpellier, CIRAD: Susper Project (CIRAD-AVRDC).

Slovic, Paul. 1987. "Perception of risk." *Science* 236:280–285.

Sylvander, Bertil. 1995. "Conventions de qualité, marchés et institutions: le cas des Produits de Qualité Spécifique." In *Agrolimentaire: une économie de la qualité.*, edited by F Nicolas and E. Valceschini, 167–183. Paris: INRA, Economica.

Tuong, Vu. 2009. The Political Economy of Avian Influenza Response and Control in Vietnam. Brighton: STEPS report.

Tuong, V. 2010. Power, Politics and Accountability: Vietnam's Response to Avian Influenza. In Scoones, I. (Ed.), *Avian influenza: Science, Policy, Politics*. 93–129. London: Earthscan, 52.

Tuyen Le Danh, Mai Le Bach, Muriel Figuié, Nicolas Bricas, Bernard Maire, Marie-Claude Dop, Chung Nguyen Dinh, and Khan Nguyen Cong. 2004. "Evolution de la consommation alimentaire et de l'état nutritionnel des populations urbaines au Vietnam au cours des vingt dernières années." *Cahiers Agricultures* 13:31–38.

USDA – United States Secretary of Agriculture. 2008. Vietnam retail food sector 2008. Gain Report. USDA.

USDA – United States Secretary of Agriculture. 2013. Vietnam retail foods; Sector report 2013. Gain Report. USDA.

Vietnamnet. 2014. Vietnam predominantly makes fresh milk from imported powder milk. Posted 30/01/2014. http://english.vietnamnet.vn/fms/business/93854/vietnam-predominantly-makes-fresh-milk-from-imported-powder-milk.html

Vorley, Bill, Paolo Cravero, Paule Moustier, Lan Dinh Tuong, and Delphine Marie-Vivien. 2015 "Food consumption, urbanisation and rural transformations (final draft)." Regional workshop report, Hanoi (Vietnam), 1–2, October 2015.

Wertheim-Heck, Sigrid, Sietze Vellema, and Gert Spaargaren. 2014. "Constrained consumer practices and food safety concerns in Hanoi." *International Journal of Consumer Studies* 38 (4):326–336. doi: https://doi.org/10.1111/ijcs.12093.

Wertheim-Heck, Sigrid, Sietze Vellema, and Gert Spaargaren. 2015. "Food safety and urban food markets in Vietnam: The need for flexible and customized retail modernization policies." *Food Policy* 54:95–106.

6

Between Food Safety Concerns and Responsibilisation: Organic Food Consumption in Ho Chi Minh City

Nora Katharina Faltmann

Declared organic food is a rather new phenomenon in Vietnam and constitutes a dynamic and high-priced niche market in the country's urban centres. The emergence of organic sectors in the Global North—where the majority of research on organic consumption has been focused (Grosglik 2016)—has often been associated with wider societal movements for the environment (Johnston et al. 2009; Barendregt and Jaffe 2014; Poulain 2017). Yet while the organic niche in Vietnam could at first sight look like yet another local manifestation of a global trend towards 'green' ethical consumption, it has to be contextualised locally and historically in order to comprehend the underlying societal processes and drivers. Consequently, this chapter deals with the question of how the emergence of an organic sector can be understood within broader dynamics and discourses in the contemporary Vietnamese food system[1] and the interplay of market, state and individuals.

This chapter will show how both the historical emergence of declared organic farming in Vietnam as well as the motives for consuming organic

N. K. Faltmann (✉)
Department of Development Studies, University of Vienna, Vienna, Austria
e-mail: nora.faltmann@univie.ac.at

© The Author(s) 2019   **167**
J. Ehlert, N. K. Faltmann (eds.), *Food Anxiety in Globalising Vietnam*,
https://doi.org/10.1007/978-981-13-0743-0_6

food prove to be different from developments of organic markets elsewhere. Organic demand and supply in current-day Vietnam must be viewed in light of the trajectories of the country's food system and the actors operating within it. The current state of the food system is shaped by a variety of food safety issues which have led to an increased public awareness of and desire for safe food options, with organic food being one such choice. Not only is organic food consumption in the case of Vietnam revealed to be deeply intertwined with such omnipresent food safety concerns, it also illustrates broader insecurities over questions of responsibility in shifting relations between consumers, the market and the state. The at-times conflicting interests of these actors within the organic sector must therefore be seen against the backdrop of emerging neoliberal discourses of free trade, choice and responsible individualism with the simultaneous continuing presence of a strong state.

By zooming in on the organic niche market of Ho Chi Minh City (HCMC), this chapter is specifically interested in the debates around trustworthiness, certification and responsibility regarding organic production and consumption, as they are inherently about power structures and relations between state, society and market. The aim of this chapter is thus to unravel how contemporary consumer discourses are reflected both in the structure of the organic sector and in perceptions and agency of urban organic food consumers, as well as in concomitant food safety discourses.

Based on field research conducted in Vietnam's urban metropolis of HCMC between 2015 and 2017, the data for this chapter is composed of qualitative interviews, participant observation in organic food outlets, insights from a research workshop on food safety with Vietnamese social-science students that was co-organised by the author, as well as the latest agricultural restructuring plan and media research on organic developments in Vietnam. Coming from the interdisciplinary field of development studies, this research focuses on the local embeddedness of structural (political and corporate) powers, on inner-societal as well as global imbalances and specifically on perspectives on inequalities in relation to food.

The chapter starts with background information on recent trajectories around the food system as well as consumer discourse in Vietnam, followed by an overview over the emergence of the country's organic sector contextualised within global trends around organic production. The empirical findings on organic consumption are then discussed in the context of current food concerns and a neoliberal discourse on individual responsibility of food care.

Food in (Urban) Vietnam

A System in Transition

The rapid transformation of Vietnam's food system in the past 30 years can only be understood in the context of the market reforms of *Đổi Mới* and its succeeding economic and societal transformations (see Ehlert and Faltmann, this volume). Agricultural and societal developments that accompanied the economic reforms in turn mark the needed contextualisation for shifts in provisioning and consumption patterns and discourses around food that are at the centre of this chapter.

Since the former socialist planned economy began transforming towards a decentralised market economy, starting in the late 1980s (all the while remaining under communist one-party rule), the food situation in Vietnam changed fundamentally as well. While centrally planned agriculture, state-managed shops and ration coupons for scarce food supplies characterised the years before the economic reforms (Figuié and Moustier 2009), there are now growing, yet unequally accessible, foodscapes of plenty (Figuié and Bricas 2010, 181). Standards of living have risen and global cultural and corporate influences have entered the country, including its food environments, for example, with foreign restaurants, fast food chains, supermarkets and convenience products (Pingali 2007; Figuié and Moustier 2009; Bitter-Suermann 2014).

Structurally, rural-urban migration and changing social structures related to industrialisation and urbanisation processes led to an increased gap between food producers and consumers. Direct contact with farmers and traceability of food are often no longer given, especially in urban contexts, constituting the 'distanciation' of a food system (Bricas 1993).

On the food production side, dynamics have been strongly shaped by the so-called Green Revolution, an agricultural turn towards agrochemicals, mechanisation and high-yielding crop varieties (Parayil 2003, 975). Agricultural intensification was pursued both in North and in South Vietnam since the 1960s (Fortier and Tran Thi Thu Trang 2013, 83). Yet due to the disruptions of the Second Indochina War, the Green Revolution in Vietnam fully picked up in the late 1970s after 1975's end of war and the country's unification, thus later than in many other Asian countries (Tran Thi Ut and Kajisa 2006). Among other measures, pesticides and chemical fertilisers achieved strong productivity gains while also leading to growing production costs, structural dependencies and unwanted side effects both in terms of human health and the environment (Carvalho 2006; Scott et al. 2009; Fortier and Tran Thi Thu Trang 2013). Moreover, land use conversions related to urban sprawl as well as small farm sizes have resulted in pressure on the environment, productivity of land and farmers (Fortier and Tran Thi Thu Trang 2013). In numerical terms, agriculture has seen a 10 per cent annual increase in the use of chemical fertilisers between 1976 and 2009 (Fortier and Tran Thi Thu Trang 2013, 84). The excessive application of agrochemicals is said to have spiked since the liberalisation of the agrochemical input market in the late 1980s and continues to be maintained in part by illegal imports of now forbidden substances (Pham Van Hoi 2010; Tran Thi Thu Trang 2012). Related food safety crises linked to high agrochemical residues in produce have occurred since the 1990s (Nguyen Thi Hoan and Mergenthaler 2005; Simmons and Scott 2007; Scott et al. 2009). Some view the over-application of chemicals in agriculture as a coping mechanism for Vietnamese small-scale farmers who attempt to increase outcomes and profits to ensure viability in the face of land concentration, class differentiation processes and economic pressures related to industrial agriculture (Tran Thi Thu Trang 2012; Fortier and Tran Thi Thu Trang 2013). In a similar vein, the establishment of 'safe' food labels, as is described below, has been identified as market- and demand-oriented, rather than focusing on issues of farmers' subsistence or food sovereignty (Scott et al. 2009, 72). Government attempts to regulate and restrict agricultural inputs have included the ban of certain agrochemical substances as well as the governmental establishment of a 'safe' food label in the 1990s guaranteeing controlled use of agrochemicals. Yet little profitability for farmers meant a low market share of 'safe' vegetables, and the absence of consequences for producers in cases of non-compliance led to scepticism among consumers

(Moustier et al. 2006). As a result, the programme was discontinued after 2001 (Moustier et al. 2006) and succeeded by VietGAP, the Vietnamese version of a globally prevalent standard of 'good agricultural practice' under governmental decree[2] (Nicetic et al. 2010). Whereas VietGAP products are sold in supermarkets, many supermarket chains also offer their own 'safe' food labels (Moustier et al. 2010). Generally, all vegetables sold in modern retail outlets require a certification that they conform to the government's safe vegetable production guidelines (Wertheim-Heck et al. 2015, 98).

The described transformations in Vietnam's food system are further embedded in and structured by governmental modernisation and for-malisation approaches. In terms of food production and the organisation of agriculture, the Vietnamese government shares the paradigm of the Green Revolution that growing populations can only be fed through agri-cultural intensification (Fortier and Tran Thi Thu Trang 2013, 88). In line with this, the government's 2017–2020 agricultural restructuring plan aims for large-scale production areas and a decrease of the labour proportion in the agricultural sector (MARD 2017). Modernisation and formalisation attempts also structure the food retail system through supermarket expansion and the reorganisation and reduction of often informal wet markets (Wertheim-Heck et al. 2015) which targets safer food provisioning through the role of supermarkets in private safety man-agement systems and hygiene standards (Wertheim-Heck 2015, 4). Relatedly, on the consumption side, governmental modernisation efforts include the promotion of food shopping in supermarkets and in particu-lar of VietGAP products (Nicetic et al. 2010) as opposed to wet market shopping.

Overall, as recent decades have seen transformations in the economic and agricultural system as well as in the societal structure, availability of and access to food offerings has undergone enormous change and diver-sification. Within the described plethora of food supply options—some established, some of a more recent nature—people manoeuvre their way to their personal consumption decisions and habits, a task that is aggra-vated by concerns regarding the safety of food. It is in this setting of 'distanciation', differentiation and scepticism that a newly emerging niche market for organic food has emerged, a niche that is indicative of broader developments not only within the country's food environment but also of societal concerns around food as will be elaborated in the course of this chapter.

Consumer Discourse in Vietnam

In order to comprehend the trajectories of the organic sector and the perspectives of organic food consumers in contemporary urban Vietnam, discursive changes in terms of corporatisation and consumption in the country's recent past prove to be illuminating. In the transition from pre-reform central planning to post-*Đổi Mới* liberalisation, the country has seen a marketisation and globalisation of its economy which has been intertwined with the emergence of what could be referred to as neoliberal logics (Nguyen-vo Thu-huong 2008, xi). In keeping it with Schwenkel and Leshkowich (2012), neoliberalism in this chapter is not understood as a uniform project but rather as a "globally diverse set of technical practices, institutions, modes of power, and governing strategies … that continually work to reframe and at times reconfirm neoliberal technologies of mass consumption, acquisition of wealth, moral propriety, regimes of value, and systems of accountability" (Schwenkel and Leshkowich 2012, 380f.). Acknowledging the historical and cultural particularities of such institutions and strategies (Schwenkel and Leshkowich 2012, 380) also allows us to look for neoliberal logics within an officially socialist one-party state. Part of neoliberal ideologies emerging in the globally connected market in Vietnam have been discourses on free trade, privatisation as well as freedom of choice (Nguyen-vo Thu-huong 2008, xiii; Schwenkel and Leshkowich 2012, 382). Meanwhile, a generalised understanding of post-*Đổi Mới* Vietnam as following a 'neoliberal' blueprint based on the model of Global North societies can be contested on various grounds: within a market economy with a socialist orientation, the Vietnamese state has remained politically and economically all-encompassing, as well as the biggest stakeholder in the Vietnamese economy (Nguyen-vo Thu-huong 2008, xix). More generally, neoliberal practices intersect with and at times contradict continuing socialist political visions and illiberal practices (see Gainsborough 2010; Schwenkel and Leshkowich 2012).

Thus, increasingly prevalent notions of private, individualised choice and self-interest exist alongside a strong state that continues to govern self-interests from the distance, which has been coined as "socialism from afar" (Ong and Zhang 2008, 3, for the case of China).

Since market liberalisation, discourse on consumption in Vietnam has seen a vigorous turn from governmental condemnation of conspicuous consumption as a threatening form of capitalist imperialism (Vann 2005, 468) towards an insistence on the neoliberal liberty of choice for individuals in their role as consumers or entrepreneurs (Nguyen-vo Thu-huong 2008, xiii). Thus newly 'discovered' consumers now find themselves in the position to choose from diversified markets with the corporate promotion of modern consumption (Ehlert 2016). The notion of consumer choice in turn also includes a moral imperative of making the 'right' choice (Parsons 2015). Thus as responsible neoliberal citizen, the individual is expected to be in charge of his or her well-being and health, a discourse referred to as 'responsible individualism' (Parsons 2015, 1). This is of particular interest for this chapter in the field of food and questions of the responsibility of healthy and safe food choices.

As has been noted, these neoliberal tendencies among trajectories of corporatisation and responsible individualism are embedded in at-times conflictive state powers, thus Vann (2005) speaks of "incomplete neoliberal projects" (Vann 2005, 484). As such, contemporary Vietnam evinces a plurality of governing and economic logics of which neoliberal ideologies are one component (Schwenkel and Leshkowich 2012), producing its own kinds of particularities, dynamics and challenges between state, emerging markets and consumers.

Development of Organic Sectors in Global and Local Contexts

Before diving into the specific developments and synergies of the organic sector in Vietnam, a look at organic in global contexts will establish background information against which to understand the specifics of Vietnam's situation.

Organic in Global Contexts: A Brief Overview

Organic food production in the broadest sense entails a mode of farming based on the principles of health, ecology, fairness and care (IFOAM 2005). As an integrated farming approach, it aims to maintain the vitality of plants, soils, animals and human health and make use of on-farm and local resources (Vogl et al. 2005, 6; Scott et al. 2009, 63). Explicit organic farming ideas emerged in the early twentieth century in the Global North as a critique of the effects of petrochemical agricultural inputs on the environment as well as human health (Scott et al. 2009, 63). Throughout the twentieth century, organic farmers in many countries began to organise themselves through associations, within which organic standards were agreed upon democratically (Vogl et al. 2005, 9). The certification of organic products then was a response to growing citizen interest in organic food in the 1960s and 1970s (Scott et al. 2009, 63). The early emergence of organic markets and consumer interest in organic food in the Global North were often related to broader environmental movements concerned with eco-central societal transformations towards sustainability and systemic change (Barendregt and Jaffe 2014, 5). For instance, the USA of the 1960s witnessed an organic food movement striving for small-scale food production, ecological responsibility and community engagement (Johnston et al. 2009, 510). In Western Europe, organic consumption gained considerable momentum as part of a wider environmental movement against the ecological impacts of industrialised food systems in the 1970s, itself originating in anti-establishment student uprisings (Poulain 2017, 66). While eating organic in these contexts was often embedded in environmental activism and attempts to establish an alternative to the conventional food system, large parts of the organic sector in North America and Europe have transformed into what Johnston et al. (2009) have termed the 'corporate-organic foodscape'. The term refers to the institutionalisation and corporatisation of organic agriculture, resulting in often large-scale industrial organic farms and their integration into global commodity chains (Raynolds 2004). This integration of organic farming into corporate and globe-spanning food systems and commercial consumption since the 1990s (Johnston et al. 2009) was in line with wider global trends emphasising consumerism and individual responsibilisation of health and food choices (Parsons 2015; see Ehlert and Faltmann, this volume). As organic farming is considered an alternative to the agricultural model of the Green Revolution (Vogl et al. 2005, 6), critics point out that this corporatisation, institutionalisation and the global transport of organic goods stands in contrast to the social, ecological and anti-institutional ideals of the original organic movements (Goodman and Goodman 2001; Guthman 2004).

The transformations in the organic sector are also reflected in the history of organic standards: while associations of organic farmers in many world regions followed their own private standards until the 1990s, organic agriculture has since then seen increasing standardisation and regulation (Vogl et al. 2005). Thus nowadays, organic can comprise a range of practices: small-scale farming without synthetic inputs following organic principles potentially without explicitly being termed organic, often referred to as 'organic by default' (Vogl et al. 2005, 10) or various forms of certified organic agriculture following specific guidelines (Simmons and Scott 2008, 3f). The latter can be differentiated between internally carried out certification processes[3] or external certification by authorised bodies. Such authorising bodies can be state-centred,[4] or private third-party certification bodies (Boström and Klintman 2006). This formalisation of organic agricultural practices, intended for consumer and producer protection and the regulation of trade (Vogl et al. 2005), at the same time poses financial and bureaucratic burdens for farmers through cost-intensive certification processes which have to be renewed periodically (Johnston et al. 2009). Moreover, with the development of certified organic farming being rooted in the Global North, structural imbalances in global organic supply chains between Global North retailers and suppliers on the one and Global South producers on the other hand are problematised as much as the question of appropriateness of organic standards developed in the Global North for ecological conditions in the Global South (Scott et al. 2009, 68).

Nowadays, in many countries of the Global North one can find organic food on the shelves of transnational supermarket chains as well as in less institutionalised and rather bottom-up forms such as Community-Supported Agriculture (CSA) or self-organised food cooperatives

(Johnston et al. 2009). The range of organic offers is also reflected in the clientele whose spectrum ranges from individualised middle-class organic lifestyles often interwoven with means of distinction (Barendregt and Jaffe 2014) to more politicised and collective forms of alternative food initiatives (see Hassanein 2003; Little et al. 2010; Oliveri 2015). Thus, while the described early organic niches were associated with social movements concerned with environmental sustainability, this ethicopolitical factor has not been obtained in all cases. Even more, the market logic behind the idea of contributing to environmentalism through consumption inherently contrasts the mentioned more radical environmentalist approaches to systemic change in the 1960s and 1970s (Barendregt and Jaffe 2014, 5f). Nontheless, the perception of organic farming as environmentally friendly still constitutes a major motivation for organic consumption (Seyfang 2006; MacKendrick 2014). Despite the increasing industrialisation, corporatisation and depoliticisation of large segments of Global North organic sectors, governments and organisations from the Global North often justify their support and establishment of organic initiatives abroad with ethical ideas of environmental sustainability and climate change mitigation -as is the case in Vietnam.

Foreign Influences Behind Vietnam's Organic Development

Whereas the export of organic products from Vietnam to markets with strong purchasing power (such as Europe and the USA) has been in existence since the 1990s (APEC 2008), organic production for the domestic market is rather new and still scarce. Organically certified exports include commodities ranging from tea and coffee to rice, shrimp and fish, and make up around 90 per cent of organic production in the country (Simmons and Scott 2008, 2ff). Often with a particular emphasis on low costs of labour and production, (foreign) corporate interest in the export of organic agricultural products from Vietnam is on the rise (see Biz Hub 2016; Viet Nam News 2017a).

Pioneering in the field of organic farming for a Vietnamese market was CIDSE, an umbrella organisation of Catholic development agencies, which supported the launch of the first organic production project in 1998 (APEC 2008). In the following year and with some funding from international NGOs, the private company Hanoi Organics of two Vietnamese and a Dutch person began linking organic producers in the outskirts of the capital with Hanoian consumers (IFOAM 2003; APEC 2008). Between the enterprise's initiation and the lapse of certification due to financial difficulties in 2004, 'Hanoi Organics' was certified by 'Organic Agricultural Certification Thailand' (Moustier et al. 2006, 301). Between 2005 and 2010 a project by the Danish NGO 'Agricultural Development Denmark Asia' (ADDA) in cooperation with the 'Vietnam National Farmer's Union' (VNFU), funded by the 'Danish International Development Agency' (DANIDA), also aimed for the production and promotion of organic agriculture in Vietnam and developed an internal certification system (APEC 2008; Nguyen Sy Linh 2010, 128; Whitney et al. 2014). A further actor is the Belgian NGO 'Rikolto' (formerly VECO) that carries out activities that promote sustainable agriculture in Vietnam through projects with farmers as well as the initiation of an online platform 'Safe & Organic Food Finder' in Hanoi (VECO 2016). Meanwhile, organic production for export markets in many cases enjoys foreign support, such as in the case of an organic tea project in the early 2000s in Northern Vietnam, funded by the New Zealand government, which aimed for poverty reduction among the participating smallholders (APEC 2008). Moreover, there exist different organic shrimp projects in Ca Mau Province which were assisted by the German Federal Ministry of Environment, Nature Conservation and Nuclear Safety and by the Netherland Development Organisation, projects whose support is justified with their environmental benefits, developmental capacities and climate change mitigation potential (Omoto 2012; Brunner 2014; Viet Nam News 2014; Baumgartner and Tuan Hoang Nguyen 2017).

Such initiatives reflect larger paradigm shifts in the dissemination of agricultural models by Global North donors whose promotion of sustainable farming has at times replaced former support for Green Revolution agriculture in the name of productivity gains (Conway and Barbier 1990).

Such shifts have also been observed on a corporate level: whereas agricultural inputs in line with the Green Revolution have a history of strong corporate support, the significant involvement of corporate—particularly supermarket—interest in the purchase of organic products is a more recent phenomenon and one that enhances corporate structural power within the organic segment and its commodification (Scott et al. 2009, 85).

In sum, many initiatives involved in the development of the organic sector in Vietnam are foreign-led. Organic initiatives by foreign NGOs and development agencies often have an explicit emphasis on the environmental benefits and developmental mights of organic farming. Operating modes vary as some organic initiatives establish rural-urban producer-consumer links, thus focusing on organic food within the domestic context whereas other Global North-led projects establish certified organic production for export markets, thus bearing the implicit element of international market development. Moreover, Vietnam increasingly attracts corporate interests to produce organic products for export markets. At the same time governmental support for an organic sector for the Vietnamese market has been peripheral in the past, as will be discussed now.

Vietnamese Perspectives on Organic Agriculture

As regards the Vietnamese government, written national organic standards were introduced in 2007 (Scott et al. 2009, 72), yet no regulation on organic production and trade is in place (Nguyen Sy Linh 2010, 128). With respect to certification, there is neither a domestic third-party certification organisation (Ngo Doan Dam n.d., 1; Moustier et al. 2006, 300) nor are there governmental plans to initiate a national organic certification body (interview with staff of Ministry of Agriculture and Rural Development (MARD), 10/2016). Thus, if desired, certification needs to be sought from abroad, making the process lengthy as well as costly and not accessible for small-scale production. Unlike, for example, in neighbouring Thailand where the national government plays an active role not only in the promotion but also the certification of organic agriculture, Vietnam's organic sector is predominantly driven by the private sector and foreign NGOs, as well as by some government-affiliated organs such as the Farmer's Union and local government authorities (Scott et al. 2009, 82). The question of driving forces behind organic sectors also reflects in civil society[5] involvement and public discourses about organic food and its production. The wider spectrum of actors such as within alternative agriculture movements both in Thailand and in Indonesia have resulted in debates around corporate control of the organic sector in these countries (Scott et al. 2009, 84). In Thailand there is an established local food sovereignty initiative which utilises organic farming and local marketing also as a means of resistance against structural dependencies and ecological destruction as a consequence of industrialised agriculture (Heis 2015). In Vietnam, where the organic sector is mostly shaped by corporate and foreign influences and according to the logic of the market, such critiques of corporate control or the establishment of grassroots organisations striving for food sovereignty are weak or non-existent (Scott et al. 2009). Despite issues of environmental pollution (see Pham Binh Quyen et al. 1995; Pham Thi Anh et al. 2010) and even though the effects of climate change on agriculture are beginning to be noticeable (Fortier and Tran Thi Thu Trang 2013), widely formalised environmental movements—of which organic advocacy could be an element—have not been established in Vietnam. Of course, this must also be seen in the socio-political context of tightly controlled formal civil society organisations (Wells-Dang 2014). While civil society action against environmental pollution certainly exists (see Tran Tu Van Anh 2017), an occurrence in 2016 made obvious the often restricted space for organised politicised expression of opinion. After a mass of fish dying on Vietnam's central coast related to a Taiwanese steel factory and people in major cities going to the streets against the slow government response towards this pollution scandal, the initiating protests were suppressed (Radio Free Asia 2016).

Meanwhile, there could be a change in direction in the attention organic farming is receiving from the government: at an international forum on organic agriculture in Vietnam in 2017—co-organised by MARD—Prime Minister Nguyễn Xuân Phúc presented the increasing demand for organic products as a chance for development of organic farming in the country. Phúc thus called for the adoption of global organic standards in Vietnam, seeing the target groups among high-income domestic groups as well as in global organic markets. At the same event the Minister of Agriculture and Rural Development pointed out that few Vietnamese businesses were internationally certified organic, increasing mistrust towards their organic products (Saigon Times 2017; Vietnam Economic News 2017; Viet Nam News 2017b). Moreover, the country's newest agricultural restructuring plan—besides mentioning large-scale production and labour productivity increase—now includes the encouragement of clean and organic agriculture (MARD 2017). Thus while such calls for organic farming are new on the side of the Vietnamese government, food safety and health (Scott et al. 2009, 84ff) as well as the promotion of VietGAP standards and the country's overall modernisation, industrialisation and intensive farming for food security remain the overall aim (see Gorman, this volume).

In the Vietnamese discussion on the organic food sector, a clear definition or protected terminology is often missing. Media articles frequently use the terms 'organic food' (*thực phẩm hữu cơ*) and 'safe food' (*thực phẩm an toàn*) interchangeably (Simmons and Scott 2008, 4), a confusion that, coupled with the novelty of marketed organic food, impacts consumers' perceptions of the concepts as well (Moustier et al. 2006, 300; Simmons and Scott 2008, 4). During the student workshop conducted in the course of research for this chapter, the terms 'safe' and 'organic' food were also discussed interchangeably by the Vietnamese students and without differentiation of the particularities in production (field notes, 08/2017). Such differentiation is essential though, since the requirements for organic farming forbid the use of chemical inputs altogether whereas in farming for marketed 'safe' vegetable production such as VietGAP, the moderate use of certain chemicals and fertilisers is permitted (Simmons and Scott 2007, 23). Despite this difference, the promotion and sale of products as 'organic' while originating from so-called safe food production has at times been observed[6] (Moustier et al. 2006; field notes, 11/2015). Regarding financial accessibility, the prices for organic products in Vietnam are substantially, at times in multiples, above the market average of comparable non-organic products (Tran Tri Dung and Pham Hoang Ngan 2012, 1). One reason for the very limited domestic market for organic products (Scott et al. 2009, 72) could lie in this premium price for organic food, whereas another inhibition could lie in the low, yet rising, share of organic agriculture among Vietnam's total agricultural land.[7] Besides the growing but small externally certified organic production, there are only a few internally certified initiatives which link farmers with Vietnamese consumers, concentrated mostly around Hanoi (PGS IFOAM, n.d.).

In line with the weak ties to civil society and (thus far) low governmental attention, Vietnam's organic sector leads a niche existence, yet it is gaining momentum. Thus, if the newest governmental statements mark a paradigm shift towards growing support for alternative agricultural systems or are merely lip service remains to be seen. With all this in mind, what does the organic niche market look like in urban Vietnam and how does it relate to or contrast with prevailing consumer paradigms and the motives of foreign and domestic support for Vietnam's organic sector?

HCMC's Organic Food Sphere

In HCMC, the attentive observer will first notice the corner shops with green signs advertising 'organic' food scattered across the city, or more precisely across certain districts. Moreover, a major street in the city centre hosts a large organic store selling a variety of imported organic products, predominantly from Germany, as well as produce that is not actually organic but VietGAP certified (field notes, 08/2017). Yet organic consumption opportunities do not end there. Besides the array of shops, there exists a range of organic delivery services, artisanal cosmetic brands and air-conditioned organic juice-shops, offering their services in the more wealthy districts of the city or advertising them at events and on social media. A range of occasional markets enabling consumers to purchase food directly from farmers or from small businesses have become increasingly popular. Among signposted organic produce on offer in HCMC, *certified* organic production is the exception to the rule. At the time of research, there were three shops offering organically certified fruits and vegetables of Vietnamese origin in HCMC, whereas other enterprises labelled 'organic' follow organic production without certification and yet others sell certified 'safe' rather than 'organic' produce (field notes, 2015–2017; online research, 02/2017). Moreover, some of the enterprises have a short half-life with many having disappeared within the three years of field research. Organic food production in a broader sense also extends into homes and event venues: small plots of land can be rented in a private urban garden area doubling as vegetable fields, leisure venue and setting for nature education courses for children (Word Vietnam 2016; field notes, 07/2016). Also less spacious options for chemically untreated food are being utilised by many urban inhabitants in the form of smallest-scale home cultivation of sprouts, herbs or vegetables (see Kurfürst, this volume). Such practices of vegetable cultivation (at home or on a rented plot) could be subsumed under organic food consumption and at times are viewed as such. Yet this chapter examines organic consumption in a more narrow sense in outlets which specifically market organic products. In such corporate settings where citizens manoeuvre as consumers, trust and knowledgeability are negotiated very differently than in (semi-)private settings. Thus, what drives people to opt for organic food in their shopping will be explored next.

Organic Food Consumption in HCMC

Moving from the structural aspects and macro-level actors within Vietnam's organic sector to the perceptions and agency of individuals, this section zooms in on consumers of organic food in HCMC. The aim of the analysis of empirical data on organic food consumption is to compare and contrast the narratives of the interviewees with the structures and trajectories of the country's (organic) food system as it exists today.

Before going into the underlying motivations of customers and entrepreneurs of organic food, these will be briefly portrayed. The basis for the portrayal are 13 interviews with customers of an organic shop in the city centre, as well as 2 interviews with organic entrepreneurs. One of the entrepreneurs, whom I will refer to as Hoa,[8] is the owner and founder of a number of organic shops—one of which was a site for the customer interviews—that sell organic produce from affiliated farms within Vietnam as well as certified imported organic goods. At the time of the interviews, the farms were in the process of becoming certified as some of the first for the Vietnamese market. The other entrepreneur, Minh, is the founder of a service delivering uncertified organically produced fruits and vegetables from his farm to customers in the city centre.

All but one of the interviewees were women, a gender imbalance that complied with general observations in food outlets, whether organic shops, markets, or supermarkets in the city. Although increasing participation of men in food shopping has generally been observed, especially in more aspirational urban lifestyle places such as supermarkets, food shopping is still often considered a predominantly female task (Wertheim-Heck and Spaargaren 2016). On closer examination many of the female customers also turned out to be mothers or other caretakers of young children—a characterisation shared by the founder of the organic delivery service: Minh estimated that 95 per cent of his customers were mothers of babies, feeding organic produce to their children while often not consuming organic themselves (Interview, 10/2015). Age-wise the interviewed customers ranged from early 20s to mid-60s, with mothers in their 30s most strongly represented. Except for one older lady, the interviewees were all in employment or university students, an observation very much in line with the advice of the shop's staff for the author to come after 5 p.m. in order to encounter respondents after office closing hours. Most interviewees were either in the process of acquiring higher education degrees or working in occupations requiring such, indicating a high level of education among the respondents. The often exceptionally high English skills of many of the customers—half of whom preferred to lead the interviews in English[9]—furthermore hinted at a potentially private education and/or an international work environment. When asked to portray the company's customer base, one of the organic entrepreneurs described managers or business owners, having middle to high incomes, with high being estimated at USD 1000 per capita and month. Yet, people with lower incomes were not ruled out as potential customers: "Low income means it's around USD 500 per month, it's okay. But if you just can earn USD 50 or 100 per month it's difficult [to buy organic]" (Interview, 10/2015). Compared to Vietnamese average incomes,[10] the estimated 'low' monthly income of USD 500 would still position the customers of this business well above the national average.

The common view that consumers of organic food necessarily have high incomes was challenged by the other interviewed entrepreneur who did not see income as the major factor among organic customers:

> Mostly many people think that the rich people have money to buy organic products. But I think it's not good based on, you know, I think many people, many customers they are still young. Students and young people. I think that they are not rich people but they still pay for organic products because they care about their health, their family health, future also …. But mostly people are medium, I mean average income. (Interview 01/2016)

Besides the income aspect the quote addresses a number of crucial aspects of organic food consumption, with the portrayal of consumers not only as young and often educated but also united in their concern for health, an observation that will be contextualised further on. While far from being a homogenous group, many of the interviewed customers did share certain characteristics in terms of gender, education, income as well as their motivations for organic consumption.

Organic Consumption for Environmental Concerns?

As elaborated previously, environmental considerations as well as concerns for the well-being of farmers or the future of the agricultural system were and are often part of the motivation for organic consumption elsewhere. Some of the (limited) existing research on the consumer side of organic food in Vietnam has also pointed out environmental concerns as one of a range of reasons for organic consumption (Ho Thi Diep Quynh Chau 2015; VECO 2016). Yet when asked about their motives for organic consumption, such environmental concerns were not brought up independently as a reason for choosing organic by any of the costumers interviewed by the author. Interestingly, a baseline study among vegetable consumers in Hanoi carried out came up with contrasting results. According to the survey, the main reasons for buying safe or organic vegetables were health (91 per cent) and environmental protection (38 per cent), followed by better taste (20.5 per cent) (VECO 2016, 2).[11] Whereas health in this survey emerged as the leading priority, which will be discussed later on, it is striking that one third of the survey respondents stated environmental concerns as a motivation for organic consumption whereas this aspect was not brought up once by the interviewees of the authors' research. The difference is even more remarkable as the interviewee demographic of both research projects was similar, comprising mostly female, middle to high income, respondents (VECO 2016, 1). A quantitative survey among consumers in different food outlets in HCMC also showed a relation between environmental concern and the intention to purchase organic food (Ho Thi Diep Quynh Chau 2015). Here, contrasting the methodologies of quantitative and qualitative research has explanatory potential: in the case of the baseline study a structured questionnaire provided predetermined answers, stating environmental protection as one potential reason for organic consumption, while the qualitative open-ended questions underlying this research did not offer such predetermined response categories. Expecting and assuming that environmental concerns are a motive to purchase organic food might be a predetermined notion shaped by a Global North conception of organic consumption which potentially diverges from the Vietnamese context. Hence, the open-ended character of the interviews for this study allowed for exploring the interviewees' subjective sense of and views on organic consumption of their own accord, potentially diverging from the researcher's personal associations with and knowledge of organic farming.

The semi-structured interviews underlying this chapter also asked if consumers paid attention to the food's origin when buying organic. In the cases in which origin was stated to be of importance at all, it was referred to in terms of product safety or international food standards in the countries of origin. Meanwhile, the issue of carbon footprints related to potentially long transport distances was not mentioned as a reason to pay attention to origin. While the reduction of environmental impact through 'local' consumption is often a component in organic consumption (see Brown et al. 2009), food miles were not an aspect that was expressed by any of the interviewed consumers.

As vegetables and, to a lesser degree, fruits—which happened to be from organically managed farms within Vietnam—were among the most purchased goods among the interviewees, the factor of food miles might simply not have been of any personal relevance here. At the same time, the origin of the mainly imported processed goods on offer, for which the question of environmental costs of transportation would apply, was also not brought up by the interviewees.

Entrepreneur Hoa stressed having consumer education on sustainable agricultural development and the environmental benefits of organic agriculture on her agenda, which unearthed a discrepancy between the entrepreneur's assessment of her customers' environmental aspirations and the views the customers themselves voiced. While Hoa assumed that her customers "think that if they buy organic they can contribute to agricultural development in Vietnam" (01/2016), such a motive was not named once by her customers.

The absence of environmental concerns in the motivations of organic customers not only marks a contrast to the narrative of the Vietnamese organic entrepreneurs. It also differs from the motives behind early organic niche markets in the Global North which—as elaborated before—have been intertwined with environmental citizen movements. Moreover, the customers' non-priority of environmental protection contrasts the foreign supporters of organic development in Vietnam who proclaim environmental benefits at the core of their support.

Health & Food Safety

Health concerns appeared as a central topic among the interviewed consumers with their own health as well as that of their families being stated as the number one reason to purchase organic. The main fear here was of the long-term effects from consuming chemically contaminated food, mostly vegetables and meat, resulting in cancer as one customer expressed:

> I think organic food is very good for your health, sort of you can protect, avoid the cancer. So the organic food they don't use too much chemicals so they are very good. (Interview, 10/2015)

To avoid chemically contaminated food, consumers would resort to organic products in the knowledge that chemical inputs were not utilised. Besides the general thematisation of chemical usage in farming, the widespread narrative of farmers spraying produce with certain chemicals that would make them grow unnaturally fast was also taken up by some of the interviewees. Thanh, 64 years old and regular customer at the shop, refers to this practice of growth acceleration: "I have a relative in the countryside, he told me that each two to three days people harvest chili, so horrible" (Interview, 10/2015). Organic vegetables on the other hand were believed to be grown slower and without such chemical enhancers. Besides the application of chemicals in farming, concerns regarding growth hormones in meat were also frequently voiced. Here a university student, shopping vegetables for her family, explained why she has been restricting her meat consumption:

> Because I know it's not good to eat because they have poison in the meat. It means that instead if you raise a pig or a buffalo you need about six months to grow it ... and now usually they're just three months I think and a few weeks before they sell for the meat company they will get food that helped the pig grow fast in two weeks. (Interview, 10/2015)

Generally, the interviews coincide with existing research stating an increasing demand for organic produce in Vietnam, especially for health reasons and among people with higher incomes (Moustier et al. 2006; Thien T. Truong et al. 2012). The centrality of the health factor in organic consumption in turn must be put in relation to the overall food safety situation in current Vietnam in which the fear of unsafe, health-damaging substances in food is very prevalent. Especially in urban settings where people rely on external and anonymous food supplies, the complexity and anonymity of the food chain is often cause for concern. Anxieties over the safety of food mainly focus on high agrochemical residues in vegetables (Moustier et al. 2006, 297; Mergenthaler et al. 2009a, 267; Pham Van Hoi 2010, 3) and antibiotic remnants in meat (Figuié and Moustier 2009, 213)—the same concerns that were also voiced in the interviews with the customers. Practices of fraud such as the selling of counterfeit and sub-standard products are another source of insecurity over unsafe food (Figuié and Bricas 2010, 181). Products with a particularly critical reputation are foods of Chinese origin (Mergenthaler et al. 2009b, 429) as they are said to be the target of overly chemical treatment and preservation as well as substandard controls (see Zhang, this volume).

Besides concerns over the quality of products, the interviewees' concerns also related to questions of food hygiene in certain outlets. In general debates, food hygiene concerns in Vietnam predominantly concern street food or large-scale canteens, for example, in factories, some of which have been reported to produce cases of mass food poisoning (Viet Nam News 2016). While questions of hygiene of pre-cooked meals is less related to the purchase of organic foods for home-cooking, said concerns regarding certain food outlets did come up in the interviews in the context of food avoidance, proving to be of relevance for the customers.

The purchase of organic food was generally seen as the safe alternative to unsafe food. Meanwhile, customers' explanations of organic farming varied widely, ranging from detailed knowledge about organic standards and practices to the more common description of organic farmers not using chemicals. In this regard, the internet was often named as the source of information on organic agriculture, yet the press as well as social media and friends played a role as information sources as well. It was also the recommendation of friends or internet research that led many of the customers to this specific shop, whereas others encountered it by chance. This customer, who is an employee at a bank and a mother of two children aged one and five, frequents the shop as the owner is her friend, whose information on organic farming she seems to trust:

> The quality of these vegetables, when they grow, until they collect the vegetables in the field they control the quality from the company. And I know about it, because my friend [shop owner] told me personally. (Interview, 10/2015)

Others stressed that they could not be sure if the shop's food was actually safe or not, yet believed in it "based on a feeling" (Interview, 10/2015). The element of uncertainty arose in a number of the interviews and was at times met with trial and error as Thanh describes:

> We had food here several times as a trial. And then we stopped in short time because the food was so expensive, and we bought food in normal market for [a] meal … but we had [food] poison[ing]. Finally we use food faithfully in this shop …. I believe because no shop I can trust in like this shop. (Interview, 10/2015)

In this case it is not a general belief in the quality of organic food but trust in this very specific shop after trial and error and comparing it with another organic store which she found out to be better in advertisements than in reality.

Pivotal Moments Towards Organic Consumption: The Centrality of Responsibility

In addition to a general awareness of and anxieties towards food safety issues which could lead to the wish to consume organic food, some of the interviewees reported events that can be understood as pivotal moments or turning points towards organic consumption. For many of the interviewed mothers as well as for others in familial care-taking roles, this pivotal moment was the responsibility for small children. The wish to provide harmless and healthy food to the children was often expressed: "Sometimes I go to another organic shop to buy the same food [as in this shop] because now I have a child. My son is six months. Today is the first day of his weaning." As Bich, regular customer, university lecturer and mother of two young children indicates here, the stop at the organic shop constitutes a task often in addition to regular grocery shopping which is done elsewhere. Moreover, opting for organic food on the first day of weaning suggests the importance put on the high food quality intended for the child from the very first bite. Thanh, who was accompanied by her four-year old grandson, depicted the interlaced events of expecting a baby in the family with a case of food poisoning, leading the whole family to change their consumption habits:

> When my daughter was pregnant, I bought green cauliflower and water spinach and string bean, my daughter had these foods, and had [food] poison[ing]. So we decided that we just use the amount of food we can buy here, depending on our money. (Interview, 10/2015)

Regarding organic food for children it was noticeable that oftentimes due to financial reasons kids would be the only recipients of organic food in a household. "Because it's high quality vegetables it's also quite expensive. So just for my children" (Interview, 10/2015), Bich explains.

Concomitantly, the choice of products in such contexts was often very selective, limited predominantly to vegetables and fruits for the children.

Going the extra length financially and by adding to the regular shopping routine in order to provide the family's children with the perceived safest food not only indicates the weight that is put onto the children's health. It also hints at a form of responsibilisation in which it is the task of the individual to protect the health of those unable to exercise choice by themselves, namely children.

The role of responsibility for the family's health as a pivotal moment was not limited to the interviewed shoppers but also voiced by the organic entrepreneurs. Minh, founder of the organic delivery service started farming based on organic principles on family land in order to provide himself, his family and friends with healthy food: "Because I care [for] my health and [for] my family's health. And I think some of my friends they need my products" (Interview, 10/2015), a decision that later evolved into a business. Organic entrepreneur Hoa explicitly described expecting a baby as the pivotal moment that drew her attention to the health aspects of eating:

> So before 2013 I was not concerned about what I eat, I don't care, I don't know about organic. But when I was pregnant in the first 3 months I was sick, sickness of pregnancy, so I did not eat anything except raw vegetables. So whenever my mom or my husband bought vegetables from outside to bring home we always need many things to clean it. Take time to clean it and people still worry about vegetable chemical effects [being] not good to my baby and my health. So I spent time on the internet to find out, to discover about safe food and organic. So I thought that organic is the highest safety standard in the world. (Interview, 01/2016)

For both entrepreneurs the concern for their family's health was said to have been the first reason to turn towards organic agriculture as a source of chemical-free and safe food, with the business idea having followed. In the case of the pregnancy, the general element of responsibility for the health of oneself and one's family is complemented with another layer of concern: the incorporation of unsafe food would not only harm oneself but also the well-being of the unborn baby.

Not only did the element of responsibility and care prove to be central for organic shopping, it also points towards a related aspect that was described earlier in the gender ratio of shoppers: the responsibility for the bodily integrity of the family's children through food consumption appears to be a gendered one. In the majority of cases it is not simply parents but specifically mothers or other female relatives who take on the responsibility of 'safe' shopping for the health of the children. Females have no less than the responsibility to protect their children's health through their shopping choices, or as Cairns et al. (2013) in their work on mothering the 'organic child' have put it: "the organic child ideal reflects neoliberal expectations about childhood and maternal social and environmental responsibility by emphasizing mothers' individual responsibility for securing children's futures" (Cairns et al. 2013, 97). These gendered notions of food work have been addressed elsewhere (see Beardsworth et al. 2002; Cairns et al. 2013; Ehlert, this volume) yet their centrality for organic consumption in Vietnam has not been addressed in prior research. As mentioned, food shopping in Vietnam remains a predominantly female task, yet labour division alone does not reveal how far this gendered responsibility stretches into the realms of family care.

Summarising Remarks: Organic Food Consumption as Individualised Responses to Food Safety Concerns

What the empirical data revealed is the widespread concerns around questions of food, its safety and overall health effects. Growing public discourse on health problems related to food increases pressure on individuals for the micro-management of themselves as well as everyday foodways (Parsons 2015, 80). This notion of responsible individualism reflected in the three empirical sections discussing questions of environmental concern, food safety and health as well as responsibility and care.

Environmental concerns do not appear to be of priority for consumers of organic food in Vietnam. Neither the environmental aspect of organic agriculture nor questions of food miles of imported organic products were raised by the customers. The critique of long transport routes within the corporate-organic foodscape as defeating the purpose of organic agriculture was not a topic of concern. Rather than regarding more abstract and distant concerns for the environment, the empirical data suggests that organic consumption in urban Vietnam is driven by more individualised concerns, namely for the integrity of people's health.

Health and food safety concerns that were at the core of the interviewees' motivation for purchasing organic food reflect deep insecurities in the arena of food more broadly. One can say that the topic of food safety in contemporary Vietnam is a contested field with manifold warnings and guidelines on sides of the government, the media as well as private enterprises. Fuelled by constant media coverage and social media debates (see Talk Vietnam 2016; VietNamNet 2016; Viet Nam News 2016), issues of food safety are ingrained into the public's awareness and result in people worrying for their bodily well-being in a seemingly unsafe environment. It is in this context that organic food consumption becomes an individualised attempt by urban consumers to respond to their food safety concerns by consuming what is perceived to be a safe and healthy food option. By being interlaced with food safety, explicitly organic food can be seen as one component in a wider trend also comprising 'safe' and hygienic foods that become increasingly common in Vietnam and more generally in Southeast Asia (Scott et al. 2009, 69).

Safety and health concerns became particularly prominent in relation to certain pivotal moments—either in terms of one's health or the care and responsibility for children's well-being. Under these circumstances, people's individual responsibility to choose harmless and healthy food was further emphasised, again pointing towards notions of the responsible consumer as well as the role of health concerns within organic food consumption. Moreover, responsible individualism and food safety concerns proved to be important drivers for the interviewed entrepreneurs, whose business ideas started from the quest for safe food for themselves and their families that could not be met by the existing food sphere.

Moreover, the interviews revealed certain patterns of trust negotiation, often through the personal element of friends' recommendations or by trial and error; customers did not blindly trust in organic but often rather relied on their social relations or their senses to assess the food's qualities. This can be seen in light of the at-times inflationary usage of the term organic within HCMC's foodscape as well as a mistrust towards food labels in Vietnam more generally that in turn relate back to topics of food safety (see Figuié et al., this volume).

Conclusion: Questions of Responsibilisation and Food Anxiety in Vietnam's Organic Sector

After zooming in on particularities of organic food consumption in HCMC, the conclusion now zooms out again to put the city's organic niche into the wider perspective of the discussed trajectories of Vietnam's organic sector more broadly. Working out the particularities of organic food shopping for urban consumers in HCMC has allowed for illustration of the differences in motivation between customers of the organic niche market in Vietnam and other world regions as well as between respective Vietnamese customers and (foreign) actors of organic initiatives in Vietnam. As discussed, the organic sector in Vietnam emerged under very different circumstances than in countries of the Global North, namely often with foreign (donor-funded) NGO and corporate involvement with respective agendas as well as in a context of a rapidly transforming food system characterised by a range of food safety concerns. As the empirical section has shown, individual motivations of consumers for buying organic generally differ widely from the official rationale of environmental protection behind foreign-financed organic initiatives as well as some of the domestic initiatives. Rather than relating their organic purchases to the environmental benefits of organic farming, customers' choices of organic food have proven to be deeply intertwined with concerns about the well-being of themselves and/or the ones they feed. This concern with individual health and physical integrity then must be put in the context of the current discourse around food safety in Vietnam and people's concomitant food anxieties.

With a governmental focus on food productivity, the organic sector leads a niche existence that only recently received increased attention from the state. Latest governmental statements indicate a clear corporate-oriented focus with the target of the organic sector catering to high-income groups within Vietnam as well as affluent export markets.

Meanwhile, the political climate of the one-party state towards (environmental) social movements and protests is not exactly favourable, which could be one factor for the organic sector being rather corporate-oriented and accommodating less critical voices and movements towards the corporate-organic foodscape than is the case in some other southeast Asian contexts (Scott et al. 2009).

Within the constellation of the state, the market and individuals that show neoliberal tendencies such as the responsibilisation of the individual alongside a strong socialist state, responsibilities and competencies are not always clear and create ambivalences and insecurities. As has been described for the case of China—which in this regard is not dissimilar from Vietnam—"[t]he breathless pace of market reforms has created a paradox in which the pursuit of private initiatives, private gains, and private lives coexists with political limits on individual expression" (Ong and Zhang 2008, 1). Similarly, agency of individuals in this system predominantly takes place within market logics and less so through civil society, a dynamic that was observable within Vietnam's organic sector as well. Agency being confined to the realms of the market further speaks to the initial mention of potential inequalities in regard to food. In light of HCMC's organic sphere—whose spatial concentration in high-income districts was described earlier—the socio-economic and educational background of organic customers seems neither surprising nor incidental. Organic food shopping for individual health and safety reasons is a shape of corporatised agency not available to wide masses of the current population—not only within HCMC but also nationwide with organic being an urban and high-priced phenomenon.[12]

Moreover, this chapter has shown how consumers manoeuvre between domestic food safety and consumer discourses, internationally acquirable information, and global discourses on environmentalism in regard to organic farming that is growing increasingly accessible in globalising Vietnam. The overlapping and at-times contradictory multitude of discourses and questions of responsibilisation constitute a source of anxiety—in terms of food safety but also concerning more general questions of who is in charge and trustworthy in the current food system.

Thus for a range of reasons, the future development of Vietnam's organic sector will continue to deserve academic attention. Particularly in light of the findings that among urban consumers of organic food, it was often trial and error or personal recommendations rather than an organic label that established trust in organic products, the question of the future of certification within the Vietnamese market arises. Others have already recommended small bottom-up food initiatives due to the importance of social relations, word of mouth advertisement as well as widespread mistrust towards governmental action on issues of sustainability and a certain reluctance to follow governmental regulations (de Koning et al. 2015, 617). Therefore, in the current food system of ambivalences, anxieties and conflicting interests, it remains to be seen what will happen to perceptions of organic food if the state implements the expressed plans of getting further involved in the country's organic sector.

Acknowledgements This research was made possible through funding of the Austrian Science Fund (FWF) as part of the research project 'A Body-Political Approach to the Study of Food – Vietnam and the Global Transformations' (P 27438). I would like to thank my colleagues Judith Ehlert, Carina Maier and Petra Dannecker for their valuable feedback on earlier drafts of this chapter. Moreover, I am grateful for the support of Hoa Lai in desk research and for the consistent help of Nguyen Thi Bao Hà as my interpreter.

Notes

1. 'Food system' here is understood very broadly as a system entailing the production, processing, packaging, distribution, retail and consumption of food (Ingram 2011).
2. GLOBALG.A.P. is a certification scheme and standard for 'good agricultural practice' in 80 countries which aims to reduce hazards in production, harvest and handling of produce. In Vietnam the Ministry of Agriculture and Rural Development (MARD) has authorised primarily private providers to certify compliance with VietGAP. The criteria of VietGAP are slightly lower than those of GLOBALG.A.P. (Nicetic et al. 2010).
3. An established form of internal certification are Participatory Guarantee Systems (PGS). PGS is an organic quality assurance system through social control, participation and knowledge building rather than through

third-party certification. Mostly used within local economies, PGS offers low-cost quality assurance which is often more viable for small-scale farmers than third-party organic certification which poses cost and bureaucratic barriers (IFOAM n.d.).

4. Examples for common governmental organic standards are the United States Department of Agriculture (USDA) National Organic Program, the Japanese Agricultural Standards and the EEC Regulation No. 2092/91 of the European Union (Scott et al. 2009, 76).

5. I am aware that 'civil society' is a controversial term in the context of Vietnam, as under an authoritarian regime there is limited space for political expression of civil society or social movements, partly as there are no registered civil society organisations which are completely autonomous from the Vietnamese state (Wells-Dang 2010, 2014). Yet if widening the gaze from legally registered NGOs to including more informal networks, one does find a range of civil society activities (Wells-Dang 2014).

6. If the phenomenon of advertising food as organic which does not adhere to organic standards goes back to a confusion of terminology, or is a problem of free riders, remains to be answered clearly and could be of interest for future research on organic provision in Vietnam.

7. Estimates on the share of certified organically managed agricultural land among Vietnam's total agricultural land vary. The Research Institute of Organic Agriculture (FiBL) survey 2008 estimated the share of organic agricultural land in Vietnam to be 0.2 per cent (Willer et al. 2008, 235) whereas the FiBL survey 2017 estimated the organic share to already make up 0.7 per cent (Willer and Lernoud 2017, 315). Others have estimated the share of organic agricultural land as high as 1 per cent (Nguyen Sy Linh 2010, 128). As the available figures are based on certified organic farming only, the overall share of land under organic cultivation might be much higher.

8. All interview partners mentioned in this research were anonymised.

9. The interviews in Vietnamese were conducted with the help of an interpreter and are quoted here in their English translation.

10. According to the General Statistics Office of Vietnam, the average urban per capita income in 2012 was around VND 2.9 million monthly, or almost USD 1700 yearly. Yet due to discrepancies between official and unofficial incomes, medium salaries in Vietnam are challenging to pinpoint and room for potential inaccuracy should be remembered (de Koning et al. 2015, 610).

11. Other survey-style research on the motivations of urban organic consumers in the region at times also came to the conclusion that the environmental friendliness of organic production was part of people's reason to buy organic, for instance in Bangkok (Roitner-Schobesberger et al. 2008) or Shanghai (Hasimu et al. 2017).
12. Issues of food safety in relation to social inequality in contemporary Vietnam constitute the main focus of the author's PhD research.

References

APEC, 2008. APEC regional development of organic agriculture in term of APEC food system and market access, APEC#209-AT-01.6.

Barendregt, B.A., Jaffe, R., 2014. The Paradoxes of Eco-Chic. In: Barendregt, B.A., Jaffe, R. (eds.). Green consumption: the global rise of eco-chic., London; New York: Bloomsbury Academic, 1–16.

Baumgartner, U., Tuan Hoang Nguyen, 2017. Organic certification for shrimp value chains in Ca Mau, Vietnam: a means for improvement or an end in itself? *Environment, Development and Sustainability* 19, 987–1002.

Beardsworth, A., Bryman, A., Keil, T., Goode, J., Haslam, C., Lancashire, E., 2002. Women, men and food: the significance of gender for nutritional attitudes and choices. *British Food Journal* 104, 470–491.

Bitter-Suermann, M., 2014. Food, modernity, and identity in Ho Chi Minh City, Vietnam. Dissertation, Saint Mary's University, Halifax, Nova Scotia.

Biz Hub, 2016. Fruit producer Vinamit get US, EU organic certification [WWW Document]. Việt Nam News. URL http://bizhub.vn/news/fruit-producer-vinamit-get-us-eu-organic-certification_282833.html (accessed 02.25.18).

Boström, M., Klintman, M., 2006. State-centered versus Nonstate-driven Organic Food Standardization: A Comparison of the US and Sweden. *Agriculture and Human Values* 23, 163–180.

Bricas, N., 1993. Les caractéristiques et l'évolution de la consommation alimentaire dans les villes africaines. In: Muchnik, J. (ed.). Alimentation, techniques et innovations dans les régions tropicales. Paris: L'Harmattan, 127–160.

Brown, E., Dury, S., Holdsworth, M., 2009. Motivations of consumers that use local, organic fruit and vegetable box schemes in Central England and Southern France. *Appetite* 53, 183–188.

Brunner, J., 2014. Organic shrimp certification: A new approach to PES. VNFF Newsletter No 2 Quarter II/2014. Vietnam Forest Protection and Development Fund, Hanoi, 7–11.

Cairns, K., Johnston, J., MacKendrick, N., 2013. Feeding the 'organic child': Mothering through ethical consumption. *Journal of Consumer Culture* 13, 97–118.

Carvalho, F.P., 2006. Agriculture, pesticides, food security and food safety. *Environmental Science & Policy* 9, 685–692.

Conway, G.R., Barbier, E., 1990. After the green revolution: sustainable agriculture for development. London; New York: Earthscan Publications.

de Koning, J.I.J.C., Crul, M.R.M., Wever, R., Brezet, J.C., 2015. Sustainable consumption in Vietnam: an explorative study among the urban middle class. *International Journal of Consumer Studies* 39, 608–618.

Ehlert, J., 2016. Emerging consumerism and eating out in Ho Chi Minh City, Vietnam. The social embeddedness of food sharing. In: Sahakian, M., Saloma, C.A., Erkman, S. (eds.), 2016. Food consumption in the city: practices and patterns in urban Asia and the Pacific, Routledge studies in food, society and the environment. London; New York: Routledge, 71–89.

Figuié, M., Bricas, N., 2010. Purchasing Food in modern Vietnam. In: Kalekin-Fishman, D., Low, K.E.Y. (eds.), Asian Experiences in Every Day Life: Social Perspectives on the Senses. Burlington: Ashgate, 177–194.

Figuié, M., Moustier, P., 2009. Market appeal in an emerging economy: Supermarkets and poor consumers in Vietnam. *Food Policy* 34, 210–217.

Fortier, F., Tran Thi Thu Trang, 2013. Agricultural Modernization and Climate Change in Vietnam's Post-Socialist Transition: Agricultural Modernization and Climate Change. *Development and Change* 44, 81–99.

Gainsborough, M., 2010. Present but not Powerful: Neoliberalism, the State, and Development in Vietnam. *Globalizations* 7(4), 475–488.

Goodman, D., Goodman, M., 2001. Sustaining Foods: Organic Consumption and the Socio-Ecological Imaginary. In: Cohen, M.J., Murphy, J. (eds.), Exploring Sustainable Consumption. Oxford: Elsevier Science, 97–119.

Grosglik, R., 2016. Citizen-consumer revisited: The cultural meanings of organic food consumption in Israel. *Journal of Consumer Culture* 17, 732–751.

Guthman, J., 2004. Back to the Land: The Paradox of Organic Food Standards. *Environment and Planning A* 36(3), 511–528.

Hasimu, H., Marchesini, S., Canavari, M., 2017. A concept mapping study on organic food consumers in Shanghai, China. *Appetite* 108, 191–202.

Hassanein, N., 2003. Practicing food democracy: a pragmatic politics of transformation. *Journal of Rural Studies* 19, 77–86.

Heis, A., 2015. The alternative agriculture network Isan and its struggle for food sovereignty – a food regime perspective of agricultural relations of production in Northeast Thailand. *ASEAS – Austrian Journal of South-East Asian Studies* 8(1), 67–86.

Ho Thi Diep Quynh Chau, 2015. CÁC YẾU TỐ ẢNH HƯỞNG ĐẾN Ý ĐỊNH MUA THỰC PHẨM HỮU CƠ CỦA NGƯỜI TIÊU DÙNG TẠI TP.HCM., Master Thesis, Ho Chi Minh City Open University.

IFOAM, 2003. Developing Local Marketing Initiatives For Organic Products In Asia, A Guide for Small & Medium Enterprises. IFOAM, Germany, 2003.

IFOAM, 2005. The Principles of Organic Agriculture. Preamble. IFOAM, Bonn, available under https://www.ifoam.bio/sites/default/files/poa_english_web.pdf (accessed 02.22.17).

IFOAM, n.d. PGS General questions [WWW Document]. URL https://www.ifoam.bio/en/pgs-general-questions (accessed 02.20.18).

Ingram, J., 2011. A food systems approach to researching food security and its interactions with global environmental change. *Food Security* 3, 417–431.

Johnston, J., Biro, A., MacKendrick, N., 2009. Lost in the Supermarket: The Corporate-Organic Foodscape and the Struggle for Food Democracy. *Antipode* 41, 509–532.

Little, R., Maye, D., Ilbery, B., 2010. Collective Purchase: Moving Local and Organic Foods beyond the Niche Market. *Environment and Planning A* 42, 1797–1813.

MacKendrick, N., 2014. Foodscape [WWW Document]. contexts. understanding people in their social worlds. URL https://contexts.org/articles/foodscape/ (accessed 02.23.17).

MARD, 2017. Prime Minister approves agricultural restructuring plan in 2017–2020 [WWW Document]. Cổng thông tin điện tử Bộ NN và PTNT. URL https://www.mard.gov.vn/en/Pages/prime-minister-approves-agricultural-restructuring-plan-in-2017-2020.aspx (accessed 02.21.18).

Mergenthaler, M., Weinberger, K., Qaim, M., 2009a. Consumer Valuation of Food Quality and Food Safety Attributes in Vietnam. *Review of Agricultural Economics* 31, 266–283.

Mergenthaler, M., Weinberger, K., Qaim, M., 2009b. The food system transformation in developing countries: A disaggregate demand analysis for fruits and vegetables in Vietnam. *Food Policy* 34, 426–436.

Moustier, P., Figuié, M., Nguyen Thi Tan Loc, Ho Thanh Son, 2006. The role of coordination in the safe and organic vegetable chains supplying Hanoi. In: I International Symposium on Improving the Performance of Supply Chains in the Transitional Economies 699, 297–306.

Moustier, P., Phan Thi Giac Tam, Dao The Anh, Vu Trong Binh, Nguyen Thi Tan Loc, 2010. The role of farmer organizations in supplying supermarkets with quality food in Vietnam. *Food Policy* 35(1), 69–78.

Ngo Doan Dam, n.d. Production and supply chain management of organic food in Vietnam, Field Crops Research Institute (FCRI), Vietnam Academy of Agricultural Sciences (VAAS), 1–6.

Nguyen Sy Linh, 2010. Viet Nam: Organic Development. In: Willer, H., Kilcher, L., (eds.), 2010. The World of Organic Agriculture. Statistics and Emerging Trends 2010. IFOAM, Bonn and FiBL, Frick, 128–130.

Nguyen Thi Hoan, Mergenthaler, M., 2005. Food safety and development: how effective are regulations. In: Proceedings of Deutscher Tropentag, 11–13.

Nguyen-vo Thu-huong, 2008. The ironies of freedom: sex, culture, and neoliberal governance in Vietnam, Critical dialogues in Southeast Asian studies. Seattle: University of Washington Press.

Nicetic, O., van de Fliert, E., Ho Van Chien, Vo Mai, Le Cuong, 2010. Good Agricultural Practice (GAP) as a vehicle for transformation to sustainable citrus production in the Mekong Delta of Vietnam. 9th European IFSA Symposium, 4–7 July 2010, Vienna, Austria. WS 4.4 – Transition towards sustainable agriculture: from farmers to agro-food systems, 1893–1901.

Oliveri, F., 2015. A Network of Resistances against a Multiple Crisis. SOS Rosarno and the Experimentation of Socio-Economic Alternative Models.

Omoto, R., 2012. Small-scale producers and the governance of certified organic seafood production in Vietnam's Mekong Delta. Dissertation, University of Waterloo.

Ong, A., Zhang, L., 2008. Introduction: Privatizing China. Powers of the Self, Socialism from Afar. In: Li Zhang, Aihwa Ong, (eds.), 2008. Privatizing China: socialism from afar. Ithaca: Cornell University Press.

Parayil, G., 2003. Mapping technological trajectories of the Green Revolution and the Gene Revolution from modernization to globalization. *Research Policy* 32, 971–990.

Parsons, J.M., 2015. Gender, class and food: families, bodies and health. London; New York: Palgrave Macmillan (Palgrave Macmillan Studies in Family and Intimate Life).

PGS IFOAM, n.d. Participatory Guarantee Systems Worldwide [WWW Document]. URL https://pgs.ifoam.bio/ (accessed 02.20.18).

Pham Binh Quyen, Dang Duc Nhan, Nguyen Van San, 1995. Environmental pollution in Vietnam: analytical estimation and environmental priorities. *TrAC – Trends in Analytical Chemistry* 14, 383–388.

Pham Thi Anh, Kroeze, C., Bush, S. R., Mol, A.P.J., 2010. Water pollution by intensive brackish shrimp farming in south-east Vietnam: Causes and options for control. *Agricultural Water Management* 97, 872–882.

Pham Van Hoi, 2010. Governing pesticide use in vegetable production in Vietnam Dissertation, Wageningen University, Wageningen.

Pingali, P., 2007. Westernization of Asian diets and the transformation of food systems: Implications for research and policy. *Food Policy* 32, 281–298.

Poulain, J.-P., 2017. The Sociology of Food: Eating and the Place of Food in Society. London; New York: Bloomsbury Academic.

Radio Free Asia, 2016. Two Arrested in Connection With Vietnam Fish Death Protests [WWW Document]. URL https://www.rfa.org/english/news/vietnam/two-arrested-in-connectin-05022016164927.html (accessed 01.23.18).

Raynolds, L.T., 2004. The Globalization of Organic Agro-Food Networks. *World Development* 32, 725–743.

Roitner-Schobesberger, B., Darnhofer, I., Somsook, S., Vogl, C.R., 2008. Consumer perceptions of organic foods in Bangkok, Thailand. *Food Policy* 33, 112–121.

Saigon Times, 2017. Vietnam seeks to develop sustainable organic agriculture – News from the Saigon Times [WWW Document]. URL http://english.thesaigontimes.vn/57556/Vietnam-seeks-to-develop-sustainable-organic-agriculture.html (accessed 01.23.18).

Schwenkel, C., Leshkowich, A.M., 2012. Guest Editors' Introduction: How Is Neoliberalism Good to Think Vietnam? How Is Vietnam Good to Think Neoliberalism? *positions* 20(2), 379–401.

Scott, S., Vandergeest, P., Young, M., 2009. Certification Standards and the Governance of Green Foods in Southeast Asia. In: Clapp, J., Fuchs, D. (eds.): Corporate Power in Global Agrifood Governance. Cambridge: MIT Press, 61–92.

Seyfang, G., 2006. Ecological citizenship and sustainable consumption: Examining local organic food networks. *Journal of Rural Studies* 22, 383–395.

Simmons, L., Scott, S., 2007. Health concerns drive safe vegetable production in Vietnam. *Leisa Magazine* 23(3), 22–23.

Simmons, L., Scott, S., 2008. Organic agriculture and "safe" vegetables in Vietnam: Implications for agro-food system sustainability. Department of Geography, University of Waterloo; Ontario, Canada, 1–21.

Talk Vietnam, 2016. Street food near schools poses high risks [WWW Document]. URL https://www.talkvietnam.com/2016/04/street-food-near-schools-poses-high-risks/ (accessed 05.29.17).

Thien T. Truong, Yap, M.H.T., Ineson, E.M., 2012. Potential Vietnamese consumers' perceptions of organic foods. *British Food Journal* 114, 529–543.

Tran Thi Thu Trang, 2012. Food Security versus Food Sovereignty: Choice of Concept, Policies, and Classes in Vietnam's Post-Reform Economy. *Kasarinlan – Philippine Journal of Third World Studies* 26, 68–88.

Tran Thi Ut, Kajisa, K., 2006. The Impact of the Green Revolution on Rice Production in Vietnam: *The Developing Economies* 44, 167–189.

Tran Tri Dung, Pham Hoang Ngan, 2012. Organic vegetable supply chain in Vietnam: Marketing and finance perspectives. Vietnamica Monitor.

Tran Tu Van Anh, 2017. Civil Society Action against Industrial Water Pollution in Vietnam: the Case of the Đồng Nai River Basin. Doctoral Thesis at Faculty of Arts, University of Bonn.

Vann, E.F., 2005. Domesticating consumer goods in the global economy: Examples from Vietnam and Russia. *Ethnos* 70, 465–488.

VECO, 2016. Habits, concerns and preferences of vegetables consumers in Hanoi. Findings from the "Safe & Organic Food Finder" baseline study, available under https://vietnam.rikolto.org/en/news/case-study-habits-concerns-and-preferences-vegetables-consumers-hanoi (accessed 02.21.17).

Vietnam Economic News, 2017. Organic farming – important part of Vietnam's agriculture [WWW Document]. VIETNAM ECONOMIC NEWS. URL http://ven.vn/organic-farming-important-part-of-vietnams-agriculture-30251.html (accessed 02.21.18).

VietNamNet, 2016. Why is unsafe food rampant in Vietnam? [WWW Document]. URL http://english.vietnamnet.vn/fms/special-reports/155277/why-is-unsafe-food-rampant-in-vietnam-.html (accessed 02.21.17).

Viet Nam News, 2014. Shrimp project helps create 'organic coast' [WWW Document], URL http://vietnamnews.vn/sunday/features/250091/shrimp-project-helps-create-organic-coast.html (accessed 05.29.17).

Viet Nam News, 2016. Food poisoning kills two in Yên Bái [WWW Document], URL http://vietnamnews.vn/society/295193/food-poisoning-kills-two-in-yen-bai.html (accessed 02.09.17).

Viet Nam News, 2017a. Japanese firms plan organic farms in An Giang [WWW Document], URL http://vietnamnews.vn/economy/377026/japanese-firms-plan-organic-farms-in-an-giang.html (accessed 05.29.17).

Viet Nam News, 2017b. PM opens door for organic farmers [WWW Document]. vietnamnews.vn. URL http://vietnamnews.vn/society/419571/pm-opens-door-for-organic-farmers.html (accessed 02.22.18).

Vogl, C.R., Kilcher, L., Schmidt, H., 2005. Are Standards and Regulations of Organic Farming Moving Away from Small Farmers' Knowledge? *Journal of Sustainable Agriculture* 26, 5–26.

Wells-Dang, A., 2010. Political space in Vietnam: a view from the 'rice-roots'. *The Pacific Review* 23, 93–112.

Wells-Dang, A., 2014. Civil society networks in Cambodia and Vietnam. A comparative analysis. In: Waibel, G., Ehlert, J., Feuer, H. (eds.), 2014. Southeast Asia and the civil society gaze: scoping a contested concept in Cambodia and Vietnam, Routledge studies on civil society in Asia. London; New York: Routledge, 61–76.

Wertheim-Heck, S.C.O., 2015. We have to eat, right? Food safety concerns and shopping for daily vegetables in modernizing Vietnam. Dissertation, Wageningen University.

Wertheim-Heck, S.C.O., Spaargaren, G., 2016. Shifting configurations of shopping practices and food safety dynamics in Hanoi, Vietnam: a historical analysis. *Agriculture and Human Values* 33, 655–671.

Wertheim-Heck, S.C.O., Vellema, S. and Spaargaren, G., 2015. Food safety and urban food markets in Vietnam: The need for flexible and customized retail modernization policies. *Food Policy* 54, 95–106.

Whitney, C. W., den Braber, K., Nhung Tu Tuyet, Jørgensen, S. T., 2014. Farm Management Schemes within Organic PGS Survey and Analysis in Sóc Sơn, Hanoi, Vietnam. In: Rahmann, G., Aksoy, U. (eds.). *Building Organic Bridges*, Volume 4, Sweden – Viet Nam, Thünen Report, No. 20(4), 1187–1190.

Willer, H., Lernoud, J. (eds.), 2017. The World of Organic Agriculture. Statistics and Emerging Trends 2017. FiBL & IFOAM – Organics International: Frick and Bonn.

Willer, H., Yussefi-Menzler, M., Sorensen, N. (eds.), 2008. The World of Organic Agriculture. Statistics and Emerging Trends 2008, IFOAM, Bonn and FiBL, Frick.

Word Vietnam, 2016. Family Garden [WWW Document]. URL http://word-vietnam.com/food-drink/top-eats/family-garden (accessed 02.22.18).

7

Urban Gardening and Rural-Urban Supply Chains: Reassessing Images of the Urban and the Rural in Northern Vietnam

Sandra Kurfürst

Introduction

This chapter examines the sites of production of what consumers in Vietnam perceive to be *rau sạch, rau an tòan* (clean and safe vegetables). First, it focuses on the spaces and practices of gardening in the city. Second, it examines the practices and images that constitute and underlie the rural as a signifier of fresh and clean food.

The twenty-first century has been termed the "Asian urban century" with half of the urban world population living in Asia (UN-Habitat 2012, p. 28). Roy (2014, p. 14) comprehends the Asian urban century as the "historical conjuncture", at which the urban becomes a matter of government. Urbanism then is "produced through the practice of state-craft and the apparatus of planning" (Roy 2014, p. 14).

After extensive phases of zero-urban growth and de-urbanization during the Indochina Wars, Vietnam is now on the threshold of becoming

S. Kurfürst (✉)
Global South Studies Centre (GSSC), University of Cologne,
Cologne, Germany
e-mail: s.kurfuerst@uni-koeln.de

© The Author(s) 2019
J. Ehlert, N. K. Faltmann (eds.), *Food Anxiety in Globalising Vietnam*,
https://doi.org/10.1007/978-981-13-0743-0_7

205

an urbanized society. In 2016, 34 per cent of the population was living in urban areas with 1.2 million people moving to the city each year, as compared to 1960, when only 15 per cent of the population was residing in cities (Thanh Nien News 2016; World Bank 2018). Recognizing the city's capacity as a hub of economic growth and remedy for economic crisis (UN-Habitat 2012), the development of "modern and civilized" cities (*đô thị hiện đại văn minh*)[1] throughout the country has become a state priority. Historically, the royal city in Northern Vietnam was defined by the confluence of officialdom and sacrality. In the eleventh century, Hanoi was founded as a sacred city—its centre being defined by the location of the royal palace and temple in the rectangular and enclosed space of the citadel (Kurfürst 2012a, p. 35). By contrast, the countryside in Vietnam is associated with the village that is regarded as the cradle of Vietnamese civilization. Nguyen Tu Chi (1993, p. 47) defines the village in Northern Vietnam as the "basic cell of Vietnamese society". Northern Vietnamese village communities have evolved as tropes of autonomy from state power and independence from colonial domination, both exerted from the city (Marr 2004; Phan Huy Le 2006). Today the urban is still considered the locus of political power and a hub of modernization. While rural areas are valued for their productivity, nurturing the nation, rural spaces and residents have also increasingly come to be designated as backward (To Xuan Phuc 2012; Salemink 2018). Harms (2011b, p. 457) concludes that the rural is addressed with "both reverence and paternalitistic subordination to the urban centre".

Although the division between the city and the countryside cannot be properly physically located, the binary categories of the urban and the rural still inform the ways that people imagine space (Harms 2011a, p. 84). Accordingly, designations of the rural and the urban are crucial to both the politics of place and belonging and the politics of space and rent-seeking. For those living in the city and the countryside, the urban and the rural are important markers of identity and belonging. By contrast, the state holds the classificatory authority over these spaces. Designating a space as rural or urban ultimately alters and determines its use function and economic value.

Focusing on the sites of production of clean and safe vegetables, that is, urban gardens and rural areas, the paper argues that while the boundaries between the rural and the urban are constantly crossed in everyday practice, they are maintained as socially constructed—though often ambivalent—binaries.

Urban Gardening

Urban gardening can be observed in cities around the globe (Follmann and Viehoff 2015). It comprises diverse forms of small-scale agricultural production in the city, conducted in public space, private gardens or on rooftops. Some municipalities even explicitly promote urban gardening in the form of municipal projects, such as the "eatable city".[2] However, the spaces and their meanings vary widely according to the socio-economic and political context in which they are based. According to Lefebvre (1991) every society has its own space. Space is socially produced and thus relations of production are manifested in space (Lefebvre 1991, pp. 33, 129). In much of the literature, urban gardening is conceptualized as a political act, particularly a critique of the neoliberal system (Certomà 2011; Schmelzkopf 2002; Staeheli et al. 2002). For example, the term "guerrilla gardening" refers to individuals' or groups' appropriation of private or public spaces without the landowner's permission by planting flora (Flores 2006). Accordingly, guerilla gardening has come to denote a political practice in public space (Adams and Hardman 2014). The formation of collective gardens, such as the community gardens in Great Britain and Australia or *Prinzessinnengärten*[3] in Berlin further hint at urbanites' interest in the origin of agricultural products and their distrust in anonymous commodity chains (Bendt et al. 2013; Evers and Hodgson 2011; Witheridge and Morris 2016; Participant observation Berlin 2015). Moreover, these social gardens do have a communicative function as well. They serve as a basis of social cohesion in an estranged urban environment (Firth et al. 2011). What initially started out as a temporary occupation of highly valued fallow urban land is frequently sought to be transformed into sustainable green spaces (Follmann and Viehoff 2015). Citizens negotiate land tenure with the municipality or the private owner of the land lot to maintain the garden. That is how individuals and collectives transform urban space through their gardening activities into urban commons. In fact, the creation of gardens on urban land counters the very linkage between urbanization and capitalism. According to David Harvey (2012, p. 42) urbanization takes over a particular role "in the dynamics of capital accumulation because of the long working periods and turnover times and the long lifetimes of most investments in the built environment". In other words, urban gardens occupy land that could otherwise be used for real estate development, which would contribute to private rent-seeking.

The particular discussion of urban gardening as an expression of the right to the city is very much informed by research on cities of the Global North (Certomà and Tornaghi 2015). On the contrary, small-scale agricultural production or urban farming in the cities of the Global South has long been discussed in the context of poverty alleviation, urban informality and thence with a focus on the urban poor (Bakker et al. 2000; Ngome and Foeken 2012; Simiyu and Foeken 2014). Overcoming the developed versus developmental divide in urban and development studies (Robinson 2006; Parnell and Robinson 2013), this chapter alludes to the cultural history of urban gardens in Hanoi. In effect, it suggests, for private gardens in particular, a transformation from a sacred function to a utilitarian one. What is more, urban gardening in Hanoi, like in many Northern cities, can, at times, be an expression of the right to the city, too. By occupying public spaces for gardening, urbanites actively shape the urban landscape, challenging the state's planning apparatus.

Actors in urban gardening are frequently driven by their concern for food safety. Interviewees, all of them belonging to the urban middle class,[4] mentioned a longing for clean and safe vegetables, as well as the relaxation achieved through gardening, as major motives for growing their own produce. In particular, families with small children are concerned about the safety of the produce they use to cook meals for their children (see Faltmann, this volume). This is particularly the case for the ingredients of the rice soup *cháo*, such as greens, mushrooms and soy sprouts (Le Huu Viet and Tra Giang 2014). The aspect of care for the family appears to be crucial in the decision to grow fresh produce at home. Additionally, interviewees try to ensure food safety by drawing on their urban-rural ties. This chapter links the empirical findings on urban gardening and the rural-urban supply chains to the broader discussion on the rural-urban dichotomy in Vietnam (Drummond 2003; Fuhrmann 2017; Gillen 2016; Harms 2011a, b; Kurfürst 2012a; Labbé 2016). It concludes that the socially constructed oppositions of the rural and the urban not only inform the way people imagine (urban) space (Gillen 2016; Harms 2011a), but also what they imagine to be clean and safe vegetables.

The data presented in this chapter were gathered through qualitative methods comprising semi-structured and narrative interviews with practitioners of urban gardening, site visits to gardens, as well as expert interviews with botanists, agronomists, historians and social anthropologists, conducted between September 2014 and October 2015 in Hanoi. The selection of the gardens and interviewees was based on snowball sampling. Since the concern for food safety is omnipresent, I was directed to different interview partners by my colleagues and friends in Hanoi, once I had introduced my research topic of clean and safe vegetables. The names of the interviewees have been altered in order to make them anonymous. In addition, content analysis of Vietnamese language newspapers such as Tiền Phong and online fora was conducted. To achieve comparisons with urban gardening in cities of the Global North, additional site visits were conducted to gardens in Berlin. In April 2015, I visited the aforementioned public-access community garden *Prinzessinengärten* as well as the *Tempelhofer Feld*. The latter is a former airfield that primarily served as a US military base until German reunification in 1990. In 2014, it was decided by referendum to transform the airfield into an open green space, with some of the area allotted to urban gardening (Dannenberg and Follmann 2015).

Agricultural Production in the City: Continuity and Change

The cultivation of vegetables around the house, in home gardens or on the sidewalks is nothing new, neither in Ho Chi Minh City nor in Hanoi (Le Huu Viet and Tra Giang 2014). The continuity of the rural within the urban—comprising both spaces and practices—is a particularly important feature of Hanoi's urbanism. Since the foundation of the capital Thăng Long in the eleventh century, agricultural villages have been central to the city's food supply system. In particular the 13 farms (*thập tam trại*) located west of the royal citadel—in today's Ba Đình District—provided the royal city with agricultural products such as vegetables, flowers and medicinal herbs (Kurfürst 2012a). In addition, villages north of the royal city, located on the stretch of land surrounded by West Lake and the Red River used to produce speciality plants, such as *đào* and *quất* trees, the traditional Vietnamese Lunar New Year tree, as well as rice and vegetables for the city (Leaf et al. 1999; Leaf 2002).

Only through the urban sprawl and the densification of the inner city—particularly during the 1990s—were these former spaces of agricultural production turned into land for construction (see Gorman, this volume). While the cultivation of speciality plants was moved beyond the dike to the fertile grounds on the banks of the Red River (Leaf et al. 1999), food production for the city was confined to the urban hinterland. Yet, with the growing gardening activities in the inner city, practices associated with rural areas, such as agricultural production or animal breeding seem to re-enter the city.

The chapter focuses on the gardening activities in two districts that used to be sites of agricultural production: first, the area located around West Lake, in what is nowadays Tây Hồ District; and, second, the area known as Bắc Từ Liêm, which only became a part of Hanoi through the adjustment of the city's administrative boundaries in 2008.[5]

Gardening in Private Space

Gardening in private space, on a land lot belonging to the household, has a long tradition in Vietnam. In rural areas, families used to have a private garden adjacent to their house. The garden made up one-third of the land lot and was used for growing vegetables. A further site of cultivation was the house's courtyard, in which ornamental trees were grown (Expert Interview with Social Anthropologist, Hanoi October 2015; Nguyen Khac Tung 1993). While the garden was a space of production, the courtyard referred to the realm of aesthetics. This functional division is also represented linguistically. While agricultural production translates into *trồng rau*, literally meaning growing vegetables, the art of growing bonsai trees is called *chơi cây cảnh*, translating into "playing bonsais". The semantics reveal a differentiation between an everyday necessity, namely the cultivation of vegetables, and the joyous endeavour of planting ornamental trees.

With the move to the city, house owners often maintained the planting of ornamental trees. In Hanoi's narrow tube houses, bonsai trees are grown on little balconies or on the rooftop.

Home gardens were also promoted by the socialist state from the 1960s onwards in order to produce medicinal herbs, which are required to produce Southern medicine (*thuốc Nam*). Southern medicine corresponds to Traditional Chinese Medicine in the way that it is based on elements extracted from the local flora and fauna.[6] In fact, the Vietnamese state sought to promote people's self-sufficiency, particularly in rural areas, by encouraging them to grow medicinal plants for the treatment of the most common ailments such as headache and diarrhoea (Wahlberg 2012a, pp. 216–217). That is why today, still, many Vietnamese are familiar with the domestic production of medicinal herbs.

The following examples shed light on the spaces, plants and motivations for gardening in private. When speaking of gardening in private, this chapter refers to the private space of the home. In Vietnam, an individual or private company can acquire land-use rights for a particular lot. According to the Vietnamese Land Law all land belongs to the entire population, but the right to management is held by the state. The state issues land-use rights to individuals, thus allowing them to use the land (Anon. 2001, p. 7; Nguyen Van Suu 2004, p. 270). Such land-use rights also determine the specific use of a lot. That is why only few private gardens do still exist in the inner-city districts as most of the land has been transformed from land for agricultural production into construction land. Therefore the following examples focus on private rooftop gardens. The first rooftop garden is located in the aforementioned new residential area of Bắc Từ Liêm. The second rooftop garden is located right in the city centre, close to Hanoi's Ancient Quarter.

Bắc Từ Liêm is a new residential area in the West of Hanoi with spacious detached houses and broad sidewalks. The area was only developed ten years ago on former paddy fields. Mai and her husband live together with their two sons in a four-storey house. On each floor is a room with a small balcony facing the street. On the balconies, the family cultivates different kinds of foliage plants, mainly ornamental trees. Through a small window in the attic, the family can access the roof. On the rooftop, Mai grows diverse herbs, such as mint. She used to cultivate different kinds of vegetables, but her harvest was destroyed by a rat. That is why she turned to the cultivation of fragrant greens, which, she explains, rats do not like to eat. The mother of two grows her own vegetables because she is concerned about her children's health. Although she has to purchase additional fresh produce from the market, she says "at the market you can never be sure if the vegetables are really clean and where they come from. The sales woman at the market might get it one day from one supplier and the next day from another" (Interview October 2015, translated from Vietnamese).

Urban gardening in Hanoi is also conducted right in the city's historical centre. In Hanoi's central Hoàn Kiếm District is a narrow two-storey house owned by a retired couple. The couple lives on the first and second floors, while the ground floor is occupied by a photo shop. The second floor is divided into an inner space as well as an outer space, featuring the rooftop garden. The inner space houses a big altar with a picture of Buddha in the centre. Outside, the garden comprises a mixture of vegetables, medicinal herbs and ornamental trees. In the middle of the outer space, there is even a small pond. The house owner, named Thắng, explains that his garden is a miniature world, a symbol of love for nature (*yêu thiên nhiên*) and "longevity"—using the English term (Interview October 2015). Plants, stones and water are arranged according to the principles of *feng shui* (*phòng thủy*). Ornamental trees are decorated together with precious stones in the shape of a Buddhist monk, a lingam or a holy animal (*con vật thiêng*). Accordingly, the rooftop garden becomes a spatial continuity of the inner sacred space of worship. In between the pots of ornamental trees stand pots and boxes of leafy greens such as *lá lốt* (piper lolot), *rau răm* (known as Vietnamese coriander) and *rau xương sông* (*blumea lanceolaria*).[7] Thắng explains that he likes to garden and wants to have access to clean vegetables. Apart from vegetables, he cultivates different kinds of medicinal herbs, which are essential to the production of Southern medicine. Thắng cultivates herbal plants for the treatment of low blood pressure and arthrosis. In addition to curing diseases, some medicinal plants also have ritual functions. He gives the example of the tree *cây dây mỏ quạ* (*Dischidia major*) that is used to prevent bad spirits from entering the house. Consequently, Thắng's rooftop garden unites the realm of profane domestic production with the realm of the sacred, in the form of holy trees and stones, as well as medicinal plants.

Gardening in Public Space

The occupation of public space by individuals for private activities is a crucial feature of Hanoi's urbanism. Drummond (2000, p. 2377) refers to the blurring of private and public in Vietnam as "inside out" and "outside in". The former denotes private activities in public space, whereas the latter designates the state's intervention into the private domestic space of the home, such as the state's happy family campaign or policies on family planning.[8] In particular, the occupation of the sidewalks of the Ancient Quarter for private economic activities, such as petty trade, cafés and restaurants, has been well received in the literature on Hanoi (Anh Dung Ta and Manfredini 2017; Drummond 2000; Koh 2006; Kurfürst 2012b; Thomas 2002). This research shows that the boundaries between private and public space are often fluid and constantly re-negotiated between citizens and local authorities. Such negotiation is made possible through so-called mediation space (Koh 2006, p. 15). Mediation spaces open up when local officials face a moral dilemma. On the one hand, they are part of the local community and want to be compassionate towards their neighbours; on the other hand, they are responsible for implementing the regulations on the use of the sidewalks (Koh 2006, p. 9). While emphasizing the importance of the sidewalks as a space for pedestrians, the municipality of Hanoi nonetheless introduced a regulation in 2008 allowing for the private economic exploitation of the pavements in case a fee is paid to the district (Kurfürst 2012a, p. 104).

The private appropriation of public space can also be observed in the context of urban gardening. In Bắc Từ Liêm, families occupy the wide sidewalks in front of their houses with styrofoam boxes and pots, in which they grow vegetables and herbs for private consumption. Asked about why residents are allowed to block the sidewalks, Mai says "It is in front of their house. So they can use it. As long as they [the vegetable boxes] stay in front of their houses no one cares." She goes on to explain that she can tell from the vegetables where families with little children live (Interview October 2015, translated from Vietnamese). First, the quotation shows that it is acceptable to cultivate on the sidewalks, as long as the vegetable boxes are placed in front of the owner's house entrance and do not intrude into the public space in front of the neighbour's house. Second, it points to the existence of mediation space, since local officials seem to tolerate the occupation of the sidewalks for private production and consumption (Fig. 7.1).

In Tây Hồ District, unlike in Bắc Từ Liêm, the sidewalks are rather narrow or non-existent. Instead, residents garden on fallow urban land.

Fig. 7.1 Private appropriation of the sidewalk in Bắc Từ Liêm. (Copyright to image: Sandra Kurfürst)

For example, in Yên Phụ members of the neighbourhood cultivate vegetable lots on land located in the middle of the street. Although the gardening activity occurs in public space, the lot is not accessible to everyone. Access to the land and the permission to harvest are subject to the social control within the neighbourhood. Only those who cultivate the land are also allowed to harvest (Participant Observation September 2014, October 2015).

The temporary usage of fallow land for gardening is very common in Hanoi and can be frequently encountered in the newly developed residential areas, so-called New Urban Areas of Hanoi (Le Huu Viet and Tra Giang 2014). For land belonging to the municipality, a development plan is often already in existence. Yet, as long as construction work has not started, this kind of interim usage is tolerated by the authorities. In sum, citizens actively shape the urban landscape through their gardening practices. They appropriate urban land dedicated to private rent-seeking and temporarily transform it into an urban common, thereby undermining the state's planning policies and development plans of private investors.

Apart from the sidewalks and fallow urban land, gardening can also be observed in public and particularly sacred institutions, such as the Buddhist pagoda and the communal house. As Hanoi developed from an agglomeration of villages, many urban wards still have their own communal house (*đình*), Buddhist pagoda (*chùa*) and Taoist temple (*đền*). Traditionally, the communal house is the residence of the village deity and thence a place where the neighbourhood assembles on occasions such as the deity's birth and death day. Likewise, many Vietnamese visit one of these sacred institutions on the occasion of the first and fifteenth of the lunar month, praying and making offerings for their family's fortune. This chapter presents the gardening activities in Láng Pagoda and Yên Phụ communal house.

Láng Pagoda (*Chùa Láng*) is located in the same-named street Phố Chùa Láng in Hanoi's Đống Đa District. The Buddhist pagoda, also known as *Pagodes des Dames*, was built in the twelfth century under the reign of King Lý Anh Tông. According to members of the pagoda, it is the largest pagoda in Hanoi, occupying 10,000 square metres of land. The whole area surrounding the pagoda used to be famous for the cultivation of fresh vegetables and herbs, particularly Vietnamese Basil (*rau húng*) due to the high-quality soil. A 70-year-old member of the pagoda contemplates "the herbs of Láng Pagoda are a speciality" (Interview October 2015, translated from Vietnamese). They were well known for their fragrance (*thơm*). However, in the scope of urbanization, all the vegetable fields surrounding the pagoda were transformed into land for construction. Today only a few vegetables are still grown on pagoda land, but even here the amount of cultivable land has diminished. The pagoda's allotment garden can be accessed from the main courtyard through a small gate. In between the green small stupas reach into the sky. The land is carefully divided into small lots separated from one another by moats. Each plot is used to cultivate a different kind of vegetable or herb. For example, in October 2015 the pagoda's famous basil as well as cabbage and green onions were grown on the different parcels of land (Fig. 7.2).

Fig. 7.2 Gardening in *Chùa Láng* (Láng Pagoda). (Copyright to image: Sandra Kurfürst)

Given the densification of the area located in between Kim Mã, Nguyễn Chí Thanh and Láng Roads, it is actually the institution of the pagoda that guarantees the persistence of gardens. Because the gardens are situated on pagoda land, they cannot be easily transformed into land for construction. Another factor in support of the gardens' persistence is the fact that, during the subsidy era (*thời bao cấp*), they belonged to the local cooperative (*hợp tác xã*). Like China, the Vietnamese government used land collectivisation as a means to achieve the overall aim of the transition to socialism (Nguyen Van Suu 2004). As a consequence, the pagoda land used to be operated by the local cooperative. Tuấn, a member of the pagoda, reports that, even today, former members of the cooperative still come to crop (Interview October 2015). During the period of collectivisation, individuals had to participate in the collective production of vegetables. Additionally, families were allowed to use a small lot of land for cropping for the family's own consumption.[9] Initially acknowledged by the economic reform programme *Đổi Mới*, this practice of subsistence production still continues on sacred land. In other words, belonging to both the cooperative during the subsidy era and the pagoda community nowadays determine access to the garden, as well as its persistence on pagoda land. Through membership to the pagoda, newcomers to the area like Tuấn, who migrated from his rural home town to Hanoi after de-collectivisation, are also integrated in this very "community of practice" (Lave and Wenger 1991, p. 53).

The members of this community of practice have come to know each other on the basis of face-to-face interaction in the garden and often help each other out: "We exchange. For example if I grow onions, but I would like to have cabbage, I will ask someone who grows cabbage, to exchange with me" (Interview October 2015, translated from Vietnamese). Also the care-taking of the plants is organized among the gardeners. Plants are watered twice a day, in the morning and afternoon, by a person carrying two watering cans on his or her back. While the watering is collectively organized and the gardeners exchange their harvests, they still cultivate for private consumption.

Gardening in sacred space is also conducted in Tây Hồ District. Yên Phụ Ward used to be a village located on the banks of West Lake. Today, some of the old village structures, including the village gate and the communal house still exist. Likewise, the name that the residents refer to when speaking of their housing area connotes its past as a village (*làng* Yên Phụ with *làng* meaning village). The communal house of the area comprises a garden bordering West Lake. The garden displays both sacred and profane features. Close to the main sanctuary are ceramic pots with ornamental trees and miniature temples. Closer to the lake are two vegetable patches, one containing cabbage and the other several boxes of styrofoam containing different kinds of herbs, for example, chive. On the lake's banks, banana trees rise into the sky. The garden is taken care of by elderly women, who are members of the communal house. They cultivate fresh produce for the communal house's holidays. For example, on the occasion of the first and fifteenth of the lunar month it is customary for the worshippers to receive a small bag with banana and sticky rice after having prayed and donated to the communal houses. Accordingly, the community is fed with the products of the communal house's garden. A man who regularly comes to the space of the communal house to fish explains "This is the garden of the communal house. Retired women come here." Asked about whether everyone from the village is allowed to garden, he answers "No. Only those people that have been serving the communal house for a long time come here" (Interview September 2015, translated from Vietnamese). Gardening on land belonging to a sacred institution has become a common practice. Also in the New Urban Area of Linh Đàm, in which a village structure including the communal house still exists, residents produce cabbage and morning glory on the land belonging to the communal house. Often, communal houses and pagodas occupy large stretches of land that are not allowed to be used for construction. The interviewed gardeners on sacred ground repeatedly answered that they gardened there because it was *đất chúng* (communal land). In effect, conversations with historians revealed that former village statutes (*hương ước*) were still intact today, guaranteeing villagers the right to exploit common land (Expert interviews with Historians September, October 2015).

Consequently, belonging to a particular community of practice appears to be a necessary prerequisite for cultivating and harvesting the land. Membership to the former cooperative, the communal house or the pagoda community defines the right of access and participation.

Gardening: Transgressing the Boundaries between Private and Public

Urban gardening activities in Hanoi point to the permeability and flexibility of the local conceptions of private and public.

First, the case studies show that sidewalks and fallow urban land in New Urban Areas are appropriated by residents to cultivate vegetables and herbs for their own consumption. This finding is in line with previous studies on the usage of public spaces for private economic activities. Similarly, members of a former cooperative and/or sacred institution garden on communal land belonging to the Buddhist pagoda and the communal houses. The members of these communities of practice garden primarily for private consumption. However, the fresh produce cultivated on communal land is used for ritual purposes, too. On festival days and sacred holidays the produce from Yên Phụ communal house's garden is fed back to the community.

Second, adhering to the historical continuity of home gardens in Vietnam, the chapter identified a semantic shift in the practice of gardening in the light of food anxiety. This shift is represented in the functional transformation of home gardens from aesthetics to utility, in which ornamental trees and holy stones are increasingly being replaced by boxes of vegetables and herbs that are perceived as safe and clean as compared to the produce offered at the market.

Rural Practices in Urban Space

When cultivating vegetables in the city, urbanites literally adopt rural practices. Other than in many cities of the Global North in which the cultivation of vegetables on fallow urban land is commonly referred to as "urban gardening", the Vietnamese gardeners would stick to the term *trồng rau* (growing vegetables), which is based in agriculture.

Furthermore, the interviewed gardeners often referred to their rural past when asked about their gardening skills. Many stressed that they had acquired the skills and knowledge for the cultivation of herbs and vegetables in the countryside. Thirty-six-year-old Lan Anh explains "I assisted my grandmother gardening when I was a child. Therefore I acquired some basic skills. In addition, I retrieve information from the internet before I start cultivating a particular kind of vegetable" (Interview January 2015). Consequently, it is through the training and apprenticeship back home in the countryside that they acquired their gardening skills. Yet, as the quotation reveals, they complement this embodied knowledge with "global" knowledge distributed through digital networks, such as social networking sites and blogs (Interviews October 2015). Such complementary adoption of different forms of knowledge actually indicates rural migrants' "urban insinuation", that is, their "transition from ruralites to urbanites" (Nguyen Tuan Anh et al. 2012, pp. 3, 6). That said, the reference to the rural is, in a general sense, a crucial marker of identity politics in Vietnam. Rural-urban migration to Hanoi dates back to the medieval ages, when artisans and craftsmen from the Red River Delta migrated to Hanoi, establishing the guild area that is known today as the 36 Streets or the Ancient Quarter. What is more, the early years of state socialism in Northern Vietnam saw a wave of migration from the countryside to the city. As independence was in fact won from the countryside, revolutionary cadres from rural areas were encouraged to move to the city.[10] A further migration wave was introduced through economic liberalization as well as the relaxation of the household registration system, which had previously restricted migration within the country (Nguyen Tuan Anh et al. 2012). In search for higher income opportunities, many people from rural areas moved to the city. Accordingly, most urban dwellers still have rural ties. These connections to kin in the countryside are reevaluated in the urbanites' search for clean and safe vegetables.

Rural-Urban Supply Chains

In order to ensure food safety, urbanites might also draw on their social relations in the countryside. The sending of remittances by family members from the city to the countryside is a common practice in Vietnam (Earl 2014, p. 197). In the light of growing distrust towards obscured production networks, the sending of food supplies from rural areas to the city has gained in importance, too. Interviewees report that they receive boxes of fresh vegetables and meat (pork and beef) from their relatives back home in rural areas.

For example, Trung, a father of two, receives a box each month with fresh seafood, such as shrimps and crabs, as well as some vegetables from his family residing in Hạ Long Bay in Quảng Ninh Province. His family sends him the box of fresh food supply by car, while others reported that the goods were sent to them via the diverse bus lines operating throughout the country. Since many people residing in Hanoi regularly visit their places of origin (về quê) in the countryside on occasions such as weddings, anniversaries of deaths and particularly the Vietnamese lunar New Year, they bring vegetables from their rural places upon returning to Hanoi. For example, Duy comes from a rural area of Vĩnh Phúc Province, located 40 km outside the city. When he returns home to visit his parents, he brings herbs and vegetables for his friends with small children in Hanoi. While Duy acts as an intermediary of perceived safe produce for his friends, Anh is on the receiving end of such a rural-urban food supply. The father of two reported that he would mainly buy the fresh produce from his relatives and friends, or from friends' relatives. The two examples of Duy and Anh point to the relevance of trust in the supplier-consumer relationship (see Figuié et al., this volume). Urbanites like Trung and Anh actually embed their food supply into trust-based relationships drawing on their social ties to the countryside. They receive the fresh produce either directly from family members or friends, or through middlemen like Duy, who have relatives residing in the countryside. Wertheim-Heck and Spargaaren (2016, p. 659) make similar observations, when identifying "kinship shopping" as a way to ensure food safety. According to them, this strategy builds on the trust in a relative's good intentions, as well as on the belief that producers in rural areas have the necessary knowledge to produce safe vegetables.

The prevailing idea that people from rural areas know how to cultivate safe produce is further illustrated by the case of Thảo.

Thảo, a young Hanoian woman, reports that her mother has, for years, been buying from one particular street vendor who delivered the goods right to their doorstep. The vendor maintained that the vegetables were fresh, coming directly from her village. Thảo told her mother that the vegetables did not come from the countryside but from the urban Long

Biên Island in the Red River or were even imported from China. Nonetheless, her mother kept on buying from the street vendor. The mother insisted that the vendor would not dare to cheat on the origin of her produce since she knew the trader well. Through the daily interaction with the vendor and the ability to touch and smell the fresh produce, she established a relationship of trust. The case illustrates how "fresh", "clean" and "safe" have come to connote the products' rural origin. In order to be fresh and safe, vegetables are considered to have to come directly from rural areas, or more precisely the village, and not peri-urban areas such as Long Biên Island. Yet this longing for the produce's rural origin does not withstand the real flow of agricultural commodity chains, since over two-thirds of vegetables consumed in Vietnam's capital originate from Hanoi's peri-urban region. The remainder is imported from Đà Lạt in the Southern part of the central highlands or China (Gerber et al. 2014). Interviewees frequently reported that they purchased vegetables, herbs and fruits for their own consumption directly from the countryside. For example, Nhiên, a 38-year-old teacher, buys vegetables in her home province of Thái Nguyên or when she visits the countryside for business. Wertheim-Heck and Spaargaren (2016, p. 659) refer to this form of consumption as "farmer shopping". In their account it is the label "local farmer produce" that is regarded a qualifier of food safety. However, this qualifier is solely based on trust. Consumers have neither visited the actual sites of production, nor do they have any information on the methods of agricultural production and the flow of commodity chains.

In sum, consumers draw on personal trust-based relationships and the rural origin to ensure food safety. They do so when attaining produce through kinship shopping, farmer shopping or when purchasing at local markets. However, the end consumers themselves seem to have little knowledge about the actual production sites, having no means to verify the methods of production except for the reports of those from whom they receive their supplies. Overall, respondents considered the rural as a signifier of freshness and safety. This image of the rural is socially constructed in opposition to the city that is often associated with pollution, alienation and disorder (Drummond 2003; Fuhrmann 2017; Kurfürst 2012a; Labbé 2016).

Reassessing Images of the Rural and the Urban in Vietnam

Although spatial distinctions between the city and the countryside increasingly seem to dissolve, with more and more people from rural areas moving to the city and urbanites building weekend villas in the countryside, binaries of the rural and the urban continue to inform the way people imagine (urban) space (Gillen 2016; Harms 2011a). Actors designate spaces and practices as either rural or urban, thence (re)producing the binaries in their social interactions. In other words, they continuously draw on the binary categories of the rural and the urban to make sense of their life worlds (Habermas 1995).

According to Harms (2011a), the binaries of the city and the countryside are charged with symbolic meanings. A closer look at the discursive practices constituting this spatial dichotomy reveals that the rural and the urban are actually ascribed with quite ambivalent meanings. On the one hand, the city is considered both a signifier of modernization (*hiện đại*) and civilization (*văn minh*). On the other hand, the city is perceived as a place of environmental pollution and moral corruption. In contrast, the countryside is imagined as a place of tradition, with intact social ties and close contact to nature. But at the same time, the countryside is also regarded a place of backwardness that requires guidance and development from the centre (Drummond 2003, p. 163; Fuhrmann 2017, p. 144; Harms 2011b, pp. 457–458).[11] In the national narrative, rural life is presented as the cradle of Vietnamese culture, mediating an image of the rural as the place of both a functioning collective and an undamaged nature. In her study of environmental change in Vietnam, Fuhrmann shows that the countryside is associated with a clean environment and a beautiful landscape full of fresh air and green trees. Furthermore, rural people are considered to be in close contact to nature as they regularly interact with nature through plantation and harvest (Fuhrmann 2017, pp. 145–146). This connection to nature in particular, is important to a reading of urbanites' striving for safe and clean produce. According to Fuhrmann (2017, p. 141) the rural is associated with "effortless access to fresh food". Consequently, the countryside is regarded as the purveyor of safe foods.

Finally, the rural does not so much refer to a specific geographical location, but appears rather to be an imagined space accompanied by a set of specific symbols (Fuhrmann 2017; Gillen 2016; Harms 2011a). The symbols associated with the rural, such as freshness, cleanliness and safety also seem to inform urbanites' consumption decisions in the light of increasing food anxiety. The receiving of boxes of fresh produce from the countryside or local farmer shopping appear to be based on this very idea of the rural, as well as on social bonds to the countryside. As a consequence, bearing the label "rural" sets vegetables apart from other fresh produce, not indexed as such and sold at urban markets, and ascribes them with a different value. However, as already pointed out, the indexicality of the rural does not necessarily mean that the fresh produce meets national or global standards of food safety, but is a valuation based on local perceptions of fresh and clean food.

According to Ehlert and Voßemer (2015, p. 20), actors draw on different forms of knowledge when evaluating the freshness and safety of the produce they consume, such as rational information on food and emic perceptions of freshness and food quality.

Conclusion

This chapter examined the production sites of clean and safe vegetables, looking at the physical spaces of urban gardening and the practices *in situ*, as well as at the discursive and consumptive practices constituting rural space. In fact, the chapter focused on the recombination of the dimensions of the rural and the urban within the city of Hanoi.

The case studies presented in this chapter point to the persistence of the socially constructed—though often ambivalent—binary concepts of the rural and the urban. Empirically, the two dimensions are important since social actors apply them to make sense of their lifeworld. As Harms (2011a, p. 84) put it:

Objectively speaking, these categories and associations of rural and urban cannot be physically located on the landscape in any fixed manner. Yet people continue to reproduce them as if they were utterly real, tangible, seemingly material truths.

Conceptions of the urban and the rural inform what people consider clean and safe vegetables, too. Actually most of the vegetables consumed in Hanoi are produced in the peri-urban region. However, indexing vegetables as rural, as well as receiving vegetables through social networks in the countryside qualify them as safe foods. Additionally, the presented narratives of the countryside in Vietnam and the individual biographies of migration point to the relevance of the rural for identity politics and the feeling of belonging. In fact, those who receive vegetable boxes are only able to do so because they have strong social ties to their rural hometowns. The feeling of belonging is furthermore expressed in urban gardeners' responses of how they acquired their gardening skills, with many explaining that they were able to cultivate their own produce because they grew up in the countryside. Hoa, a home gardener, even says "Truth be told, urbanites lack [gardening] experience" (Interview October 2015, translated from Vietnamese). In sum, urban gardeners combine their skills acquired through apprenticeship back home, with knowledge retrieved from the internet. Consequently, members of the urban community of practice adapt rural practices to the urban-built environment, generating and distributing knowledge through diverse information artefacts. In sum, the boundaries between rural and urban areas are actually blurred and flexible, as they are continuously negotiated through the exchange of commodities, knowledge, people and practices between the two. As Krause (2013, p. 237) affirms "Livelihoods rarely work in sync with the physical properties of places but remain connected to them in complex ways."

Likewise, the urban is characterized by the constant reworking of private and public spaces. In the private space of the home, spaces originally dedicated to spirits, geomancy and aesthetics are turned into spaces of food production. Vegetable boxes placed on the outer extension of the space of worship increasingly replace holy plants, stones and water ponds. What is more, land belonging to sacred institutions, such as the communal house or pagoda, is used for both private and collective consumption, with access being determined by membership to a particular community of practice, for example, the communal house, Buddhist pagoda or former cooperative.

By using the few open spaces in the city for gardening, citizens actively shape the urban environment, thereby executing their right to the city. They employ what the city offers, such as waste land, waste products in the form of Styrofoam boxes, water bottles or milk packages, to grow vegetables and herbs. In this regard, the city that is otherwise a place associated with environmental pollution can become a place of sustainability, too. Accordingly, the presented urban gardening practices are not actually so different from the manifestations of urban gardening observed in the cities of the Global North. Overall, the presented cases are an expression of citizens' lack of trust in anonymous commodity chains and food supply systems.

Notes

1. The socialist state propagates the development of modern and civilized cities. The policies linked to this modernization discourse frequently aim at eradicating mobile vendors from the urban landscape in order to establish urban order (*trật tự đô thị*) (Kurfürst 2012a; Schwenkel 2012).
2. The municipality of Andernach in Germany introduced the project of the "eatable city". For further information see: http://www.andernach.de/de/leben_in_andernach/essbare_stadt.html
3. Bendt et al. (2013) identify *Prinzessinnengärten* as a public-access community garden which is open to anyone and collectively managed. *Prinzessinnengärten* was founded in 2009 on a land lot in Berlin's Kreuzberg District, the land rented from the state of Berlin.
4. In her monograph *Vietnam's New Middle-Class,* Catherine Earl (2014) identifies the accumulation of cultural capital, and thence education and employment, as crucial to the achievement of middle-class status. Moreover, she shows that "conspicuous consumption" (Veblen 1899), particularly indoor-leisure activities, are a marker of class distinction.
5. Through readjustment, the surrounding provinces of Hà Tây, Vĩnh Phúc, Hưng Yên, Bắc Ninh, Hải Dương, Hà Nam und Hòa Bình that used to constitute the capital's hinterland were integrated into the Hanoi Capital Region. Today Bắc Từ Liêm is a part of Cầu Giấy District.
6. The fourteenth-century Buddhist monk Tuệ Tĩnh, author of "Nam Dược Thần Hiệu", which is the first known script on Vietnamese medicine, explained the value of Southern medicine to the Vietnamese by

pointing out the compatibility of medicine derived from the local flora and fauna with Vietnamese bodies (Wahlberg 2014, p. 48). Indeed, Wahlberg (2012b, p. 157) argues that "traditional medicine" is a very recent invention as it is the outcome of a process of institutionalization of health care for all conducted by the socialist state. In this regard, the production of herbal medicine at home was also a cheap and effective way to grant basic health care to all.

7. *Xương sông* is used to make spices or to cook soup. It is also served in combination with raw fish.

8. The so-called happy family campaign, launched in 1994, was a major tool of birth control, ascribing the reproductive responsibility to women, rather than men (Bélanger and Barbieri 2009).

9. Kerkvliet (1993, p. 11) reports that since the practice of cooperatives began, 5 per cent of arable land was reserved for private use. Since households were allowed to keep the harvest for themselves, many concentrated their efforts more on the cultivation of their private land plots than on the collective. In the North, the encroachment of private households onto collective land became a common strategy to extend private land plots.

10. As Lentz (2011, p. 564) explains, the revolution was won by the landless rural people who were exploited by landlords. Accordingly, the national founding myth of the socialist state is based on the revolutionary power of the countryside.

11. On the common perception of highlanders as backward and primitive see Salemink (2018).

References

Adams, David, and Michael Hardman. 2014. "Observing guerrillas in the wild: Reinterpreting practices of urban guerrilla gardening." Urban Studies 51, no. 6: 1103–1119.

Anh Dung Ta, and Manfredo Manfredini. 2017. "Mobilized Territories in More-Than-Relational Public Spaces. Sidewalk Territories of Resistance in Hanoi, Vietnam." Conference Paper. 10th IFOU—International Forum on Urbanism Conference Hong Kong, December 14–16, 2017.

Anon. 2001. A Selection of Fundamental Laws of Vietnam. Latest Legislation. Hanoi: The Gioi.

Bakker, Nico, Marielle Dubbeling, Sabine Guendel, Ulrich Sabel-Koschella, and Henk de Zeeuw. 2000. Growing Cities, Growing Food, Urban Agriculture on the Policy Agenda. DSE.

Bélanger, Danièle, and Magali Barbieri (2009). "Introduction. State, Families and the Making of Transitions in Vietnam." In Reconfiguring families in contemporary Vietnam, edited by Danièle Bélanger and Magali Barbieri, 1–46. Stanford University Press.

Bendt, Pim, Stephan Barthel, and Johan Colding. 2013. "Civic greening and environmental learning in public-access community gardens in Berlin." Landscape and Urban Planning 109, no. 1: 18–30.

Certomà, Chiara. 2011. "Critical urban gardening as a post-environmentalist practice." Local Environment 16, no. 10: 977–987.

Certomà, Chiara, and Chiara Tornaghi. 2015. "Political gardening. Transforming cities and political agency." Local Environment 20, no. 10: 1123–1131.

Dannenberg, Peter, and Alexander Follmann. 2015. "Ringen um Grün in der Stadt." Standort 39, no. 2–3: 94–100.

Drummond, Lisa. 2000. "Street scenes: practices of public and private space in urban Vietnam." Urban Studies 37, no. 12: 2377–2391.

Drummond, Lisa 2003. "Popular television and images of urban life." In Consuming urban culture in contemporary Vietnam, edited by Lisa Drummond and Mandy Thomas, 155–169. London: Routledge Curzon.

Earl, Catherine. 2014. Vietnam's new middle classes: Gender, career, city. Copenhagen: Nias Press.

Ehlert, Judith, and Christiane Voßemer. 2015. "Food sovereignty and conceptualization of agency: A methodological discussion." Austrian Journal of South-East Asian Studies 8, no. 1: 7–26.

Evers, Anna, and Nicole L. Hodgson. 2011. "Food choices and local food access among Perth's community gardeners." Local Environment 16, no. 6: 585–602.

Firth, Chris, Damian Maye, and David Pearson. 2011. "Developing 'community' in community gardens." Local Environment 16, no. 6: 555–568.

Flores, Heather. 2006. Food not Lawns: How to Turn Your Garden and Neighbourhood into a Community. Chelsea Green: White River Junction.

Follmann, Alexander, and Valérie Viehoff. 2015. "A green garden on red clay. Creating a new urban common as a form of political gardening in Cologne, Germany." Local Environment 20, no. 10: 1148–1174.

Fuhrmann, Eva. 2017. Perceptions of Change in Vietnam. Human Environmental Values in a Peri-urban Area of Southeast Vietnam. Berlin: Regiospectra.

Gerber, Jonathan, Sarah Turner, and Lynne B. Milgram. 2014. "Food Provisioning and Wholesale Agricultural Commodity Chains in Northern Vietnam." Human Organization 73, no. 1: 50–61.

Gillen, Jamie. 2016. "Bringing the countryside to the city: Practices and imaginations of the rural in Ho Chi Minh City, Vietnam." Urban Studies 53, no. 2: 324–337.

Habermas, Jürgen. 1995. Theorie Kommunikativen Handelns. Frankfurt a. M.: Suhrkamp.

Harms, Erik. 2011a. Saigon's edge. On the margins of Ho Chi Minh City. Minneapolis: University of Minnesota.

Harms, Erik. 2011b. "Material symbolism on Saigon's edge: Symbolic transformation of Ho Chi Minh City's periurban zones." Pacific Affairs 84, no. 3: 455–473.

Harvey, David. 2012. Rebel Cities. London: Verso Book.

Kerkvliet, Benedict. 1993. State-village relations in Vietnam. Contested cooperatives and collectivization. Working paper Centre of Southeast Asian Studies, No. 85. Clayton: Monash University.

Koh, David. 2006. Wards of Hanoi. Singapore: ISEAS.

Krause, Monika. 2013. "The Ruralization of the World." Public Culture 25, no. 2 70: 233–248.

Kurfürst, Sandra. 2012a. Redefining Public Space in Hanoi. Places, Practices and Meaning. Zürich: LIT.

Kurfürst, Sandra. 2012b. "Informality as a strategy: Street traders facing constant insecurity." In Urban Informalities: Reflections on the Formal and Informal, edited by Colin McFarlane and Michael Waibel, 89–111. Farnham, Surrey: Ashgate.

Labbé, Danielle. 2016. "Critical reflections on land appropriation and alternative urbanization trajectories in periurban Vietnam." Cities 53: 150–155.

Lave, Jean, and Etienne Wenger. 1991: Situated Learning. Legitimate Peripheral Participation. Cambridge: Cambridge University Press.

Le Huu Viet, and Tra Giang. 2014. "Thuê 'kỹ sư osi' chăm sóc rau sạch tại gia." Accessed March 28, 2014, http://www.tienphong.vn/kinh-te/thue-ky-su-osin-cham-soc-rau-sach-tai-gia-670939.tpo.

Leaf, Michael. 2002. "A tale of two villages. Globalization and Peri-Urban Change in China and Vietnam." Cities 19, no. 1: 23–13.

Leaf, Michael, and Students of Plan 545. 1999. "Urbanization on the periphery: a Hanoi case study." Asian Urban Research Network Working Paper Series, No. 24, UBC Centre for Human Settlements, Vancouver.

Lefebvre, Henri. 1991. The Production of Space. Oxford: Blackwell.

Lentz, Christian. 2011. "Mobilization and State Formation on a Frontier of Vietnam." In: Journal of Peasant Studies 38, no. 3: 559–586.

Marr, David. 2004. "A brief history of local government in Vietnam." In Beyond Hanoi. Local Government in Vietnam, edited by Benedict Kerkvliet and David Marr, 28–55. Copenhagen: NIAS.

Ngome, Ivo, and Dick Foeken. 2012. "'My garden is a great help': gender and urban gardening in Buea, Cameroon." GeoJournal 77, no. 1: 103–118.

Nguyen Khac Tung. 1993. "The village: Settlement of Peasants in Northern Vietnam." In The traditional village in Vietnam, edited by Phan Huy Le, 7–43. Hanoi: The Gioi Publishers.

Nguyen Tu Chi. 1993. "The traditional Viet village in Bac Bo: Its organizational structure and problems." In The traditional village in Vietnam, edited by Phan Huy Le, 44–62. Hanoi: The Gioi Publishers.

Nguyen Tuan Anh, Jonathan Rigg, Luong Thi Thu Huong, and Dinh Thi Dieu. 2012. "Becoming and being urban in Hanoi. Rural-urban migration and relations in Viet Nam." Journal of Peasant Studies 39, no. 5: 1103–1131.

Nguyen Van Suu, 2004. "The politics of land: Inequality in Land Access and Local Conflicts in the Red River Delta since Decollectivization." In Social inequality in Vietnam and the challenges to reform, edited by Philip Taylor, 270–296. Singapore: ISEAS.

Parnell, Susan, and Jennifer Robinson. 2013. "(Re)theorizing Cities from the Global South: Looking Beyond Neoliberalism." Urban Geography 33, no. 4: 593–617.

Phan Huy Le. 2006. "Research on the Vietnamese Village: Assessment and Perspectives." In Viet Nam. Borderless histories, edited by Tran Nhung Tuyet and Anthony Reid, 23–41. Madison: University of Wisconsin.

Robinson, Jenny. 2006. Ordinary cities. Between modernity and development. London, New York: Routledge.

Roy, Ananya. 2014. "Worlding the South: towards a post-colonial urban theory." In The Routledge handbook on cities of the Global South, edited by Susan Parnell and Sophie Oldfield, 9–20. London: Routledge.

Salemink, Oscar. 2018. "The Regional Centrality of Vietnam's Central Highlands." In Oxford Research Encyclopedia of Asian History, edited by David Ludden, 1–30: Oxford University Press.

Schmelzkopf, Karen. 2002. "Incommensurability, land use, and the right to space: community gardens in New York City." Urban Geography 23, no. 4: 323–343.

Schwenkel, Christina. 2012. "Civilizing the City. Socialist Ruins and Urban Renewal in Central Vietnam." Positions 20, no. 2: 437–470.

Simiyu, Romborah R., and Dick Foeken. 2014. "Urban crop production and poverty alleviation in Eldoret, Kenya: Implications for policy and gender planning." Urban Studies 51, no. 12: 2613–2628.

Staeheli, Lynn, Don Mitchell, and Kristina Gibson. 2002. "Conflicting rights to the city in New York's community gardens." GeoJournal 58, no. 2/3: 197–205.

Thanh Nien News. 2016. "1.2 million Vietnamese move to the city every year." Accessed September 13, 2017, www.thanhniennews.com/society/12-million-vietnamese-move-to-cities-every-year-report-64140.html.

Thomas, Mandy. 2002. "Out of Control: Emergent Cultural Landscapes and Political Change in Urban Vietnam." Urban Studies, 39, no. 9: 1611–1624.

To Xuan Phuc. 2012. "When the *Đại Gia* (Urban Rich) go to the Countryside: Impacts of the Urban-Fuelled Rural Land Market in the Uplands." In The Reinvention of Distinction. Modernity and the Middle Class in Urban Vietnam, edited by Van Nguyen-Marshall, Lisa Drummond and Danièle Bélanger, 143–154. ARI: Springer Asia Series.

UN-Habitat. 2012. State of the World's Cities, 2012–2013. Nairobi: UN-Habitat.

Veblen, Thorstein. 1899. The theory of the leisure class. New York: A. M. Kelley.

Wahlberg, Ayo. 2012a. "A revolutionary movement to bring traditional medicine back to the grassroots level: On the biopolitization of herbal medicine in Vietnam." In Global Movements, Local Concerns: Medicine and Health in Southeast Asia, edited by Laurence Monnais-Rousselot and Harold J. Cook, 207–225. Singapore: NUS Press.

Wahlberg, Ayo. 2012b. "Family Secrets and the Industrialisation of Herbal Medicine in Postcolonial Vietnam." In Southern medicine for Southern people. Vietnamese medicine in the making, edited by Laurence Monnais-Rousselot, Claudia Michele Thompson und Ayo Wahlberg, 153–178. Cambridge Scholars Publishing.

Wahlberg, Ayo. 2014. "Herbs, Laboratories, and Revolution: On the Making of a National Medicine in Vietnam." East Asian Science, Technology and Society 8, no. 1:43–56.

Wertheim-Heck, Sigrid, and Geert Spaargaren. 2016. "Shifting configurations of shopping practices and food safety dynamics in Hanoi, Vietnam: a historical analysis." Agri Hum Values 33:655–671.

Witheridge, Jennifer and Nina J. Morris. 2016. "An analysis of the effect of public policy on community garden organisations in Edinburgh." Local Environment 21, no. 2: 202–218.

World Bank. 2018. "Urban population." Accessed January 25, 2018. https://data.worldbank.org/indicator/SP.URB.TOTL.IN.ZS

Part III

The Politics of Food Security

8

From Food Crisis to Agrarian Crisis? Food Security Strategy and Rural Livelihoods in Vietnam

Timothy Gorman

In 2007 and 2008, the world was gripped by a dramatic food crisis, as a confluence of factors—including the rising price of oil and oil-derived inputs like fertilizer and the dwindling of reserve food stocks across the Global South—conspired to drive the prices of staples like wheat and rice to record heights (Brown 2012). The crisis revealed new sources of instability lurking within the global food system, as grain traders took advantage of financialized commodity markets to reap speculative profits, driving up staple prices in the process, and as a growing reliance on food imports left countries around the world fully exposed to volatility in world price levels (Clapp and Cohen 2009). Across the Global South, high prices and scarce supplies touched off food riots and social unrest, culminating most dramatically in the uprisings that rocked the Arab world (Naylor 2014, p. 15; Barrett 2013; Patel and McMichael 2014).

Even Vietnam, a country that has made massive strides in strengthening its food security in recent decades, was not immune to the contagion.[1]

T. Gorman (✉)
Department of Sociology, Montclair State University, Montclair, NJ, USA
e-mail: gormant@montclair.edu

© The Author(s) 2019   **235**
J. Ehlert, N. K. Faltmann (eds.), *Food Anxiety in Globalising Vietnam*,
https://doi.org/10.1007/978-981-13-0743-0_8

Over the course of just a few days in April of 2008, the price of rice in Ho Chi Minh City doubled, reaching more than 20,000 Vietnamese Dong (VND) (or USD 1.3) per kilo, driven in part by the hoarding of supplies and the diversion of the rice harvest to export markets, where prevailing prices were even higher (Ngan 2010, p. 220). A contemporary account in the Saigon Economic Times (*Thời báo Kinh tế Sài Gòn*) described the scene: "In the past 20 years, we have not seen the sight of people lining up, shoving, and even fighting one another over a bag of rice. This may be the first time since 1989," claims the author, Hồng Văn, referring to the last years of socialist-era economic planning, "when people have had to line up to buy rice" (Văn 2008). Economist Peter Timmer, who has written extensively on the political economy of rice in Asia, expressed disbelief over the extent of the "panic" in Vietnam in a 2011 interview: "In Ho Chi Minh City, for heaven's sake, the center of the second-largest rice exporting surplus in the world, supermarkets and rice markets got cleaned out in two days" (Charles 2011).

The response of urban consumers to the rapid rise in rice prices and the perception of impending shortages illustrates the high degree of anxiety that continues to persist around rice and rice supplies in Vietnam, despite two decades of relative abundance that have followed the implementation of market reforms in the late 1980s. These anxieties were manifested not just in the queues that formed outside supermarkets in Ho Chi Minh City, but in the Vietnamese government's response to the crisis. In the face of rapidly rising rice prices, the government first moved to block rice exports; taking advantage of the structural legacies of the socialist era, in March 2008, the Prime Minister ordered the state-owned companies that dominate Vietnam's rice exports to cut outbound shipments and refrain from signing new contracts with foreign buyers (Alavi et al. 2012; Ngan 2010). Simultaneously, the government sought to crack down on the smaller private export sector by reducing quotas, raising minimum export prices above market levels, and implementing an export tax (Ngan 2010). This immediate attempt to stabilize the price and supply of rice was supplemented in 2009 by the promulgation of Resolution No. 63/NQ-CP, which sets out a long-term strategy aimed at ensuring Vietnam's food security and reducing the country's exposure to the volatility of global rice markets (see Zhang, this volume).

This chapter is a critical examination of the post-crisis food security strategy outlined in Resolution 63. The first half of the chapter consists of a close analysis of the text of the resolution itself, and focuses specifically on how "food security" is defined in the document and how this conceptualization reflects the cultural, historical, and political context in which it was formed. The second half of the chapter then draws from the perspectives of critical agrarian studies, and especially the concepts of "agrarian transition" (Byres 1977) and "agrarian crisis" (De Janvry 1981), to examine how the food security strategies encapsulated in Resolution 63 have reshaped the nature of agriculture and impacted rural communities in Vietnam. To do so, it draws on survey data collected from rural households in Bạc Liêu province, in the Mekong River Delta, to argue that the implementation of Resolution 63 has resulted not just in increased rice production, but also in an erosion of living standards among small farmers, a growing exodus from agriculture and into precarious forms of wage labor, and the concentration of agricultural land in the hands of a small number of large-scale commercial farmers.

Defining the Crisis and Framing the Response: "National Food Security" in a Vietnamese Context

Resolution (*Nghị quyết*) No. 63/NQ-CP on Ensuring National Food Security (*Đảm Bảo an Ninh Lương Thực Quốc Gia*) was issued by the Prime Minister of Vietnam, Nguyễn Tấn Dũng, on December 23, 2009. The resolution consists of five sections: a preamble which lays out the successes that Vietnam has achieved to date in terms of food security, but also acknowledges the "limitations and shortcomings" which remain to be resolved; a section setting forth basic premises or "viewpoints" (*quan điểm*) on Vietnam's food security, which affirms that "food security must be part of a general socio-economic development strategy" characterized by industrialization and modernization of the agricultural sector, and that rice and rice production are central to that strategy; a section that lays out "objectives" (*mục tiêu*) to be achieved by the year 2020, including specific targets for the rate of growth in agricultural output, the area of land under rice cultivation, malnutrition rates, food consumption and caloric intake, and farmers' incomes; a section on "major tasks and solutions" (*nhiệm vụ, giải pháp chủ yếu*), including an overhaul of the land-use planning system and new investments in infrastructure, agronomic research and extension, support for rice farmers and traders, and new guidelines on rice trading and export; and finally, a fifth section which assigns responsibility for realizing this strategy to the relevant authorities, including the Ministry of Agriculture and Rural Development and various provincial governments. While it has been supplemented in the intervening years by various decrees outlining concrete actions to be taken by these authorities, Resolution 63 remains the clearest and most-succinct formulation of Vietnam's national food security strategy, and the guiding document around which policy interventions continue to be formulated (Yen et al. 2017). The following section consists of a close analysis of its text, paying particular attention to the way in which "food security" is defined, as well as to exploring the historical and political context through which this conceptualization has taken form.

Food Security as Rice Security

The concept of "food security" is framed in the text of Resolution 63 not around "food" in an abstract or general sense, but around rice specifically. This is implicit even in the term for "food security" used in the text: *an ninh lương thực*, which directly translates to "security" (*an ninh*) of "staple grains" (*lương thực*), which in the Vietnamese context strongly implies rice. Resolution 63 not only employs this terminology, but specifically highlights rice as the crop and foodstuff most central to Vietnam's long-term food security. The section laying out the government's "viewpoints" on food security, for example, asserts that the "principal task" facing the country is to "bring into play" the country's advantage in rice production (*phát huy lợi thế về cây lúa*) while one of the "objectives" listed is the intensification of rice farming in the Mekong and Red River Deltas (Government of Vietnam 2009, pp. 49–50). The section on "major tasks and solutions," meanwhile, calls for the development of "planning zones of food production with great outputs of rice," the "strict protection" of rice-growing land, and large investments in irrigation canals, sea dykes, and other forms of infrastructure meant to facilitate and protect intensive rice cultivation, while the guidelines offered on scientific research, extension services, and the food trade similarly focus on rice over other foodstuffs (Government of Vietnam 2009, pp. 50–54).

The centrality of rice to Vietnamese food security policy—and the anxieties provoked among both urban consumers and policymakers during the rice price crisis of 2008—reflects the continued primacy of rice to Vietnamese diets and to culturally shaped conceptions of what "food" is and what kinds of food are essential to a well-balanced diet.[2] Even today, as Vietnam has become more affluent and as diets have shifted accordingly, the average Vietnamese person consumes most of her calories in the form of rice; on average, this translates to 1400 calories per day, equivalent to approximately 170 kg of rice per capita per year (Hai 2012, p. 3; Tsukada 2011, p. 59). The importance of rice to the Vietnamese diet is especially acute when it comes to the rural poor and urban working class, who are most dependent on this relatively cheap staple (Coxhead et al. 2012), and for whom rice represents a major expenditure, making them extremely sensitive to fluctuations in its price (Ha et al. 2015).

Rice is not just central to Vietnamese diets, but to Vietnamese cultural practices as well. In the Vietnamese language, the word *cơm*, which literally translates as "cooked rice," is used as general term for food. For example, a speaker of Vietnamese would not say whether she has "eaten yet," but whether she "has eaten rice yet" (*ăn cơm chưa*) (Hendry 2009, p. 185). In a country where the daily meals are referred to as *cơm sáng*, *cơm trưa*, and *cơm tối* (literally, "morning rice," "noon rice," and "evening rice"), the Vietnamese conception of a filling and nutritious meal thus hinges upon the presence of rice, without which one might not feel sated. Despite the degree to which baguettes and other foreign foods have been assimilated into Vietnamese culinary culture "a square meal for most, if not all, Vietnamese people" is, as cultural historian Vu Hong Lien notes, "still a meal with rice" (Vu 2016, p. 8). For these reasons, Vietnamese consumers are, as was amply demonstrated in the spring of 2008, extremely sensitive to shortages and price volatility in the rice market, both due to reliance on the grain as a staple and to cultural perceptions around its centrality and irreplaceability.

Food Security as Food Output and Abundance

Food security is defined in the resolution not around access or distribution, but around the supply and output of rice. Resolution 63 takes as its central aim that "adequate food supply sources" be achieved and maintained in order to "put an end to food shortage and hunger" (Government of Vietnam 2009, p. 50). In doing so, the Vietnamese government fixates on what food security scholar Per Pinstrup-Andersen calls the "supply side of the equation," while ignoring the fact that mere "availability does not ensure access" (Pinstrup-Andersen 2009, p. 5). This focus on food supply and availability goes against the tendency—at least in academic and global policy circles—to focus on issues of food access and distribution, rather than output figures alone.[3]

This focus on output over access, however, does have some basis in the experiences of post-war Vietnam, in which the intensity of hunger and privation has closely tracked fluctuations in overall food supply. In the decade following reunification in 1975, for example, food shortages were endemic, due to the stagnation of rice production, particularly in the Mekong Delta, in the face of attempts at collectivization by the new socialist authorities (Long 1993). These shortages were greatly alleviated by the *Đổi Mới* economic reforms of the late 1980s, which reintroduced markets for agricultural commodities and re-privatized land and other factors of agricultural production such as irrigation infrastructure, leading to an explosion of rice production; whereas Vietnam produced fewer than 20 million tonnes of paddy (unprocessed rice) in 1991, that number had increased by more than 50 percent, to over 30 million tonnes, by the end of the decade (Food and Agriculture Organization 2017; see Fig. 8.1). With the explosive growth of Vietnam's agricultural output and the general increase in living standards, the incidence of hunger fell drastically. In 1991, 46 percent of the population was undernourished, but by 2005, that figure had decline to less than 20 percent (Food and Agriculture Organization 2017).

More than a decade of rapid growth in rice output has, however, not completely relegated concerns about food security to the ash heap of history, and in the wake of the rice price crisis, they soon re-emerged, driven

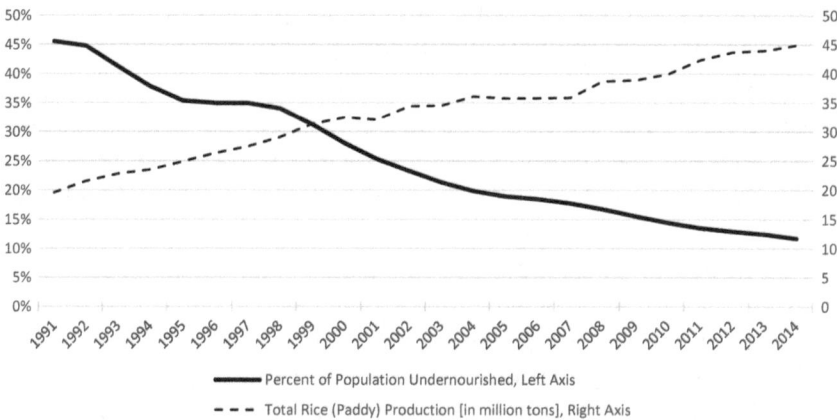

Fig. 8.1 Rice production and undernourishment in Vietnam, 1991–2014. (Source: Food and Agriculture Organization (2017))

by fears that Vietnam's rice output had begun to level off. After rising steadily over the 1990s, paddy production stagnated over the first years of the new millennium, falling off from a high of 36 million tonnes in 2004 and remaining below that peak in the three years leading up to the rice crisis. While such a level of output remained sufficient to meet domestic rice consumption needs, this arrested growth is framed as a major threat to Vietnam's continued food security in Resolution 63. In response, the resolution calls attention to three trends that had contributed to the stagnation of rice output, framing the reversal of these trends as essential to Vietnam's long-term food security.

The first of these trends is the decline in area under rice production. According to a report by the Ministry of Planning and Investment, published at the height of the rice crisis, almost 500,000 hectares of agricultural land were converted to other uses between 2000 and 2008, representing a loss of more than 5 percent of the country's base of agricultural land (Central Institute for Economic Management 2008, p. 20). This rapid loss of agricultural land raised alarm at the highest echelons of the Vietnamese political establishment; in an interview with the newspaper *Sài Gòn Giải Phóng* in December of 2008, the Minister of Agriculture, Cao Đức Phát, remarked "that the reclamation of agricultural land and its conversion to other uses is one of the most important threats to food security" in Vietnam (Nam 2008). Based on projections from Vietnam's Ministry of Agriculture and Rural Development, this trend was expected to continue further, with the total area of rice-growing land continuing on a steady decline from 4.3 million hectares in 2000 to 4 million in 2008 to an anticipated total of 3.6 million in 2020 (Hai 2012). Resolution 63 directly addresses this trend, and declares that 3.8 million hectares should be kept in rice production as a permanent "fund" (*quỹ*) of rice-growing land, to be "kept and strictly protected" by the government, at both the national and local levels (Government of Vietnam 2009, p. 51).

The second threat to rice output that is targeted in the resolution is the stagnation of rice yields in Vietnam. After rising steadily, they too began to level off in the years before the rice crisis (Yu et al. 2010), compounding the effect posed by the dwindling base of rice-growing land. To achieve such yield gains, the Resolution outlines two major policy thrusts: the first being new investment in development and dissemination of new, higher-yielding seed varieties (including genetically modified organisms), and the second the promotion of mechanization, especially of the rice harvest (Government of Vietnam 2009, p. 52). At present, the resolution states, the continued reliance on manual labor allows for significant losses in the harvesting process; it thus sets as a target for 2020 the use of mechanical combines on at least 50 percent of the harvested area, setting the bar significantly higher, at 80 percent, for the Mekong Delta (Government of Vietnam 2009, p. 52).

The third threat to rice output identified in the resolution is potentially the most severe: that of climate change and sea-level rise, which stand to impact food security by degrading agricultural capacity in key rice-growing regions, particularly the Mekong Delta (Government of Vietnam 2009, p. 52). As the seas rise, the tides push salt water up the mouth of the Mekong and into the canals that crosshatch the delta, making the cultivation of rice increasingly difficult, especially during the dry season, when this phenomenon, known as saline intrusion, is most severe. At present, approximately 1.8 million hectares in the Mekong Delta, or about 45 percent of the region's total land area, are affected by saline intrusion (Smajgl et al. 2015, p. 167). By 2050, that figure is projected to increase to 2.1 million, and nearly 300,000 hectares of rice-growing land are expected to become uncultivable due to saline intrusion (Yu et al. 2010; Mekong River Commission 2011, p. 175). According to estimates, the adverse impacts of climate change will reduce rice output in the Mekong Delta by 2.7 million tonnes by 2050, representing a 13 percent decrease from 2007 levels (Yu et al. 2010, p. 8). To combat this threat, Resolution 63 calls for broad investment in the construction and improvement of infrastructure systems designed to counteract the threat of sea-level rise and its impact on national food security. These include dikes and other measures to physically seal off vulnerable areas, such as the Mekong Delta, from the rising tides and thus to "protect production and the assets of the state and the people" from the impact of sea-level rise, as well as irrigation canals to ensure the year-round availability of fresh water in "concentrated food production regions" (Government of Vietnam 2009, p. 51).

"National" Food Security as Self-Sufficiency in Rice

Food security is conceptualized in Resolution 63 as "national food security" (*an ninh lương thực quốc gia*), a framing which calls further attention away from issues of access and distribution to the overall balance of food supply and demand at the level of the territorially bounded nation-state. Seen from this perspective, the decline in harvested area and the stagnation of rice yields are problematic because Vietnam's population has continued to grow, threatening the country's continued capacity to meet its own consumption needs without resorting to rice imports. Thus, the resolution takes as its general objective that the growth in rice output overtake the rate of population growth by 2020 (Government of Vietnam 2009, p. 50), reflecting the evident concern of policymakers over the country's ability to feed a population that is expected to grow to 100 million in 2020, and potentially reach 130 million by 2030, up from just 50 million at the country's reunification in 1975 (McPherson 2012, p. 139). This projection informs the minimum target of 3.8 million hectares of rice-growing land set out in the resolution, which should, if intensively cultivated, provide sufficient rice output to feed Vietnam's projected future population.

This embrace of self-sufficiency goes against several decades of policy orthodoxy by policymakers and economists at multilateral development institutions, such as the World Bank and the Food and Agricultural Organization (FAO), which have encouraged countries in the Global South to shift production from staple grains to high-value cash crops, and then use the proceeds from exports to finance food imports. As the chairman of Cargill, one of the world's largest food traders, remarked in 1993, rather than "develop the capacity to grow food for local consumption," countries in the Global South should simply "produce what they produce best – and trade" (Kneen 2002, p. 10). Through structural adjustment agreements and the strictures of free trade agreements like the General Agreement on Tariffs and Trade (GATT), these institutions served to re-orient agriculture in the Global South from self-provisioning and national food security to an "export industry producing 'non-traditional exports' for sale to the developing world" (McMichael and Schneider 2011, p. 122); examples of such non-traditional exports include fresh fruits and vegetables, as well as meat and farmed seafood.

The cost of such specialization in non-traditional exports is, however, an increased reliance on imported staples, and with it an intensified exposure to the vicissitudes of global food markets. While all staples have demonstrated some price volatility in recent years, the global rice market is "notoriously unstable," in the words of economist Peter Timmer, due to the relatively small volume of rice that is traded internationally in proportion to global demand (Timmer 2015, p. 49). This instability was on abundant display during the price crisis of 2007–2008, when the global rice price increased by more than 300 percent in a matter of months. The renewed push for self-sufficiency encapsulated in Resolution 63 reflects, therefore, not just concerns over falling output, but rising anxieties on the part of Vietnamese policymakers over Vietnam's integration into global food markets, and increasing skepticism that such markets could be relied upon as a source of rice imports in times of global economic crisis. A food security strategy document drafted by the Center Institute for Economic Management (part of the Ministry of Planning and Investment) at the height of the crisis in 2008 pointed, for example, to the "global turmoil" and the "chaotic situation of the food market that is now playing out in many countries," as a reason for which the Vietnamese state and communist party must re-affirm their commitment to "ensuring food security for the future" so as not to become reliant on such markets for supplies of vital staples such as rice (Central Institute for Economic Management 2008, p. 16).

Vietnam was not alone in reaffirming its commitment to food self-sufficiency and limiting its exposure to global market forces in the aftermath of the crisis. Indeed, as Timmer observes, the crisis drove "policymakers in rice-consuming countries," especially those in Southeast Asia, "to insulate their domestic rice economies from the world market" (Timmer 2015, p. 49), as by promoting the settlement of new agricultural land in Malaysia and building new irrigation infrastructure in the Philippines (McCulloch and Timmer 2008; Trethewie 2012; Alavi et al. 2012, pp. 79–80). This trend was so pervasive that a 2012 World Bank report on the crisis and policy response in Southeast Asia attributed these efforts to a "perception, deeply embedded in the Asian culture and political psyche, that food security is best defined as self-sufficiency, especially in rice" (Alavi et al. 2012, p. 34).

Food Security as Political Imperative

Finally, Resolution 63 affirms the leading role and responsibility of the Vietnamese state in ensuring "national food security," as defined within the parameters outlined above. By nature of its relatively dense population and scarcity of arable land, and of its exposure to environmental hazards such as drought, floods, and typhoons, Vietnam has always been vulnerable to food shortages. Throughout its history, Vietnam has also been heavily influenced by Confucian political thought, which places a strong emphasis on the prevention of famine as central to the responsibilities of the sovereign and necessary to the maintenance of a well-ordered society. Confucius is recorded, for example, as listing the key "requisites of government" as "sufficiency of food, sufficiency of military equipment, and the confidence of the people in their ruler" (Confucius 1971, p. 254). If, by contrast, the government was unable to ensure adequate supplies of food, it was taken as a sign that the king had lost the "mandate of heaven," and thus his legitimacy (Woodside 1989). Indeed, famine was a potent driver of unrest and rebellion throughout Vietnam's pre-colonial history, and the maximization of rice production remained a consistent concern of its kings (see Peters, this volume). In 1460, for example, when Lê Thánh Tông took the throne, he immediately issued an edict "exhorting rural people to grow as much rice as possible," and "repeatedly reminded" local officials "to check that all available land was in production" (Taylor 2013, p. 218). Centuries later, the kings of the Nguyễn dynasty pursued the settlement and clearance of the Mekong Delta as a means of relieving demographic pressures and increasing the food supply by bringing new lands under cultivation (Nguyen-Marshall 2005, pp. 22–23).

The capacity for food shortages to spark social unrest and catalyze political change has, if anything, intensified in recent decades. In the waning days of World War II, the disruption of south-north shipping by Allied bombing and the hoarding of rice by French and Japanese authorities touched off a horrific famine that killed upwards of a million in northern Vietnam, setting the stage for Ho Chi Minh's abortive seizure of power and declaration of Vietnamese independence in September of 1945 (Gunn 2014). In light of the evident ability of food shortages to spark social unrest and political upheaval, the Vietnamese Communist Party has, since coming to power in the 1950s, focused on "self-reliance" in food as one of its primary concerns, and made great "efforts to industrialize the agricultural sector as a way to achieving food self-sufficiency" (Tran Thi Thu 2011, p. 71). Even these efforts, however, were not enough to ward off endemic rice shortages in the 1980s. These shortages eventually culminated in the storming of warehouses and granaries by hungry peasants in the Red River Delta in 1986, an event which contributed to the promulgation of the *Đổi Mới* reforms in that same year (Kerkvliet 2005, p. 208).

The political potency of hunger and food insecurity is, of course, not unique to Vietnam, a fact demonstrated in abundance at the peak of the food price crisis in 2008. Across the Global South, high prices and scarce supplies touched off food riots and social unrest, culminating in the uprisings of the Arab Spring. That the uprisings in Egypt and elsewhere, as with the 2007 "Saffron Revolution" in Myanmar, were triggered in part by rising food prices, could not have been lost on Vietnamese policymakers (Coe 2014; Kingston 2008). As a recent review of Vietnam's food security policies, composed by senior staffers at the Ministry of Planning and Investment, put it, "solving the problem of food insecurity" comprises the "fundamental base for Vietnam's social and political stability" (Yen et al. 2017, p. 44). To this end, the re-affirmation of self-sufficiency in rice as a strategic goal in the aftermath of the 2008 price crisis reflects the view, long held by the country's leadership, that the supply and price of rice are "far too important" to Vietnam's social and political stability "to be left to the whims of an unstable world market" (Timmer 1993, p. 200), and that instead the country must continue to rely on domestic production to satisfy demand for this crucial staple (see Zhang, this volume).

From Food Crisis to Agrarian Crisis: Self-Sufficiency at What Cost?

The way in which food security is defined by the Vietnamese government in Resolution 63—in terms of rice output and the balance between consumption and production at the national level—directly shaped the policies pursued in the aftermath of the rice price crisis. This section first examines three of these policy interventions, including the embrace of land-use planning as a means of ensuring Vietnam's long-term self-sufficiency in rice production, renewed investment in infrastructure projects meant to stave off the impacts of climate change and to facilitate the intensification of rice production, and the use of subsidies and other supports to encourage the modernization and mechanization of rice production. The remainder of the section then looks at the ways in which these concrete policy interventions have shaped social conditions in rice-growing areas, drawing on survey data from Bạc Liêu province in the Mekong Delta.

Policy Initiatives: From Conceptualization to Implementation

The first policy intervention outlined in Resolution 63 is the endorsement of land-use planning as a means to achieve food security and self-sufficiency, an effort which builds on the socialist-era legacy of centralized natural resource management. In the language of the resolution, "national food production must be based on the utilization of the advantages of each region, the efficient use of land and water resources, with priority given to planning zones of food production with large output in rice … in order to achieve national food security targets" (Government of Vietnam 2009, p. 50). Of such zones, the one to which the resolution attaches the greatest importance is the Mekong Delta, the nation's largest rice-producing area.

As McPherson notes, the principal means by which the Vietnamese government aims to achieve its vision of food security and goal of rice self-sufficiency is through "explicit controls over rice land" (McPherson 2012, p. 138). Thus, the vision of planning endorsed in Resolution 63 is primarily a negative one, aimed at halting the further conversion of rice-growing land to other uses and thus ensuring that the area under rice cultivation does not fall below the 3.8-million-hectare minimum set forth in the resolution. A subsequent policy document, Decree (*Nghị định*) No. 42/2012/ND-CP on the Management and Use of Rice-Growing Land (*Quản lý, Sử dụng Đất Trồng Lúa*), elaborates on the restrictions laid out in Resolution 63, forbidding the transfer of land out of rice production except "for purposes of national defense and security," or in other cases of "national and public interest" (Government of Vietnam 2012, p. 2).

While vague on many points of implementation, Resolution 63 does set out, in detail, a new set of procedures by which local and provincial governments must realize the rice cultivation targets of the central government through the planning apparatus: first, local authorities must draft detailed land-use plans, which set aside specific areas for rice, as well as the cultivation of perennial crops, forestry, aquaculture, and industrial and residential use; then, these detailed plans must be submitted to the Prime Minister for approval; once the plans are finalized, any additional changes to the plan that involve the conversion of rice-growing land to other uses must be resubmitted to the Prime Minister's office for approval, essentially centralizing control of even the most minute details of agricultural land-use planning at the uppermost levels of the government. The Resolution, however, assigns the primary responsibility for "strictly managing the fund of agricultural production land, especially planned rice land" to the provincial authorities, who are to punish any violators of the land-use plan through fines and other means. Although the enforcement of such restrictions may vary, it has been noted elsewhere that, on the whole, "land use planning is most strictly enforced in rice cultivation" (Giesecke et al. 2013, p. 1202).

The second intervention outlined in Resolution 63 is a call for greater investment in infrastructure, to both support the intensification of existing rice agriculture and to offset the potential damage posed by climate change. The resolution includes specific calls for the development of irrigation infrastructure to serve at least 3.2 million hectares of rice-growing land, as well as for "investment in building new dike systems" as a means of "coping with sea level rise" (Government of Vietnam 2009, p. 51). The reliance on infrastructural solutions to Vietnam's long-term food security challenges, as outlined in Resolution 63, is reflected in a number of large-scale water control projects launched in the aftermath of the food price crisis. In 2012, the Prime Minister's office issued a new water resources development plan for the Mekong Delta region, which committed VND 107,700 billion (equivalent to over USD 5 billion) to the construction of sea dykes, flood control systems, and irrigation canals intended to mitigate the impact of climate change and to maintain the region's high level of agricultural output (Benedikter 2014, pp. 115–116).

The third intervention outlined in the resolution is a new set of measures aimed at supporting the modernization and mechanization of agriculture through enhanced subsidies and supports. In broad terms, this allocation of resources illustrates the commitment of the Vietnamese state to maximizing rice production and achieving its stated goal of rice self-sufficiency not solely through the use of coercive land-use policy, but also through positive inducements designed to make rice production more rewarding for individual producers. These measures include a subsidy of VND 500,000 to 1 million (equivalent to approximately USD 25–50) per hectare per year for land under rice production, the exemption of agricultural land from taxation, a reduction on tariffs for imported machinery, pesticides, and fertilizers, and the indefinite suspension of irrigation charges (Hai 2012; Yen et al. 2017; Thang and Linh 2015). Additionally, the Vietnamese government has subsidized loans taken out by farmers for the purchase of agricultural inputs (Yen et al. 2017, p. 55),

supplied support to rice farmers hit by natural disasters and disease outbreaks, and provided subsidies for expenses involved in "reclaiming" or
clearing land for rice cultivation (Thang and Linh 2015).

From Intervention to Impact: Food Security Policy and Agrarian Transition in Bạc Liêu

This section draws on key concepts from the field of agrarian studies to
argue that the implementation of the food security strategy outlined in
Resolution 63 has intensified an ongoing process of "agrarian transition"
in the case study area (Byres 1977). As defined by T. J. Byres, an agrarian
transition is a process by which "capitalism becomes the dominant mode
of production in agriculture" (Byres 1977, 258). While the form taken by
capitalist agriculture varies from context to context, its distinguishing
factor is the "central importance of productive capital" in farming and
the reinvestment of profits in "an endless cycle of accumulation" whereby
such capital, such as land and machinery, is continuously acquired and
productive capacity expanded (Bernstein 2010). In the Mekong Delta,
this transition has been defined by the shift toward more intensive and
mechanized rice production on relatively large farms. With this transition have come both changes in the nature of rice production itself and
in the broader social relations around agriculture, leading to increasing
social polarization and bringing adverse consequences to the smallholder
farmers who once comprised the social base of rice production in the
study site. To explore these changes, this section focuses on a single village
in Bạc Liêu province, in the Mekong Delta, drawing on household surveys from the periods before and after the rice crisis and the issuance of
Resolution 63.

Bạc Liêu province (see Fig. 8.2) is an ideal location in which to examine the impacts of the food security strategy laid out in Resolution 63,
since it is heavily impacted by two trends identified in the resolution as
major threats to Vietnam's long-term food security: the conversion of
rice-growing land to other uses and the adverse impact of saline intrusion
and sea-level rise on intensive rice cultivation. Between 1996 and 2006,
the production of farmed salt-water shrimp, mainly tiger prawn (Penaeus

VIETNAM

Bạc Liêu Province

Fig. 8.2 Location of Bạc Liêu province in Vietnam. (Source: Generated by author using shapefile from the GADM Database of Global Administrative Areas, Version 2.8 (http://www.gadm.org). Used with permission by Robert J. Hijmans, database developer)

monodon) in Bạc Liêu increased more than tenfold, from under 6000 tonnes per year to more than 60,000. Over the same period, the surface area used for aquaculture ponds nearly tripled, from 42,600 hectares to 120,200 (see Fig. 8.3). As shrimp production exploded, rice production in the province declined, from a high of 893,500 tonnes of paddy in 2000 to an average of just 655,000 over the five-year period between 2004 and 2007, a decline mirrored by a drop in the area of rice harvested per year (see Fig. 8.4). By virtue of its proximity to the coast and its location in the Cà Mau peninsula, Bạc Liêu is heavily affected by saline intrusion, as tidal forces drive salt water inland via rivers and irrigation canals

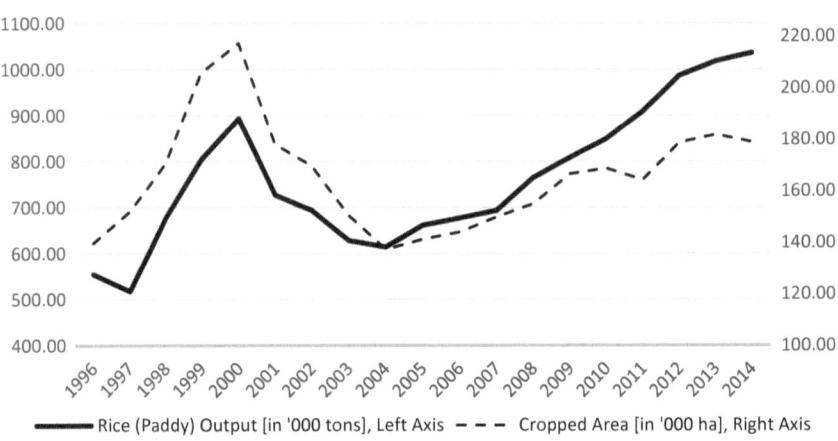

Fig. 8.3 Rice output and cropped area, Bạc Liêu province, 1996–2014. (Source: http://fsiu.mard.gov.vn/data/trongtrot.htm)

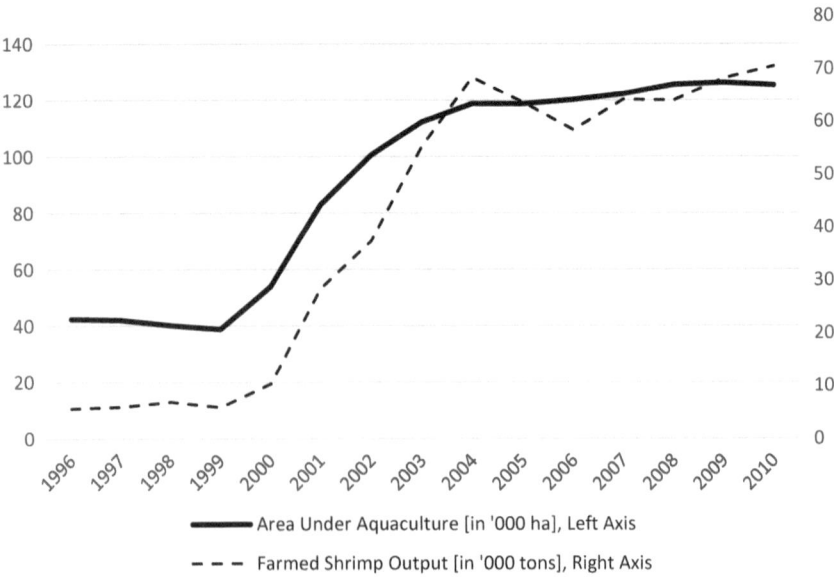

Fig. 8.4 Farmed shrimp production and area under aquaculture, Bạc Liêu province, 1996–2010. (Source: http://www.gso.gov.vn/default_en.aspx?tabid=469)

(Kotera et al. 2008). As the seas rise, this phenomenon will only intensify, putting the future of rice cultivation in Bạc Liêu at risk, unless significant investments are made in protective infrastructure (Tuan and Chinvanno 2011; Smajgl et al. 2015).

To arrest the decline in rice production and rice area in Bạc Liêu, Vietnamese authorities have relied on land-use planning and on the construction of physical infrastructure meant to blunt the adverse impact of global climate change. In 2010, 77,610 hectares, or about one-third of the province's total area, was under intensive rice cultivation; according to the land-use plan developed by the province and approved by the national government in 2012, however, this area is to be expanded to 83,000 hectares by the year 2020 (Government of Vietnam 2013). To make the expansion and intensification of rice agriculture possible, the national government has since 2009 invested VND 691 billion (or approximately USD 35 million) in a system of 66 sluice gates, designed to seal off irrigation canals and block the inflow of salt water into the rice-growing areas of Bạc Liêu (Ministry of Agriculture and Rural Development 2017). The active measures taken by the Vietnamese government in recent years to protect and intensify rice production in Bạc Liêu have borne significant fruit, as evidenced by the dramatic uptick in both overall rice output and total area cropped since 2010 (see Figs. 8.4 and 8.5). In 2013, for example, paddy production in Bạc Liêu surpassed, for the first time, 1 million tonnes per year, up from a low of 614,000 tonnes in 2004.

Against this backdrop of increased rice production—and the seeming success of efforts to ensure Vietnam's food security and self-sufficiency by boosting rice output in places such as Bạc Liêu—the remainder of this section seeks to assess the impact of such land-use planning and infrastructural measures on the social and class relations around agriculture, using a village, identified here by the pseudonym "Hòa Bình" (after the district in which it is located), as a case study (see Fig. 8.5). This case study draws on socio-economic survey data from 2001, collected by Tran Thi Ut and researchers from the International Rice Research Institute (Tran Thi Ut 2004), as well as a follow-up survey conducted by the author and research assistants from Cần Thơ University in 2014. In each iteration, every household in Hòa Bình village was surveyed, for a total of 162

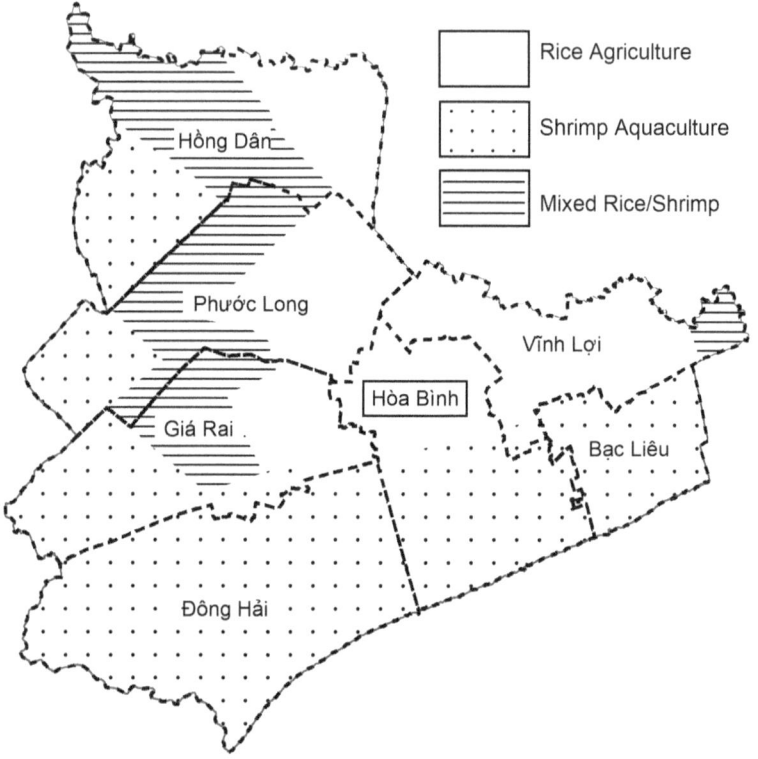

Fig. 8.5 Land-use map of Bạc Liêu province with district names and case study site (Hòa Bình). (Source: Generated by author using shapefile from the GADM Database of Global Administrative Areas, Version 2.8 (http://www.gadm.org). Used with permission by Robert J. Hijmans, database developer)

households in 2001 and 223 in 2014, allowing for a comparison of socio-economic conditions and agrarian livelihoods in the period before the food crisis in 2007–2008 and that which followed the issuance of Resolution 63 in 2009.

The first and most glaring result which may be gleaned from these data is a dramatic upsurge in rice production, surpassing even the significant gains made at the provincial level. In 2001, for example, households in the village cultivated a total of 219.5 hectares of rice land, almost all of which was used to produce two crops per year, and harvested a total of 1880 tonnes of rice. By 2014, however, the area under rice cultivation had increased from 219.5 hectares to 322.5 hectares, as new irrigation and salinity-control works made more of the land in the village suitable for rice agriculture, and as the stringent enforcement of the land-use plan constricted alternative cropping practices, such as aquaculture or the cultivation of fruit and vegetable gardens. By the time of the re-survey in 2014, all of the rice-growing households in the village (both those with large and small holdings) had switched from growing two crops of rice to three per year, in response to changes to the land-use plan and exhortations by local authorities, as well as to the newly built sluice gates, which afforded protection from saline intrusion and thus made the cultivation of an additional dry-season crop feasible.

As a result, the total harvest in Hòa Bình village increased more than threefold during the period between the two surveys, reaching a total of 6006.5 tonnes in 2015. This dramatic increase in agricultural output, however, belies a significant reduction in the social basis of rice production, and in particular the relative decline of farming as a primary means of livelihood and of smallholder owner-operators as a class. This can be seen first by examining the rate of participation in rice agriculture. In 2001, 91 percent of households in the village (147 of 162) were directly involved in rice production. By 2014, that share had dropped to 81 percent (or 181 of 223 households), but this fails to capture the full extent of the decline in the primacy of rice farming as a livelihood.

A closer examination of the data on household income sources illustrates, in more striking detail, the shift away from smallholder rice farming. In 2001, more than three quarters of the households in the village (122 of 162) were primarily self-employed agriculturalists: that is, they derived more than half their total household income from agriculture and less than half of their income from wages, both in the agricultural sector and beyond (see Fig. 8.6). By 2014, however, fewer than half of all households in the village (or 109 out of 223) were primarily self-employed farmers, while the share of households primarily dependent on non-agricultural wage labor (such as construction or factory work) increased dramatically, from 3.7 percent to 25.6 percent.

This movement out of agriculture is in keeping with a broader trend, observed across the Global South, of "de-agrarianization," whereby rural households derive a decreasing share of their incomes from farming

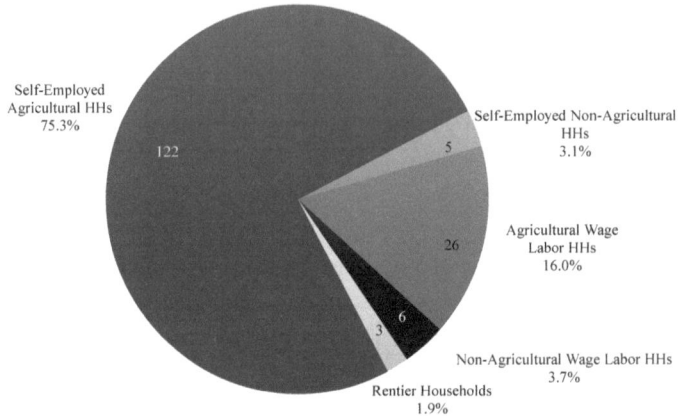

Class Structure in 2001

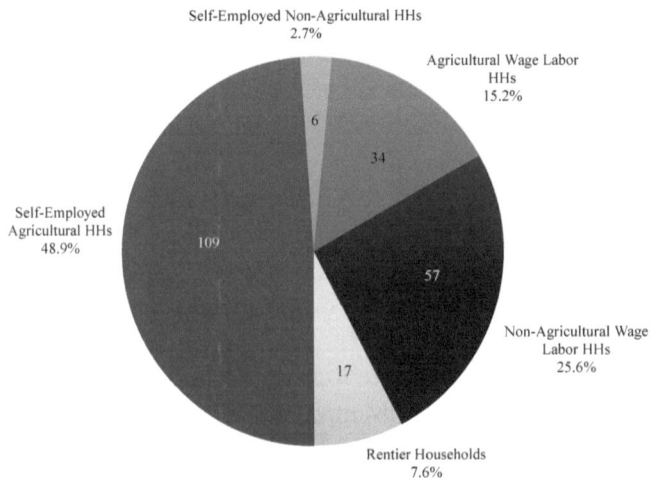

Class Structure in 2014

Self-Employed Agricultural Households
Receive >50% of Income from Agri-/Aquaculture &
Receive <50% of Income from Wages

Non-Agricultural Wage Labor Households
Receive <50% of Income from Agri-/Aquaculture &
Receive >50% of Income from Wages

Agricultural Wage Labor Households
Receive >50% of Income from Agri-/Aquaculture &
Receive <50% of Income from Wages

Self-Employed Non-Agricultural Households
Receive <50% of Income from Agri-/Aquaculture &
Receive <50% of Income from Wages

Rentier Households
Receive >30% of Income from Renting out Land and Machines

Fig. 8.6 Changing class structure in Hòa Bình village. (Source: 2001 survey data collected by Tran Thi Ut (2004); 2014 data collected by author)

(Bryceson 1997; Rigg 2006). As the social base of agriculture declines (i.e. as fewer and fewer households are involved in agriculture itself, even as the overall output and cultivated area increase), there occurs a concomitant process, also widely discussed in the field of agrarian studies, of concentration and accumulation, especially of land. Such a phenomenon has been widely observed in Vietnam over the past two decades, and has been especially pronounced in the Mekong Delta (Akram-Lodhi 2005; Prota and Beresford 2012; Gorman 2014).

Hòa Bình village is no exception to this broader trend, as evidenced by an increase in the percentage and number of households without land. In 2001, only 7 households in the village (or 4.3 percent of the total) were functionally landless, meaning that they had less than 500 square meters of agricultural land. By 2014, that number had grown to 24 (or 11 percent of the total). Alongside this increase in landless households came the growing concentration of land in the hands of larger farmers. In 2001, for example, the top 20 percent of households owned 105 hectares of agricultural land (or 45 percent of the total agricultural land in the village) while in 2014 that figure had increased to 161 hectares (or 50 percent of the total). This increasing concentration of land can be quantified using the Gini coefficient, which assigns a numerical score (ranging from 0 to 1) to assess how equally an asset is distributed among a population, with higher scores indicating more inequality. In 2001, the Gini coefficient for agricultural land was 0.408, but by 2014, it had increased to 0.487 (see Fig. 8.7).

What we see occurring in Hòa Bình village is thus a reflection of a broader process of "agrarian transition," now underway in the Mekong Delta, whereby large, highly mechanized, and commercially oriented farms displace the previously dominant model of smallholder, or "peasant," agriculture (Byres 1977; De Koninck 2004). The reasons for this transition can be traced to downward pressures on per-hectare profits, as prices for fertilizer, fuel, pesticides, seeds, and other inputs rise while output prices remain stagnant. As a result of this "price squeeze" (or *ép giá* in Vietnamese), the profit margin for rice agriculture is thin; in Hòa Bình village, a typical farmer can make a profit of roughly VND 40–50 million, or USD 2000–2500, per hectare per year, assuming that he or she grows three crops and does not experience any significant losses

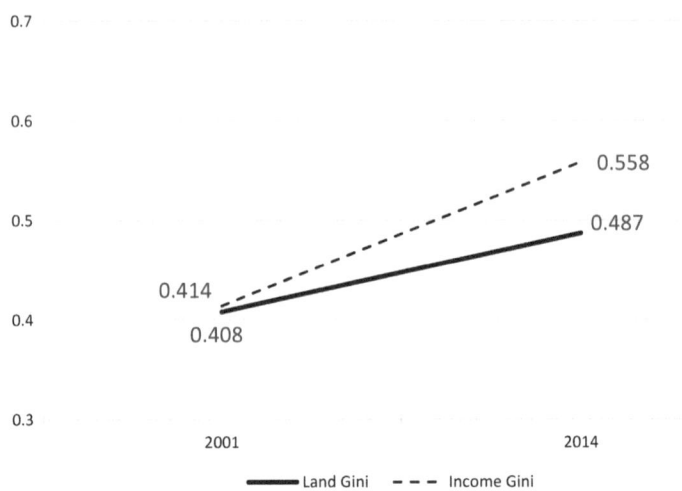

Fig. 8.7 Gini coefficients for land and income, Hòa Bình Village. (Gini coefficients calculated using ineqdec0 module in Stata, weighted by household size). (Source: 2001 survey data collected by Tran Thi Ut (2004); 2014 data collected by author)

due to drought, pest outbreaks, storms, or saline intrusion. For small farmers in Hòa Bình, one hectare is a typical holding, and many have even less land; in a country where average gross domestic product (GDP) now exceeds USD 2000 per capita, such a sum is wholly insufficient to meet the needs of an entire family, especially given the rising costs of healthcare and education.[4]

As a result, many households that formerly relied on rice agriculture have become increasingly dependent on other livelihoods and income sources, such as petty trading, casual construction labor in the district town, and, increasingly, remittances from sons and daughters in the industrial zones of Bình Dương and Đồng Nai, located a few hundred kilometers away to the north of Hồ Chí Minh City. While some of these households remain involved in agriculture as a sideline economic activity, many have sold all or part of their farmland to larger operators. As described elsewhere (Gorman 2014), this emerging class of capitalist farmers consists of local villagers who typically received larger plots during the process of post-socialist land privatization in the 1980s and 1990s, and who have been able, through further acquisitions, to amass farms ranging from 5 to 30 hectares. By utilizing economies of scale, these farmers are able to reap significant gains through intensive rice production, gains they have re-invested in the acquisition of more land and of machinery such as tractors and combine harvesters.

The end result of such accumulation has not just been increasing inequality in the distribution of land, but of income as well: in 2001, the Gini coefficient for income distribution in Hòa Bình village stood at 0.414 and, by 2014, it had increased to 0.558 (see Fig. 8.7). What this rising inequality reflects is an increasing gap between the incomes of those households engaged in large-scale rice farming, which frequently exceed VND 50 million (or USD 2500) per capita per year, and those of the former farmers now relegated to non-agricultural wage labor, for which the average income is only VND 13 million (or USD 650) per household member, a figure far below the national average as well as the global poverty threshold of USD 1.90 per person per day used by the World Bank (World Bank 2015).

Conclusion: From Food Crisis to Agrarian Crisis?

The data from Hòa Bình village illustrate the fundamental paradox of Vietnam's food security strategy: by fostering the development of "modern," mechanized, and large-scale rice production through policy initiatives (such as per-hectare subsidies for rice producers and support for the purchase of mechanical inputs such as combines and tractors) that clearly favor large producers over smallholders, and by promulgating land-use plans and constructing physical structures (such as sluice gates) designed to promote and facilitate intensive rice production, the government of Vietnam has achieved dramatic successes in raising rice output and forestalling the next food crisis. At the same time, however, these interventions have prevented smallholders from engaging in alternative production strategies, such as the cultivation of fruits and vegetables or even the conversion of agricultural land to salt-water ponds for shrimp aquaculture, that might offer higher returns per hectare than rice and thus provide a more viable source of livelihood for those with limited land resources. In this way, the implementation of policies designed to boost rice production in the name of national food security have at the same time undermined the position of small farmers who have traditionally comprised the backbone of Vietnamese agriculture.

For those small farmers now being pushed out of rice agriculture at a rapid pace, both in Hòa Bình village and in the Mekong Delta more broadly, there are few attractive economic alternatives. This is especially true for older household members, given the preference for younger workers (and especially women) in the factories of Vietnam's industrial zones. This lack of options is compounded by the disappearance of wage labor opportunities in the agricultural sector itself. In the course of the author's fieldwork, many poorer farmers in the village recounted that they were once able to supplement their incomes by performing seasonal work on the farms of their neighbors, especially at harvest time. With the recent turn to mechanized combine harvesters, however, this source of income has evaporated. As a result, households that once relied primarily on rice agriculture now find themselves dependent on casual manual labor and remittances from family members, both of which provide relatively low, and erratic, income streams compared to farming.

In sum, then, the interventions made by the Vietnamese state in the name of food security, defined for political, historic, and cultural reasons as national self-sufficiency in rice, have contributed to the declining viability of smallholder rice agriculture and to the general air of agrarian crisis in the countryside. Vietnam's unfolding agrarian crisis, though distinct in its particulars, parallels developments elsewhere, such as Latin America and India, where small farmers have found themselves crushed under the weight of rising costs, falling profits, and ballooning debt (De Janvry 1981; Lerche 2011; Shah 2012). In their survey of the current state of agrarian studies and of the key challenges facing agrarian communities in the Global South, Akram-Lodhi and Kay trace the contours of such agrarian crises, wherein "an exclusive emphasis on farming" no longer presents an "adequate survival strategy" for rural households, who instead become dependent on "a plethora of fragmentary and insecure sources" of non-agricultural income, including "the sale of temporary and casualized waged labor," as well as "handicraft manufacture, petty merchant trading, the provision of petty services, and … remittances arising from migration" (Akram-Lodhi and Kay 2010, p. 179). Though written in broad terms to capture a generalized phenomenon, this summation captures perfectly the situation now unfolding in the rice-growing areas of the Mekong Delta. The question, however, remains of whether the Vietnamese state will, almost a decade on the rice price crisis of 2007–2008, continue to prioritize the maximization of rice output as the linchpin of its food security strategy—in the hope of averting the kind of urban unrest that has toppled comparable regimes elsewhere in the world—and by doing so, risk unraveling the social fabric of rural areas in the Mekong Delta and beyond.

Notes

1. As shown in Fig. 8.1, based on data from the Food and Agriculture Organization, the incidence of malnutrition in Vietnam has plunged since the 1990s, while overall output of food (especially rice) has increased dramatically.
2. A similar point about the cultural centrality of rice in Japan is made by Ohnuki-Tierney (1993).
3. For example, at the 1996 World Food Summit, "food security" was officially defined not as the quantitative abundance of food, but the condition that "exists when all people, at all times, have physical and economic access to sufficient safe and nutritious food that meets their dietary needs and food preferences for an active and healthy life" (Food and Agriculture Organization 1996).
4. According to Vietnam's General Statistics Office, the cost of healthcare and education services rose by 129.28 percent and 131.54 percent, respectively, between 2009 and 2015. In contrast, consumer prices as a whole increased by 59.51 percent (General Statistics Office of Vietnam 2017).

References

Akram-Lodhi, A. H. (2005) 'Vietnam's Agriculture: Processes of Rich Peasant Accumulation and Mechanisms of Social Differentiation', *Journal of Agrarian Change,* 5(1), 73–116.

Akram-Lodhi, A. H. and Kay, C. (2010) 'Surveying the agrarian question (part 1): unearthing foundations, exploring diversity', *The Journal of Peasant Studies,* 37(1), 177–202.

Alavi, H. R., Htenas, A., Kopicki, R., Shepherd, A. W. and Clarete, R. (eds.) (2012) *Trusting trade and the private sector for food security in Southeast Asia* (Washington, D.C.: World Bank).

Barrett, C. B. (ed.) (2013) *Food security and sociopolitical stability*, First edition (Oxford: Oxford University Press).

Benedikter, S. (2014) *The Vietnamese hydrocracy and the Mekong Delta: water resources development from state socialism to bureaucratic capitalism* (Berlin: Lit Verlag).

Bernstein, H. (2010). *Class dynamics of agrarian change* (Sterling, Virginia: Kumarian Press).

Brown, L. R. (2012) *Full planet, empty plates: the new geopolitics of food scarcity*, First Edition (New York: W.W. Norton & Company).

Bryceson, D. F. (1997) *Farewell to farms: de-agrarianisation and employment in Africa* (Aldershot: Ashgate).

Byres, T. J. (1977) 'Agrarian transition and the Agrarian question', *The Journal of Peasant Studies*, 4(3), 258–274.

Central Institute for Economic Management (2008) *Đảm bảo An ninh Lương thực trên Thế giới và ở Việt Nam (Ensuring Food Security Globally and in Vietnam)*, Hanoi: Ministry of Planning and Investment.

Charles, D. (2011). How Fear Drove World Rice Markets Insane. In *All Things Considered*: National Public Radio.

Clapp, J. and Cohen, M. J. (eds.) (2009) *Global Food Crisis: Governance Challenges and Opportunities* (Waterloo: Wilfrid Laurier University Press).

Coe, C. A. (2014) 'Minding the Metaphor. Vietnamese State-Run Press Coverage of Social Movements Abroad', *Journal of Vietnamese Studies*, 9(1), 1–35.

Confucius (1971) *Confucian analects, The great learning, and the doctrine of the mean*, (Translated by: Legge, J.) (New York: Dover Publications).

Coxhead, I., Linh, Vu Hoang and Tam, Le Dong (2012) 'Global market shocks and poverty in Vietnam: the case of rice', *Agricultural Economics*, 43(5), 575–592.

De Janvry, A. (1981) *The agrarian question and reformism in Latin America* (Baltimore: The Johns Hopkins University Press).

De Koninck, R. (2004) 'The Challenges of the Agrarian Transition in Southeast Asia', *Labour Capital and Society*, 37(1&2), 285.

Food and Agriculture Organization (1996) *Rome Declaration on World Food Security and World Food Summit Plan of Action*. Rome (92-5-503939-3).

Food and Agriculture Organization (2017) *FAOSTAT Database*. Rome. Available at: http://www.fao.org/faostat/ (Accessed: May 10 2017).

General Statistics Office of Vietnam (2017) *Consumer price index, gold and USD price indexes, December 2015* Available at: https://www.gso.gov.vn/default_en.aspx?tabid=625&ItemID=15502 (Accessed: May 10 2017).

Giesecke, J. A., Tran, Nhi Hoang, Corong, E. L. and Jaffee, S. (2013) 'Rice Land Designation Policy in Vietnam and the Implications of Policy Reform for Food Security and Economic Welfare', *The Journal of Development Studies,* 49(9), 1202–1218.

Gorman, T. (2014) 'Moral Economy and the Upper Peasant: The Dynamics of Land Privatization in the Mekong Delta', *Journal of Agrarian Change,* 14(4), 501–521.

Government of Vietnam (2009) *Resolution No. 63 NQ-CP of December 23, 2009, on National Food Security.* Hanoi: Government of Viet Nam. Available at: http://extwprlegs1.fao.org/docs/pdf/vie95278.pdf (Accessed: May 10 2017).

Government of Vietnam (2012) *Nghị định số 42/2012/ND-CP về Quản lý, Sử dụng Đất Trồng Lúa (Decree No. 42/2012/ND-CP on the Management and Use of Rice-Growing Land).* Hanoi: Government of Vietnam. Available at: http://vnu.edu.vn/upload/vanban/2012/09/28/2012_05_11-42_2012_ND-CP_Ve-quan-ly-su-dung-dat-tron g-lua.pdf (Accessed: May 10 2017).

Government of Vietnam (2013) *Nghị quyết số 51/NQ-CP về việc quy hoạch sử dụng đất đến năm 2020 và kế hoạch sử dụng đất 5 năm kỳ đầu (2011–2015) tỉnh Bạc Liêu (Resolution 51/NQ-CP on Land Use Planning to 2020 and the 2011–2015 Five-year Land Use Plan of Bạc Liêu Province).* Hanoi: Government of Vietnam.

Gunn, G. C. (2014) *Rice wars in colonial Vietnam: the Great Famine and the Viet Minh road to power* (Lanham, Maryland: Rowman & Littlefield).

Ha, Pham Van, Nguyen, Hoa Thi Minh, Kompas, T., Che, Tuong Nhu and Trinh, Bui (2015) 'Rice Production, Trade and the Poor: Regional Effects of Rice Export Policy on Households in Vietnam', *Journal of Agricultural Economics,* 66(2), 280–307.

Hai, Le Trong (2012) *The Rice Situation in Vietnam*, Manila: Asian Development Bank.

Hendry, J. B. (2009) *Rural Vietnam: the small world of Khanh Hau* (New Brunswick: AldineTransaction).

Kerkvliet, B. J. (2005) *The power of everyday politics: how Vietnamese peasants transformed national policy* (Ithaca, N.Y.: Cornell University Press).

Kingston, J. (2008) 'Burma's Despair', *Critical Asian Studies,* 40(1), 3–43.

Kneen, B. (2002) *Invisible giant: Cargill and its transnational strategies,* 2nd ed. (London and Sterling, Va.: Pluto Press).

Kotera, A., Sakamoto, T., Nguyen, Duy Khang and Yokozawa, M. (2008) 'Regional consequences of seawater intrusion on rice productivity and land use in coastal area of the Mekong River Delta [Viet Nam]', *JARQ – Japan Agricultural Research Quarterly*, (4), 267–274.

Lerche, J. (2011) 'Agrarian Crisis and Agrarian Questions in India', *Journal of Agrarian Change*, 11(1), 104–118.

Long, Ngo Vinh (1993) 'Reform and Rural Development: Impact on Class, Sectoral, and Regional Inequalities', in Turley, W.S. & Selden, M. (eds.) *Reinventing Vietnamese socialism: doi moi in comparative perspective* (Boulder, Co.: Westview).

McCulloch, N. and Timmer, P. C. (2008) 'Rice Policy in Indonesia', Bulletin of Indonesian Economic Studies, 44(1), 33–44.

McMichael, P. and Schneider, M. (2011) 'Food Security Politics and the Millennium Development Goals', *Third World Quarterly*, 32(1), 119–139.

McPherson, M. (2012) 'Land Policy in Vietnam: Challenges and Prospects for Constructive Change', *Journal of Macromarketing*, 32(1), 137.

Mekong River Commission (2011) *Assessment of Basin-wide Development Scenarios: Main Report, Basin Development Plan Programme* (Vientiane, Lao PDR: Mekong River Commission).

Ministry of Agriculture and Rural Development (2017) *Thông tin dự án: Hệ thống phân ranh mặn ngọt tỉnh Bạc Liêu – Sóc Trăng (Project Description: System to Demarcate the Saline-Fresh Boundary in Bac Lieu and Soc Trang Provinces)*. Hanoi. Available at: http://mic.mard.gov.vn/Project/1051.aspx (Accessed: May 10 2017).

Nam, Thành (2008) *Bộ trưởng Bộ NN-PTNT Cao Đức Phát: Thế mạnh của nước ta hiện nay vẫn là nông nghiệp (Minister of Agriculture and Rural Development Cao Đức Phát: The Strength of our Country is Still Agriculture)*. Sài Gòn Giải Phóng Online. Available at: http://www.sggp.org.vn/bo-tru-ong-bo-nnptnt-cao-duc-phat-the-manh-cua-nuoc-ta-hien-nay-van-la-nong-nghiep-276243.html (Accessed: May 10 2017).

Naylor, R. (ed.) (2014) *The evolving sphere of food security* (Oxford: Oxford University Press).

Ngan, Pham Hoang (2010) 'The Vietnamese rice industry during the global food crisis', in Dawe, D.C. (ed.) *The rice crisis: markets, policies and food security* (London: Earthscan).

Nguyen-Marshall, Van (2005) 'The Moral Economy of Colonialism: Subsistence and Famine Relief in French Indo-China, 1906-1917', *The International History Review*, 27(2), 237–258.

Ohnuki-Tierney, E. (1993) *Rice as self Japanese identities through time* (Princeton, N.J.: Princeton University Press).

Patel, R. and McMichael, P. (2014) 'A political economy of the food riot', in Pritchard, D. & Pakes, F.J. (eds.) *Riot, unrest and protest on the global stage* (Basingstoke: Palgrave Macmillan).

Pinstrup-Andersen, P. (2009) 'Food security: definition and measurement', *Food Security*, 1(1), 5–7.

Prota, L. and Beresford, M. (2012) 'Emerging Class Relations in the Mekong River Delta of Vietnam: A Network Analysis', *Journal of Agrarian Change*, 12(1), 60–80.

Rigg, J. (2006) 'Land, farming, livelihoods, and poverty: Rethinking the links in the Rural South', *World Development*, 34(1), 180–202.

Shah, E. (2012) '"A life wasted making dust": affective histories of dearth, death, debt and farmers' suicides in India', *The Journal of Peasant Studies*, 39(5), 1159–1179.

Smajgl, A., Toan, T., Nhan, D., Ward, J., Trung, N., Tri, L., Tri, V. and Vu, P. (2015) 'Responding to rising sea levels in the Mekong Delta', *Nature Climate Change*, 5(2), 167–174

Taylor, K. W. (2013) *A history of the Vietnamese* (Cambridge: Cambridge University Press).

Thang, Tran Cong and Linh, Dinh Thi Bao (2015) *Rice Policy Review in Vietnam*: Food and Fertilizer Technology Center for Asia and Pacific Region. Available at: http://ap.fftc.agnet.org/ap_db.php?id=406.

Timmer, C. P. (1993) 'Food Policy and Economic Reform in Vietnam', in Ljunggren, B. & Perkins, D.H. (eds.) *The Challenge of reform in Indochina* (Cambridge, MA: Harvard University Press).

Timmer, C. P. (2015) *Food security and scarcity: why ending hunger is so hard*, (Translated by, 1st ed. (Philadelphia: University of Pennsylvania Press).

Tran Thi Thu, Trang (2011) 'Food security versus food sovereignty choice of concept, policies, and classes in Vietnam's post-reform economy', *Kasarinlan: a Philippine journal of Third World studies*, 26(1), 68–88.

Tran Thi Ut (2004) 'Land and Water Resource Management in Coastal Areas: Assessing the Socio-economic Impact of Government Intervention, Bac Lieu Province, Mekong Delta, Vietnam', RCSD Working Paper.

Trethewie, S. (2012) In Search of Food Security: Addressing Opacity and Price Volatility in ASEAN's Rice Sector, Singapore: RSIS Center for Non-Traditional Security Studies.

Tsukada, K. (2011) 'Food Security in a Rice-Exporting Country', in Shigetomi, S., Kubo, K. & Tsukada, K. (eds.) *The world food crisis and the strategies of Asian rice exporters* (Chiba-shi, Japan: Institute of Developing Economies, IDE-Jetro).

Tuan, Le Anh and Chinvanno, S. (2011) 'Climate Change in the Mekong River Delta and Key Concerns on Future Climate Threats', in Stewart M., Coclanis P. (eds) *Environmental Change and Agricultural Sustainability in the Mekong Delta. Advances in Global Change Research, vol 45* (Dordrecht: Springer), 207–217.

Văn, Hồng (2008) *Cơn sốt gạo – cơ hội để nhìn lại ("Rice Fever" – An Opportunity to Reflect).* Thời báo Kinh tế Sài Gòn (Saigon Economic Times Online) (Accessed: May 10 2017).

Vu, Hong Lien (2016) *Rice and baguette: a history of food in Vietnam* (London: Reaktion Books).

Woodside, A. (1989) 'History, Structure, and Revolution in Vietnam', *International Political Science Review/Revue Internationale de Science Politique,* 10(2), 143.

World Bank (2015) *FAQs: Global Poverty Line Update.* Available at: http://www.worldbank.org/en/topic/poverty/brief/global-poverty-line-faq   (Accessed: May 10 2017).

Yen, Vu Hoang, Nhung, Nguyen Hong and Dung, Tran Anh (2017) 'Overview of Vietnam's food security policies', in Petersen, E. (ed.) *Vietnam Food Security Policy Review* (Canberra: Australian Centre for International Agricultural Research), 44–66.

Yu, Bingxin, Zhu, Tingju, Breisinger, C. and Hai, Nguyen Manh (2010) *Impacts of climate change on agriculture and policy options for adaptation: The Case of Vietnam,* Washington: International Food Policy Research Institute.

9

When Food Crosses Borders: Paradigm Shifts in China's Food Sectors and Implications for Vietnam

Hongzhou Zhang

Introduction

The paradigm shift of China's overall food security strategy as well as the Chinese consumers' growing anxiety over the safety and affordability of domestically produced food products have important implications for global food security and food markets beyond its borders, particularly its Southern neighbor—Vietnam. While Chinese agricultural presence in other Southeast Asian countries, particularly Myanmar, Cambodia, and Laos, has received a significant amount of attention from academics and research organizations during the past few years (Baird and Barney 2017; Chheang 2017; Fox and Castella 2013; Lu and Schönweger 2017; Schoenberger 2017), the close yet complicated food ties between China and Vietnam have appeared much less frequently in discussions, and the

H. Zhang (✉)
S. Rajaratnam School of International Studies (RSIS), Nanyang Technological University, Singapore, Singapore
e-mail: ishzzhang@ntu.edu.sg

© The Author(s) 2019
J. Ehlert, N. K. Faltmann (eds.), *Food Anxiety in Globalising Vietnam*,
https://doi.org/10.1007/978-981-13-0743-0_9

analysis of the potential impacts of the recent changes in China's overall food security strategy and consumption patterns on Vietnam's food sectors is also lacking.

Against this background, this chapter aims to provide a preliminary overview of the macro trends that are emerging in regard to the Chinese food security strategy at the national level and the food preferences at the household level and its implications for Vietnam. Moving away from the traditional micro-perspective analysis which focuses on the economic, social, and environmental impacts of various forms of Chinese agro-capitalism, this chapter adopts a macro-perspective: examining how Vietnam fits into China's new food security strategy as well as the shifting dietary preferences of Chinese consumers and its potential implications for Vietnam's food sectors. Conceptually, this chapter wishes to highlight trans-border aspects of food anxiety. While most of the data used in this chapter are from China's Bureau of Statistics and the Food and Agriculture Organization of the United Nations (FAO) and sources such as government reports, news articles, and existing Chinese and English literature, some insights were drawn from the author's field research observations. From November 5, 2013, to November 14, 2013, the author visited Nanning City in China, Hanoi in Vietnam and the border regions between two countries. During the field study trip, the author had extensive interviews with local scholars, grain traders, farmers, and government officials in both countries. Given the references used, this chapter mainly pronounces the Chinese perspectives and domestic discourses on the country's role in global food trade and food initiatives having a spillover effect beyond its national borders.

The chapter is structured as follows. The section "Paradigm Shift in China's Overall Food Security Strategy" concisely reviews China's food security strategy and its recent changes. Then, the section "Major Changes in Chinese Food Consumption Patterns" analyzes the major changes in Chinese food consumption patterns. After providing a brief background of the various aspects of the food ties between China and Vietnam, the section "Implications for Vietnam" studies the potential implications of the macro changes in China's food security strategy and consumption patterns for Vietnam. A short conclusion is given in the last section.

Paradigm Shift in China's Overall Food Security Strategy

For decades, influenced by the painful memories of periodic famines and distrust toward the international market, China has embarked on a policy of achieving self-sufficiency in grain. Largely reacting to Lester Brown's 1994 article "Who Will Feed China"[1] (Qureshi 2008), China issued the country's first ever food security White Paper in 1996 (Brown and Halweil 1998; Goldenberg 2015). In this white paper, China officially announced the 95 percent self-sufficiency rate as the bottom line of its food security strategy, and also pledged to achieve absolute self-sufficiency in cereals, including wheat, rice, and corn (State Council, PRC 1996). Significant reduction in China's grain output in the early 2000s led both domestic and international audiences to doubt China's ability to feed itself (Zha and Zhang 2013). During the 2007–2008 global food crisis, China promulgated the first ever *National Mid- to Long-Term Food Security Plan (2008–2020)* in which the government reiterated its commitment to achieving a 95 percent self-sufficiency rate in grain supply and 100 percent cereal self-sufficiency (State Council, PRC 2008).

With strong political commitment and policy support from the government, China has achieved 12 years of consecutive grain production increase since 2003 (see Table 9.1). Its total grain production reached 616 million tonnes in 2016, over 40 percent higher than that of 2003. In spite of the remarkable growth in domestic grain production, China's total grain imports surged during the same period, reaching 125 million tonnes in 2015. Besides, official targets of the 95 percent self-sufficiency rate for grain and 100 percent for cereals have been breached. Looking into the future, forecasts by international organizations and local institutes indicate that domestic grain demand and the production gap will continue to widen (see Table 9.2).

Imports of other agricultural products also soared. Regarding overall agricultural trade, China was still a net exporter of agricultural products, with USD 2.4 billion trade surplus in 2003. By 2015, China had become the largest importer of agricultural products, with an agricultural trade deficit of USD 50 billion (Ministry of Commerce, P.R. China

Table 9.1 China's annual grain production and imports

Year	Total production (million tonnes)	Grain total imports (million tonnes)	Grain imports as % of China's total production
2003	431	25.3	5.87
2004	470	33.5	7.13
2005	484	36.5	7.54
2006	498	37.1	7.45
2007	502	37.3	7.43
2008	529	41.3	7.81
2009	531	52.2	9.83
2010	547	67	12.25
2011	571	63.9	11.19
2012	590	80.3	13.61
2013	602	86.5	14.37
2014	607	100	16.47
2015	621	125	20.13
2016	616	114	18.50

Source: National Bureau of Statistics, P.R. China (2017, 11–7, 12–1)

Table 9.2 China's grain production and demand forecasts by different organizations

Organization	Base year	Total demand in 2020 (estimated), million tonnes	Targeted production by 2020, million tonnes	Self-sufficiency rate
OECD/FAO	2013	746	550	73.7%
Food and Agricultural Policy Research Institute	2011	726	550	75.8%
United States Department of Agriculture	2013	775	550	71.0%
State Bureau of Statistics, P.R. China	2013	725	550	75.9%
Institute of Agriculture Economy, China	2013	741	550	74.2%

Source: Trade Promotion Center of the Ministry of Agriculture, P.R. China (2016, 53–59)

2002–2016). China is now the largest importer of pork, rubber, cotton, dairy and dry whole milk powder, to name but a few.

It is increasingly clear that domestic production has fallen short of rapidly rising demand. Faced with these challenges, in December 2013,

China began to reform its food security strategy. For the first time, China opted for "domestic supply with moderate imports". While rhetorically, top leaders including the Chinese President Xi Jinping have repeatedly said that China must rely on itself to achieve food security, the basis of China's food security strategy has shifted from grain self-sufficiency to self-sufficiency of overall grain-producing capacity (Ren 2015; Ministry of Agriculture, P.R. China 2017). In other words, China is implementing a new food production policy, which is based on farmland management and application of technology, to ensure the effective supply of agricultural products and grain security. It aims to enhance the crop producing capacity through better land management and utilization of advanced agro-technologies, rather than to have all the food crop at hand and in the barn (FAO 2016). This means more attention will be given to protecting the critical resources, arable land and water in particular, instead of boosting actual grain production through intensive farming. In the meantime, better utilization of international agricultural resources has become an integral part of China's food security strategy.

Although self-sufficiency is still at the center of China's food security strategy, some major changes have taken place. On the one hand, the definition of grain has been redrawn. The central focus of the food security strategy has shifted from ensuring grain self-sufficiency (which covers not only rice, wheat, and corn, but also soybean, root tubers such as potatoes, and coarse grains) to basic self-sufficiency in cereals (wheat, rice, and corn) *and* absolute security of the staples (rice and wheat). In other words, the new food security strategy demands optimal allocation of resources to safeguard supplies of the country's staples—rice and wheat. Over the past two years, while absolute security of staples has repeatedly been stressed, the country's overall grain-producing capacity, rather than the actual output of a particular year, has become the goal of China's new food security strategy (Ren 2015). In 2016, it is announced that China does not seek a consecutive increase in grain output during the next five years, and the country will focus on consolidating and improving grain output capacity. On the other hand, "moderate imports" officially form part of the national food security strategy. It is the first time in history that "moderate imports" as a policy option have been explicitly accepted. It calls for "more active utilization of the international food market and agricultural resources to effectively coordinate and supplement the domestic grain supply" (Cheng and Zhang 2014).

Boosting Domestic Food Production and Global Consequences

Investing in agricultural technology is considered vital for addressing China's food security problems. China will increase investment and subsidies for the agricultural technology sector to improve land yield, resource efficiency, and labor productivity. In particular, with very limited land and water resources, yield improvement has consequently become the most promising solution to China's food security problem, and China has placed great emphasis on agricultural technologies, particularly Genetically Modified (GM) technologies. To promote the development of GM technology, China made it a development priority in its 12th Five-Year Plan (2011–2015) and the state has invested billions of dollars into GM technology development. In November 2015, China National Chemical Corp (ChemChina) entered talks to buy the Swiss-based Syngenta (one of the biggest seeds and pesticides company in the world) for USD 41.7 billion. Subsequently, ChemChina increased its offer to more than USD 43 billion, and successfully acquired Syngenta in May 2017. This is the largest overseas acquisition by a Chinese company to date. Being the world's largest agricultural producer and leading food importer, China's attitude toward GMOs will have a far-reaching impact on future GM research and investment and the global agricultural industry (Zhang 2016a).

Confronted with limited land and fresh water resources, China is turning toward its "blue lands" (including its territorial waters and Exclusive Economic Zones—EEZs) for food. At the 18th Party Congress, Chinese leaders pledged to enhance China's capacity for exploiting marine resources. Development of aquaculture and offshore fishing is being prioritized. In fact, the food security concern has been the main driver for two key structural changes that are taking place in China's fishery sector: the rapid growth of the aquaculture sector and outward expansion of the marine fishery sector. While these structural changes tend to have a positive contribution to China's food security strategy at least in the short term, they are generating consequences which go beyond the fishery sector and the national boundary. For instance, more and more fishing incidents involving Chinese fishermen have triggered greater conflicts in regional waters. The outward and rapid expansion of China's marine fishery sector has put further pressure on the already limited stocks in the world and could further weaken the already fragile marine ecology (Greenpeace 2015; Mallory 2013; Zhang 2016b).

Furthermore, while China recognizes that the agricultural sector must be modernized, the prevalence of small, fragmented land plots and unproductive farms render the task daunting, as pointed out by Chen Xiwen (2017), the former head of the Chinese Communist Party Office on rural policy and deputy head of the party's office of financial affairs. China's household-based smallholding agriculture has inherent limitations. Chief among these are the high costs and risks in gaining the capital, the skills, and especially the market access needed for commoditized agriculture, which deterred many small agriculturalists from making the transition. As such, China began to formulate and implement its agricultural modernization program in the mid-1990s, which aimed to transform the country's small-scale, household-based agriculture into a modernized agriculture, with the emphasis on increased scale, specialized production of higher-value goods, and market-orientation (Zhang 2012).

Agriculture Goes Global

China's outward-looking food security approach has three major aspects. First, China aims to import more food from the international market. In the coming years, not only imports of soybeans, cotton, edible crops, sugar, dairy, and other agricultural products will increase, more cereal, mainly maize, will also be imported from the international market. With China's increasing reliance on imports, the country's agricultural import diversification will become critical for global agricultural development. China's current agricultural imports are limited to a few agricultural products and national suppliers, particularly the United States. Such diversification entails import of various agricultural products via multiple channels, regions, and approaches. Its purpose is to reduce risks caused by overdependence on a few suppliers, particularly the United States (Wu and Zhang 2016).

The second aspect is the expansion of overseas agricultural investment. Stated-owned agribusiness, private companies, and even individual farmers from China have ventured abroad through leasing or purchasing foreign agricultural land ranging from Southeast Asia to Russia's Far East, Central Asia, Australia, New Zealand, Africa and Latin America. China is supporting its agricultural companies—both the state-owned enterprises such as COFCO and the Beidahuang Group as well as private companies such as Shuanghui and Bright Groups—to become global players that can compete with established global agribusiness giants such as Cargill. It is estimated that over the past five years, China's overseas food-related mergers and acquisitions (M&A) reached USD 20 billion. This includes Shuanghui International's USD 4.7 billion takeover of American company Smithfield Food in 2013, the acquisition of Dutch grain trader Nidera and Singapore-based Noble Group's agribusiness by China National Cereals, Oils, and Foodstuffs Corporation, and ChemChina's USD 41.7 billion purchase of Syngenta (Zhang 2016a).

Pushing forward the new model of global agricultural cooperation is the third aspect of China's global agricultural policy. China aims to further liberalize its agricultural sector to enhance the country's food security. Based on the principle of mutually beneficial cooperation, China gives economic and technological support to developing the agricultural sector in neighboring countries. China is also enhancing connectivity with neighboring countries by establishing more cross-border trade centers and free trade zones, and improving diplomatic ties for cross-border investment under the framework of China's Belt and Road Initiative—the trillion-dollar economic integration undertaking proposed by China that focuses on connectivity and cooperation between Eurasian countries As the most populous country in the world and a major food trader, China's food security is highly dependent on global food trade and global food security. For this reason, the Chinese government believes it has both interest and responsibility to contribute to global food security. Strengthening global food security is seen as a critical means to safeguard China's own food security. Apart from providing agricultural assistance to developing countries to enhance their agricultural production, China is emerging as a major donor of food in the world. In 2011, when the food security situation exacerbated in East Africa, China provided close to USD 70 million worth of food aid to help countries combat hunger. China has increased its donations to the Food and Agricultural Organization (FAO), the World Food Program and the International Agricultural Consultative Group, and now plays a stronger role in the newly reformed FAO Committee on Food Security (Zha and Zhang 2013). Nevertheless, it should be noted that some are quite critical of China's global agricultural engagement. On the one hand, as the food security emerges as a top international concern after the global food crisis in 2007/2008, many feared that China had embarked on a state-sponsored quest to lock up vast tracts of land in developing countries of Africa, Southeast Asia, Latin America, and Central Asia to grow food to feed itself (Financial Times 2008). Many news reports and studies accused China of playing a leading role in land-based foreign investment in agriculture, usually being criticized as a so-called land grabber or neocolonial power (Hofman and Ho 2012).

Major Changes in Chinese Food Consumption Patterns

Moving Away from Grains

Since the Reform and Opening up in 1978, China's economy has experienced phenomenal growth. Per capita income of Chinese residents increased remarkably as well. The per capita annual income of urban residents reached USD 4890 in 2015, up from merely USD 52.7 in 1978; per capita annual income of the rural residents amounted USD 1657 in 2015, representing over 90 times of increase as compared to that of 1978 (National Bureau of Statistics, P.R. China 2017). In the meanwhile, China also experienced very rapid urbanization. In the late 1970s, over 80 percent of Chinese lived in rural areas, yet, by 2015, China's urbanization rate reached 56.1 percent (National Bureau of Statistics, P.R. China 2017).

Table 9.3 Trend in per capita consumption of major food products of China (kg)

	1980	1986	2010	2020f
Grain	190.3	207.1	148	128.4
Vegetables	134	na	175.4	209.2
Fruits	6.3	na	55.9	92
Edible oil	1.7	na	12.6	na
Sugar	1.6	na	5.6	8.3
Poultry and meat	12.6	na	48.9	62.9
Aquatic products	2	na	21.2	28.3
Milk	1.4	na	26.9	45.9
Eggs	1.8	na	12.1	14.5

Source: Han (2014, 59)

Against extraordinary income growth and rapid urbanization, the Chinese dietary pattern has changed notably, and the trend is still ongoing.

As shown in Table 9.3, the Chinese diet is moving away from grain. China's per capita grain consumption has been declining steadily since it peaked in 1986. By 2010, per capita grain consumption has fallen by nearly 30 percent as compared to the peak level of 1986 and it is forecasted to drop further to 128.4 kg by 2020. By contrast, per capita consumption of the major non-grain food products has all increased, though at varied rates. While per capita consumption of vegetables has modestly increased to 175 kg per capita from 134 kg in 1980, which is expected to reach 209.2 kg in 2020, the per capita consumption of fruits, meat, sugar, aquaculture products, milk, and eggs have experienced explosive growth during the same period. From 1980 to 2010, China's per capita annual consumption of fruits had increased 7.8 times, poultry and meat 2.8 times, aquatic products 9.6 times, milk over 18 times. The shift in the Chinese diet is expected to continue as seen in Table 9.3.

A Widening Dichotomy in Food Consumption Patterns

Beneath the overall shift of China's diet as discussed above, a widening dichotomy in China's food consumption patterns is surfacing along with the growing income and a huge rural-urban divide. Similar to the experience of other countries, China's rapid economic growth in the past decades is associated with soaring inequality among its citizens. China's income inequality has exploded over the past decades. In 1980, China's Gini coefficient (a measure of inequality) stood at 0.3, according to People's Daily; in 2012, it was at 0.49 and the World Bank considers a coefficient above 0.40 to represent severe income inequality. Although the official statistics indicate China's Gini coefficient has dropped slightly since 2012, it is still among the highest in the world, and some scholars even suggested the official number is an underestimation. For example, an estimate by economists at the Southwest University of Finance and Economics in Chengdu put the Gini coefficient at 0.61 in 2010 (Wildau and Mitchell 2016). Despite the controversies regarding China's Gini coefficient, what is clear is that while the size of China's middle and high-income group is expanding, a significant number of Chinese remain poor. One-third of the country's wealth is owned by the top 1 percent of households, while the bottom 25 percent account for only 1 percent of wealth (Xie and Jin 2015). Furthermore, based on China's new poverty line, there are still over 100 million Chinese living under it. This income inequality has thus created a dichotomy in food consumption patterns of the Chinese consumers.

On the one hand, the affluent middle-income and high-income consumers are experiencing growing anxieties over the quality and safety of the food products, particularly those produced domestically. For three consecutive years, food safety has been ranked as number one social concern by the Chinese, according to opinion polls. The 2014 China Comprehensive Moderate Prosperity Index Survey revealed that 53.3 percent of the interviewees were dissatisfied with China's food safety situation (Center for Coordination and Innovation of Food Safety Governance 2014).

In 2015, the Chinese Ministry of Environmental Protection and the Ministry of Land and Resources released the first ever results of a nationwide soil pollution survey that took place from 2005 to 2013. The survey result indicates that 16.1 percent of China's soil and 19.4 percent of its arable land showed contamination with inorganic chemicals like cadmium, nickel, and arsenic (BBC 2014). Contamination of food by heavy metals—particularly cadmium, lead, mercury, and arsenic—is of great concern as it affects staple foods including rice and vegetables. People who consume high levels of heavy metals over an extended time can develop organ damage and weakened bones, among other medical conditions (Larson 2014).

Shaped by growing distrust toward domestic food produce as well as rising demand for a different variety of food products, Chinese consumers are increasingly turning away from domestic produce to imports, including agricultural products from Southeast Asian countries. For example, according to *Taobao*—China's biggest online shopping website—spending by the average e-shopper on organic and imported food and beverages has expanded eightfold over the past three years as many popular online offerings, such as organic baby foods, rice, and tea, are not available in local stores (Youchi 2016).

On the other hand, the poor's food anxiety is attributed to the rising food prices, particularly grain and meat products. The Chinese government heavily relies on price interventions and trade restrictions—raising domestic purchase prices for rice, wheat, corn, pork, beef, sugar, and so on, and limiting imports to boost domestic production. As a result, domestic food prices have risen significantly over the past few years, and high domestic food prices have generated constant anxiety from lower income groups over the affordability of food in China (Source). Taking rice and wheat, for example, since the introduction of the minimum grain purchase price policy in 2004, the grain market has been tightly controlled by the government which places grain production increase as the ultimate objective. Since 2004, China has gradually raised the grain purchase prices to boost grain production, particularly amid the global food crisis in 2007/2008. As seen in Table 9.4, China's minimum purchase price for Japonica rice has more than doubled between 2007 and 2014.[2] In the past three years, the minimum purchase price for Japonica rice has remained unchanged which has been against the background of a significant drop in global rice prices. The same pattern is being observed in the case of wheat. Given the dominating effects of government's minimum grain purchase price on the domestic grain markets, the domestic retail prices have increased significantly over the past few years. It is revealed by Chinese top government officials, that on average, the current domestic grain prices are 50 percent higher than the international grain prices (Chen 2017). The high domestic grain prices become a huge burden for domestic consumers, and it is estimated that the Chinese con-

Table 9.4 China's minimum grain purchase price for rice and wheat (RMB/kg)

Year	Japonica rice	Mixed wheat
2004	1.50	Nil
2005	1.50	Nil
2006	1.50	1.38
2007	1.50	1.38
2008	1.64	1.44
2009	1.90	1.66
2010	2.10	1.72
2011	2.56	1.86
2012	2.80	2.04
2013	3.00	2.24
2014	3.10	2.36
2015	3.10	2.36
2016	3.10	2.36

Source: National Development and Reform Commission, P.R. China (2004–2016)

sumers are paying over USD 40 billion a year due to the grain price gaps. Given the fact that the share of grains, rice, and wheat in particular is much higher in the poor consumers' diet, high domestic grain prices have been motivating the poor consumers to switch for cheap rice and wheat from foreign countries, such as Vietnam, Thailand, and Myanmar (Li 2015). The cheap foreign imported and smuggled grains are not only favored by low-income urban consumers but also desired by the rural residents, including rice and wheat farmers. For instance, the investigation reports of several high-profile rice smuggling cases (primarily from Vietnam) revealed that the smuggled rice was often purchased by farmers who prefer to sell their own produce to the government at higher prices set by the government and rely on the cheap smuggled rice for their own consumption. In some cases, farmers purchased the smuggled rice and resold it to the government to make a profit (GrainNews 2015).

Not only grains are being tightly controlled, other key food products such as pork and sugar have been closely regulated by the government as well. Taking pork as an example, China has built a pork reserve following a fatal outbreak of PRRS (also known as porcine blue-ear disease) in 2006 that left millions of pigs dead and pork prices going through the roof. As a result, owing to a supply and demand gap as well as rapidly rising production costs, domestic pork price has skyrocketed in recent years, despite intermittent ups and downs (Lockett 2016).

Again, as in the case of grain, with the soaring pork price and limited liberalization of China's pork markets, the price gap between China's and the international pork market has widened quickly. By the end of 2016, China's domestic pork price was more than 2.5 times of the price level in the United States (Gale 2017). Not surprisingly, the pork price rises have become so large that they hurt the affordability of domestic consumers particularly the low-income consumers. The huge domestic and international price gap has spurred China's pork imports and smuggling of frozen meats, which is preferred by the price sensitive consumers despite potential safety and quality concerns.

Implications for Vietnam

As China continues to grow, albeit at a lower rate, and opened its borders under the country's high-profile Belt and Road Initiative (BRI), the effects on the agricultural sector and food security of Vietnam will be much more significant. Taking the rice sector as an example, China's annual rice production is over 200 million tonnes. This represents more than 25 percent of global rice production and nearly five times the size of the world's export market, in which Vietnam is one of the biggest suppliers. Given the scale of China's rice production and consumption as well as the thinly traded market for rice, changes in China's food security strategy, rice policy, in particular, will have profound impacts on Vietnam not least owing to Vietnam's reliance on rice both as a staple and a source of export revenue (Vietrade 2016). While rice may be the most visible agricultural commodity, this same story may well be replicated across a range of food products, such as fishery, sugar, fruits, and vegetables. The rest of the section reviews various aspects of food ties between China and Vietnam, including not only the formal agricultural trade and investment ties, agricultural technology and input cooperation but also the massive food smugglings and illegal farm labors across the land borders, and discusses how these trends are shaped and will continue to be shaped by the changing dynamics in China's food systems.

Formal and "Informal" Agricultural and Food Trade

Agricultural trade between China and Vietnam, in parallel with the overall trend of trade between China and Southeast Asian countries, has expanded phenomenally over the past decade, particularly since the signing of "the Framework Agreement on Comprehensive Economic Cooperation between the People's Republic of China and the Association of Southeast Asian Nations" in Phnom Penh, Cambodia in 2002. As seen in Table 9.5, China's agricultural trade with Vietnam has increased from USD 430 million in 2004 to over USD 6.7 billion in 2016, hence jumped up by over 1300 percent during this period. Among the bilateral agricultural trade, China's agricultural exports to Vietnam reached USD 3.87 billion in 2016, up from USD 240 million in 2004, whereas agricultural imports from Vietnam increased from USD 191 million in 2004 to USD 2.84 billion in 2016.

In terms of agricultural trade structure, China's main exports to Vietnam include oranges, apples, garlic, soybean meal, feathers, prepared intestines; and Vietnam is the top supplier of rice, fruits, and nuts as well as sugar to China. According to data of China's Ministry of Commerce, although Vietnamese rice exports to China in 2016 inched down against the previous year, Vietnam remained China's largest rice supplier (Ministry of Commerce, P.R. China 2002–2016). From January to April 2017, Vietnam's total fragrant rice exports amounted to over 355,000 tonnes, with China alone accounting for a staggering 46 percent (Vietnamnet 2017a). China is also becoming one of the key markets for Vietnam's cashew and fishery exports. China is currently the third largest

Table 9.5 China and Vietnam agricultural trade (USD million)

China agricultural exports to Vietnam					
	2004	2005	2014	2015	2016
Vietnam	240.02	305.59	2988.63	3430.61	3869.65
ASEAN	2118.33	2422.46	13,539.20	14,753.72	15,377.70
China agricultural imports from Vietnam					
	2004	2005	2014	2015	2016
Vietnam	191.46	206.59	2249.98	2717.57	2837.32
ASEAN	3715.30	3681.67	16,032.88	15,806.56	14,500.31

Source: Ministry of Commerce, P.R. China (2002–2016, 20)

importer of Vietnamese cashew (Vietnam's cashew exports, nearly USD 3 billion, account for over 40 percent of the global total); and, in the first quarter of 2017, China overtook the United States as the largest importer of Vietnamese catfish (Vietnamnet 2017b).

Apart from agricultural products, bilateral trade of agricultural inputs, including seeds, fertilizers, pesticides, and food additives are booming as well. For instance, Vietnam spends on average USD 774 million each year on imports of pesticides and insecticides, 90 percent of which come from China (An 2016); and Vietnam imports nearly 70 percent of hybrid rice seeds from China (Pham 2017). In order to promote the agricultural product trade, China and Vietnam signed a memorandum of understanding on cooperation in the field of trade of agricultural products in 2013 (Zhao 2015).

The phenomenal agricultural trade between the two sides is attributed to a variety of reasons including China's domestic production shortage, diversification of the Chinese diet, price differences, and distrust toward domestic food produce. In the case of sugar, the persistent domestic demand and supply gap has been the key factor that contributes to large sugar imports (Ministry of Agriculture, P.R. China 2015). Regarding rice, after the outbreaks of several safety scandals related to toxic rice, more and more Chinese consumers have been buying imported rice. While some are willing to pay up to ten times the price for the imported Japanese rice, others are buying rice from Southeast Asian countries, particularly Thailand and Vietnam as an alternative. In the past few years, the domestic and international rice price difference has also been one of the key drivers behind China's massive imports of rice from Southeast Asian countries, particularly for the state-owned grain traders who are granted with China's rice import quota. Regarding fruits, diversification of diet has been the primary driver. With the Chinese consumers' growing taste for fresh fruit, demand for tropical fruits from Southeast Asian countries, particularly Thailand and Vietnam, has been on the rise as well. More and more Chinese consumers purchase durian, longan, mangosteen, and coconut from Southeast Asia. Southeast Asian countries are the biggest sources of fruit imports for China, with Vietnam and Thailand accounting for 46 percent of China's total fruits and nuts imports in 2015 (Ministry of Commerce, P.R. China 2002–2016).

On the other hand, as Chinese consumers' food preferences change, some of the domestic food products, particularly the low end manufactured and processed food products, are being increasingly shipped to neighboring countries including Vietnam. Taking the instant noodle, for example, as Chinese consumers are turning away from instant noodles, Chinese producers are entering growing markets like Vietnam. In the past, for hundreds of millions of peasant workers in China, instant noodles were a convenient choice for a meal because they were available for a few cents in every convenience store. However, rising wages have improved living standards and expectations for millions of peasant workers who are increasingly willing to pay more for better and healthier food, instead of a 25-cent bowl of instant noodles. To make the matter worse, instant noodles have developed a bad reputation in China owning to scandals and rumors and a 2012 food-poisoning incident and long-standing allegations that instant noodles are contaminated with plasticizers (Minter 2016). As a result, China's instant noodle makers are struggling to re-start growth. One option is to export noodles to other emerging Asian economies such as Vietnam, where consumption is still growing along with the manufacturing sector (Minter 2016).

In addition to the formal agricultural trade, the changing food dynamics in China have also resulted in pervasive smuggling of food products via the land borders between Vietnam and Myanmar and China's Yunnan and Guangxi provinces. Rice has been the most common food product which is being smuggled into China from Southeast Asian countries. For instance, in 2014 it was estimated that over 3 million tonnes of rice have been smuggled from Vietnam and Myanmar to China via the land borders. Despite a series of anti-smuggling campaigns, in 2015, around 2.6–2.7 million tonnes of rice were smuggled into China (see Table 9.6). The former chief of China's cabinet-level State Council's rural policy Unit-Chen Xiwen also admitted that it is likely that more rice is being smuggled into China than the volume sent in legal shipments. Rice is first brought from Vietnam and Myanmar to China's border cities in Guangxi and Yunnan province. From there it is shipped by rail to China's inland provinces for sale. Smuggled rice is sold to processors or mills, processed and sold, or mixed with domestic rice.

Table 9.6 China's rice imports and smuggling

	2014	2015
China's official import data	2.6	3.4
FAO import data	5.9	6.1
Data from rice exporters	Nil	6.0
Smuggled amount	3.3	2.6–2.7

Source: Ministry of Commerce, P.R. China (2016, 11); FAO (2016)

There are multiple reasons why so much rice is being smuggled into China. For a start, with growing diversification of the Chinese diet, Thai rice is gaining popularity in China among the middle-income consumers. Secondly, as the domestic rice price rose, cheap rice from Vietnam and Myanmar is being preferred by low-income consumers in the cities and by rural residents. Third, the widespread concerns over the heavy metal contamination of domestic rice further pushed consumers to opt for foreign rice. In China, rice can be priced up to USD 154 per tonne higher than in rice-growing countries in Southeast Asia. As discussed earlier, this is largely due to Chinese authorities setting a high government purchasing price to protect farmers' interests. Also, under China's rice trading system, the quota is mostly being granted to state-owned enterprises, which leave the private rice processors with very limited access to cheap foreign rice. As a result, some opt to purchase smuggled rice. The massive rice smuggling has been recognized as a major threat to China's food security and consumer safety (General Administration of Customs of China 2014).

For similar reasons, sugar and frozen meats are also being smuggled into China via the land borders on massive scales. As much as 2 million tonnes of sugar were smuggled into the country in 2015–2016, up from 800,000 tonnes a year earlier. While the government has sought to curb the practice in recent years, the large gap between domestic and global prices makes it hard to control. Most smuggled sugar is believed to be produced in India and Thailand and then transshipped to Myanmar or Vietnam before entering China, it said in an April report (Bloomberg News 2016). As for beef, it was estimated that over 2 million tonnes of frozen beef were smuggled into China in 2013, which made up over 20 percent of total domestic consumption in 2013. In the past, frozen beef was smuggled to China via sea ports such as Guangzhou. However, due to the government's crackdown, more frozen beef began to find its way into China via the land borders between Vietnam and Yunnan and Guangxi provinces in China. The smuggled pork, however, is mostly from Southeast Asian countries, Vietnam in particular. Since 2003, due to Foot and Mouth disease of swine, China has banned the import of pork from Vietnam. Yet in recent years, due to a rapid surge in China's domestic pork price (see above), the pork price in China has become much higher than that of Vietnam. For instance, as of November 2016, this price gap is about USD 615 per tonne. Driven by this high potential profit, pork smuggling has surged. In November 2016, official reports indicate that as high as 10,000 pigs could be smuggled into China via the land borders on a daily basis. Similar to other products, the smuggled pork would be quickly distributed to other Chinese provinces. In the past, there were even reports suggesting that foreign "zombie" (frozen meat which has been stored for decades) meats were also smuggled into China (Yu 2015). While the government has taken considerable efforts to combat the meat smuggling and the general public has been duly informed about the potential safety risks of the smuggled meat, meat smuggling is still flourishing as these cheap meats are being demanded by pork processors, meat retailers, and restaurants, given the large number of Chinese consumers who are still very sensitive to meat prices. The rising concerns over the excessive use of growth enhancer and lean meat powder in the domestic hog sector have further motivated Chinese consumers to switch to imported meats, including the smuggled frozen meats (Cai et al. 2015).

Looking into the future, the agricultural trade between China and Vietnam is expected to expand even further as China is seeking to reduce its over-reliance on the United States for food imports under its new food security strategy. Aiming for USD 100 billion in bilateral trade turnover, Vietnam also intends to export more of its processed agricultural products, seafood, and electronic and consumer products to the Chinese market (VietnamNet 2017). However, as China is determined to achieve self-sufficiency in staples, including wheat and rice, it is unlikely that Vietnam's formal rice exports to China will expand even further. This is particularly the case as concerns are mounting on adverse impacts of imported rice on China's domestic rice production. In the meanwhile, as

Chinese consumers are willing to pay more for better and healthier food and the Chinese government is looking to curb the country's overuse of pesticides and chemical fertilizers that have largely contributed to the large scale contamination of arable land, overcapacity in the low end food manufacturing sector (including the counterfeited food sector) and fertilizer and pesticide sectors have pressured these manufactures to explore new markets, particularly fast-developing Vietnam.

Close agricultural and food trade with China presents both opportunities and challenges to the Vietnamese food sectors. On the positive side, booming agricultural and food trade has not only greatly enriched the diet of the people from both sides but also contributed to income growth of farmers as well as food security of the region. On the other hand, however, the huge formal and informal agricultural and food trade between the two countries create enormous challenges to Vietnam as well. Given the critical role of rice farming in the agricultural sector and rice consumption in the Vietnamese diet, over-reliance on China as the main export market breeds risks for the Vietnamese rice sector. In times of rice glut, Vietnam will be at the mercy of China's rice import policies. In the past few years, oversupply of rice in the global market has been dragging down prices in the world market, affecting rice exporters including Vietnam. Worse still, China's decision to diversify its rice import sources and curb massive rice smuggling from Vietnam via the land borders have created further hardships for the Vietnamese rice producers and traders. In times of supply shortages, however, huge demand from China could contribute to surge in domestic rice price as in the case of the global food crisis in 2007/2008, resulting in panic buying and large scale food anxiety in Vietnam (see Gorman, this volume). In 2007/2008, Vietnam introduced a rice export ban to ensure stability of domestic rice supply. Yet, with China as the biggest buyer of Vietnamese rice and pervasive border smuggling, it will be politically, diplomatically, and practically challenging for Vietnam to ban rice export to China, should another food crisis occur.

Furthermore, it is evidenced that when China took tougher action against counterfeited and substandard food products in the cities, many of these products quickly flooded the rural markets where surveillance is lacking and farmers are much more price sensitive. Given the lax control over cross-border trade and Vietnamese consumers' relative sensitivity to prices, these products could also be exported or smuggled to Vietnam via the land borders, posing safety threats to local consumers. Already, some of the substandard Chinese food products were found in the Vietnamese market (VietNamNet Bridge 2016a). In the past few years, rumors of tainted milk, fake chicken eggs from China and rice paper wraps made from plastic have horrified consumers in Vietnam. In Vietnam, it was suggested that surge in cancer was related to massive food smuggling from China into Vietnam for sale in local markets due to widespread corruption among Vietnamese border guards (Thuy 2012). Many smuggled food products are believed to be adulterated or containing cancer-causing agents, kept in toxic plastic bags or stored without any concern for minimum hygienic standards or health safety regulations. A related issue is the use of fertilizers, pesticides, insecticides, and food additives. In recent years, excessive use of chemical inputs, mostly imported or smuggled from China, has been identified as one of the leading cause for environmental pollution and blamed by authorities for the rocketing cancer rate (An 2016). In fact, given the close food ties between the two countries, news or rumors related to food safety scandals in China could quickly hit home for many Vietnamese consumers (as they already have, see Part II, this volume).

Investment, Agricultural Technologies, and Fishery

By the end of 2015, China's accumulated overseas Agricultural Foreign Direct Investment reached USD 11.74 billion. It is estimated that there were over 1300 Chinese agricultural companies operating in 85 countries, ranging from plantation to animal husbandry, to fishery and related sectors. By the end of 2013, China's agricultural investment in Asia produced 53 million tonnes of grain and 41.5 million tonnes of cash crops (Zhang and Cheng 2016). Apart from the direct investment, more and more Chinese companies are expanding their presence overseas via Merger and Acquisition (M&A). From 2010 to 2014, China's agricultural related M&A totaled USD 18.5 billion.

In November 2016, China issued the country's five-year plan for the rural economy which includes four paragraphs on "coordinated utilization of domestic and foreign markets and resources" (National Development and Reform Commission, P.R. China 2016). It specified that China's agricultural going global would be based on the periphery through deepening cooperation with "neighboring countries" while strengthening agricultural ties with South America, consolidating agricultural cooperation with Africa, and thinking globally. This emphasizes the importance of its southern neighbors as key targets for China's agricultural investment and aids.

China's agricultural investment in continental Southeast Asia dates back to the 1990s. Although China's agricultural investment has mainly concentrated in Laos and Myanmar under China's Opium Replacement Program since the 1990s and recently in Cambodia, China's investment in Vietnam's agricultural sector has been impressive as well. By the end of 2014, China had 112 agricultural investment projects in Vietnam, with total contracts amounting to nearly USD 280 million (Ministry of Commerce, P.R. China 2016). During the visit of Vietnam's President Tran Dai Quang to China in May 2017, he said Vietnam hopes China could invest more in Vietnam's agriculture, one of the seven priority sectors (Van 2017). It can be expected that under China's Belt and Road initiative, China's investment in Vietnam's agricultural and food sector will continue to expand.

As an agricultural country rich in agricultural products and seafood, but with a low level of variety improvement, storage, and processing technology (Vietnam Business Forum 2014), Vietnam opts for large scale investment in its agricultural sectors to enhance food production and reduce rural poverty (Viet Nam News 2017). In this aspect, China's renewed interest in developing the region's agricultural sector thus provides a huge opportunity for Vietnam to boost agricultural productivity and diversification and build sustainable food supply chains. Nevertheless, large inflow of Chinese investment into Vietnam's agricultural and food sectors inevitably generate social, economic and even political concerns, particularly at the local level. As being witnessed in Cambodia, Laos, and Myanmar, with large Chinese presence in these countries' agricultural sectors, local and international media spawns debate in land grabbing discourse concerning issues of national sovereignty and independence. Furthermore, as many of the agricultural investment deals involve large pieces of land, there are growing concerns of the negative impacts of Chinese investment on local small-scale farmers. For instance, in

Northern Myanmar, China's agricultural investment has caused environmental, social, and political conflict with local farmers who have been forcibly displaced from their land (Woods 2014).

What's more, Chinese investment in the region's agricultural sector, if not properly managed, could lead to displacement of local farmers and environmental degradation. Next, as the biggest rice producer and consumer in the world, technological development in China could have a direct impact on Vietnam's rice production and consumption. For decades, to boost rice production, China has invested heavily in hybrid rice technologies. Currently, well over half of China's total rice-growing area is planted with rice hybrids, making the country by far the world's largest producer of the crop. While hybrid rice plantation has greatly contributed to the phenomenal expansion of China's total rice production, in recent years, some serious problems emerged. Among these problems, as discussed in the previous section, rice contamination by heavy metal, has become a top threat to consumer safety. While industrial pollution and overuse of chemical inputs are among the main causes of heavy mental contamination, it is also discovered that some of the hybrid rice varieties, such as Indica-Japonica Hybrids-Super-rice, have a high propensity to absorb cadmium (Forum on Health, Environment and Development—FORHEAD 2014). As Vietnam's hybrid rice seed sector relies heavily on imports from China, with rapid industrialization and urbanization, "cadmium rice" could be soon found in Vietnam. Perhaps, a bigger challenge would be the GM rice. China's embrace of GM rice technologies could have major implications on Vietnam's rice sector. As the powerhouse for GM rice technology, China could easily dominate Vietnam's GM rice production as in the case of hybrid rice. This could trigger national security concerns. While the Vietnamese government has been quite supportive of GM technologies, the social resistance is considerably high (Lien 2015). As in the case of China, many Chinese security experts claim that GM food is the United States' bioweapon against the Chinese people, the "China factor" (Zhang 2016c) could further complicate the domestic debates on GM food. Last but not least, while a lot can be learned by Vietnam from China's experience in agricultural development over the past decades, some of the bad practices from China could also be replicated in Vietnam either through Chinese agricultural investors or through tens of thousands of legal and illegal Vietnamese farmers working in China, as food ties between the two sides become ever closer. In fact, there were reports suggesting that some Vietnamese went to China to learn the gutter oil techniques,[3] and some of the illegal chemical additives found in Vietnamese food sectors originated from China (VietNamNet Bridge 2016b).

Furthermore, as China is determined to expand its fishery sector to meet the country's rising demand for food, competition between China and Vietnam over the limited fishery resources from the disputed waters in the South China Sea[4] could intensify. Traditionally, inshore fishing has been the major marine fishing operation in China, as nearly 90 percent of China's total marine catch in 1985 was inshore. However, by 2002, this figure dropped to 64.5 percent (Bureau of Fisheries of Ministry of Agriculture, P.R China 1986, 2003). While data at the national level is unavailable after 2002, data from local levels continues to suggest the shift from inshore to offshore fishing. The production of inshore fishing dropped to 60 percent of Guangzhou city's total marine catch in 2006, and 50.5 percent in Hainan province by 2007 (Zhang 2016b). Due to overfishing, pollution and land reclamation, fish stocks in China's traditional fishing grounds are depleted. Seventy percent of China's beaches are polluted and 50 percent of tidal wetlands have disappeared. The Bohai fishing ground, Zhoushan fishing ground, the other fishing grounds near coastal waters in the South China Sea, and the Beibu Gulf fishing grounds now exist in name only (Tang 2016). In particular, big fish in China's Bohai are almost completely gone and the annual production of small fish is less than 10 percent of its peak amount (Beijing Times 2015). As the depletion of fishery resources mainly occurs in inshore waters, China consequently focuses more on expanding offshore fishing.

To ensure a stable supply of fishery products and to protect the fishermen's livelihood, China encourages its fishermen to go further out to sea. According to President Xi Jinping, Chinese fishermen need to "build bigger ships and venture even further into the oceans and catch bigger fish" (Chan 2013). In practical terms that means offshore fishing in waters near the Spratly islands and distant water fishing. However, offshore fishing in waters near the Spratly Islands is not covered by China's South China Sea fishing ban (May 16 to August 1 annually). Fishermen who go there would receive additional fishing-fuel subsidies under *the Special*

Fishing-Fuel Subsidy for Fishing In The Spratly Islands Programme introduced in 1995 (Zhang 2016b).

Similarly for Vietnam, due to overfishing and excess capacity in its coastal and inshore fishery, the country has implemented strategies since the late 1990s to limit coastal fishing effort and develop offshore fisheries. In 1998, construction of new vessels less than 20 horsepower was banned and a financial subsidy was provided to build bigger vessels capable of sailing to offshore waters (Pomeroy 2010; Pomeroy et al. 2009). The outward expansion of Vietnamese marine fishery has been remarkable. In 2012, the near-shore and offshore catching output was in balance, with a rate of 50.6 percent and 49.4 percent. This is a significant change compared to that in 2001, when near-shore fishing accounted for 69.2 percent of the total marine catch. Furthermore, Vietnam is expected to reach a rate of 64 percent offshore—36 percent inshore by 2020 (Le 2016). In a recent development, so-called Vietnamese blue boats have become active in illegal fishing in the South Pacific (Forum Fisheries Agency 2017). As a result, in recent years, there have been a growing number of maritime incidents involving the two countries' fishermen in the South China Sea. Some of the maritime incidents even triggered diplomatic and even security tensions between China and Vietnam. For instance, in July 2016, Vietnam has accused the Chinese coastguard of sinking a fishing boat in the disputed waters of the South China Sea and demanded compensation from China (Straits Times 2016).

Conclusion

The paradigm shifts of China's overall food security strategy and the Chinese consumers' food preferences have important implications for global food security and food markets beyond its borders, particularly Vietnam (see Gorman, this volume). China's renewed interest in developing the region's agricultural sector could provide huge economic opportunities for Vietnam's agricultural and food sectors. Nevertheless, as food ties between the two countries strengthen, Vietnam's food markets will also be increasingly subject to forces beyond its borders. For instance, food shortages in China could easily trigger panic buying in Vietnam. Moreover, the

Chinese consumers' growingly diversified tastes for different varieties of food products as well as concerns toward safety and quality of domestic produce could create further demands for food products from Vietnam, which could generate more income for the farmers. However, what should be noted is that the massive smuggling of the food products such as rice, sugar, and frozen meat, though providing considerable benefits to both countries, could eventually hamper the agricultural ties between the two sides in the future, if left unmanaged. For example, massive rice smuggling across the land borders is damaging the reputation of Vietnamese rice in the Chinese market.

Furthermore, some of the emerging trends in China's food sectors could become big challenges for Vietnam. First, as the biggest rice producer and consumer in the world, China's embrace of GM food technologies could have major implications on the rice sector of Vietnam. Next, as China is determined to expand its fishery sector to meet the country's rising demand for food, competition between China and Vietnam over the limited fishery resources from the disputed waters in the South China Sea could intensify. Furthermore, some of the bad practices, such as the overuse of fertilizers and pesticides, and illegal additives in China's food sectors could also be replicated in Vietnam either through Chinese agricultural investors, farmers, or agricultural laborers at the border regions who frequently cross the national borders as agricultural traders or labors. Last, if China takes tougher action against counterfeited and substandard food products within its borders, some of these products could be exported or smuggled to Vietnam via the land borders, posing safety threats to local consumers, given the lax control over the cross-border trade.

Notes

1. In this article Brown argued that China's rising food inputs will put unbearable strain on the global grain export capacity, push up worldwide prices of nearly all major commodities, and make food expensive for everyone.
2. RMB is converted in this chapter using the exchange rate as of December 31, 2015, when USD 1 was traded at RMB 6.5.

3. "Gutter oil" is a term used in mainland China, Hong Kong, Macao, and Taiwan to describe illicit cooking oil which has been recycled from waste oil collected from sources such as restaurant fryers, grease traps, slaughterhouse waste, and sewage from sewer drains.
4. Due to geopolitical reasons, in Vietnam it is called the "East Sea" (*Biển Đông*).

References

An, Hong, 2016. *Chinese chemicals flood Vietnam's agricultural sector.* [Online] Available at: http://e.vnexpress.net/news/news/chinese-chemicals-flood-vietnam-s-agricultural-sector-3472977.html [Accessed 20 August 2017].

Baird, I.G., Barney, K., 2017. The political ecology of cross-sectoral cumulative impacts: modern landscapes, large hydropower dams and industrial tree plantations in Laos and Cambodia. *The Journal of Peasant Studies* 44, 769–795. doi:https://doi.org/10.1080/03066150.2017.1289921

BBC, 2014. *Report: One fifth of China's soil contaminated.* [Online] Available at: http://www.bbc.com/news/world-asia-china-27076645 [Accessed 23 December 2016].

Beijing Times, 2015. 鱼类资源不足峰值*1/10*渤海污染严重亟待防治 *[Fish stock below 10% of the peak level, pollution in Bohai must be addressed].* [Online] Available at: http://epaper.jinghua.cn/html/2015-03/11/content_176274.htm [Accessed 23 December 2016].

Bloomberg News, 2016. *Smuggling Crackdown Seen Spurring China Sugar Reserve Sales.* [Online] Available at: https://www.bloomberg.com/news/articles/2016-09-14/smuggling-crackdown-seen-spurring-china-sugar-reserve-sales [Accessed 24 December 2016].

Brown, L.R., Halweil, B., 1998. China's water shortage could shake world food security. World Watch 11, 10–21.

Bureau of Fisheries of Ministry of Agriculture, P.R China, 1986. *China Fishery Statistical Yearbook 1985.* Beijing: China Agricultural Press.

Bureau of Fisheries of Ministry of Agriculture, P.R China, 2003. *China Fishery Statistical Yearbook 2002.* Beijing: China Agricultural Press.

Cai, L., Pongrace, A., Butts, C., Wang, S., 2015. China's Astounding Appetite for Pork: Recent Trends and Implications for International Trade. *Penn Wharton Public Policy Initative.* URL http://publicpolicy.wharton.upenn.edu/live/news/644-chinas-astounding-appetite-for-pork-recent-trends (Accessed 31 December 2017).

Center for Coordination and Innovation of Food Safety Governance, 2014. *Food Safety Governance,* Beijing: Renmin University of China.

Chan, M., 2013. *Xi's fishermen visit seen as warning to South China Sea neighbours.* URL http://www.scmp.com/news/china/article/1211086/xi-jinping-pledges-makes-seas-safer-fishermen (accessed 23 April 2016).

Chen, X., 2017. 今日头条|陈锡文:不加强农业国际竞争力农民生存空间会越来越小The Paper. URL http://www.thepaper.cn/newsDetail_forward_1806853 (accessed 10 October 2017).

Cheng, G. & Zhang, H., 2014. *China's Global Agricultural Strategy: An Open System to Safeguard the Country's Food Security,* Singapore: RSIS.

Chheang, V., 2017. The Political Economy of Chinese Investment in Cambodia (Trends in Southeast Asia), Trends in Southeast Asia. ISEAS – Yusof Ishak Institute, Singapore.

FAO – Food and Agriculture Organization, 2016. *China's view on implementation and performance of agroecology,* Rome: FAO.

Financial Times, 2008. UN warns of food 'neo-colonialism'. *Financial. Times.* URL https://www.ft.com/content/3d3ede92-6e02-11dd-b5df-0000779fd18c (Accessed 17 October 2017).

Forum Fisheries Agency, 2017. "Rai Balang Surveillance Sweep Nabs IUU Fishers: Blue Boats Spotted in PNG EEZ", 17 March 2017, available at http://www.ffa.int/node/1905 [Accessed 23 December 2016].

Forum on Health, Environment and Development (FORHEAD), 2014. *Food Safety In China: A Mapping Of Problems, Governance and Research,* New York, United States: Social Science Research Council (SSRC).

Fox, J., Castella, J.-C., 2013. Expansion of Rubber (Hevea brasiliensis) in Mainland Southeast Asia: What are the Prospects for Small Holders? The Journal of Peasant Studies 40(1), 155–170. doi:https://doi.org/10.1080/03066150.2012.750605

Gale, F., 2017. *China's Pork Imports Rise Along with Production Costs,* Washington DC: USDA.

General Administration of Customs of China, 2014. 粮食走私危及国内食品安全. Gen. Adm. Cust. China. URL http://www.customs.gov.cn/publish/portal0/tab68121/info715322.htm (accessed 11.5.17).

Goldenberg, S., 2015. Lester Brown: "Vast dust bowls threaten tens of millions with hunger." The Guardian.

GrainNews, 2015. 我国成"大米走私"重灾区 *[China Rice Smuggling Pervasive].* [Online] Available at: http://www.grainnews.com.cn/a/news/2015/07/13-24721.html [Accessed 23 December 2016].

Greenpeace, 2015. *Africa's Fisheries' paradise at a Crossroad: Investigating Chinese Companies,* Amsterdam: Greenpeace.

Han, J., 2014. *China: Food Security and Agricultural Going Out Strategy Research.* Beijing: Development Press.

Hofman, I., Ho, P., 2012. China's "Developmental Outsourcing": A critical examination of Chinese global "land grabs" discourse. *The Journal of Peasant Studies* 39, 1–48. https://doi.org/10.1080/03066150.2011.653109

Larson, C., 2014. *China's Polluted Soil Is Tainting the Country's Food Supply.* [Online] Available at: https://www.bloomberg.com/news/articles/2014-12-08/china-s-polluted-soil-is-tainting-the-countrys-food-supply [Accessed 23 December 2016].

Le, Minh Tri., 2016. *Offshore fishing and Vietnam's sovereignty protection.* [Online] Available at: http://english.vietnamnet.vn/fms/marine-sovereignty/165364/offshore-fishing-and-vietnam-s-sovereignty-protection.html [Accessed 23 December 2016].

Li, X., 2015. 中国粮食收购:肥了国企,坑了全民 *[China's Grain Purchase: Benefits the State-owned grain companies but hurt the people].* [Online] Available at: http://www.chinagrain.cn/liangyou/2015/7/7/2015779425929934.shtml [Accessed 21 December 2016].

Lien, Hoang, 2015. Vietnam Debates GMO Crops With Eye on History [WWW Document]. VOA. URL https://www.voanews.com/a/vietnam-debates-gmo-crops-with-eye-on-history/2917662.html (accessed 11.5.17).

Lockett, H., 2016. *Beijing taps emergency pork reserves as prices hit record high.* [Online] Available at: https://www.ft.com/content/cb86e098-e495-3deb-890b-5cc783d157e5 [Accessed 23 December 2016].

Lu, J., Schönweger, O., 2017. Great expectations: Chinese investment in Laos and the myth of empty land. Territory, Politics, Government (forthcoming), 1–18. doi:https://doi.org/10.1080/21622671.2017.1360195.

Mallory, T. G., 2013. China's Distant Water Fishing Industry: Evolving Policies and Implications. *Marine Policy,* Volume 38, pp. 99–108.

Ministry of Agriculture, P.R. China, 2015. *China Agricultural Trade Development Report,* Beijing: Ministry of Agriculture, P.R. China.

Ministry of Agriculture, P.R. China, 2017. *China's Number 1 Document in 2017.* [Online] Available at: http://www.moa.gov.cn/ztzl/yhwj2017/zywj/201702/t20170206_5468567.htm [Accessed 12 February 2017].

Ministry of Commerce, P.R. China, 2002–2016. *China Monthly Imports and Exports Statistical Report-Agricultural Products,* Beijing: Ministry of Commerce, P.R. China.

Ministry of Commerce, P.R. China, 2016. Report on China's Outward Investment and Economic Cooperation 2016. Ministry of Commerce, P.R. China, Beijing.

Minter, A., 2016. *China's Progress Is Killing the Instant Noodle.* [Online] Available at: https://www.bloomberg.com/view/articles/2016-09-29/china-s-progress-is-killing-the-instant-noodle [Accessed 20 August 2017].

National Bureau of Statistics, P.R. China, 2017. *2017 China Statistical Abstract.* Beijing: China Statistics Press.

National Development and Reform Commission, P.R. China, 2016. *National Rural Economic Development 13th Five Year Plan,* Beijing, China: National Development and Reform Commission, P.R. China.

Pham, Thai Ha, 2017. *Country Report: Seed Industry in Vietnam.* [Online] Available at: http://www.kosaseed.or.kr/Vietnam.pdf [Accessed 23 December 2016].

Pomeroy, R., 2010. *Addressing Overcapacity in the Small-Scale Marine Fisheries of Vietnam,* Malaysia: WorldFish Center.

Pomeroy, R., Kim Anh Thi Nguyen & Thong, H. X., 2009. Small-scale marine fisheries policy in Vietnam. *Marine Policy,* Volume 33, p. 419–428.

Qureshi, A., 2008. *Food Security in China.* [Online] Available at: http://hir.harvard.edu/article/?a=1750 [Accessed 23 July 2017].

Ren, Z., 2015. Solving China's Food Problem is the Top Priority of the Government. *Qiushi Journal,* Volume 9.

Schoenberger, L., 2017. Struggling against excuses: winning back land in Cambodia. *The Journal of Peasant Studies* 44, 870–890. doi:https://doi.org/10.1080/03066150.2017.1327850

State Council, P.R. China, 1996. The Grain Issue in China. China.org. URL http://www.china.org.cn/e-white/grainissue/index.htm [Accessed 23 July 2016].

State Council, P.R. China, 2008. *China Mid-long Term Grain Security Plan* (2008–2020). State Council, P.R. China, Beijing.

Straits Times, 2016. *Vietnam says China 'sank' fishing boat in South China Sea.* [Online] Available at: http://www.straitstimes.com/asia/east-asia/vietnam-says-china-sank-fishing-boat-in-south-china-sea [Accessed 23 July 2016].

Tang, F., 2016. Depletion of Fishery Resources along China's Coast. *Cultural Geography,* Volume 9, pp. 41–49.

Thuy, Thanh, 2012. *Vietnamese markets flooded with cancer-causing food from China.* [Online] Available at: http://www.asianews.it/news-en/Vietnamese-markets-flooded-with-cancer-causing-food-from-China-25678.html [Accessed 20 August 2017].

Trade Promotion Center of the Ministry of Agriculture, P.R. China, 2016. Food Security and Non-Necessity Import Control Study. *Issues in Agricultural Economy,* Volume 7, pp. 53–59.

Van, Yen, 2017. President Tran Dai Quang active in China. En-Cdnqdndvn. URL http://en-cdn.qdnd.vn/foreign-affairs/bilateral-relations/president-tran-dai-quang-active-in-china-480851 (accessed 11.5.17).

Vietnam Business Forum, 2014. Identifying Opportunities, Challenges of Agro-processing Industry. Vietnam Business Forum. URL http://vccinews.com/news_detail.asp?news_id=31542 (Accessed 31 December 2017).

Viet Nam News, 2017. *Agriculture need more investments and technology, say experts.* [Online] Available at: http://vietnamnews.vn/economy/349898/agriculture-need-more-investments-and-technology-say-experts.html#6PwgFh4HbmmQ3iJW.97 [Accessed 23 July 2017].

VietNamNet Bridge, 2016a. *How unsafe food reaches Vietnamese's dining-table?* [Online] Available at: http://english.vietnamnet.vn/fms/special-reports/149451/how-unsafe-food-reaches-vietnamese-s-dining-table-.html [Accessed 23 December 2016].

VietNamNet Bridge, 2016b. *Why is unsafe food rampant in Vietnam?* [Online] Available at: http://english.vietnamnet.vn/fms/special-reports/155277/why-is-unsafe-food-rampant-in-vietnam-.html [Accessed 23 December 2016].

VietnamNet, 2017. *President attends Vietnam-China economic, trade cooperation seminar.* [Online] Available at: http://english.vietnamnet.vn/fms/business/178246/president-attends-vietnam-china-economic%2D%2Dtrade-cooperation-seminar.html [Accessed 20 August 2017].

Vietnamnet, 2017a. *China emerges as Vietnam's largest fragrant rice importer.* [Online] Available at: http://english.vietnamnet.vn/fms/business/178656/china-emerges-as-vietnam-s-largest-fragrant-rice-importer.html [Accessed 20 August 2017].

Vietnamnet, 2017b. *China emerges as biggest importer of Vietnam tra fish.* [Online] Available at: http://english.vietnamnet.vn/fms/business/177959/china-emerges-as-biggest-importer-of-vietnam-tra-fish.html [Accessed 20 August 2017].

Vietrade, 2016. Rice export of Vietnam: successful achivements in the first 6 months of 2016. Vietrade. URL http://en.vietrade.gov.vn/index.php?option=com_content&view=article&id=2531:rice-export-of-vietnam-successful-achivements-in-the-first-6-months-of-2016&catid=270:vietnam-industry-news&Itemid=363 (accessed 11.5.17).

Wildau, G. & Mitchell, T., 2016. *China income inequality among world's worst.* [Online] Available at: https://www.ft.com/content/3c521faa-baa6-11e5-a7cc-280dfe875e28 [Accessed 23 December 2016].

Woods, K., 2014. *Foreign Investment in Agriculture in Myanmar: FDI, Stakeholders Mapping and National Legal and Policy Assessment,* Hong Kong: Oxfam.

Wu, F., Zhang, H., 2016. China's Global Quest for Resources: Energy, Food and Water. Routledge.

Xie, Y. & Jin, Y., 2015. Household Wealth in China. *Chinese Sociological Review,* 47(3), pp. 203–229.

Youchi, K., 2016. *3 great forces changing China's consumer market.* [Online] Available at: https://www.weforum.org/agenda/2016/01/3-great-forces-changing-chinas-consumer-market/ [Accessed 23 December 2016].

Yu, E., 2015. *China's latest stomach-churning food scandal: Frozen meat from the 1970s.* [Online] Available at: http://edition.cnn.com/2015/06/24/asia/china-smuggled-meat/ [Accessed 23 December 2016].

Zha, D. & Zhang, H., 2013. Food in China's International relations. *Pacific Review,* Volume 26, pp. 455–479.

Zhang, Q.F., 2012. The Political Economy of Contract Farming in China's Agrarian Transition. J. Agrar. Change 12, 460–483. doi:https://doi.org/10.1111/j.1471-0366.2012.00352.x

Zhang, H., 2016a. *China's Global Food Quest.* [Online] Available at: http://the-diplomat.com/2016/03/chinas-global-food-quest/ [Accessed 23 December 2016].

Zhang, H., 2016b. Chinese fishermen in disputed waters: Not quite a "people's war". *Marine Policy,* 68(c), pp. 65–73.

Zhang, H., 2016c. IPP REVIEW – The GMO Controversy in China: More than Food Security. IPP Rev. http://ippreview.com/index.php/Home/Blog/single/id/70.html (accessed 11.5.17).

Zhang, H. & Cheng, G., 2016. China's food security strategy reform: an emerging global agricultural policy. In: F. Wu & H. Zhang, eds. *China's Global Quest for Resources: Energy, Food and Water edited by Fengshi Wu and Hongzhou Zhang (Routledge, 2016).* London: Routledge.

Zhao, T., 2015. *China, Vietnam see booming trade in agricultural products.* [Online] Available at: http://www.chinadaily.com.cn/business/2015-11-05/content_22376636.htm [Accessed 15 August 2017].

10

Concluding Remarks: Anxiety as Invariant of Human Relation to Food

Jean-Pierre Poulain

Several sociologists have pointed to risk as a characteristic of modern societies (Giddens 1991; Le Breton 1995; Beck 1995; Martucelli 1999). Ulrich Beck has proposed the concept of "risk society" to describe modern societies. However, this idea has sparked debates. The first concerns modernity. What Europe experienced during the nineteenth and twentieth centuries took place in two generations in some Asian countries. Kyung-Sup Chang (2010) has proposed the concept of "compressed modernity" to account for this phenomenon. The second concerns the concept of risk itself, which, in the field of food, is charged with reducing the problem to its health-related dimensions.

In the last three decades, the West has faced several big food crises, especially that of bovine spongiform encephalopathy (BSE). In this context, the question of "risk" in food safety has taken a particularly important place, in both scholarly and secular conceptions. This hegemonic

J.-P. Poulain (✉)
University of Toulouse, Toulouse, France

Taylor's University, Kuala Lumpur, Malaysia
e-mail: poulain@univ-tlse2.fr; jean-pierre.poulain@taylors.edu.my

© The Author(s) 2019
J. Ehlert, N. K. Faltmann (eds.), *Food Anxiety in Globalising Vietnam*,
https://doi.org/10.1007/978-981-13-0743-0_10

framework has led to a hierarchy of risks: "important" risks and "less important" ones. The former lead to mortality or morbidity and the latter are more qualitative and are in part social, political, and cultural choices. The risk paradigm focuses attention on the health and tends to reject the other dimensions, though it has the merit of promoting the institution-alisation of food risk management bodies. But contemporary crises can-not be reduced to the question of food safety; they interact with food security, food fraud and social controversies. Poulain (2018) showed how the approach in terms of concerns and anxiety could be a way to over-come this hierarchisation of risks by giving them an equivalent status.

This book presents a double interest. Vietnam is a very good example of "compressed modernity", and the author's epistemological perspective gives "food anxiety" a central position in the theoretical framework (see Ehlert and Faltmann, this volume). Some food sociologists have pointed to the fact that, whereas the concept of "risk" can be seen as a conse-quence of modernisation, "food anxiety" could be an anthropological invariant (Beardsworth 1995; Poulain 2017 [2002]). Far from being con-tradictory, these two perspectives focus on complementary dimensions of the relation of the human being to food. They allow a better understand-ing of contemporary food crises and create the conditions of a more global analysis.

Food and "Compressed Modernity"

The transformation of the food system organisation and of the social representations and meanings associated with food during the process of modernisation, gives food a crucial place in the social and political arena of modernised societies. In addition to the "classical" food safety and food security concerns, more controversial issues have emerged like the use of "genetically modified products", animal "cruelty", as well as junk food and its supposed connections with obesity development. Nothing seems self-evident anymore. Food industries are targeted; even the farm-ers, who once had the confidence of city dwellers, are now attacked on various fronts. Lobbying groups are accused of manipulating scientists, the media, politicians, and consumers for their own benefit. The system is not running as smoothly as it once did. A certain tension is rising within the "food social space"[1] over concerns extending from intergenerational responsibility—"What kind of planet are we leaving for our children?"—to intra-generational issues—"How to divide resources between global North and South, and within societies, between rich and poor?"

We have already explored in previous publications (Poulain 2012b) the trends in modernised societies, such as the medicalisation of food, its judicialisation, development of environmental concerns, culinary and gastronomic heritage, or the transformation of human-animal relationships, which are challenging the hitherto dominant "feeding model" of food. So, it's imperative for the authorities in charge of food policies as well as all agents along the agro-food chain, to listen to and understand the reactions of consumers and citizens.

In most Asian countries that have experienced rapid or compressed modernisation, food anxiety is exacerbated. What Western countries have undergone in one and a half centuries, Asia experienced in less than 50 years. In two generations, Vietnam, similar to some other Asian countries, has faced rapid structural transformations in the domains of economy, housing and urbanisation, transportation, and "food social space". The transition from concern for food security to food safety characterises the evolution of the Western context. This reduced concern for famine and more for the quality of food, did not happen in modernised Vietnam where these two issues of food safety (see Part II, this volume) and food security (see Gorman, this volume) coexist at the same time.

To eat is an act of trust that supposes a certain social consensus all along the food chain, from the farmer or the stockbreeder to the eaters themselves; trust in all the actors that contributed to produce, transform and market the products (Lahlou 1998; Kjærnes et al. 2007). Therefore, we can also interpret the exacerbation of contemporary food anxieties as the result of a breakdown of "consensus" between the different actors interacting in the "food social space".

To describe the fast modernisation of certain Asian countries, Chang has proposed the concept of compressed modernity. It corresponds to a "civilisational context in which economic, political, cultural and social changes occur in an extremely condensed manner both in space and in time" (Chang 2017, 33). Moreover, in compressed modernity, disparate historical and social elements coexist, contributing to the construction and reconstruction of a complex social system characterised by fluidity (Chang 2017). The compression of time and space was already described by David Harvey (1990) as the result of technological innovations in the sectors of communication (telegraph, telephone, fax, internet, etc.), as well as transport and travel (high speed trains, democratisation of air transport), which both came to reduce spatial and temporal distances.

Beck and Grande (2010) have tried to articulate "compressed modernity" and Beck's "first" and "second" stages of modernity. "First modernity" is defined as a rise in rationality and the "de-traditionalisation" of societies, and the second as a weakening of the legitimacy of the "normative system", leading to an "individualisation of lifestyles". "Second modernity" corresponds to post-traditional societies, in which the normative models have lost a part of their strength and legitimacy. Not only South Korea, Malaysia, and China but also Vietnam, even though at a lower level, fit more or less into this framework. This stage of modernity is accompanied by the coexistence of issues related to food security and food safety, to which is added a certain level of fraud in the international market, creating a specific context (see Figuié et al., this volume).

So, "compressed modernity" corresponds to the telescoping of these two forms of modernity. Chang (2017) describes two sub-phenomena that have an impact on both the time and space dimensions: "condensation" and "compression". The first, condensation, refers to the phenomenon that the physical process required for the movement or change to take place between two time points (eras) or between two locations (places) is abridged or compacted (Chang 2017, 33–34). The second, compression, corresponds to a "phenomenon that diverse components of multiple civilisations that have existed in different areas and/or places coexist in a certain delimited time-space and influence and change each other" (Chang 2017, 34). Reduction of distance in space increases the mobility of food and populations at the national level (between regions and between rural and urban areas) but also at an international level (between countries). Through this mobility, the interlinking or crossover of food cultures is developed and, in certain contexts, the hybridising or creolisation of cultures (Tibère 2016). Reduction of time also pushes the process of designating food cultures as heritage. At the same time, it also promotes the development of cosmopolitan cultures, with compression superimposing different food cultures in the same social space.

It is possible to add a new source of anxiety to the traditional distinction between "food security" and "food safety", namely "controversial risks". This concept covers the problems generated by the emergence of hazards linked either to technological innovations to food (such as the application of genetic engineering or molecular engineering, nanotechnologies, etc.), or to the evolution of knowledge, which in itself elucidates and makes visible new dimensions of an issue. These risks are not based on the same body of knowledge and their management is not safeguarded by the same scientific, administrative, and political actors. Moreover, the issue of fraud finds favourable conditions in societies that have been rapidly modernised. On the one hand the state agencies in charge of the suppression and prosecution of fraud are weakly developed and on the other hand technological progress offers new possibilities.

So, we can identify four main categories of crises:

- **Food security crisis.** Shortage of food or accessibility issues for a certain segment of a population.
- **Food fraud crisis.** A situation where the normal, legal, and/or traditional characteristics of the products are not respected. This can be falsified products or totally "fake food" produced with technologies that are intended for producing real "artefacts" that simulate food. The food fraud crisis is a legal issue and can also be, in addition, a safety issue.
- **Food safety crisis.** Contamination of either chemical or microbiological origin is likely to have adverse health consequences either in the short term or in the long term. The issue could also come from the presence of foreign object in the food.
- **Controversial crisis.** Impossibility of scientifically adjudicating the problem. This impossibility can be momentary, if scientific progress allows the possibility of elucidating the nature of the risk, or permanent, if the nature of the risk is not scientifically determinable.

One of the characteristics of "compressed food modernity" is the intermingling of these different sources of crises (Poulain 2018).

Compressed Food Modernity in Vietnam

Vietnam is a good example of compressed modernisation. Since the economic reforms of *Đổi Mới*, in 1986, a middle class has emerged, and the traditional ways of life are changing very fast. In a few decades, this country has passed from under-nutrition to over-nutrition, and experiences now what epidemiologists call the "epidemiological transition" and the "double burden" of malnutrition (Gillespie and Haddad 2003). The first burden is the transition from mortality rates based on epidemic diseases, whose severity was reinforced by food scarcity, to a higher incidence of mortality through non-communicable diseases ((NCD), like cardiovascular diseases, cancers, etc.), for which obesity is a significant risk factor. The second burden is the coexistence of under- and over-nutrition problems, at the same time and for the same population. What a contrast between Vietnam of the early 1980s, suffering from 'hunger and poverty' and the present concerns of public health authorities over the increase of obesity and NCDs.

But the history of Vietnam has some particular features—such as wars of decolonisation and migrations—that have undoubtedly contributed to the intensification of certain aspects of "compressed modernity". The fall of Dien Bien Phu in May 1954, marks the end of the First Indochina War and the beginning of the French decolonisation. After the partition of the country, along the 17th Parallel in the following July, the first migrations began, mainly to France and European countries. Twenty years later, the victory of North Vietnam over the South and the "Paris Peace Accords" were accompanied by a second wave of migration. United States, Canada and to a lesser extent Europe are the receiving countries. Finally, the 1980s were marked by a migration of poverty, with the more than two million so-called boat-people who fled by boat to escape starvation and—for some—the communist regime.

These three migratory flows did not affect the same layers of society. The first two concerned mainly social categories in relation with the colonial authorities or with the American and Western supporters of the Republic of Vietnam in the South. The last stream, the "boat-people", was composed mainly of poor and rural people.

From the point of view of food, the break with colonial Vietnam is characterised by a distancing from part of the national food culture; in particular, the gastronomic practices of the elites, including those of the Hue court. These cuisines and gastronomies, once considered part of the lifestyles of a "corrupted elite", were blacklisted for many years. Those are the Vietnamese lifestyles that the two first waves of migrations brought with them to other countries and that they kept alive in the first generation of Vietnamese restaurants overseas. Even the food habits of ethnic minorities of Vietnam, regarded as more or less "primitives", had no place in this Vietnamese food culture.

Since the late 1990s, these issues have become topics of research, with the first conference dedicated to them taking place in Hanoi entitled "Food practices and cultural identities" co-organised by University of Toulouse, and Universities of Hue and Hanoi (Poulain 1997a, b). Gastronomic Vietnamese cultures are today viewed as a much more complex heritage and cross different regional, social, and ethnic levels.

The migratory three waves towards different countries have also contributed to the fame of Vietnamese cuisine and gastronomy all over the world, and have had an influence on the gastronomic culture in the receiving countries themselves (Poulain 1997b). Indeed, tourists who since the 1990s have come to Vietnam in ever greater numbers arrive with certain "knowledge" of Vietnamese cuisine, learnt in restaurant in their own countries. The adaptation by Asian restaurants overseas to the Western organisation of the meal has accelerated the individualisation of dishes. The traditional distinction between *nuoc-nam* (Vietnamese) and soya sauce (non-Vietnamese) have almost disappeared. Both are now found on the tables of restaurants in Vietnam. What was once a simple adaptation to the demands of tourists is increasingly used by young Vietnamese people.

Economic isolation and the sidelining of a part of Vietnam's historical gastronomic inheritance have effected a reduction of the food culture. In that context, the fast opening up of the economy to the global food and tourism markets was a powerful accelerating factor of modernisation. What we now see in the metropolis is a "compacted" food culture, that is, the coexistence of different Vietnamese food cultures plus a lot of foreign restaurants, from fast food to fine dining and international cuisines. The rapid shift of an impoverished food environment (through economic closure and the sidelining of some national food patterns and cuisines) to a context where food cultures are multiplying, intertwining, and becoming more complex is a potential source of concern and anxiety. The switch from a simplified food environment to a more complex one, in which certain influences coming from the outside are claimed by Vietnamese, has multiple and interacting effects: an increase in food anxiety, the destabilisation of regulatory devices, and a questioning of social identities.

The feeling of anxiety is reinforced by the multiplication of crises and scandals that, as in many Asian countries, make the front pages of Vietnamese newspapers and the headlines of TV news. Here too, the different levels of crisis are entangled: food safety and health risks, food security (exacerbated since the international food security crises of 2008 and the Vietnamese stock building policies), fraud, and other controversies. In the face of the growing number of scandals due to the use of banned products in livestock and/or agriculture and the press reports, the Municipality of Ho Chi Minh City has announced the establishment of a "special committee" in charge of food safety (Hồng Nga 2016). Controversies over GMO rice led the Vietnamese Food Association and its Thai counterpart to commit to zero GMO production (Rice Trade Cooperation 2006).

The Contribution of the Food Anxiety Paradigm

To conceptualise their diet, eaters mobilise an intellectual way of functioning that anthropologists call 'magical thinking'. This was thought, at the beginning of the discipline, to be a characteristic of 'primitive' societies. Today we know that 'magical thinking' is used also by modern eaters in their reasoning and coexists with other forms of rationality. An outline of magical thinking is easy to formulate: symbolic qualities of everything that comes into contact with food—whether it is tools, other natural products, packaging, and also individuals producing, handling, cooking, and selling them qualities of all those objects and individuals—are passed on through 'symbolic contamination' to the food itself. The American psycho-sociologist Paul Rozin demonstrated this phenomenon of symbolic contamination experimentally. For instance, one only has to put a dead and disinfected cockroach—as such bacteriologically safe—into a glass of milk and then remove it in order to make this product "undrinkable", nevertheless perfectly drinkable from a strictly objective point of view. An even more striking experiment, if one suggests to someone to write 'danger cyanide' on an adhesive label and to stick this on a glass, and then to fill this labelled glass with any (potable) liquid, for a great number of people this drink becomes unfit for consumption (Rozin 1976). This can be applied to the contemporary dietary context. All technological interventions (handling, culinary changes, operations that go with commercialisation) and all the professionals who carry them out have symbolical influence on the identity of food; so it is advisable to study in order to try and understand them. Through the act of eating, a food enters us, and takes part in our intimate physical life. It crosses the border between the world and us. That is why food gives us the feeling of control over our everyday life. With this in mind, we can better understand why the uncertainties, the fears concerning food intensify echo uncertainties about the eater's own future.

Anxiety and the Ambivalences of Human Diet

Several authors have developed the idea that the opposition between 'neophilia' and 'neophobia' might result from the contradiction between the biological obligation to consume varied food and the cultural constraint: to eat only known, socially identified, and demonstrated foods (Rozin 1976; Fischler 1988). This double constraint characteristic of human's omnivorous status, which is named *the omnivore's paradox* is the source of a fundamental anxiety in the human diet. Food anxiety is thus not new or linked to the present economic climate; it is permanent and must continually be regulated. This is the role of the 'culinary system', that subset of the cultural system made of a series of rules defining the order of the edible, and the conditions of preparation and consumption.

This allows the acceptance of a new food by 'marking' it gustatively, seasoning it literally 'with the sauce' of a cultural space. Inserted in a culture, the eater has only a few decisions to take. It is the culinary system of its society that dictates the decisions to the eater. The culinary system resolves the 'double bind' or paradoxical injunction, peculiar to omnivorous status.

Dietary modernity and the anxieties that attend it are then interpreted on the mode of a crisis of the regulating function of culinary systems. The weakening of social constraints weigh heavily on the eater, associated on the one hand with the increase of individualism, and on the other hand with the industrialisation of food production, transformation, and marketing that cut the link between humans and their food. These generate a context within which 'dietary anxiety' dominates. It is possible to distinguish different dimensions of the ambivalence of human diet to which particular forms of anxiety correspond (Beardsworth 1995; Poulain 2017 [2002]).

The first ambivalence is between *pleasure and displeasure*. It accounts for the fact that diet can be at the same time a source of sensuality, plenitude, intense sensorial pleasure, but also cause a whole range of disagreeable sensations, going from simply 'unpleasant' to disgust that can cause nausea, if not vomiting. Anxiety then has sensorial and hedonic components.

A further ambivalence is linked to the complexity of the link between diet and *health or illness*. It is rooted in the fact that food is a source of energy, vitality, health, but at the same time a vector of poisoning, a potential cause of illness, of disorders. The effects of these disorders can appear on a very short timescale. But the risks for the health can also be felt over the medium or even the long term, as it is the case for some toxins (e.g. micro-toxins) of deficiency or extra load in some nutriments or new contaminating agents as prions, responsible for BSE. The anxiety that goes with incorporation here is of a sanitary order. It is from this that we find the contradiction between two principles connecting diet with health, the first one formulated by Hippocrates, '*Thou shall do your medicine from food*', and the second by the adage '*man digs his grave with his teeth*'.

The last ambivalence takes root in the *relationship with life and death*. It holds in the fact that the dietary act is an absolute and inescapable necessity in order to live, but that implies, most of the time, the death of animals that are considered as edible. Some cultures clear up this paradox by putting an interdiction on food that requires the death of an animal by advocating vegetarianism. In most of the cases, dietary murder is surrounded by a series of rituals of protection or social devices the function of which is to legitimise the animal's death. Then anxiety comes from the conflict between the need to eat meat and the fact of having to impose suffering on animals and take their life in order to do so.

To eat, then, is an act that imposes choices, decisions, but also the need to take objective and symbolical risks. Those different paradoxes generate the three forms of specific anxiety that dietary cultures try to manage. Regulation of the ambivalence of *pleasure-displeasure* is maintained by culinary culture, what Levi Strauss named the 'culinary system', that is to say the set of social rules that define forms of preparation, cooking, seasoning, and so on. New food is introduced in a culture by being prepared according to ways of cooking, preparation, or by being associated with strongly identified seasoning, which reassures the eater by giving this product a familiar taste. More generally, a mode of preparation or seasoning already known has a reassuring effect by inserting the new food in the normative dietary system.

The management of the second ambivalence *health-illness* is one of the most interesting questions in the anthropology of food. The capacity of humans to build knowledge simply in order not to poison themselves and maintain their survival is a real cognitive enigma. All cultures have at their disposal a "traditional" dietetic functioning as a science of categories that structures the order of the edible. It can be organised around a binary system like: yin and yang of a macrobiotic diet, the five elements of the Chinese and Vietnamese "order" of nature (Poulain 1997a-I), or categories of 'warm', 'cold', 'humid' or 'dry', used in different cultural universes such as Hippocratic European medicine (Flandrin and Montanari 2013), fishermen of the Malay peninsula (Wilson 1967), natives from Central America (Messer 1984), or some Indian ethnic groups (Mahias 1985). The membership of one of these categories gives to food particular qualities that justify their consumption in some contexts or recommend them to some individuals. Those profane dietetics allow eaters to conceptualise the link between diet and health. This knowledge is often presented as magic reasoning; these analyses suggest that apparently irrational knowledge could have adaptive qualities.

The ambivalence of *life and death* asks the question of the moral acceptability of killing animals, among others, those having nervous systems, and as such as being able to feel pain and to show it. Killing for food is a source of anxiety and, on this point, different modes of regulations are possible. In societies of hunters, there are several examples of rituals, prayers, or apologies addressed to the soul or the spirit of the animal (Frazer 1911; Kent 1989). Some like Chipewyan, Ameridians from the North of Canada, think that the animal can be killed only with its consent (Sharp, quoted by Beardsworth 1995). Another attitude consists of killing the animals in a sacrificial framework. In numerous societal situations (the Greek world, certain "ethnic proto-Indochinese" societies (Condominas 1954)) the animal is not killed to be consumed, or rather not killed *only* to be consumed, but it is put to death in a ritual setting where there is communication with the 'world beyond'. The explicit objective of putting the animal to death is not so it can be eaten but that its death serves to set up a relationship with the spirits or beings from this world beyond, in order to garner favours or forgiveness by offering the slain animal to the deities. The soul of which escapes the body of the animal at the moment of death is seen as a support for the message sent to the spirits or beings which inhabit the world beyond. The body which remains after death can then become the object of something shared, and consumed without having the act of killing weigh heavily on the conscience of those who undertook this act. The choice of the animals to be sacrificed is inscribed in the proper logic of the ritual and its significations: a chicken in certain cases, a pig in others (Condominas 1954). In Yao society, studied by Annie Hubert, all meat which is consumed must first be sacrificed and offered to the ancestors (Hubert 1985).

In the Judaeo-Christian tradition, after the fall from heaven, the authorisation is explicitly given to men in the opening of the genesis to consume animals: 'All that moves and lives will serve you as food; as well as the verdure of plants, I give you everything, only you will not eat the flesh with its blood' (Genesis 9.3.). Judaism associates with this a whole series of interdicts, as per the association of milk and meat, 'Thou shall not cook a kid in the milk of its mother' (Deuteronomy 14.21) and specifies the edible animals (pure) and non-edible (impure) by the 'people consecrated to Yahveh'. Blood is also the subject of an interdict because it is the support of the soul of the animal. Animal slaughter is put under religious control, with a rabbi controlling the procedure of killing and giving his seal of approval to 'kosher' food. It is the quite the same in Islam, where meat can be 'halal' only if the slaughter was realised according to a precise ritual and with the presence of an imam. The interest of those rituals is to operate to reassure the eater by making the death of an animal morally acceptable. In the Christian universe, the sacrifice of the 'son of God's made man' makes redundant other forms of sacrifice, and rejects the notion of dietary murder in the profane universe.

This analysis in terms of a triple ambivalence opens the way towards the comprehension of sources of anxiety and of human eaters' reasoning. At the same time this theoretical framework is useful to analyse and monitor food crises.

Anxiety as Erosion of the Modes of Management of Ambivalences in Human Diet

Contemporary food crisis can be read as the result of an erosion of the modes of regulation of dietary anxiety. Globalisation of markets, industrialisation of production, and the appearance in institutional catering of central kitchens are becoming more and more important, tending to reduce the gustative markers peculiar to certain cultures by imposing a homogenisation of tastes. Culinary particularisms and the specific tastes that accompany them do not have the same strength as identification functions. The mutation of daily eating practices and the individualisation of the decisions reactivate the pleasure-displeasure anxiety.

The links between diet and health, but also between diet and illness are put forward by modern epidemiological discourse. Progress in the methods of scientific analysis allows for deeper knowledge of the origins of food poisoning and the chemical and/or bacterial agents responsible for it. The illustration in the media of these 'dietary accidents' presented as entirely novel, reactivates the fears associated with this second type of ambivalence, without us knowing whether an instance of food poisoning is indeed new, or if it is simply a matter of our ability to detect, which is improving. The diffusion of nutritional knowledge in society intensifies both the positive link between diet and health (e.g. diet as a lever for prevention), and the negative link (i.e. diet as the cause of the disease, especially NCDs). Nutritionalisation plays a role in the exacerbation of the anxiety of health-illness.

Crisis also makes a dent in the ways of managing the issue of killing animals for food. Older works of scholarship have pointed to the particular mode of management adopted by Western laypeople in society, as, for example, the fact that slaughterhouses are kept at a distance from society, relegated to the urban periphery, a Taylorian organisation of slaughter that dilutes the responsibility for killing by dividing the technical process. In a period of about 20 years how the relationship between man and animals is imagined has deeply changed. Pets became anthropomorphised (Digard 2009). Progresses of ethology and sciences of animal behaviour have shown that they had feelings, intelligence, erasing every day a bit more of that border between men and animals (Poulain 1997b, 2007).

The crisis opened by this affair affected the prestige of the medical profession head on and weakened the trust in the relationship between politicians and the scientific experts supposed to advise them. The weakened prestige of science and the symbolical functions of the vet controlling the process of slaughter and giving their approval for the meat to be edible are both affected.

The above analyses allow a new way of reading the processes of management of risk and anxiety in terms of symbolic and social functions, either as quality conventions (process of labelling and certificating) or as devices for including public debate. They invite one to abandon the logic of reassurance that applies implicitly where "we knew a time when things happened without problems".

Risk and Anxiety

Since the 1990s, following various food crises in western countries, the food issue has come to be organised around the concept of "risk" and the theory of strategic "early warning signals" (Ansoff 1975). Food issues (safety and food security) have now gained a place on political and media agendas. Henceforth, discussion on these topics is delivered by official agencies where experts scientifically evaluate risks and try to understand the more or less rational perceptions of consumers in order to manage and communicate these risks. 'Assessment' (by experts), 'perception' (by the customers or citizens) and 'management' (by the authorities—in economic and political institutions) are the three keywords in risk monitoring.

Within the social sciences, research has been undertaken, which sometimes supports, justifies, or validates these theoretical frameworks and thus has helped to organise and legitimise the vision of administrative risk management (Slovic 1987). Sometimes these research projects also delineate and challenge the rational asymmetry on which they were based—with, on the one hand, the "experts", who are supposedly presenting the "truth", and, on the other, the "laymen", who are more or less "wrong"—by claiming the necessity to articulate the understanding of experts and citizens (Beck 1995). They point out that the diverging understanding of citizens and scientists cannot be reduced to perception bias since the former perceive dimensions that are excluded by the probabilistic calculation of the risk of mortality and morbidity (Beck 1995; Poulain 2002, 2012a, 2017 [2002]).

Some anthropological works show that as all human cultures proceed to an orderly organisation of the world, they all encounter the same problem. This concerns the definition of a remainder, that is, what must remain 'outside the scope' of conceptualising the world.

With the anxiety paradigm focuses are put on the sources of concern, mainly the ambivalence of the omnivorous relation to food: pleasure and displeasure, health or illness, and life and death. Anxiety is seen as a fundamental attitude. But anxiety has to be regulated, which means it must be maintained at an acceptable level. That is the role of food models. A food model is a particular configuration of the food social space. It corresponds to a particular order of the edible, a food system, a culinary system, a system of consumption, a system of temporality, and a set of internal differentiation. We have proposed the following definition:

Food models are socio-technical and symbolic groups that relate a human group to its environment, establish its identity and ensure the establishment of processes of internal social differentiation. They are a body of technological knowledge accumulated from generation to generation, allowing the selection of resources in natural space, to prepare them for food, then dishes and to consume them. But at the same time they are symbolic code systems that depict the values of a human group involved in the construction of cultural identities and processes of personalisation. (Poulain 2002)

A food model is a body of knowledge that aggregates multiple experiences in the form of trial and error by a human community. It comes in the form of a series of nested categories that are used daily by members of a society, without real awareness, implicitly taken as "self-evident". This "self-evident" character is the main epistemological obstacle to the study of dietary patterns.

The sociology of risk poses risk as a "new" datum on the scale of history in the development of rationality and probabilistic thinking. For the socio-anthropology of food, food anxiety is a "constant" phenomenon. It is the role of dietary patterns to maintain the intensity of anxiety at an acceptable level, and to regulate it. Thus, crises appear as a weakening of the devices of regulation and as a consequence of the erosion of food models.

The paradigmatic rupture is that anxiety is not the problem, but that 'bad' regulation is. This paradigmatic reversal is similar to that made in the sociology of organisations by Michel Crozier and Erhard Friedberg (1980), when they proposed to regard conflict not as the consequence of an organisational failure, but as constitutive of organisations. Whereas the preceding theoretical currents, Taylorism, or the current of human relations, sought to avoid conflict at all costs, the sociology of organisations postulates that the purpose of management is not about avoiding conflicts, but rather about regulating them.

Reading risk in terms of it being a consequence of modernity invites one to seek the conditions of a return to the confidence of a time before crisis. It could also in certain situations support the naïve idea of a nostalgic, lost food paradise. The approach whereby anxiety is posed as an invariant suggests a focus on the 'devices' of regulation of anxiety that are food models. While the theory of risk hierarchises the risks between vital risks, that is, the health risks on one side, and on the other, the secondary, more 'qualitative' risks, the perspective of food anxiety gives importance, not only to the health risks, but also to the questions of pleasure, social identities, ethics, human-animal relationships…

With this book, issues heretofore perceived as secondary emerge from the shadows and come to light. In doing so, it constitutes a reading frame useful for understanding and identifying the challenges of modernisation as well as for taking action, whether in public health policies or of food crises management. This book, with its different empirical examples, makes a contribution in showing that Vietnam is a privileged place to support this idea of interest of the concept of "food anxiety".

Note

1. The concept of "food social space" describes the social dimensions of food. It corresponds to the area of freedom left to human eaters by two sets of physical constraints: biological constraints related to their status as omnivores, which are essential but relatively flexible, and the ecological constraints created by the biotope in which they live, which become economic constraints in the industrialised world and which progressively tend to be reduced due to our technological control of nature (Poulain 2017 [2002]). "Food social space" is in line with the Maussian notion of a "total social fact", that is, which "sets in motion ... the totality of the society and its institutions" (Mauss 1950). It is possible to distinguish various dimensions of social food space: the edible order, the food system, the culinary space, the consumption patterns, food temporality and the social differentiation space. Its main interests are to show the variations of the social dimensions of food between two cultures and in the frame of one culture, and to study the interaction between social and biological infrastructure of nutrition as well as the environment (for a systematic presentation see Poulain 2017 [2002]).

References

Ansoff, H. I. (1975): Managing Strategic Surprise by Response to Weak Signals. *California Management Review* V.XVIII(2), 21–33.

Beardsworth, A. (1995): The Management of Food Ambivalence: Erosion and Reconstruction? In: Maurer, D. and Sobal, J. (eds.): Eating Agendas: Food and Nutrition as Social Problems. New York: Aldine de Gruyter, 117–141.

Beck, U. (1995): World Risk Society. Cambridge: Polity Press.

Beck, U. and Grande, E. (2010): Varieties of Second Modernity: Extra-European and European Experiences and Perspectives. *The British Journal of Sociology* 61(3), 409–443.

Chang, Kyung-Sup (2010): The Second Modern Condition? Compressed Modernity as Internalized Reflexive Cosmopolitization. *The British Journal of Sociology* 61(3), 444–464.

Chang Kyung-Sup (2017): Compressed Modernity in South Korea: Constitutive Dimensions, Manifesting Units, and Historical Conditions. In: Kim, Y. (ed.): The Routledge Handbook of Korean Culture and Society. London and New York: Routledge, 31–47.

Condominas, G. (1954): Nous avons mangé la forêt. Paris: Mercure de France.

Crozier, M. and Friedberg, E. (1980): Actors and systems: The politics of collective action. Chicago: University of Chicago Press.

Digard, J.-P. (2009): Raisons et déraisons des revendications animalitaires. Essai de lecture anthropologique et politique. *Pouvoirs* 131, 97–111.

Fischler, C. (1988): Food, Self and Identity. *Social Science Information* 27(2), 275–292.

Flandrin, J. L. and Montanari, M. (eds.) (2013): Food: A Culinary History. New York: Columbia University Press.

Frazer J. (1911): Le Rameau d'or. Paris: Laffont.

Giddens, A. (1991): Modernity and Self-identity. Cambridge: Polity Press.

Gillespie, S. and Haddad, L. (2003): The Double Burden of Malnutrition in Asia: Causes, Consequences, and Solutions. New Delhi: Sage Publications India.

Harvey, D. (1990): The Condition of Postmodernity: An Enquiry into the Origins of Cultural Change. Cambridge: Blackwell.

Hông Nga (2016): En finir avec les substances toxiques dans les aliments. In: Le courrier du Vietnam, 03/05/2016.

Hubert A. (1985): L'Alimentation dans un village Yao de Thaïlande du Nord: de l'au-delà au cuisiné. Paris: CNRS Éditions.

Kent S. (1989): Cross-cultural perceptions of farmers as hunter and the value of meat. In: Kent, S. (ed.): Farmers as hunters: the implications of sedentism. Cambridge: Cambridge University Press, 1–17.

Kjærnes, U., Harvey, M. and Warde, A. (2007): Trust in food: A Comparative and Institutional Analysis. Hampshire: Palgrave Macmillan.

Lahlou, S. (1998): Penser manger: alimentation et représentations sociales. Paris: PUF.

Le Breton, D. (1995): La sociologie du risque. Paris: PUF.

Mahias M.-C. (1985): Délivrance et convivialité: le système culinaire des Jaina. Charenton-le-Pont: Éditions de la Maison des sciences de l'homme.

Martucelli. D. (1999): Sociologies de la modernité. Paris: Gallimard.

Mauss, M. (1950): Sociologie et anthropologie. Paris: PUF.

Messer E. (1984): Anthropological perspectives on diet. *Annual Review of Anthropology* 13, 205–249.

Poulain, J.-P. (ed.) (1997a): Eating and drinking habits and cultural identities. *Vietnamese Studies*, Special issues I, 55(3), 5–190 and II, 55(4), 5–251.

Poulain, J.-P. (1997b): La nourriture de l'autre: entre délices et dégoûts, Réflexions sur le relativisme de la sensibilité alimentaire. *Internationale de l'Imaginaire* 7 (Cultures, nourriture), 115–139.

Poulain, J.-P. (2002): De la sociologie du risque à l'étude des modèles alimentaires. In: Lledo, P.-M. et al. (eds.): Manger pour vivre? Paris: PUF, 85–116 (Forum Diderot).

Poulain, J.-P., (ed.) (2007): L'homme, le mangeur, l'animal. Qui nourrit l'autre? Paris: Les cahiers de l'OCHA (Observatoire Cidil des Habitudes Alimentaires).

Poulain, J.-P. (2012a): Risques et crises alimentaires. In: Poulain, J.-P. (ed.): Dictionnaire des cultures alimentaires. Paris: PUF, 1168–1185.

Poulain, J.-P. (2012b): The Affirmation of Personal Dietary Requirements and Changes in Eating Models. In: Fischler, C. (ed.): Selective Eating: The Rise, Meaning and Sense of Personal Dietary Requirements. Paris: Odile Jacob, 253–264.

Poulain, J.-P. (2017 [2002]): Sociology of Food. Eating and the Place of Food in Society. London: Bloomsbury Academic [translation of Poulain, J.-P. (2002): Sociologies de l'alimentation, les mangeurs et l'espace social alimentaire. Paris: PUF].

Poulain, J.-P. (2018): Beyond Weak Signal Listening Theory: From Risk Analysis to the Management of Alimentary Concerns. In: Augustin, J. L. and Poulain, J.-P. (eds.): Food and Risks in Japan and China. London: Routledge.

Rice Trade Cooperation (2006): Working Record of the Rice Trade Cooperation Meeting between the Rice Exporters Association of Thailand and the Vietnam Food Association. Bangkok, 16 November 2006.

Rozin, P. (1976): The Selection of Foods by Rats, Humans, and Other Animals. In: Rosenblatt, J. S., Hinde, R. A., Shaw, E. and Beer, C. (eds): Advances in Study of Behaviour, Volume 6. New York, San Francisco, London: Academic Press, 21–76.

Slovic, P. (1987): Perception of Risk. *Science* Volume 236, Issue 4799, 280–285.

Tibère, L. (2016): Food as a Factor of Collective Identity: The Case of Creolisation. *French Cultural Studies* 27(1), 85–95.

Wilson, P. J. (1967): A Malay village in Malaysia. New Haven: HRAF Press.